T0316948

The Learning Economy and the Economics of Hope

Anthem Studies in Innovation and Development

The **Anthem Studies in Innovation and Development** aims to publish cutting-edge scholarship that pushes the boundaries of our understanding of how innovation impacts human and economic development. The aim is to promote a better understanding of innovation, evaluate ongoing approaches to analyse innovation capacity, and to generate a set of instructive readings that elaborate upon the role of innovation capabilities in enabling development, reducing inequality and eliminating poverty. The series is interested in exploring the role of technology and innovation in sustainable development (at the global or sectoral level), links between trade and innovation (including investment and intellectual property rights), the role of the state and new issues in the interface of innovation and industrial policy. The series is particularly interested in analytical approaches to institutional and evolutionary economics, new frameworks and constructs on capabilities building and economic history reviews of innovation and technological change.

Series Editors

Padmashree Gehl Sampath – United Nations Conference on Trade and Development (UNCTAD), Switzerland; Aalborg University, Denmark
Rajneesh Narula – University of Reading, UK

Editorial Board

Dan Breznitz – University of Toronto, Canada
Carlos Correa – University of Buenos Aires, Argentina
Dominique Foray – École Polytechnique Fédérale de Lausanne, Switzerland
Elisa Guiliani – University of Pisa, Italy
Raphie Kaplinsky – University of Sussex, UK
Bengt-Åke Lundvall – Aalborg University, Denmark
Keith Maskus – University of Colorado, USA
Khalid Nadvi – University of Manchester, UK

The Learning Economy and the Economics of Hope

Bengt-Åke Lundvall

ANTHEM PRESS

Anthem Press
An imprint of Wimbledon Publishing Company
www.anthempress.com

This edition first published in UK and USA 2016
by ANTHEM PRESS
75–76 Blackfriars Road, London SE1 8HA, UK
or PO Box 9779, London SW19 7ZG, UK
and
244 Madison Ave #116, New York, NY 10016, USA

British Library Cataloguing-in-Publication Data
A catalogue record for this book is available from the British Library.

Library of Congress Cataloging-in-Publication Data
Names: Lundvall, Bengt-Åke, 1941– author.
Title: The learning economy and the economics of hope / by Bengt-Åke Lundvall.
Description: London; New York, NY: Anthem Press, [2016] |
Includes bibliographical references and index.
Identifiers: LCCN 2016038800 | ISBN 9781783085965 (hardback)
Subjects: LCSH: Knowledge economy. | Information technology –
Economic aspects. | Technological innovations – Economic aspects.
Classification: LCC HC79.I55 L86 2016 | DDC 303.48/3 – dc23
LC record available at https://lccn.loc.gov/2016038800

ISBN-13: 978-1-78308-596-5 (Hbk)
ISBN-10: 1-78308-596-7 (Hbk)

This title is also available as an e-book.

CONTENTS

TABLES

FIGURES

PREFACE

This book brings together 12 papers written over a period of 30 years (1985–2015). I have added an introduction (Chapter 1) where I indicate the context of the papers and their relationship to each other and an essayistic Postscript (Chapter 14) where I reflect upon normative implications.

Anyone who reads the book as a whole will experience some repetition. This reflects 'self-citation' and that the papers appear in their original form. This means, however, that each chapter can be read separately. I am most grateful to Shagufta Haneef who helped me with preparing the manuscript and the editing.

Several of the papers have been co-authored, and I am grateful to Anthony Arundel, Antoine Valeyre, Björn Johnson, Edward Lorenz, Morten Berg Jensen, Rasmus Lema and Shulin Gu for their collaboration and for permissions to republish those papers in this volume.

I am in intellectual debt to many other scholars who have given inspiration to my work. Thanks first to colleagues in the research group on Innovation, Knowledge and Economic Dynamics (IKE group) at Aalborg University, particularly Asger Brændgaard, Bent Dalum, Birgitte Gregersen, Björn Johnson, Esben Sloth Andersen, Gert Villumsen, Jan Fagerberg, Jesper Lindgaard Christensen and many others.

Since 1984, I have become increasingly involved in collaboration with scholars from outside Denmark. I have benefited from cooperation in European projects with Alice Lam, Daniele Archibugi, Edward Lorenz, Giovanni Dosi, Luc Soete, Maria Jao Rodrigues, Mark Tomlinson, Susana Borras and many others.

In the new millennium, I learnt a lot on how to link innovation to development from Globelics colleagues Jose Cassiolato, Judith Sutz, Gabriela Dutrrenit, K. J. Joseph, Keun Lee, Rajah Rasiah, Shulin Gu, Anna Kingiri, Bitrina Diaymett, Mammo Muchie and many others.

One of the messages in this book is that apprenticeship learning is important in all domains of knowledge, including research. I have had three 'masters' who have inspired my work: Lars Herlitz, Richard R. Nelson and Christopher Freeman.

For the title of this book, I have borrowed the concept 'the economics of hope' from Freeman's 1993 book. Christopher Freeman was an intellectual giant who not only called for a better world but also, as a scholar and a world citizen, made contributions to make it a reality.

Thanks are due also to my life companion, Birte Siim, who gave ideas for how to wrap up the work so that it could reach the publisher on time. Our numerous and often heated discussions on nation states, global citizenship and politics have served as antidotes against technology determinism and economistic perspectives.

Part I
INTRODUCTION

Chapter 1

CONTRIBUTIONS TO THE LEARNING ECONOMY: OVERVIEW AND CONTEXT

Bengt-Åke Lundvall

This book is about the economics of innovation and knowledge. One of the major conclusions drawn is that the perspectives standard economics imposes on society are biased, incomplete and inadequate. The focus on rational choice, allocation of scarce resources and equilibrium only captures some dimensions of the modern economy, notably short-term and static ones. Alternative perspectives, in which the focus is on learning as an interactive process and on processes of innovation, give visibility and direct attention to other, at least equally important and more dynamic, dimensions.

Social science is about human action and interaction, and it differs from natural science in several respects. It does not have access to laboratories where it is possible to organize controlled experiments. In spite of this, standard economics has gone far in adopting criteria and ideals from natural science, more precisely ideals that originate from Newtonian physics. This is reflected in standard economists' conception of equilibrium as an ideal reference state and their tendency to focus exclusively on quantitative relations, also paired with in its excessive use of mathematics.

In this book, I insist that economics should remain a social science while also taking into account the complexity of the strivings and hopes of human beings. People cannot be reduced to algorithms or automatons. The basic assumption about rational behaviour in economic models (in which individuals and firms act as if they know everything about the future) is absurd and leads to equally absurd conclusions and to dubious policy recommendations.

Taking a departure from more realistic assumptions about how and why people act as they do in society has implications for what constitutes a theory in social science. In social science, a theory should be regarded as a focusing device – no more and no less. This book presents two sets of theories or focusing devices – the innovation system and the learning economy – that differ from those used in standard economics. These alternative focusing devices help us to see the core institutions in the economy (such as the market, the competition regime, the firm, the law, etc.) in a different light than that cast by mainstream economic theory.

What is currently presented as the only and necessary pathway for the economy and for economic policy aiming at competitiveness and growth at the national level actually undermines both. The only certain outcome of current national strategies with focus on fiscal balance and cost competitiveness is that the rich get richer and the poor stay poor. Using an alternative analytical perspective, where the focus is on processes of innovation and learning, points in other possible directions for institutional design and economic policy, where the focus is on collective entrepreneurship, knowledge sharing and international collaboration.

1.1 The Structure of the Book

Twelve articles have been selected for this volume; some of these are co-authored. I have chosen the papers that I regard as my main contributions to the understanding of the learning economy. The work is presented here in the order that it was published, and it spans a period of 30 years (1985–2015).

The twelve chapters are presented in five parts. Part I gives the introduction to this book and an overview of the content. Part II includes four chapters from the period 1985–95 about innovation as an interactive process and innovation systems. Part III includes four chapters from the period 2000–2010 about knowledge creation and the characteristics of the learning economy. Part IV includes three chapters that use the learning economy and the innovation system as focusing devices in an analysis of China's innovation system and policy, Europe's financial crisis and Africa's growth and structural problems and a chapter on how globalization changes the role of national innovation systems. Part V closes the book with a chapter on the learning economy and the economics of hope. In essayistic form, it regards major global challenges through the lens of the learning economy and spells out wider normative implications for public policy as well as for a research agenda.

The rest of this introduction briefly discusses the context for the original papers and presents the central ideas in each chapter. A summary of the main points of criticism of standard economics appears at the end of the chapter.

1.1.1 Part II: Innovation as an interactive process

The first chapter of this part (chapter 2) is about product innovation and user–producer interaction (Lundvall 1985). It is a think piece that was worked out as an analytical follow-up to a major empirical project on the impact of 'microelectronics' on the Danish economy, and it draws on the analysis of how technology was shaped in four distinct industrial complexes. It was presented in draft form at a seminar at the Science Policy Research Unit (SPRU) in the spring of 1984 and at the Stanford Seminar on Economics of Science and Technology in the fall of 1984. It was published as a booklet by Aalborg University Press in 1985. It is, to the best of my knowledge, the first publication that refers to the concept of 'innovation system' relating it to university–industry linkages and to the micro-phenomenon of user–producer interaction.

The chapter draws together the wider theoretical implications of what other innovation scholars have documented in empirical and historical studies. The Sappho study at SPRU (Rothwell 1972, 1977) and the historical work on the textile industry by Nathan Rosenberg at Stanford (1976) are just two examples of contributions that document that innovation is an interactive process and that users play an important role in the development of new products and processes.

As demonstrated in the very last chapter of this book, the uptake in the academic community of the ideas developed in chapter 2 has been selective. Experts in economic geography were among the first to link the analysis to the location of economic activities; marketing experts and software developers have used the ideas for developing management strategies and innovation policy experts were inspired to give more attention to the demand side. Other elements of the analysis never received much attention however. The criticism of the basic assumptions in economics has been largely neglected, and the same is true for the analysis of 'unsatisfactory innovations'.

The chapter looks different from the standard scientific journal article, and the somewhat pedestrian language reflects that it was one of my first attempts to write a paper in English. The terse style was inspired by Janos Kornai's book *Anti-equilibrium* (1971). I hope that the reader will be able to overcome these barriers. Some typos have been corrected, but for the rest, the original has been left unchanged.

Chapter 3 presents user–producer interaction and relationships as a micro-foundation for the national innovation system. The chapter was written in the context of a major collective project on technology and economic theory that brought together economists working on innovation. The fact that the resulting publication (Dosi et al. 1988) ended with a structure where there was a separate section on innovation systems with contributions from, respectively, Freeman, Nelson, Pelikan and Lundvall contributed to the wider introduction and spread of the concept in innovation studies.

Most of the ideas developed in chapter 2 are presented in a somewhat different form in the first part of chapter 3. One major difference is that in the new chapter, the interaction process is described as a process of learning rather than as a process of information exchange. A second is that there is more emphasis on the risks for lock-in in connection with establishing durable user–producer relationships. Nevertheless, the most important new contribution in the chapter is the discussion of 'national systems of innovation'.

In many respects, this first conceptualization of the national innovation system is tentative (chapters 4 and 5 introduce a more developed understanding of the concept). However, there are some nontrivial statements in this chapter that point ahead to issues that I have returned to later in my career. One of these issues is to see the innovation process as rooted in the production process. In the chapter, this is reflected in the sequence of analysis that starts from the concept of a national system of production as used by French Marxist economists.

Another issue relates to the potential role of 'final users' as including workers and consumers. In the third part of this book, those two ideas are developed in the context of the learning economy. Chapter 8 in Part III shows specifically that international differences in the participation of workers in processes of learning are as important for the explanation of differences in innovation performance as differences in national science systems.

Chapter 4 is the introduction to *National Systems of Innovation: Towards a Theory of Innovation and Interactive Learning* (Lundvall 1992). It gives a more complete picture of the innovation system concept and is based on two major assumptions. The first is that learning is the most important process and knowledge the most important resource in the modern economy. The second is that learning is a social and interactive process, and therefore, it is necessary to take into account the role of institutions and organizations when analysing economic processes.

The chapter discusses at some length if it is meaningful to analyse national innovation systems in an era of globalization. It argues that the globalization process makes it even more important to understand both the historical and the current role of the nation state for innovation. It is crucial in order to cope with the contradictions and institutional mismatch that reflect the transformation toward a more globalized economy.

One central point in the chapter is the distinction between a narrow and a wide definition of the innovation system. The first refers mainly to the linkages between research institutions and business, while the second includes and gives special attention to learning that takes place in connection with the normal operation of the production and marketing. This discussion leads to a pragmatic and broad definition of the national innovation system opening up for different definitions depending on historical and local context.

These three chapters (2–4) were written during the period 1984–92. They were inspired by empirical work as well as by interaction with many scholars. The ideas behind them were influenced by interaction with colleagues in the Aalborg University research group on Innovation, Knowledge and Economic Dynamics (the IKE-group), including Esben Sloth Andersen, Asger Brændgaard, Bent Dalum, Birgitte Gregersen, Björn Johnson, Gert Villumsen, Jan Fagerberg and several others. Of special importance was the interaction and discussions with Christopher Freeman who joined our research group as guest professor in the first half of the 1980s.

One characteristic of these contributions on innovation systems is that they increasingly refer to the role of knowledge and learning in relation to the innovation process and innovation systems. Actually the final chapter in *National Systems of Innovation* (Lundvall 1992) was presented under the heading 'Innovation Policy in a Learning Society'. The last chapter in Part II goes further in defining the characteristics of 'the learning economy'. This chapter was co-authored with Björn Johnson and was actually my first scientific journal article published in English. It appeared in 1994 in the *Journal of Industry Studies* (later under the name *Journal of Industry and Innovation*). This chapter takes further steps toward analysing the economics of knowledge and learning. It introduces a taxonomy of knowledge distinguishing between know-what, know-why, know-how and know-who and discusses how learning takes place.

1.1.2 Part III: Economics of knowledge and learning

In *Innovation as an Interactive Process – from User–Producer Interaction to National Systems of Innovation* (Lundvall 1988), I proposed to bring dimensions of work organization and labour market institutions into the analytical framework of innovation systems. Part III of this book presents four contributions that expand on these ideas. The economics of knowledge and learning is analysed, empirical studies of different modes of learning are presented and it is shown that the performance of national innovation systems reflects the degree and form of workers' inclusion in organizational learning. Finally the concept of a national system of innovation is revisited on this basis. All four of these chapters build on papers published during the period 2000–2010.

Chapter 6 was published in its current form in Christensen and Lundvall (2004). The chapter is about the production, diffusion and use of knowledge seen from an economic perspective. Fundamental distinctions between tacit and explicit knowledge and between know-how, know-why, know-what and know-who are related to distinctions between public/private and local/global knowledge. It is argued that the idea of the economy as being knowledge based in its current stage is misleading and that it is more enlightening to assume that we have moved into a learning economy where interactive learning is a key to the economic performance of firms, regions and nations.

This is one reason why a narrow economics perspective is insufficient. The most serious weakness of standard economics is that it abstracts from the fact that agents are more or less competent and that learning processes enhancing competence are fundamental for the economic performance of organizations and regions. When it comes to understanding industrial dynamics in the learning economy, it is necessary to bring in disciplines other than economics in the analysis.

Chapter 7 was first published in *Research Policy* in 2007 and co-authored with three colleagues, Morten Berg Jensen, Björn Johnson and Edward Lorenz. It introduces empirical analysis of two modes of learning – an experience-based mode that involves learning by doing, using and interacting (the DUI-mode) and a science-based mode that makes use of scientific knowledge through research and development (R&D) and interaction with research institutions reflecting a mode of innovation linking Science and Technology to Innovation (STI-mode). The paper is a follow-up on an earlier paper on the role of tacit knowledge in relation to innovation (Johnson et al. 2002).

The empirical analysis is based on survey data from around 700 Danish firms. It shows that firms using mixed strategies, that is, firms that combine a strong version of the STI-mode with a strong version of the DUI-mode, are the most successful in introducing product innovations. The distinctions made and the results obtained have important implications for innovation policy and for the analysis of innovation systems. They help to avoid biased approaches exaggerating the role of science-based innovation, while also indicating limits for experience-based innovation strategies. The basic idea that innovation requires a combination of experience-based and science-based knowledge is widely shared among experts on innovation management and is a common observation in case studies. What is unique about this chapter is that it presents econometric evidence that support this idea.

Chapter 8 was co-authored with Anthony Arundel, Edward Lorenz and Antoine Valeyre and published in *Industrial and Corporate Change* in 2007. The chapter explores the link between the organization of work and innovation through an analysis of national aggregate indicators for the EU member states of respectively organizational forms and innovation modes (how firms innovate). The analysis shows that in nations where work is organized to support high levels of discretion in solving complex problems, firms tend to be more active in terms of innovations developed through their in-house creative efforts. In countries where learning and problem solving on the job are more constrained and little discretion is left to the employee, firms tend to engage in a supplier-dominated innovation strategy. Their technological renewal depends more on the absorption of innovations developed elsewhere. The results suggest that in order to understand national systems of innovation, it is necessary to bring the predominant mode of work into the analysis. Early conceptions of national innovation systems were built on an analysis of interactive learning between producers and users. Now we show that the analysis needs to be founded also on an understanding of how people interact and learn at the workplace in different national economies. The results also suggest that European policy efforts to improve innovation performance as part of the revised Lisbon strategy would benefit from a stronger focus on the diffusion of innovative forms of work organization. A step in this direction would be to develop indicators of work organization that could be directly linked to innovation performance.

The chapter is one in a series of papers using data from the European Survey on Working and Living Conditions showing that there are dramatic differences within Europe when it comes to how work is organized and how workers learn. The first paper developing the taxonomy used was a contribution by Lorenz and Valeyre to the edited volume *How Europe's Economies Learn* (Lorenz and Lundvall 2006). This dimension of national innovation systems which is crucial for innovation performance has been largely neglected both in research and in the design of innovation policy.

Chapter 9 was written as a postscript for the new 2010 edition of the book on national systems of innovation originally published in 1992. It presents the research that constituted the background for the concept of national systems of innovation. It also discusses the diffusion of the concept and different recent interpretations of the concept. It draws the implications from research on economics of knowledge and learning presented above.

In this chapter, it is argued that during the process of diffusion there has been a *distortion* of the concept as compared to the original versions developed by Christopher Freeman and the IKE group in Aalborg. Often policymakers and scholars have applied a narrow understanding of the concept, giving rise to so-called innovation paradoxes, which leave significant elements of innovation-based economic performance unexplained. Such a bias is reflected in studies of innovation that focus on science-based innovation and on the *formal* technological infrastructure and in policies aiming almost exclusively at stimulating R&D efforts in high-tech sectors.

Without a broad definition of the national innovation system encompassing individual, organizational and interorganizational learning, it is impossible to establish the link from innovation to economic growth. A double focus is needed where attention is given not only to the science infrastructure but also to institutions/organizations that support competence building in labour markets, education and working life. This is especially important in the current era of the globalizing learning economy (Lundvall and Johnson 1994; Lundvall and Borràs 1997; Archibugi and Lundvall 2001).

One major reason for this distortion is the uncomfortable coexistence in international bodies such as the Organisation for Economic Co-operation and Development (OECD) and the European Commission of the innovation system approach and the much more narrow understanding of innovation emanating from standard economics (Eparvier 2005). Evolutionary processes of learning where agents are transformed and become more diverse in terms of what they know and what they know how to do are not reconcilable with the rational 'representative agents' that populate the neoclassical world (Dosi 1999).

1.1.3 Part IV: Continental transformations and global challenges

The fourth part of the book contains four chapters based upon recently published papers. Three of those apply the basic concepts to different continents and to major global challenges. Chapter 13 goes back to the two very first contributions that introduced the concept of a national innovation system (Freeman 1982/2004; Lundvall 1985) and shows how they can be used to span the more recent literature on the tension between national and global perspectives on innovation.

Chapter 10 relates innovation systems and the learning economy to China's ambition to develop its national innovation system so that innovation becomes less dependent on foreign sources and more oriented toward social and environmental objectives. Chapter 11 presents a critical view of the European integration project. Specifically it argues that the opportunities offered by the Lisbon Strategy to bridge the gap between Southern and Northern Europe were not exploited. Chapter 12 discusses the implications of a learning economy perspective for Africa's economic transformation. One main conclusion is that the current economic structure with extreme dependence on production and exports of natural resource–based commodities calls for efforts to diversify the economy through active industrial and innovation policies.

Chapter 10 was published in 2006 and co-authored with Shulin Gu who pioneered the study of China's innovation system in her book on China's industrial technology (Gu 1999). The chapter makes an attempt to explain the evolution of China's growth pattern and of Chinese policies aimed at promoting innovation. It refers to domestic debates in China that point to the need for a shift in the growth trajectory with stronger emphasis on 'endogenous innovation' and 'harmonious development'.

This chapter makes an attempt to capture the current characteristics of China's production and innovation system – how they were shaped by recent history and what major challenges they raise for the future. It presents data on China's postwar growth experience. It shows how the shift in policy toward decentralization, privatization and openness around 1980 established an institutional setting that, together with other factors such as the presence of a wide 'Chinese Diaspora', has resulted in extremely high rates of capital accumulation especially in manufacturing.

It also takes a closer look at how the policy shift in the 1980s affected the institutional framework shaping R&D activities, in particular, and learning and innovation, in general. The attempt to break down the barriers between the science and technology infrastructure, on the one hand, and the production sphere, on the other, was highly successful as compared to the development in the former Soviet Union. Nonetheless, the original intentions were not fully realized. Rather than establishing markets for science and technology, the reforms led knowledge producers to engage in mergers or forward vertical integration, and they became to a large extent involved in production activities.

It discusses the decision by China's government to promote endogenous innovation and harmonious development. Applying the innovation system perspective, it argues that these broadly defined objectives can be realized only through a strategic adjustment toward 'innovation-driven growth and learning-based development', and we discuss what important policy elements such a strategic adjustment needs to encompass.

The chapter concludes that imperfections in the division of labour and in the interaction between users and producers of knowledge and innovation that motivated the reforms of the 1980s remain of central concerns. In order to raise the long-term efficiency of the massive accumulation of production capital, it is necessary to promote the formation of social capital and to be more considerate when exploiting natural capital.

Chapter 11 is a critical assessment of the European integration project. The project is of great importance since it is the most ambitious attempt in the world to build transnational governance in a period when the limits of national strategies become increasingly obvious. Therefore it is important to understand why the project now is in crisis and what changes in the strategy are required to get it back on track.

While the Eurozone was originally designed to protect member countries from economic instability, it has now turned into a major source of instability for the world as a whole. When the Economic and Monetary Union (EMU) was established, there were warning voices that a monetary union without a common fiscal policy would be vulnerable to external shocks. The total budget of the EU is only a few per cent of GNP and cannot play the same role as the federal budget in the United States as an automatic stabilizer. This is especially problematic for a currency union bringing together countries at very different levels of economic development. There were elements in the Lisbon Strategy that could have reduced the gaps between Northern and Southern Europe. But the turn toward a more neoliberal strategy that took place around 2005 undermined its capacity to function as a scaffold for the Eurozone (Lundvall and Lorenz 2011).

The chapter shows that the countries in the Eurozone now most exposed to financial speculation are the ones that have the weakest industrial structure with the biggest proportion of workplaces directly exposed to competition from emerging economies. On this background, it is argued that there is a need to design Keynesian policies coordinated at the European level in such a way that they promote deep institutional change in education, labour market and industrial policy in Southern Europe. Public expenditure needs to be allocated to stimulate the learning capacity where it is weakest – this is why the solution may be referred to as a 'new new deal'. It is about redistributing learning capacities.

Chapter 12 is co-authored with Rasmus Lema and published in 2015 in the *African Journal of Science, Technology, Innovation and Development*. It takes as its starting point the discrepancy between the reporting of record growth rates for African economies and the reality of how people's living conditions have evolved over the last decade in African high growth economies. It is argued that the economic upswing as measured by high rates of registered growth in GNP in African countries needs to be used to support structural and institutional change across the economic, social and political spheres bringing them closer to what we refer to as 'learning economies'.

The widening of the gap between reality on the ground and perceptions based on growth rates reflects partly that the increasing global demand for natural resources – especially for commodities such as oil and minerals – has led to advantageous change in terms of trade and to increased export volumes and raised the rates of GNP growth while the impact on domestic employment has often been limited and sometimes negative. The expansion of the commodity sector does not automatically create new employment directly, and so far it has rarely resulted in a substantial increase in job creation in upstream and downstream manufacturing and in knowledge based services.

This is taken as a starting point for an analysis of opportunities and policy options for African countries. What kind of policies and institutions are necessary in order to transform the current increase in rents from commodities exports into industrial investment and upgrading of agriculture and agro-industrial development? Recommendations of neoclassical economists are contrasted with those derived from the classical development economics that includes scholars such as Dobb, Hirschman and Sen. The theoretical perspective proposed on this basis takes into account that we have entered a phase – the learning economy – where it is useful to take as a starting point that 'learning' is at the core of any process of development.

Chapter 13 on innovation systems and globalization goes back to the two very first publications that referred to 'innovation systems' and discusses how they have spanned different research trajectories on innovation. It also indicates a new research agenda on how innovation systems are changed through increased openness. Factors such as deregulation of financial markets, new communication and transport technologies and liberalization of trade have given rise to global networks of production and global value chains. Innovation and learning increasingly take place through transnational interactive learning or through the spread of codified knowledge across national borders.

This chapter compares and confronts two distinct approaches to economic development. Global value chain analysis tends to see participation of firms from low-income countries in global value chains as a prerequisite for economic upgrading and as an important element in moving countries out of poverty. The national innovation system approach gives more attention to building national infrastructure and innovation capabilities. It is argued that it is necessary to combine participation in global trade with building national capabilities and that it is important to combine the two perspectives both in theory and as the basis for economic development strategies. New neoliberal recipes presenting participation in global value chains as a simple and direct road to development are misleading.

1.1.4 Part V: Economics of hope or despair – what next?

Part V concludes the earlier discussions in chapter 14 and addresses global issues regarded through the focusing device 'the learning economy'. The form is brief and essayistic. The chapter begins with reflections on the basic concepts and their roots. With reference to the three chapters on China, Europe and Africa (Chapter 10, 11 and 12 respectively), it is shown that while problems and opportunities are context specific, they often originate from developments in another region. On this basis, the essay points to the need for new forms of global governance that can promote learning worldwide. It ends with ideas for a research agenda.

1.2 What Is Wrong with Economics?

In this book, the focus is on the creation of new kinds of resources (new use values) rather than on allocation of a given set of scarce resources. Further, the focus is upon how individuals and organizations learn rather than on how they make rational decisions on the basis of a given set of preferences. This double change of focus has both theoretical and practical implications. As the focus moves to innovation and learning, the need to revise the understanding of basic concepts in economic theory becomes obvious. Below I have listed 10 points where my research as it is presented in this book indicates a need for a different understanding from the one offered by neoclassical economics.

1. The concept of scarcity is at the very core of neoclassical economic theory, but it does not apply to knowledge.
2. The assumption of rationality and rational expectations cannot be applied to innovation processes.
3. Markets for innovations are not arm's length markets with prices as the major decision criterion.
4. More intense competition often goes hand in hand with more intense cooperation and in combination they tend to stimulate technical and organizational change.
5. Firms and individuals are different in terms of both skills and efforts. To assume a representative agent misses the most important dynamics.
6. Learning is a social process and hence there is a need for a socioeconomic approach to understand the economy.
7. Growing inequality has economic costs as well as social costs since it undermines the processes of learning.
8. At the core of international competitiveness are dynamic capabilities, including the capability to learn, rather than relative costs.
9. Any assessments of impact of expanding international trade should take into account how it affects the national knowledge base in the countries involved.
10. Governments have an important role to play in giving direction to new technological trajectories and in fostering economic development.

Joseph A. Schumpeter has stated that the general equilibrium approach is applicable to a circular flow economy where everything repeats itself period after period and not to a real capitalist economy (Nelson and Winter 1982). The very repetition could explain that individual agents might start to behave as if they were fully informed and made rational decisions. The following chapters support Schumpeter's view and they show that the neoclassical economic perspective is best suited for an economy without innovation. Moreover, they bring the analysis a step further by demonstrating that in order to understand economic dynamics the focus must be on processes of interactive learning taking place in all parts of the economy.

Such a shift in perspective also opens up for positive sum games where competition is combined with global cooperation and where new ways to solve major global problems creates a basis for new patterns of sustainable and equitable development. For instance, the absolute scarcity of certain crucial natural resources can be overcome when knowledge abundance is exploited through global sharing of technological and organizational knowledge. In the last chapter, I will spell out why – in spite of several deep world crises – there is hope for the future. One fundamental reason for optimism is that all people, including economists and policymakers, do have the potential to learn from experience.

References

Archibugi, D. and Lundvall, B.-Å. (eds.). 2001. *Europe in the Globalising Learning Economy*. Oxford: Oxford University Press.

Arundel A., Lorenz E., Lundvall, B.-Å. and Valeyre A. 2007. 'How Europe's Economies Learn: A Comparison of Work Organization and Innovation Mode for the EU-15'. *Industrial and Corporate Change* 16, no. 6: 1175–210.

Christensen, J. L. and Lundvall, B.-Å. (eds.). 2004. *Product Innovation, Interactive Learning and Economic Performance*. Amsterdam: North Holland.

Dosi, G. 1999. 'Some Notes on National Systems of Innovation and Production and Their Implication for Economic Analysis'. In *Innovation Policy in a Global Economy*, edited by Archibugi, D., Howells, J. and Michie, J. Cambridge: Cambridge University Press.

Dosi, G., Freeman, C., Nelson, R. R., Silverberg, G. and Soete, L. (eds.). 1988. *Technology and Economic Theory*. London: Pinter Publishers.

Eparvier, P. 2005. 'Methods of Evolutionism and Rivalry with Neoclassical Analysis. The Example of the National System of Innovation Concept'. *Journal of Economic Methodology* 12, no. 4: 563–79.

Freeman, C. 1982/2004. 'Technological Infrastructure and International Competitiveness', *Industrial and Corporate Change* 13, no. 3: 540–52.

Gu, S. 1999. *China's Industrial Technology, Market Reform and Organizational Change*. Routledge in association with the UNU Press, London and New York.

Gu, S. and Lundvall, B.-Å. 2006. 'China's Innovation System and the Move toward Harmonious Growth and Endogenous Innovation', *Innovation: Management, Policy & Practice* 8, no. 1–2: 1–26.

Jensen, M.B., Johnson, B., Lorenz, E. and Lundvall, B.-Å. 2007. 'Forms of Knowledge and Modes of Innovation', *Research Policy* 36, no. 5: 680–93.

Johnson, B., Lorenz, E. and Lundvall, B.-Å. 2002. 'Why All This Fuss about Codified and Tacit Knowledge?', *Industrial and Corporate Change* 11: 245–62.

Kornai, Janos. 1971. *Anti-Equilibrium: On Economic Systems Theory and the Tasks of Research*. Amsterdam: North Holland. Reprinted in New York: Augustus Kelley (1991).

Lorenz, E. and Lundvall, B.-Å. (eds.). 2006. *How Europe's Economies Learn*. Oxford: Oxford University Press.

Lundvall, B.-Å. 1985. *Product Innovation and User-Producer Interaction*. Aalborg: Aalborg University Press.

———. 1988. 'Innovation as an Interactive Process – from User-Producer Interaction to National Systems of Innovation'. In *Technology and Economic Theory*, edited by Dosi, G. (eds.). London: Pinter Publishers.

————. 1992. 'Introduction'. In *National Systems of Innovation: Towards a Theory of Innovation and Interactive Learning*, edited by Lundvall, B.-Å. London: Pinter Publishers.

————. 2004. 'The Economics of Knowledge and Learning'. In *Product innovation, Interactive Learning and Economic Performance*, edited by Christensen, J. L. and Lundvall, B.-Å. Amsterdam: JAI Press Ltd.

————. 2010. 'Post Script: Innovation System Research – Where It Came from and Where It Might Go'. In *National Systems of Innovation: Towards a Theory of Innovation and Interactive Learning*, 317–349, edited by Lundvall, B.-Å. London: Anthem.

————. 2013. 'The 'New New Deal' as a Response to the Euro-crisis'. In *Before and Beyond the Global Economic Crises*, 151–172, edited by Benner, M. Cheltenham: Elgar.

————. 2016. 'Innovation Systems and Value Chains in the Globalizing Learning Economy'. In *The Elgar Companion to Innovation and Knowledge Creation*, edited by Bathelt, H., Cohendet, P., Henn, S. and Simon, L. Cheltenham: Elgar.

Lundvall, B.-Å. and Borràs, S. 1997. *The Globalising Learning Economy: Implications for Innovation Policy*. Brussels: DG XII.

Lundvall, B.-Å. and Johnson, B. 1994. 'The Learning Economy'. *Journal of Industry Studies* 1, no. 2: 23–42.

Lundvall, B.-Å. and Lema, R. 2015. 'Growth and Structural Change in Africa: Development Strategies for the Learning Economy'. *African Journal for Science, Technology, Innovation and Development*. 6, no. 5: 455–66.

Lundvall, B.-Å. and Lorenz, E. 2011. 'From the Lisbon Strategy to EUROPE 2020'. In *Towards a Social Investment Welfare State: Ideas, Policies and Challenges*, 333–35, edited by Morel, N., Palier, B. and Palme, J. Bristol: Policy Press.

Nelson, R. R. and S. G. Winter. 1982. *An Evolutionary Theory of Economic Change*. Cambridge, Mass. and London: Belknap Press of Harvard University Press.

Rosenberg, N. 1976. *Perspectives on Technology*. Cambridge: Cambridge University Press.

Rothwell, R. 1972. 'Factors for Success in Industrial Innovations: Project SAPPHO – A Comparative Study of Success and Failure in Industrial Innovation', *Science Policy Research Unit*, University of Sussex, Brighton.

————. 1977. 'The Characteristics of Successful Innovators and Technically Progressive Firms'. *R&D Management* 7, no. 3: 191–206.

Part II
INNOVATION AS INTERACTIVE PROCESS

Chapter 2

PRODUCT INNOVATION AND USER–PRODUCER INTERACTION

Bengt-Åke Lundvall

2.1 Introduction

The purpose of this chapter is to demonstrate the usefulness of applying a user–producer perspective to innovation. A set of analytical and normative propositions – which are neither trivial nor conventional – is developed by focusing on the relationships and the interaction between users and producers of innovations.

The ideas presented here reflect a collective effort. Since 1977, the research program on Innovation, Knowledge and Economic dynamics (the IKE group), consisting mainly of economists but also attracting other social scientists and engineers, at the Department of Industrial Production, Aalborg University, has been working on problems relating to industrial development, international competitiveness and technical change. The approach has been heretic rather than mainstream and eclectic rather than dogmatic. It was developed partially by importing and borrowing from some different new schools with quite disparate origins.

One of the main imports came from France, where Francois Perroux and his followers have put great emphasis on the analysis of vertically organized systems of production. Another came from the United Kingdom, where Christopher Freeman and others at the Science Policy Research Unit (SPRU) have focused on industrial innovations. In Aalborg, a new combination has been tried. Innovative activities within vertically organized units, as verticals of production, industrial complexes and national systems of production, have been analysed.

The empirical work pursued so far should be regarded as exploratory. The hypotheses tested have been crude, reflecting a certain vagueness in the theoretical framework. This chapter represents a modest attempt towards a clarification. Empirical work from the IKE group will be referred to occasionally, but no comprehensive presentation will be attempted.

In developing the argument, I have leaned heavily on some central works by Nathan Rosenberg and Kenneth Arrow. Rosenberg's analysis (1972, 1976, 1982) of how users interact with producers in specific parts of the economy and under specific historical circumstances has helped to clarify many of the problems involved. Arrow's works (1962, 1969, 1973) on uncertainty and organization theory have inspired essential parts of the conceptual framework.

This chapter is divided into seven sections. Section 2.2 introduces fundamental concepts and postulates. Section 2.3 is a discussion of the relationship between market structure, innovation and transaction modes. Section 2.4 presents empirical illustrations of unsatisfactory innovations originating from specific user–producer relationships. Sections 2.5 and 2.6 apply the user–producer perspective to, respectively, locational problems and the science technology nexus. Section 2.7 relates a number of propositions to units of analysis at different levels of aggregation. In Section 2.8 some concluding remarks are presented.

The user–producer perspective has thus been applied to a broad and diverse range of phenomena. This is reflected in the presentation, which also has brought me into subdisciplines of economics, where my expertise is limited. There is ample room for users to take part in the debugging of this semi-finished product.

2.2 The Framework

In this section we shall present the central concepts used and the related propositions. Limitations regarding the validity and scope of the analysis will also be pointed out.

2.2.1 Innovation and innovative activity

It is common to regard an innovation as a distinct event, which can be dated in time. Empirical work trying to explain innovation has often taken its departure in a list of such dated events.

In this chapter we shall focus on the ongoing process of innovative activities, as well as on singular events. The outcome of this process includes both gradual technical change and discrete leaps in technical opportunities. But, the process is cumulative, and even the most conspicuous single innovation has its roots in accumulated knowledge and experience.

2.2.2 Technical opportunity and user needs

We shall regard innovations as the result of collisions between technical opportunity and user needs. We acknowledge that single innovations might result from pure accidents, but we do not see this as a normal pattern.

This implies that the innovating unit needs access not only to information about technical opportunities but also to information about user needs. We shall assume that information about user needs is differing in complexity and appropriability in the economy but that some costs and efforts always are involved in obtaining the information. The assumption that information about user needs is not a public good is of central importance for the results presented. In the first part of the next section we shall specify the need for information gathering on the part of innovating units.

2.2.3 The separation of the user from the innovating unit

Our analysis relates to the interaction between units innovating and other units, which are potential users of the innovations. This perspective is only relevant if the innovating and the using unit have been separated from each other. In the extreme case, when for example, a scientist as an integrated part of a research project, develops new methods and scientific instruments in order to solve a problem, no informational problems will be involved.

If we disregard such extreme cases, there will always be a separation between the innovating unit and the user. This will also be the case within organizations where different individuals or departments will have to interact and exchange information. It will obviously be the case, when there is a vertical division of labour between different organizations. In Section 2.3 we shall treat the special case where users and producers are separated by a market.

2.2.4 Innovation and production

Relating technical opportunities to user needs involves a logical problem. There is an immense amount of user needs in the economy, and all users might in principle be regarded as potential users of an innovation. Is it possible to define a set of users, ex ante, before the new product has been developed and procured by the users?

To overcome this difficulty, we assume that innovational activities take place in units engaged in production. We shall also assume that this production addresses a definite set of users and that the innovations are oriented towards the needs of a subset within this set. The product might be tangible – a machine tool – or intangible – a software package.

Production is a routine process resulting in a regular flow of products from producers to users. Innovation is a search process characterized by less regularity in its outcome. Production and innovations are interdependent. Information obtained in relation to production and in relation to the regular flow of products feeds the innovational process. Innovations, then in turn, reshape production and the regular flows.

This distinction between innovation and production might be difficult to apply to units designed specifically to promote innovation – R&D departments and research institutes – but even in such cases we believe that certain routine activities addressed towards a specific set of users can be identified.

The fact that innovational activities are addressed towards a specific set of users does not exclude the possibility that the result of those activities – a product innovation – might be diffused to new categories of users whose needs were not taken into account when the innovation was developed. Innovations might result in an extension of the set of users related to the innovating unit.

2.2.5 Consumers and professional users

The concept of needs is in itself a fuzzy one. Should it represent the actual behaviour in terms of effective demand and revealed preferences, or should it relate to the wants of the potential users? Actual behaviour can only give limited relevant information to the innovation process. A product innovation will typically address needs that cannot be fulfilled by existing products. Nevertheless, it also seems to be an impossible task for the producer to lay bare the indifference curves and translate them into user needs, which can be addressed by new products.

This problem will, however, take different forms depending on the nature of the user. A distinction between professional users and consumers proves to be useful. The goal function of the consumer is broad and can only be defined in very general terms such as utility maximization, satisfaction and happiness, etc. The professional user, however, is a user acting within the formal part of the economy and has a more restricted goal for his activities. In the former category, it is dubious to ascribe needs to the user and to separate needs from wants. This is less so, when the user is a professional one. If the goal function is properly defined, bottlenecks can be pointed out and new and better ways to produce goods and services could be identified or developed. An external observer might be able to discover needs that the user has not yet been able to put on to his agenda as wants.

This difference between consumer and professional user is also reflected in their respective behaviours in relation to innovations. On the one hand, the professional user is expected to be active in his search for new ways to solve his problems. He will also be expected to adapt his behaviour and qualifications when new technical opportunities come forward. This might include formal training as well as learning-by-doing. The consumer, on the other hand is expected to be more passive. He will not engage in systematic search for new products, and he will not be prone to adopt products, which involve extensive training and changes in behaviour.

This difference in (expected) behaviour is reinforced by the producer addressing the respective category of users. The producers of consumer goods will use market research to uncover the needs of the consumers, and they will use advertising both to make new products known to consumers and to influence the needs involved. They will also be conservative in their product innovations in order to minimize the change in user behaviour imposed by the new product. Product innovations in this area might be radical in terms of the technology built into the product. In terms of the interface between user and product, however, they will tend to be conservative.

In this chapter we shall mainly be concerned with user–producer relationships where the user is a professional one. This limitation makes it possible to operate with a concept of needs that is reasonably clear. Still, we can include a part of innovative activities, which has had a great impact on the overall process of technical change. Some revolutionary innovations such as the automobiles and television, etc., have, however, developed at the interface between producers and consumers, and those fall outside our framework of analysis.[1]

The distinction made above reflects the characteristic institutional arrangements for modern industrial societies. This is to not to say that those arrangements are in any sense 'optimal'. New institutions involving consumers directly or indirectly in innovative activities, might liberate new social forces stimulating the process of technical change. This is, however, a subject that will not be addressed in this chapter.

In certain areas the distinction between consumer and professional user is less clear-cut. Consumers acting as amateurs involved in hobbies might display a behaviour that is close to the one displayed by professional users. The user-clubs related to specific brands of home computers are just one example demonstrating that the amateurs might be as advanced as professionals in terms of both use and innovativeness.[2]

2.2.6 Behavioural assumptions

Our analysis will not be based on very specific behavioural assumptions. It can be applied to units optimizing under conditions of limited rationality and uncertainty as well as to satisficing units. We disregard the possibility of full information and unlimited rationality, however, and we also discard the possibility of totally erratic behaviour.

The units studied here are assumed to have certain (possibly vague) goals; we assume that they will make some efforts to reach those goals in a reasonably economic way. This implies, for example, that they will be influenced by changes in relative prices and by cost-reducing innovations. The influence might take a long time to take effect in actual behaviour and might be weak compared to other forces at work.

We believe that those rather loose assumptions are sufficient for our purpose. A more precise analysis of the impact of user–producer relationships, however, would require more strict assumptions.

2.2.7 Information

We shall make frequent use of concepts developed within information theory. We shall assume that information is flowing between units, passing through information channels and transformed into specific codes. We shall also assume that each unit has a memory consisting of accumulated information, as well as an agenda consisting of items that are scrutinized by the unit.

In a dynamic perspective, the establishment of information channels and codes can be regarded as investments. It is time consuming as well as costly to develop new channels of information and new codes. The memory is growing in volume as new information enters it, either as a result of internal experience from learning-by-doing or learning-by-using, or as a result of information brought into the organization from external units. As new information is obtained, new items might enter the agenda of the organization and old ones might be excluded.

In Section 2.5 we shall add 'distance' to this framework, a concept relating to differences in location and cultural background of the parties involved in the exchange of information. We shall also discuss the impact of instability and complexity in messages communicated between the parties.

2.2.8 Linkages and channels of information

The linkages between a user and a producer describe the regular flows of tangible or intangible products from the producer to the user. Such linkages can be described by an extended input/output table where capital goods are treated not as final demand, but as intermediate goods.

The channels of information between user and producer describe a flow of signals that are not embodied in the regular flow of products. We shall assume that the network of linkages and the network of information channels will be overlapping to a substantial degree. The linkages relate to production while the information channels relate to innovation. An important aspect of the innovation process is the exchange of disembodied information between the producer and the user via information channels. This is another way to state the close relationship between innovation and production.

The relationship between user and producer involves both linkages and channels of information. They also involve the content of the products and the information exchanged, here defined in relation to the technology involved as well as the characteristics of the user and the producer.

The interaction between user and producer takes three different forms: exchange of products, exchange of information and cooperation.

We shall regard situations where the user and the producer engage in a common project, as a situation where cooperation takes place. Cooperation can take place between different organizations as well as between separate units within an organization.

2.2.9 The stability of relationships

There are several factors reinforcing relationships once they have been established. The channels of information and the codes used within a given channel are costly to establish. As the channel and the code are established, learning takes place and the effectiveness of the exchange of information grows. Alternative channels and codes become relatively less attractive. Only when alternatives offer substantial returns will it be rational to change channels and codes. Even in such situations, inertia might prevail as long as the old channels can be operated under satisfactory conditions.

This general observation deriving from information theory is reinforced by the characteristics of technology and innovations. When the information relates to technology, the code will be complex and specific, making the change of channels and codes extra expensive.

One of the most general propositions emanating from our analysis is that the stability of user–producer relationships reinforces the innovative process in certain directions but hampers it in other directions. The interaction between innovation and user–producer relationships is far from harmonious and states of disequilibrium, reflected in unsatisfactory innovations, prevail. This subject will be illustrated in Section 2.4 by empirical examples. Before that, a classical issue in economic theory, the relation between market and organization shall be addressed in Section 2.3.

2.3 Product Innovation and the Organized Market

In this section we shall relate the interaction between user and producer to the market. We shall try to demonstrate that both the pure market and the pure hierarchy have narrow limits to their ability to promote product innovations. In this section, we define product innovations as innovations addressed towards the needs of users separated from the innovating unit by a market. Process innovations are innovations addressing the internal needs of the innovating unit. On this background we shall propose that the actual rate of product innovations can be explained only by the fact that most markets are organized involving elements of hierarchy as well as elements of cooperation and mutual trust.

2.3.1 Producer dependence – information about user needs as an input to the innovative process

The product innovating producer unit has strong incentives to monitor what is going on within user units. As we shall see, it is not primarily a question of getting an isolated signal about a new need among the users. It is a continuous process of information gathering that might involve considerable costs and resources. First, the producer will monitor process innovations within the user units. If the process innovations are successful, the producer might appropriate them and present them to other users as a product innovation.

Product innovations within user units will often imply changes in the process technology. The producer will therefore monitor the product innovations within user units. If a certain product innovation becomes successful, it might open up a new rapidly widening market for new process equipment.

Technological bottlenecks and technological interdependencies observed in user units offer potential markets for the innovating producer. Such problems might be complex and in some cases, the producer must have direct access to specific information about the production process of the user in order to contribute to a solution.

Users of complex and changing technologies will be involved in a process of learning-by-using. Access to experience and know-how accumulated in this process will be crucial for the producer. When developing a specific innovation, the producer must consider the competence and learning capacity of the users. Very advanced solutions that demand too much in relation to the users' know-how will not be diffused.

Finally, when a product innovation has been developed by the producer and adopted by some users, a more specific monitoring process takes place. In order to debug the innovation, the producer must monitor its usage, the learning-by-using taking place and the new bottlenecks, etc.

2.3.2 User dependence – information necessary to adopt and adapt product innovations

The users will also be engaged in a (more or less intensive) search for information about new technical opportunities that can result in a better performance. They will have incentives to monitor innovative activities among producers and also to monitor the competence of different producers.

To be aware of a specific product innovation is only a first step. The users have to gather information, making it possible to assess the potential impact on their own performance and the compatibility with their competence and learning capacity. Especially, if the product innovation is at an early stage of diffusion, such information will be extremely difficult to obtain and a considerable amount of uncertainty will be involved.

The users will experience specific bottlenecks in the regular production process. When developing new products, they will discover that the process technology used must be changed. To solve those problems, they might involve an independent producer in the analysis and solution. In order to do that, they must know which producer to approach. This gives them an incentive to monitor the competence of producers.

2.3.3 Incentives to exchange information

In order to get an effective solution to his problems, the user must give the producer a certain minimum amount of information about his needs. The more free access the producer gets to such information, the greater the chance for a successful solution. If the user unit is competing with other users, it might be problematic to give a producer free access to its technology and to its needs. There will be a risk that the producer might appropriate information and distribute it to other users. This places the user in a dilemma to which we shall return in the following sections.

The producers are interested in diffusing information to users about their respective competence and about their product innovations. If a producer unit is involved in competition, however, it will also face a dilemma. On one hand, it needs to convince users about the superiority of its competence, reliability and product innovations. This might demand an extensive disclosure of the product innovations involved. On the other hand, it does not want competitors to get access to its technology.

2.3.4 The need for cooperation between user and producer

Certain new products can be ordered by catalogue or bought off the shelf by the user. This will be the case for low-priced standard components. Other types of products, typically specialized and expensive capital goods, can only be adopted in a process of cooperation between the user and the producer.

The cooperation might take place in different steps. The user might present the producer with specific needs that the new product should fulfil. When the product innovation has been developed, the producer might install it and start it up in cooperation with the user. In this phase, the producer might offer training in the use of the new product. After the product has been adopted, the producer might have a responsibility for updating the product as well as for repair and service.

The extent of the cooperation necessary might vary with the type of product innovation. But we shall assume that most important product innovations involve at least some elements of cooperation. This increases the uncertainty on behalf of the user. The user unit does not only procure a product with uncertain properties, it also becomes dependent on the future behaviour of the producer. This reinforces the user's efforts to monitor competence and reliability. The choice of a specific producer might be as decisive as the choice of a specific product innovation.

We, thus find that the users and producers of product innovations are mutually interdependent in a complex way. We shall now discuss how such an interdependence will be influenced by different institutional frameworks connecting users to producers. To which degree can the market mechanism intermediate this interdependence?

2.3.5 Perfect competition and product innovations

If a great number of producers are competing and if the users are anonymous and numerous, the only information directed to producers will be price signals. It is less clear how the users will get acquainted with new products in such a market. Let us assume that they can observe new products at the marketplace by inspection.

It should be obvious that perfect competition does not induce product innovations. The producer does not get any information about user needs that are not already served by the market (the fact that we operate with professional users excludes the possibility of introspection and own use, as a substitute for such information). The user can only observe superficial characteristics of new products. The uncertainty in assessing the impact on performance will be enormous if the product is complex.

Perfect competition, thus, will imply a weak innovative capability on the part of producers and a weak incentive to develop product innovations with complex properties. Such new products will typically diffuse very slowly or not diffuse at all.

Perfect competition does not, however, affect process innovations to the same negative degree. Here the information about user needs is available within the producing unit, and the user can get full and immediate access to information about the properties of the new process. The most important limitation to process innovations will be the small scale of the operation involved. There will be no external market for the new process, and the appropriation of benefits will be related exclusively to cost reductions within the producer unit. This will put strict and narrow limits on the amount of resources allocated towards innovative activities. Process innovations will mainly result from learning-by-doing and learning-by-using (i.e. from activities that do not impose any extra costs on the producer).

It might be interesting to relate this result to the fact that product innovations are neglected within neoclassical theory. It seems as if this is quite logical as far as the basic models operate on the basis of an assumption about perfect competition.

Arrow (1962) has demonstrated that the externalities involved in relation to R&D activities will tend to result in a suboptimal allocation of investment funds to such activities. The result obtained earlier points to another mechanism that works in the same direction. It also points to the fact that a market form, assumed to be the only one guaranteeing optimal allocation of resources in a static framework, might be the one least suited to promote technical change. Only if we assume that producers have immediate access to information, not only about 'revealed preferences' but also about needs and wants in relation to products that do not exist, can this problem be overcome. But such omniscience on behalf of the producer would be in conflict with the assumption about anonymity in the relationship between user and producer.

In markets that come close to the ideal of perfect competition, we should expect that product innovations are developed by accident rather than as a result of purposeful innovative activities. Trivial changes in product design might be more easily introduced than complex product innovations. Process innovations, mainly based on learning, might take place simultaneously within all producer units, but the rate of innovation will be limited by the scale of operation involved.

Do markets characterized by perfect competition exist in the real world? Do they influence technical change in the way predicted? In markets where professional users operate, it is not so easy to find examples. Markets for vegetables and fruit, where numerous restaurant owners come and inspect the products of numerous producers, might be one example. Product innovations are not frequent in this area, and process innovations are mainly reflecting learning.[3]

This fact, however, also reflects a combination of conservative users and natural limits to product innovation. We shall argue that the potential for product innovations, in terms of the rate of change in user needs and new technical opportunities, influences the form of the market. Perfect competition can only survive where this potential is small. In the case mentioned above, a future application of biotechnology to product development might undermine the anonymous relationships between user and producer. To which extent this will become the case, will depend on the willingness to adopt new products in restaurants.[4]

Let us see why a growing potential for product development undermines perfect competition. If this potential reflects new technical opportunities, the producer unit can benefit from vertical integration with one or more user units. It will get access to information about the needs of the users, and the producer will be able to monitor the application of the new technical opportunities to those needs. On this basis, it can develop products that are superior to those of competing producers and extend the market share.

If the new potential reflects new user needs, a user can gain from vertical integration. By integrating a producer, the user unit will get immediate access to the technical competences within the producer unit, and it can gear it towards the new needs experienced. If the user unit is involved in competition with other users, it will be able to reduce costs and obtain a growing share of the market.

Vertical integration undermines perfect competition in three different ways. Directly, it diminishes the flow of goods transmitted by an anonymous market. Indirectly, it gives rise to concentration both on the producer and the user side of the market. If we assume that learning by producing and learning by using are important in relation to the new products involved, the process of concentration will be reinforced.

In the treatment of vertical integration by Oliver Williamson (1975), the main explanation for this phenomenon is said to be that transaction costs are high when 'small numbers' are involved. We shall suggest that vertical integration motivated by information problems will take place also when 'large numbers' are present. Furthermore, Williamson argues that technological factors do not play any decisive role in determining vertical integration. We shall disagree and suggest that new technical opportunities will induce vertical integration when large numbers are involved.

Our conclusion is thus: perfect competition forms an environment hostile to product innovations, and a growing potential for product innovations will undermine perfect competition.

2.3.6 Small numbers and product innovations

Within the category of nonperfect competition, several different constellations might occur:

a. One producer might relate to one user, a few users, or to numerous users.
b. A few producers might relate to one user, a few or numerous users.
c. Finally, many producers might relate to one or a few users.

Thus, we have at least eight different constellations involving 'small numbers' either on the producer or on the user side of the market. It will, of course, not be possible to go into details regarding all those constellations. Here we shall only present some general implications of small numbers in relation to product innovations. In doing so, we shall refer to the ideas developed by Williamson and use his conceptual framework as far as it applies to the problems treated. Thus, we shall accept that the actors involved are characterized by bounded rationality and that the environment is characterized by uncertainty and complexity.

Bringing in product innovations within such a framework gives interesting results. In sections 2.2 and 2.3, we specified the information needs of the producer and the user in relation to product innovations. If we take a closer look at the distribution of information in relation to those needs, we find that information asymmetry and 'information impactedness' prevail; the producer has access to information about technical opportunities, which the user does not have, and the user has access to information about user needs, which the producer does not have.

We also find that 'uncertainty and complexity' is involved not only in the environment but also in the product itself. The user units will, especially in the early stage of diffusion, have very limited possibilities to assess how the new product will affect their performance. The users will also have difficulties in assessing the future services that shall be delivered by the producer. If the producer is opportunistic, there will be ample room for 'cheating' the user. The producers might exaggerate their own competence and the capacity of the new product in order to attract users. The producers may knowingly promise to solve problems that cannot be solved and to deliver a package of services that cannot be delivered.

The room for cheating is more limited on behalf of the user. The user cannot misinform the producer without risking that it affects the effectiveness of the solution. The users can, of course, misinform the producer in relation to factors not directly related to their technical needs. The user unit can overstate its own capability to develop a substitute for the product, for example. Finally, the producer as well as the user might 'spill information' to competitors of the respective counterpart. Or they might use information obtained to invade the market of the other party. It should be observed that those specific problems, having their origin in the fact that a product innovation is involved, should be added to the general problems concerning an uncertain and complex environment.

Can a contract be written that eliminates the possibility of cheating in such a situation? I think that it is obvious that opportunistic behaviour on behalf of both parties would normally result in haggling and in tremendous transaction costs when complex product innovations are involved. This has two important implications. First, if opportunistic behaviour prevails, small-number markets might be as inefficient as perfect competition in promoting product innovations. We should expect that all, or almost all, complex innovations were process innovations (i.e., developed within presumptive user units). Second, this kind of market failure should result in a movement towards vertical integration where users and producers become joined within the same organization. We should expect that most important innovations were located within vertically organized firms. Also, we should expect a correlation in the opposite direction. The greater the potential for product innovations in a user–producer relationship, the more this relationship should be mediated by a hierarchy rather than by a market.

At this point, we do not have any systematic evidence relating to all those implications. We do know, however, that empirical studies of great numbers of important innovations indicate that the majority of those innovations are product innovations (Pavitt 1984) (i.e. innovations developed for external users separated from the innovating unit by a market rather than process innovations). This is not easily reconciled with the implications of an organizational failure framework. Later on we shall question some fundamental concepts within this framework, but first we shall take into account some factors counteracting vertical integration.

2.3.7 The limits of vertical integration

The informational problems related to product innovations can explain why vertical integration might be ineffective under certain circumstances when small numbers are involved.

If there is only one user involved and several producers, the user will be able to control the producers by playing one out against another. The room for cheating is diminished, and the incentives towards vertical integration are weak.

If there is only one producer addressing several users, an integration of one of those users will equate an invasion of the market of the users. This will increase the producer's incentives to cheat, and the risks for getting cheated will grow among the rest of the users. The rest of the users might, therefore, be expected to react either by developing their own capability in the field controlled by the producer or by stimulating the entrance of new producers. Only, if the invasion of the market of users can be expected to result in a very radical expansion of the market share of the user unit integrated, and if the rest of the users have a very limited ability to develop alternative sources for their process technology, will such a strategy be attractive for the producer. This might be the case where a radical product innovation induces a very dramatic increase in the effectiveness in user units and also involves steeply increasing returns to scale.

If there are several producers and several users, the vertical integration might be either upstream or downstream. If a user integrates a producer, the user will get access to the technical competence(s) of the producer, and uncertainty can be reduced. At the same time it is to be expected that the other users will restrict their procurements from and interaction with the integrated producer. They will be less prone to give the producer access to information about their own process technology. They will fear that the producer transfers critical information to the vertically integrated user and that the producer delivers less efficient technology than he delivers in-house As a result the producer unit will get its information input regarding user needs restricted to what can be obtained within the new organization, and this might gradually erode its technological competence(s). This means also that the user, by integrating vertically with one producer, in the long run, might get stuck with more limited technical opportunities than the other users.[5]

If a producer takes over a user unit, the same type of problems will occur. The producer unit's access to the rest of the users will become limited because it has become a competitor to the other users.

If there is only one user and only one producer involved, vertical integration might be effective in overcoming contractual and informational problems. However other limits, relating to large size, might be operating.

Our conclusion is that markets characterized by small numbers and by frequent and complex product innovations will not easily be transformed into hierarchies. Vertical integration might have detrimental effects on users as well as producers by reducing market shares and flows of information to the producer level. Only in the limiting case where there is one user and one producer operating in the market can no such negative effects be expected.

This is another way of stating that product innovations will be 'superior' to process innovations as long as the user is not a monopoly. Product innovations use a broader set of user experiences as input into the innovative process than process innovations, which only can use the experiences and needs of one single user. Here we reach a conclusion opposite to the one presented in the last section: Innovations will be stimulated by a vertical division of labour between producers and user belonging to different organizations. How to solve this apparent contradiction? We believe that the answer lies in the existence of organized markets. This concept will be treated in the next section.

2.3.8 The organized market and product innovations

In the organization failure framework, a clear-cut distinction is made between the market and the organization. Also, the coordination mechanism meant to play the most important role within the organization is hierarchy. All parties are presumed to act opportunistically, presenting false information and cheating, whenever it pays off to do so. We shall question all those assumptions and distinctions.

If a producer is going to supply to a specific set of users on a regular basis, it would be unwise to become known as an opportunistic cheater. Especially if we allow for information exchange among the users, it seems as if opportunistic behaviour will be less rewarding from the point of view of the producer. Such an information exchange will take place between professional users. Professional users often have their own organizations, which, as one important purpose, have to supply their members with such information (when the users are consumers, the room for cheating is bigger, but in this case the room for vertical integration is also more limited).

Especially when complex product innovations are exchanged, the trustworthiness of the producer becomes a decisive competitive factor. The costs inflicted on the user by a cheating producer will be considerable, and the user will often have to accept the word of the producer as the only guarantee that the innovation will perform according to specifications. Producers regarded as trustworthy will attract users, whereas producers regarded as unreliable may be offering advanced technical solutions without attracting users. This will counteract any tendency towards cheating. An important aspect of a producer strategy will be to build a relationship characterized by mutual trust with users.

This will be reinforced by the fact that producers depend on information about user needs as an input to their innovative activities. A producer who acts opportunistically risks being excluded from access to such information. That would put him into a serious disadvantage in relation to markets where there is a big potential for product innovations.

In such areas, we believe that 'codes of conduct' are imposed on users as well as producers. Such codes might be tacit and vague, but still they will make distinctions between what is acceptable and what is not. They will impose responsibility and restraint on the producers, defining limits for what is serious misinformation. They will also define limits for spilling information to the competitors of the other party. We also believe that relatively stable user–producer relationships will develop. Every single user will establish special and long-lasting relations with a subset of all producers and vice versa. This makes it easier to establish mutual trust and effective exchange of information. This vertical semi-integration differs from full integration in that it is a more easily reversible relationship that will not have as strong a negative impact on the flow of information as full integration.

Such subsets of user–producer relationships might involve elements of hierarchy. The user might dominate the innovative activities within producer units, which are formally independent and vice versa. We do not, however, believe that all user–producer relationships can be described exclusively in terms of hierarchy. If mutual trust and responsibility are totally absent, such hierarchies will be difficult to operate for the dominant part.

We shall propose that the predominance of product innovations only can be explained by the fact that markets become organized. The clear-cut distinction between market and organization might be a useful analytical tool, but it does not reflect reality. We shall also propose that the element of organization entering the market cannot be reduced to a dimension of hierarchy. Hierarchical relationships are combined with elements of cooperation and mutual trust. In markets where complex product innovations are addressed to professional users, opportunistic behaviour will be counterproductive for producers as well as users.

More generally, one might ask why opportunism should be the most dominating characteristic of human behaviour. Substantial resources are invested in bringing up children to be honest, responsible and caring for others. The reason why the result should be professional liars is not obvious. The predominance of competition and economic incentives may foster opportunistic behaviour within private firms, but even in this sphere, countervailing forces are at work. At least, this will be the case when complex product innovations are involved.

2.3.9 Williamson on innovations and technical change

In Williamson (1975), there is a chapter on market structure in relation to technical and organizational innovation. It is, however, characteristic that the part of it relating to technical innovation almost exclusively refers to how big firms perform compared to small firms. The exchange of information between user and producer relating to innovative activities is not taken into account. This might explain why Williamson concludes that his analysis 'makes it evident that it is transactions rather than technology that underlie the interesting issues of microeconomic organisations.'[6]

A user–producer perspective brings forward radically different conclusions. The interaction between users and producers exchanging product innovations and information is a process that has a strong impact on microeconomic organization. In this section we have focused on situations where the users and the producers are separated by a market. An extension of the analysis to the internal structure of organizations might also produce interesting results. Later, we shall mention some instances where differences in the internal user–producer relationships seem to influence the rate and direction of technical change.

2.4 Unsatisfactory Innovations

An economist has been characterized as one who by training, thinks of himself 'as the guardian of rationality, the ascriber of rationality to others, and the prescriber of rationality to the social world' (Arrow 1974). One of the main preoccupations of economists has been to assess how different institutional frameworks influence the performance as compared to what is 'optimal'. Mostly, however, this has been done in static framework. Welfare economics has been more geared to problems of how to allocate a given bundle of resources than to problems relating to innovations.

Microeconomics and industrial economics have focused on how different market forms influence prices and quantities produced. Antitrust policies reducing the gap between actual and optimal behaviour have been recommended. Is it possible to extend such a perspective to the dynamic efficiency properties of constellations of users and producers? Can we explain deviations from the optimal rate and direction of innovation by specific properties of user–producer relationships? Can we develop a set of policy recommendations based on such an analysis?

The first problem involved is related to defining what is optimal? Innovations might be regarded as 'invasions of unknown territories'. How should we possibly be able, ex ante, to deem if extensions in one direction are better than extensions in another? The optimal pattern of innovation is not a useful concept. However, this does not mean that any assessment of innovative performance is without meaning. It might be possible to locate situations where the actual rate and direction of innovations does deviate from the potential in a conspicuous way. A systematic analysis of technical opportunities and user needs can demonstrate that actual innovations do not exploit fully the opportunities present or do not reflect user needs.

One explanation of such deviations between a satisfactory development and the actual development might be rooted in the specific user–producer relationships prevailing. There are several factors that promote stability and even inertia in those relationships. The costs involved in establishing new channels and codes of information work in this direction. So do the organized markets, where patterns of domination and mutual trust will reinforce stable relationships and make changes difficult to achieve.

A specific constellation of user–producer relationships might foster specific trajectories of innovations. Such trajectories might prove quite insensitive to new technical opportunities and new user needs. A kind of dynamic inertia might become built into the user–producer relationships.

In this section, we shall present some results from a project on microelectronics and its impact on the Danish economy (the MIKE project). We shall illustrate the concept of 'unsatisfactory innovations' by referring to some results from four case studies, each of them analysing innovative activities within a vertical of production. In the first three cases presented, we gathered information by expert interviews and technical literature, etc. In the fourth case, this type of material was combined with a questionnaire addressed to the whole population of users.

The purpose of the presentation is to illustrate rather than to verify specific hypotheses. This permits us to present the material in a brief and anecdotic form. Each case involves a more complicated picture than the one given here. We have tried to present the skeleton rather than the full body of each case.[7]

2.4.1 Dairy processing – a case of hyper-automation

We found that dairy processing plants designed by the producers of equipment and systems were more capital intensive, more inflexible and highly automated than what corresponded to cost-effective solutions and to the needs of the users. Only recently, had the biggest of the users involved developed a capacity of its own to design and produce its own plants. The first new plant designed in-house diverged radically from earlier generations of plants and it is supposed to diminish costs substantially.

We ascribed this example of unsatisfactory innovations to some characteristics of the user–producer relationships. Two big producers dominated the supply of design and construction of plants. The number of users was high, therefore several hundreds of plants operated in Denmark. The users were organized into cooperative companies, the biggest one controlling more than half of the processing capacity. Those companies have, however, until recently been mainly oriented towards controlling the market for dairy products rather than towards coordinating the procurement of plants and equipment.

The competence of users and producers was only partially overlapping and in certain key areas it was very unequally distributed – a clear case of information asymmetry. The producers had specialized R&D departments developing electronic-based regulation systems, while the users had very limited competence in this area. The technology itself is systemic in character. The control and regulation systems built into the plant are determining how the production process becomes organized. The room for later user adjustments is relatively small.

In this relationship, a hierarchy had developed where the producers were able to impose their standards rather than adjusting to the needs of the users. But why did producers develop technology that was not cost-effective at the user level? Economic motives can be pointed out. The producers were producing not only the design of the plant but also essential elements of the hardware. The solutions developed were more intensive in terms of this hardware than what would have been satisfactory from the point of view of the users. The design of plants influenced the demand for hardware. It is difficult to substantiate, but we got the impression that noneconomic factors were even more important. It seemed as the producers were following a technological trajectory in the direction of higher and higher levels of automation. It was (implicitly) assumed that a growing level of automation would imply an increasing degree of effectiveness. Apparently, for a long period of time, such a perspective was implicitly accepted also by the users. This trajectory was developed during a phase when it was rational to substitute capital for labour. It was, however, followed long after that changes in the factor proportions and in the relative prices should have induced a new direction of innovations.

We believe that the unsatisfactory direction of innovations would have been changed earlier:

- If the users had coordinated their procurement of equipment,
- If the users had had a stronger competence in relation to electronics-based regulation systems, and
- If the technology had been less systemic and complex.

2.4.2 Clothing industry – a case of unexploited technical opportunities

Our study of the clothing industry as user of new technology was less complete, because we did not have direct access to the main producers of sewing machinery. References to a recent study of users and producers of textile machinery at the international level by Hoffman and Rush (1982) should be seen as an attempt to complete the picture in this respect.

The clothing industry resembles dairy processing in several ways. The core of the technology is produced by a small number of firms, and the users are numerous. The R&D activity and technical competence of most users is limited. On this background, one should expect that unsatisfactory innovations might occur. Studying the user industry and interviewing independent experts in Denmark revealed no obvious examples indicating that the technology did not respond to user needs. We ascribe this to the character of the technology involved.

The production process in the clothing factory is not systemic. The user remains in control of how to combine the different pieces of equipment procured from the producer. A low formal competence in process regulation is compensated by 'learning-by-combining' within the user units.

The Hoffman and Rush (1982) study indicates, however, unsatisfactory innovations in another dimension. The application of radical innovations in electronics, laser technology and chemistry to the main processes within clothing production is developing in a slow tempo. The main producers of sewing technology are reluctant to introduce radical innovations. They point to low user competence and conservatism among users as a reason for this strategy. It is argued that economic interest in securing a market for traditional products might influence the strategy.

Again, one might regard this deviation from what is satisfactory in terms of how a specific user–producer relationship fosters a trajectory that is only slowly changing in response to new needs and opportunities. The user–producer relationship in this vertical production both reflects and reinforces a process of gradual product improvement. The producers have no traditional ties, channels of information or linkages to the science-based industries where the new technical opportunities develop. The users are competing on the basis of production-based know-how rather than science-based know-how. The large number of relatively small user units makes it difficult for users to bypass the producers and develop radical process innovations on their own.

This is not to rule out that clothing technology may change radically in the future. As the gap between actual and satisfactory technology grows, either the old producers or new producers will try to close this gap (the case of quartz watches demonstrates how some new science-based producers can invade a traditional market in a dramatic way). But we shall propose that it might be a question of decades rather than months and years before such gaps are closed.

In this connection, it might be interesting to observe that the Ministry of International Trade and Industry (MITI) in Japan has developed a comprehensive research and development program oriented towards the modernization of clothing and textile technology. The main thrust in this program – as in programs in the information technology area – is to bring together users of the technology, producers of the core technology and science-based producers in electronics. Such an effort might be regarded as an attempt to compensate for the weak channels of information between producers and science-based industries and to break the inertia built into the traditional user–producer relationship. I shall suggest that an important explanation of the success of Japanese technology policy is that the importance of user–producer interaction has been realized both in the private and in the public sector.

The analysis by Sciberras and Payne (1985) on the competitiveness of the Japanese machine tools industry also points in this direction. Japanese producers of machine tools had a closer relationship both to their domestic users and to domestic producers of advanced control technology than their counterparts in the United States and Europe. Even when US producers where integrated into multidivisional corporations together with users and together with producers of control technology, they were operating at arm's length, with each unit oriented towards its own partial financial goals rather than towards strengthening the innovative capability of the whole corporation.

2.4.3 Waste water treatment – lack of interdisciplinary innovations

In order to extend our perspective from mature to new industries, we also studied users and producers of wastewater treatment technology. The users studied were 300 local authorities. Today, one domestic producer is dominating the Danish market. The product is systemic. Control and regulation technology plays an important role and the distribution of competence between users and producer is unequal. This pattern of user–producer relationships is not very different from the one we found in the case of dairy processing. We should expect a hierarchical interaction where the producer dominates the process of technical change, and solutions not reflecting the needs of the users might occur. However, we could not substantiate any clear tendency in this direction.

We found that the expertise in the field were embodied in a small number of persons, some of those were employed by the producer. Others were employed in an independent technological institute financed partially by the government, at the technical universities and in the Ministry of Environment. It was characteristic that most of the experts were 'job circulating' between those institutions and that they all knew each other personally. The experts within the Ministry of Environment assist the users in formulating standards for the systems procured from the producer. The fact that we could not observe any discrepancy between technical solutions and user needs might reflect this pattern of close-built expertise.

On one hand, it may be argued that the close interaction between the experts was effective in communicating user needs to the producers. On the other hand, one might argue that it was difficult to find truly independent experts able to evaluate the actual trajectory pursued. We believe that both mechanisms may have been at work, but we cannot say which has been the dominating one.

Another factor counteracting unsatisfactory innovations might be that the design of the plant and the production of the hardware have not been so intimately related as in the dairy case. It has been the norm that an independent engineering consultancy firm should design and coordinate the construction of the plant while the hardware should be delivered by other producers. The extreme degree of concentration on the producer side is also quite a new phenomenon; 10 years ago there were almost 10 firms operating as producers.

We found, however, a third type of unsatisfactory innovations in this area. The decisive technological bottlenecks for using new control technology were found at the interface between the mechanical, biological and chemical conditions prevailing in the wastewater and the data processing equipment used. The lack of sensors effectively transmitting information about the changes in the wastewater and the recipient was a bottleneck seriously reducing the usefulness of advanced control technology.

In spite of this fact, we found that most R&D and innovative activities were taking place either in electronic-based firms with no expert knowledge in biology, biochemistry or chemistry or in biochemical-oriented firms with little know-how relating to control technology. There are economic mechanisms at work; the immediate market might be too small to allow a specialized interdisciplinary producer to be established whereas the innovative activities mentioned were typically taking place in big firms where the activity related to waste water treatment was marginal.

But again, we shall argue that the lack of linkages and information channels plays an important role. In this case, the absence of horizontal linkages between science-based firms results in unsatisfactory innovations. Such linkages might be both easier and more difficult to establish than vertical ones. On one hand, both parties are used to communicating by scientific codes, and, on the other hand, those codes are extremely complex and diverging in content reflecting the specialization within the scientific community.

We shall suggest that there are promising arenas for potential innovations located at the interfaces between science-based industries that are not exploited today, More specifically, one can point to combinations of biotechnology and microelectronics as one such area. In our study of the Danish economy, we suggested that such new combinations might have a radical impact on traditional industries. But such interindustrial and interdisciplinary innovative efforts are hampered by the lack of linkages, information channels and common codes.

2.4.4 Software products – a case of 'hyper-centralization'

The fourth case studied was data processing and office technology in 300 kommuner – the local administrative units in Denmark. The dominating producer was one company, Kommunedata, owned by the nationwide association of local governments (Kommunernes Landsforening). The products studied were software systems related to data processing and office automation. Kommunedata has at its disposal, a very big central data processing capacity and develops programs that are designed to give the local units access to this central capacity. The local units pay for each specific program and for their use of the central processing capacity. The relationship is thus a peculiar combination of market and administrative relations.

This user–producer constellation has been extremely effective in diffusing the data processing technology to the local administrations. Today EDP is used in every single local unit, also in relatively small ones. We found, however, that the relationship had fostered unsatisfactory innovations as well. The systems and programs were more centralized in their design than both technical opportunities and user needs should infer. A number of local units had developed their own data processing capacity, and some had even broken all connections with Kommunedata. Independent expertise argued that the concept behind Kommunedata's program development does not reflect new needs for, as well as technical opportunities for, decentralization.

The most striking characteristic of the relationship between user and producer is extreme inequality in the distribution of competence. Kommunedata has more than 1,000 professionals with a formal education in relation to EDP. Only the biggest of the local units had more than one expert and the vast majority had none. The technology is systemic – meaning the programs cannot easily be changed in order to reflect local needs.

Those characteristics were reflected in the way the users adopted the systems. We found that 80 per cent of the users were passive. They had no strategy of their own either in relation to data processing or to office automation. They procured programs from Kommunedata but made no efforts to adapt the programs to their local needs. They were often frustrated in their use because of breakdowns in the central computer and because of limitations built into the programs.

In this case, we ascribed the tendency towards 'over-centralization' mainly to two factors: Kommunedata has its roots back in the 1950s and the most rapid expansion took place in the 1960s and 1970s. Its main activities were developed during a period when big mainframes offered the most economical solution to data-processing problems. The first programs widely distributed to local units were related to taxes and population statistics. In both cases, the immense flow of data involved as well as the need for central registration of data reinforced centralized solutions. Later new programs introducing elements of office automation have been developed, for example, office automation programs which link together different branches of the respective local administration. But still a majority of the professionals at Kommunedata are engaged full time in developing and maintaining the traditional programs, and those are still the 'cash cow' of the organization. The new programs seem to be influenced by the general centralized approach. The fact that the price policy has linked the income of the organization to its sale of processing capacity reinforces a trajectory of centralization that has historical roots.

The other factor at work is the lack of competence in the user units. We found that a main reason for not developing an independent local processing capacity was lack of qualified personnel. In a period with shortage in EDP expertise, it is almost impossible for the local units to attract qualified personnel. Their wage policy does not allow them to offer extreme benefits, and the environment they can offer is not necessarily the most attractive to specialists in this field.

This, we believe, reflects a more general problem. We shall argue that new basic innovations might stimulate a tendency towards an uneven distribution of competence between the producers of the new technology and its users. At the early stages of development, the producers can offer more stimulating and more rewarding working conditions for experts in the field. Users will be reluctant to offer the economic incentives necessary to compensate for a less attractive environment.

2.4.5 Concluding remarks

In all the four cases, there was a tendency towards producer dominance. In at least two of the cases, the lack of competence on the user side was reinforcing the unsatisfactory trajectory of innovations. This pattern might inspire a technology policy that is more oriented towards strengthening the competence of users than the supply-oriented technology policy dominating today. An extension of such a new orientation that encompasses the 'final users', workers and consumers might have radical implications.

In two of the cases, a lack of established linkages and channels of information reinforced unsatisfactory innovations. In one case, the linkage was between a traditional industry and a science-based industry. In the other, it was between two different science-based industries. This pattern might inspire a technology policy that brings together users and producers into new constellations. Such a concept seems to inspire the Japanese technology policy.

The fact that all four cases only illustrated producer-dominated relationships does not imply that this corresponds to a general pattern in the economy. Automobile and aerospace industries will be dominating users in relation to many smaller units producing components and process equipment. In such areas, other types of unsatisfactory innovations might develop reflecting that a few big users are able to direct the innovative process towards their own specific needs. The innovations brought forward might be less adequate for a big population of smaller users. The development of the machine tool technology might reflect such a pattern.

In our analysis, we focused on three sets of variables, namely numbers of users and producers, the distribution of competence and the character of the technology (systemic or nonsystemic). This list is to be regarded as preliminary, and further empirical work might bring forward other characteristics that are more important.

2.5 User–Producer Perspective on Location of Production

The unequal distribution of production in geographical space has been explained by agglomeration effects. In this section we shall discuss one important dimension of this concept – user–producer interaction in relation to innovative activities. We shall argue that long-distance interaction will be prohibitively costly in some phases of the technology life cycle because of the information problems involved. This contributes to an explanation of the actual division of labour between nations and regions.[8]

We shall also argue that learning by interacting reinforces historically developed user–producer linkages. This contributes to an explanation of the relative stability of the division of labour between regions and nations.

2.5.1 Distance and costs of transportation and communication

The costs of transportation and communication are growing with the distance. This is the case for goods and persons as well as for telecommunicated messages. In modern times, the innovations reducing such costs have been dramatic. Drastic reductions in the costs have been achieved and today such costs are prohibitive only for few types of products – cheap, bulky and perishable goods – and for long distances. The impact of distance on the location of production and consumption seems to vanish. At the same time, geographical concentration of production and innovative activities seems to be growing in certain areas, Silicon Valley tendencies can be observed also in Japan and Western Europe.

How can we explain this apparent paradox? We shall argue that while the development of telecommunication and other related technologies have reduced the costs of simple signals, the same has not become true for the transfer of complex and ever-changing messages. When user needs and technical opportunities are complex and going through a process of discontinuous change, geographical distance and cultural distance will make the user–producer interaction less effective.[9]

2.5.2 The cultural distance

If the cultural environment of a user is very different from that of the producer, it will be costly to establish a channel of information and to develop a common code. Not only will different national languages impair the communication, differences in culture will be reflected in different interpretations of identical signals. This will be even more so when market relations are juxtaposed with organizational relations. Codes of conduct, mutual trust and responsibility will typically be easier to establish between parties with a common cultural background.

Within the Organisation for Economic Co-operation and Development (OECD) area, the postwar period has witnessed a decrease in cultural distance across different nations. The diffusion of social innovations from the United States relating to the work process, the capital market and not least the pattern of final consumption has diminished the heterogeneity within this area. The export of management models has decreased the distance between different national corporate cultures. Still the differences persist, and still they favour national rather than international user–producer interaction. This will especially be the case, when user needs and technical opportunities are complex and discontinuously changing.

2.5.3 Paradigms and basic innovations

Within science, there is a continuous work going on aiming at the establishment of a common set of concepts. A common code is necessary in order to transmit scientific results within the scientific community. The standards of performance of a scientific unit are related to its ability to gain worldwide acknowledgement. This can only be attained if the results can be put into a code intelligible worldwide. At the same time, new paradigms develop and old paradigms become obsolete. When this happens, the old code becomes a restraint for further progress and new codes begin to develop. This will typically take place in an erratic way, and a kind of crisis develops within the scientific community. Several different codes might coexist and compete during such circumstances, some of them mixtures of the old and a new code. The producers of the new paradigm will have difficulties in communicating their results and the users will have difficulties in decoding what is going on. During such a period, long-distance communication becomes extremely difficult. Local scientific communities facilitating face-to-face contact become more well suited to overcome such difficulties than the global scientific community. Not only might the immaturity of the code make 'hands-on experimenting' necessary, the traditional criteria of scientific success might also become inadequate. Mutual trust between scientists and personal friendships might be essential in order to stimulate further progress when rational yardsticks do not work.

As a new paradigm becomes more widely accepted, a new process towards a common code develops. Long-distance communication and interaction becomes more effective as more and more users learn the new code. Scientific training has as one important function to disseminate a common code to potential users. It follows that a general diffusion of a new code normally will be time consuming, perhaps a couple of decades, corresponding to the time it takes for universities to adopt it and communicate it to new generations of students.

The introduction of science-based innovations will have effects similar to the development of new paradigms within science. The codes once learned by engineers and technicians, will not work anymore. It becomes difficult for distant users to assess specific product innovations in relation to their own needs. Conversely, distant producers addressing users engaged in the new areas will have difficulties in decoding information about user needs. Geographical and cultural proximity becomes a critical variable.

As the technology stabilizes and becomes mature, the technical code becomes simplified.

In technology, as in science, there are permanent forces working towards standardization and towards a common code. In the former case, the incentive is the potential extension of the market to a broader set of users. The importance of cultural and geographical distance declines as the technology becomes mature.[10]

The product life cycle explanation of the dynamics of international specialization can be reinterpreted in the light of a user–producer perspective. According to this explanation, the optimal factor proportions change during the life cycle. The early phase is R&D intensive, the second management intensive while the mature phase is intensive in terms of capital and unskilled labour. This explains why industries become relocated from developed to less developed countries.

A reinterpretation would suggest that the standardization and simplification of the technology make users of technology less dependent on cultural and geographical distance to the producers of technology. The fact that textile production technology has been easier to transfer than other manufacturing technologies can be ascribed to its relative stability as much as to its labour intensity. This reinterpretation does not necessarily contradict the predictions of the product life-cycle explanation. But it highlights some of the mechanisms behind this phenomenon.

2.5.4 Proximity and innovativeness

Empirical work in Aalborg, using the OECD data bank on foreign trade, has demonstrated that a substantial part of the specialization in engineering products can be explained by the degree of international specialization of domestic users of the equipment involved (see for instance IKE seminar 1981). If we regard the index of specialization for a product as an indicator of innovativeness and technical competence (this might be reasonable when the countries compared have similar factor proportions and when access to natural resources is not the decisive factor), we can relate this result to the interaction between users and producers.

One interpretation of the result is that the producers of capital goods will be better off if they have domestic innovative and competent users to interact with. The geographical and cultural proximity makes the establishment of channels and codes of information less costly and the exchange of information more effective.

An alternative interpretation is that the presence of domestic innovative and competent producers of equipment gives the users an advantage in relation to foreign competitors. Again, the geographical and cultural proximity might give the users more direct and easy access to information from domestic producers. We shall propose that both those mechanisms are at work. Both users and producers are learning by interacting. A virtuous circle with cumulative consequences is at work.

Such mechanisms will result in a rather stable pattern of international specialization reflecting historical background rather than proportions of general factors or production. Learning by interacting creates poles of competitiveness that reflect specific know-how divided between domestic users and producers. The existence of such poles of international competitiveness might prove to be rather insensitive to new technical opportunities and to changing user needs. The existing national network of user–producer interaction will only slowly adjust to external shocks. The 'virtuous circles' might become factors delaying a necessary adjustment of the national economy to new external conditions.

2.6 The Science–Technology Nexus

The interaction between producers and users of scientific results has its own properties. In this section, we shall discuss some of the specifics of this interaction. Some of the ideas presented have been inspired by the notes of Paul David on 'The Perilous Economics of Modern Science' (1984), while others are closely related to articles by Nathan Rosenberg in *Inside the Black Box: Technology and Economics* (1982).

In the first part of this section, we shall discuss how a user–producer approach relates to respectively technology push and demand pull hypotheses. In the second part, we shall outline 'a system of innovation'. In the third and fourth parts, we try to apply the user–producer perspective to science-based industries and to university–industry interaction.

2.6.1 Technology push or demand pull?

Innovational activities are often treated as a linear process starting within basic research and ending in economic growth. The results from basic research are regarded as inputs to applied research. Inventions taking place within science are supposed to give rise to innovations. As innovations become diffused they affect productivity and growth in the sphere of production. This unidirectional flow of information might be hampered by lacking competence on behalf of potential users and considerable time lags might be involved, but it is still regarded as unidirectional. Such a perspective will correspond to a technology policy supporting science and R&D activities.

Another approach has emphasized the importance of demand as a factor stimulating and directing innovations. When demand grows, it will pull R&D inventions and innovations forward and result in productivity growth. Such a perspective might give rise to policy recommendations of a laissez-faire character. Innovative activities are assumed to adjust automatically to the market forces.

A user–producer perspective raises critical objections to both of those two schools. The supply school underestimates the active role of users in the innovation process. The demand school does not distinguish demand as a quantitative category from user needs as a qualitative category. Increasing investment in R&D might give small marginal returns if the relationships to the potential users are weak and if information about user needs is costly to obtain for the producers. Increasing demand does not necessarily imply that the quality of user–producer interaction increases.

Both approaches can be accused of regarding the system of production as a black box. The supply school concentrates on the bottom of the black box where R&D is introduced and expects beneficial effects to come out at the top of the box. The demand school assumes that changes at the top of the box (i.e., changes in demand) will have beneficial effects at the bottom. A user--producer approach might be regarded as one revealing the content of the black box. The network of user producer relationships transmits signals from the top to the bottom and vice versa. We shall propose that such an approach will demonstrate that neither the demand nor the supply hypotheses have general, but possibly selective, validity in the economy.

2.6.2 A system of innovation[11]

In the economy, some key institutions are involved in different types of innovative activities. The vertical division of labour between institutions is far from clear-cut, but certain types of activities are predominating in each type of institution. The universities are centres for basic research and scientific training. At the same time, they constitute the decisive part of an academic community characterized by its own social norms, criteria of success and incentives.

Not all science is produced within the universities. Private firms as well as public agencies have their own dependent research units. Such units will typically be engaged in applied research (i.e., research aiming at the solution of problems relevant to the mother organization). In such research units the criteria of success and the incentives will be reflecting the goal of the mother organization rather than those of the academic community.

In between those two levels, there is a multitude of specialized research organizations that are neither integrated in the universities nor directly subordinated to any mother organization. Some of those are exclusively engaged in either basic or applied research; others combine the two types of activities. Such organizations might work more or less in accordance with the rules predominating within the academic community. A crucial factor determining their behaviour will be the funding mechanisms involved.

There are units closer to the process of production. R&D units operate within firms and public organizations while technological institutes operate as independent units. Their main function is to convert scientific results into practical technical solutions rather than to extend the stock of scientific knowledge. In such units the norms of the academic community will play a secondary role.

Finally, we shall consider all other professional units as engaged in production of tangible goods. Also, in these units activities related to innovation take place. Learning by doing and learning by using produce information that might be crucial to units engaged in applied research and development. The recognition of bottlenecks and other specific problems in production directs the activity of dependent and semidependent R&D units. Phenomena that cannot be accounted for by science will occur in material production and stimulate new efforts in applied as well as basic research. The agenda of the units of research and development will be influenced by what is going on in the production sphere.

We shall suggest that innovativeness and competence in the production sphere are factors that have a positive influence on the units engaged in development and research units.

We shall also suggest that the strength and form of the relationships between producing units and R&D units influence the overall innovative performance. The pattern of historically established information channels and codes will determine how easily the agenda responds to signals from the production sphere.

In order to illustrate those two propositions, we shall discuss two different sets of problems. One relates to the concept of the science-based industry, and the second to the cooperation between university and industry.

2.6.3 Science-based industries

It is obvious that some industries are using results produced by science more frequently than other parts. Electronics industry and chemical industry are R&D intensive and interact intensively with institutions pursuing research, including the universities. Other industries, such as textiles and machinery, are less R&D intensive, and they have a more distant relationship to research institutions and universities.

This fact is normally interpreted in terms of the linear unidirectional model of innovations. Scientific breakthroughs in chemistry and physics are assumed to have created the basis for basic industrial innovations. The user–producer approach might give a more balanced interpretation of the historical process, which has made some industries science-based, but not others.

Textiles, as well as machinery industries, were established on the basis of practical experience rather than on the basis of systematic knowledge during a period when scientific activities were weak and only weakly related to technological problems. The fact that they still operate at arm's length from science is not necessarily reflecting that the problems they try to solve are unsuitable to scientific treatment. It might also reflect a historical pattern of user–producer relationships, which, once established, has been reinforced.

On the one hand, the practical orientation of their innovation process might have been contagious in relation to the scientific disciplines closest to their field of operation. The lack of ability to express problems in the scientific code may have failed to stimulate the related scientific institutions. The very practical character of work within such institutions may have repelled the most ambitious and competent scientists from those fields of research. The predominance of small-scale production, making it more difficult to exploit increasing returns to R&D, may have reinforced such a tendency.

Looking at the so-called science-based industry, a reverse process might have been at work. Those industries were developed during a later historical period when the scientific institutions were more developed and more geared towards industrial problems. They were able to recruit engineers with a formal education and were from the beginning able to communicate in a scientific code. The strong innovative activity within those firms and their ability to present their problems in a form suitable to a scientific treatment stimulated the scientific institutions and disciplines most closely related to their activity. Strong and effective relationships between users and producers of science were established.

If this is true, one should expect that a new symbiosis between traditional industries and science should offer dramatic returns. Investing in making the related research activities more scientific, stimulating the ability of the industry to communicate in scientific terms and strengthening the interaction between industry and scientific institutions should be very rewarding. At the same time one should realize, however, that the investments necessary might be considerable and the lead time before the new channels of information will work effectively might be very long.

The interaction between the science-based industries and the scientific institutions is already working smoothly and will, therefore, promise higher returns in the short run, both for the parties involved and for society as a whole. The hypothesis that the distinction between science-based and traditional industries is the result of historical accident, rather than inherently based in the technology used, might therefore never be tested in practice.

2.6.4 The interaction between university and industry

One of the few instances where the importance of user–producer interaction has been explicitly recognized in policy terms relates to the interaction between university and industry. OECD has published several reports on the subject and a new ad hoc group studying regional development and technical change seems to put the linkage between university and industry at the centre of its analysis (OECD 1984). The growing interest for this linkage reflects that science-based industries have become more important for international competitiveness. It also reflects that a tendency towards a new type of agglomerations, the so-called Centres of excellence or Technopolises, where industrial development seems to be closely linked to 'excellent' universities, has been registered. The fact that most universities have rather weak relationships to industry, and that most attempts to strengthen the interaction have failed, has put this item on the agenda of national governments and international organizations.

The analysis will often end up with a call for more cooperation. The lack of cooperation is often ascribed to a lack of goodwill and especially to a certain snobbish attitude within the academic community. Without denying that such mechanisms are at work, it could be argued that the lack of cooperation reflects more fundamental ones with origin in the character of the user–producer relationships. Without recognition of the more fundamental mechanisms, attempts to link universities and industries together based on goodwill might result mainly in disappointment and frustration.

The cultural distance between the industrial community and the academic community is reflecting differences in social norms, criteria of success and incentives. While global communication of research results tends to make the products of academic science a public good, secrecy is an important element in industrial R&D. While material incentives play a subordinate role within the academic community, the contrary is the case within industry.

This cultural distance can be diminished either by changing the academic culture or changing the industrial culture. Introducing secrecy and material incentives into the academic community will in the long run impair its standard and its contribution to economic welfare, not to mention its basic critical function. Introducing the norms of the academic community on industry would imply radical change in the institutions of the market economy. A certain cultural distance seems to be inevitable and this will make it more costly to establish channels of information and an intelligible code.

Second, the scientific code that is predominating within the academic community is different from the code predominating within industry. The scientific code is developed to serve as a medium for communication between specialized scientists, while the code of industry is problem oriented. The organization of academic science into very specialized disciplines, each with its own code, is a factor making communication with industry more difficult.

In this area a reorganization of the universities, or rather of some parts of them, into interdisciplinary units might facilitate communication. Such a reorganization might also have a stimulating effect on research itself, putting new items on the agenda and giving rise to new disciplines and to new paradigms within the old disciplines. A total disruption of the discipline orientation of academic research would, of course, be unacceptable but a mixture of research units oriented towards the traditional disciplines and problem-oriented units might be beneficial both to the academic community itself and to its ability to communicate with external users.

Taking into account all the difficulties in communication involved, the fact that centres of excellence, where university and industry cooperate, do develop might seem difficult to understand. Is it not true that Stanford University has played an important role in promoting the growth of hi-tech industry in the Silicon Valley? In order to solve the apparent contradiction we have to take into regard the role of the users in the interaction.

First, we shall argue that the users involved in Silicon Valley – primarily the electronics industry – have certain specific characteristics that have facilitated the interaction. The culture of this industry has been less distant from that of the academic community. The problems to be solved have been easier to pose in terms of specific scientific disciplines. As a consequence, the costs of establishing channels of information and common codes have been relatively less.

Second, we shall question the idea that the excellence of the university has been the driving force behind the Silicon Valley phenomenon. The innovativeness of the electronics industry and its ability to communicate with the university has brought new items on the agenda of academic research. The fact that the industry has been at the forefront of science, often having a lead in relation to worldwide academic research, has meant that the items brought on the agenda have been real challenges to academic science. The ability to communicate those problems in a scientific code has made it easier to address them from a scientific point of view. This has made Stanford University an environment more attractive to ambitious and competent academic scientists. Everything equal, it is easier to produce Nobel Prizes in such an environment than at universities having less advanced users. The excellence of the university reflects the excellence of its users.

This is not to deny that an impact working in the opposite direction has been important. The interaction has been to the mutual benefit of user and producer, again a virtuous circle with cumulative effects has been at work. Our argument is rather one directed against simplistic ideas which exaggerate the role of the university in relation to industrial development. Not all kinds of university–industry interaction will result in mutual benefits. If the industry involved is traditional rather than innovative, distant from the culture of the academic community and not able to communicate in scientific code, an interaction will be difficult to establish. Such an interaction might even have serious detrimental effects on the universities. The new questions entered on their agendas might be trivial and posed in terms not well suited for scientific treatment. The industry might get responses difficult to decode and adopt to their problems, for instance.

A policy recommending a closer cooperation between university and industry must take those complications into account. One implication might be that the first step must be the strengthening of the competence of the users. Making recruitment of labour with academic training more attractive to traditional industries might be a necessary step in this direction. This would diminish the cultural distance and increase the capability to communicate with the academic community. If this analysis is correct, the establishment of an effective interaction between universities and traditional industries will take some time. In the meantime, we might witness how well-intended efforts to cooperate create frustration both in the academic and in the industrial community.

We have argued elsewhere that one of the secrets behind the successful Japanese industrial policy is a more fundamental understanding of the user–producer relationships. It is, therefore, interesting to note that Japan, according to a recent OECD document, is planning to establish a new type of geographical agglomerations – the so-called technopolises. This concept does not put the main emphasis on the role of universities but seems to give at least equal weight to the user side of the relationships.[12]

2.7 Units of Analysis and Propositions

The traditional units of analysis in economics are horizontal rather than vertical. The economy is regarded as composed of sectors like agriculture, manufacturing and services and each sector will be decomposed into industries and subsectors. A user–producer perspective brings into focus vertically organized units of analysis, which typically cross the traditional borders between main sectors and subsectors.[13]

In this section, we shall relate to each other such vertically organized units and related propositions. This brief recapitulation might also be regarded as a series of research proposals brought forward by a user–producer perspective.

The world economic system might be regarded as a complex network of user–producer relationships connecting units dispersed in economic and geographical space. This network is a product of historical development, and it will only slowly adapt to exogenous and discontinuous change. When change of this kind occurs, we should expect a growing gap between actual performance and satisfactory performance. The oil price shock and the dramatic development in new all-pervasive technologies as microelectronics have undermined the effectiveness of the existing global network. This has diminished the positive impact of the basic innovations. A policy that stimulates the reshaping of user–producer linkages will diminish the performance gap and stimulate innovative activities and economic growth. 'Long waves' in economic development might reflect the inertia of user–producer relationships (Perez 1983).

International specialization might be regarded as reflecting competition between verticals of production rather than competition between national industries. The relative or absolute advantages of a specific national industry reflect not only its own efforts but also the innovativeness and competence of domestic producers delivering process equipment, and domestic users delivering information inputs about user needs to the industry. A policy that aims at strengthening a specific industry should be based on an analysis of all stages within the vertical of production. In the long run, the competences of users might be as important as the competences of producers.

National systems of production will be more or less competitive and differ in their innovative capacity. The existing network of user–producer linkages, including linkages between applied science and basic science as well as linkages between the scientific and the technological sphere, will have an impact on innovative capacity and international competitiveness. In a specific historical period, certain user–producer linkages might become of strategic importance. A policy aiming at strengthening the international competitiveness should address such strategic linkages. What is and what is not strategic linkages will depend on the existing network of user–producer relationships as well as on new needs and opportunities.

Industrial complexes related to a broad set of needs (the military–industrial complex) or to a specific primary sector (the agro-industrial complex) are semi-autonomous networks of user–producer relationships. They are closely knit together internally, and their linkages to the rest of the economy are relatively weak. Such complexes might have great innovative capabilities because of the historically stable and close relationships between clusters of users and producers. They might also represent, however, a strong resistance to radical change in the network, the code and the channels of information used, etc. This will be reinforced when they become a basis for social and political alliances encompassing broad segments of the population. The case of Danish environmental industry gave an illustration of the impact on technological trajectories of a closely knit network of experts.

During a period when needs and technical opportunities change radically, the existence of such industrial complexes might become conservative elements that delay the restructuring of the economy. A policy that aims at securing dynamic efficiency should be addressed to the creation, reshaping and demolition of industrial complexes.

The interindustrial user–producer relationship involves two different steps in a vertical of production. It corresponds to what is at the centre of microeconomic theory – the market where firms confront with consumers. We shall suggest that this is an area where a user–producer perspective brings forward several interesting results:

- Perfect Competition – anonymity in the relation between user and producer – is an environment hostile to product innovations. Uncertainty and lack of channels of information transmitting qualitative information has a negative influence on the process of innovation as well as on the diffusion of innovations.
- When small numbers are involved, market failure will result when product innovations occur. Uncertainty and limited rationality will prevail in such situations.

- The logical outcome is an economy where no product innovations take place. All innovations should be in-house process innovations. This does not correspond to historical evidence. Product innovations are introduced on the market place.
- This paradox can only be resolved if we accept that the distinction between market and hierarchy becomes blurred in the real world. In markets where product innovations are frequent and important anonymity is eliminated, pure markets become infiltrated with organizational linkages.
- Organizational relationships might in some instances be described in terms of a hierarchy where the producer dominates the user or vice versa. Certain constellations of user–producer relationships cannot, however, be explained in such terms. Elements of cooperation and mutual trust must be introduced in order to explain why product innovation takes place when the user and the producer are of equal strength.
- The interaction between an innovating producer and a user might be captured better by a model of a cooperative positive sum game than by models emphasizing conflicts of interests.

Microeconomic theory assumes that the single firm is adjusting its behaviour to signals in the form of prices and quantities. A user–producer perspective introduces the need for qualitative information about new use values, treated as inputs, and about the needs of users. More realistic models describing firm behaviour introduce the environment of the firm as a factor influencing its conduct and performance. We shall suggest that a breakdown of this environment into user–producer relationships can clarify the analysis of firm behaviour.

An important aspect of firm strategies is related to user–producer relationships. The existing forward and backward linkages will act as strong restraints on what the firm can do, the opening up of new channels of information and the development of new codes will involve investment costs and the outcome is uncertain. The acquisition of formerly independent units operating in a different network of user–producer relationships is not necessarily motivated primarily by the production capacity acquired. It might be motivated by the access it gives to new channels of information and to new codes.

Internal user–producer relationships might differ between different firms. The ability of the internal organization to transform internal and external user needs into innovations might reflect different organizational arrangements, different incentive systems and different cultural characteristics. Is the competitiveness of Japanese firms an expression for their ability to establish proximity between users and producers within the multidivisional firms? Is the US model, characterized by arm's length relations between profit centres, detrimental to innovation?

How do the 'final users' – workers and consumers – influence innovational activities? A strengthening of their competence and influence might have dramatic effects on the innovative capability of the economy. Which types of reforms are necessary in order to realize such effects?

2.8 A Final Remark

What has been introduced here is neither a general nor a pure theory. One of the more general results obtained in our empirical work has been that user–producer interaction works in different ways in different parts of the economy. The fact that we focus on use value rather than exchange value introduces a strong historical element in the analysis.

In this chapter, we have studied user–producer relationships where the user is professional and the innovations involve a certain degree of complexity. The results obtained, therefore, have specific rather than general validity.

We do not, however, regard this only as a weakness of the user–producer perspective (Kornai 1971, 28–29). Especially in innovation theory, it has proven difficult to produce hypotheses of general validity. Attempts to reduce innovative activities to be either supply- or demand-induced have failed. Attempts to devote to respectively small and big firms special innovative abilities have not been successful.

Regarding innovative activities from a user–producer perspective might be a way to open up the black box and disclose the mechanisms that are at work. In doing so, it might become possible to develop hypotheses which have at least a specific and specified validity.

Important work in this direction has been pursued at SPRU, UK, where Keith Pavitt (1984) has used an extensive database on UK innovations to develop a taxonomy of innovation. The user–producer relationships reflected in his taxonomy are related primarily to interbranch rather than to the interorganizational interaction treated here (1984). We believe that a combination of the two approaches will prove useful.

Notes

1 This point was made by Kenneth Arrow at a private conversation when I visited Stanford University 1984.
2 This has become an increasingly important phenomenon analysed in depth by von Hippel (2005).

3 It is interesting to note that Kirman and Vriend (2000) demonstrate this even for consumer markets (their main case is the fish market in Marseille), where there is little 'innovation' and sellers and customers develop relationships of loyalty and trust. This case agrees with the patterns analysed in this chapter that there is information asymmetry – the supplier has more insight in the quality of the product than the customer.

4 The basic idea in this section, that pure markets are dynamically inefficient, has been developed further in a broader discussion of the limits of the pure market economy (see Johnson and Lundvall 1989).

5 Here I could have referred to the importance for innovating firms to have access to a diverse set of customers/suppliers as a special case of 'the strength of weak ties' Granovetter (1973).

6 The criticism of the transaction theory approach and its neglect of innovation and learning have been developed further in Lundvall (1992a).

7 The concept of unsatisfactory innovations was developed further and linked to macroeconomic stagnation in a paper presented at the OECD conference on the productivity slow-down in Paris 1990 (Lundvall 1991).

8 The role of innovation and user–producer interaction in determining location has been further developed in Lundvall (1999) and in Lundvall and Maskell (2000). The specific problems involved in establishing international user–producer interaction where discussed in Lundvall (1992b).

9 The role (and limitations) of information technologies in facilitating long-distance communication has been developed further in Lundvall (1997).

10 The interplay between innovation and standardization has been further developed in Lundvall (1995).

11 This may be the first use of the concept 'innovation system' in a publication with ISBN No. As referred to in Lundvall (2004). Chris Freeman introduced the innovation system concept in an unpublished paper for OECD already in 1982.

12 The interaction between universities and industry is covered in much more depth in Lundvall (2002).

13 Using the user–producer perspective to link input–output analysis to innovation may be seen as one way to operationalize the ideas in this chapter (Lundvall 1996).

References

Arrow, K. J. 1962. 'Economic Welfare and the Allocation of Resources for Invention'. In *The Rate and Direction of Inventive Activity* (pp. 699–625). Princeton, NJ: Princeton University Press.

———. 1969. 'The Economic Implications of Learning by Doing'. *Review of Economic Studies in Readings in the Theory of Growth* (pp. 131–149). London: Palgrave Macmillan UK.

———. 1974. *The Limits of Organization. University of Pennsylvania, Fels Center of Government.*

———. 1973. *Information and Economic Behavior* (No. TR-14). Cambridge MA: Harvard University Press.

David, P. 1984. 'The Perilous Economics of Modern Science', mimeographed draft presented at the TIP workshop, October.

Ergas, H. 1983. 'The Interindustry Flow of Technology: Some Explanatory Hypotheses', mimeo. Paris: OECD.

Freeman, C. 1982. *The Economics of Industrial Innovations*, 2nd Edition. London: Francis Pinter.

Freeman, C., J. Clark, and L. Soete. 1982. *Unemployment and Technical Innovations: A Study of Long Waves and Economic Development*. London: Frances Pinter.

Granovetter, M. 1973. 'The Strength of Weak Ties'. *American Journal of Sociology* 78: 1360–80.

Hoffman, K. and H. Rush. 1982. 'Microelectronics and the Garment Industry: Not Yet a Perfect Fit'. *IDS–Bulletin* 13, no. 2: 35–41.

IKE-Seminar. 1981. 'Technical Innovation and National Economic Performance'. Contributions by C. Freeman, S. Kjeldsen-Kragh, E. S. Andersen, G. Dalum and G. Willumsen. Aalborg: Aalborg University Press.

———. 1981. 'Technology and Employment – The Impact of Microelectronics'. Contributions by C. Freeman and the MIKE project. Aalborg: Aalborg University Press.

Johnson, B. H. and B.-Å. Lundvall. 1989. 'Limits of the Pure Market Economy'. In *Samhallsvetenskap, ekonomi och historia*, edited by B. Fridén, H. Kihlström and M. Rantanen. Gothenburg: Daidalos.

Kirman, A. P. and N. J. Vriend. 2000. 'Learning to be Loyal: A Study of the Marseille Fish Market'. In *Interaction and Market Structure. Essays on Heterogeneity in Economics, Lecture Notes in Economics and Mathematical Systems*, edited by D. Delli Gatti, M. Gallegati and A. P. Kirman. Berlin: Springer, 484.

Kornai, J. 1971. *Anti-equilibrium: On Economic Systems Theory and the Tasks of Research*. Amsterdam: North-Holland.

Lundvall, B-Å. 1991. 'Innovation, the Organised Market and the Productivity Slow-down'. In *OECD: Technology and Productivity: The Challenge for Economic Policy*. Organisation for Economic Cooporation and Development, OECD, 447–57.

———. 1992a. 'Explaining Inter-firm Cooperation and Innovation: Limits of the Transaction Cost Approach'. In *The Embedded Firm: On the Socioeconomics of Industrial Networks*, edited by G. Grabher. New York: Routledge.

———. 1992b. 'User-Producer Relationships, National Systems of Innovation and Internationalisation'. In *National Systems of Innovation: Towards a Theory of Innovation and Interactive Learning*, edited by B.-Å. Lundvall. London: Frances Pinter Publishers Ltd, 45–67.

———. 1995. 'Standards in an Innovative World'. In *Standards, Innovation and Competitiveness*, edited by R. Hawkins, J. Skea and R. Mansell. Aldershot: Edward Elgar.

———. 1997. 'Information Technology in the Learning Economy'. *Communications & Strategies* 28: 117–92.

———. 1999. 'Spatial Division of Labour and Interactive Learning'. *Revue d'Economie Regionale et Urbaine* 3: 469–88.

———. 2002. 'The University in the Learning Economy'. DRUID Working Paper, No. 6, Aalborg: Aalborg University.

———. 2004. 'Introduction to "Technological Infrastructure and International Competitiveness" by Christopher Freeman'. *Industrial and Corporate Change* 13, no. 3: 531–39.

Lundvall, B.-Å. and P. Maskell. 2000. 'Nation States and Economic Development: From National Systems of Production to National Systems of Knowledge Creation and Learning'. In *The Oxford Handbook of Economic Geography* (pp. 353–72), edited by G. L. Clark, M. P. Feldman and M. S. Gertler. Oxford: Oxford University Press.

OECD. 1984. 'Analytical Report on Research, Technology and Regional Policy'. OECD/ DSTI/SPR/84.20, mimeo, Paris: OECD.

Pavitt, K. 1984. 'Sectoral Patterns of Technical Change: Towards a Taxonomy and a Theory'. *Research Policy* 13, no. 6: 343–73.

Perez, C. 1983. 'Structural Change and Assimilation of New Technologies in the Economic and Social Systems'. *Futures* 15, no. 5: 357–75.

Rosenberg, N. 1972. *Technology and American Economic Growth*. New York: Harper Torch Books.

———. 1976. *Perspectives on Technology*. Cambridge: Cambridge University Press.

———. 1982. *Inside the Black Box: Technology and Economics*. Cambridge: Cambridge University Press.

Scherer, F. 1982. 'Inter-Industry Technology Flows in the United States'. *Research Policy*.

Sciberras, E. and B. D. Payne. 1985. *Machine Tool Industry, Technical Change and the International Competitiveness*. Harlow, Essex: Longman.

Von Hippel, E. 1976. 'The Dominant Role of Users in the Scientific Instrument Innovation Process'. *Research Policy* 5, no. 3: 213–39.

———. 1982. 'The Appropriability of Innovation Benefit as a Predictor of the Source of Innovations'. *Research Policy* 11, no. 2: 95–115.

———. 2005. *Democratizing Innovation*. Cambridge, MA: MIT Press.

Williamson, O. E. 1975. *Markets and Hierarchies: Analysis and Antitrust Implications*. New York: The Free Press.

Chapter 3

INNOVATION AS AN INTERACTIVE PROCESS: FROM USER–PRODUCER INTERACTION TO THE NATIONAL SYSTEMS OF INNOVATION

Bengt-Åke Lundvall

3.1 Introduction

This chapter focuses on the interactive nature of the process of innovation. The analysis takes as its points of departure two important characteristics of an industrial economy: the highly developed vertical division of labour and the ubiquitous and all-pervasive character of innovative activities. It analyses the implications from the fact that a substantial part of innovative activities takes place in units separated from the potential users of the innovations.

Here we shall argue that the separation of users from producers in the process of innovation, being 'a stylized fact' of a modern industrial society (capitalist or socialist), has important implications for economic theory. When we focus on innovation as an interactive process, the theoretical and practical problems tend to present themselves differently than in mainstream economic theory.

The interactive aspects of the process of innovation can be studied at different levels of aggregation. First, we discuss the 'microeconomics of interaction'. Second, we present some preliminary ideas on how the understanding of a national system of innovation can be developed.

3.2 The Micro-Foundation: Interaction between Users and Producers

In standard microeconomics the agents – firms and consumers – are assumed to behave as maximizers of profits and utility. Perfect competition with numerous buyers and sellers, and the flow of information connecting them encompassing nothing but price signals, is the normative and analytical point of reference of the theory. Monopolistic structures and complex client relationships are regarded as deviations from this normal and ideal state.

The kind of 'microeconomics' to be presented here is quite different. While traditional microeconomics tends to focus on decisions made on the basis of a given amount of information, we shall focus on a *process of learning*, permanently changing the amount and kind of information at the disposal of the actors. While standard economics tends to regard optimality in the allocation of a given set of use values as the economic problem, *par preference*, we shall focus on the capability of an economy to produce and diffuse *use values with new characteristics*. Moreover, while standard economics takes an atomistic view of the economy, we shall focus on the *systemic interdependence* between formally independent economic subjects.

3.2.1 Product innovations in a pure market

In an economy characterized by vertical division of labour and by ubiquitous innovative activities, a substantial part of all innovative activities will be addressed towards users outside the innovating units. In such an economy, successful innovations must be based on knowledge about the needs of potential users, and this knowledge is as important as knowledge about new technical opportunities (Freeman 1982, 124, *passim*).

When an innovation has been developed and introduced, it will diffuse only if information about its use-value characteristics is transmitted to the potential users of this innovation. Within organizations, this constitutes an intraorganizational problem to be solved through interaction and information exchange involving different individuals and departments belonging to the organization.

Here, however, the focus will be on those innovative activities that are oriented towards new products to be presented to a market. For simplicity, we shall label such innovations as 'product innovations' keeping in mind that they might constitute new materials and new process equipments, as well as new consumer products. Further, we shall not primarily treat innovations as single events. By using terms such as 'the process of innovation' and 'innovative activities', we indicate that the traditional separation between discovery, invention, innovation and diffusion is of limited relevance in this specific context.

How can the mutual information problem be solved when the producer and the user are separated by a market? If the market is 'pure', in the neoclassical sense, the problem must remain without a solution. In such a market the only information exchanged relates to products already existing in the market, and it contains only quantitative information about price and volume. Anonymous

relationships between buyer and seller are assumed. In such a market the innovating units as well as the potential users will operate under extreme uncertainty. Producers have no information about potential user needs, and users
have no knowledge about the use value characteristics of new products. If the
real economy was constituted by pure markets, product innovations would be
haphazard and therefore exceptional.

It is interesting to note that the pure market hailed by most neoclassical
economists, for its ability to establish an efficient allocation of resources on the
basis of very limited amount of information, forms an environment hostile to
innovative activities. Second, that product innovations would be all but absent
in a capitalist economy characterized by perfect competition. At an abstract
level, a socialist economy might be expected to overcome this crucial information problem more easily through a planning mechanism, taking into account
the need for the exchange of qualitative information. According to a study of
innovations in the Soviet Union, however, the lack of efficient user–producer
interaction seems to be a major problem in the 'real existing socialist countries' (Amann and Cooper 1982).

Anne P. Carter (1986) points to the neglect of product innovation in production models as a general and serious weakness. But this neglect is consistent with
the microeconomic assumption of pure markets as the norm. In a world where
all products were characterized by constant use-value characteristics, pure markets could survive, and those pure markets would tend to reproduce the existing
set of use values. Introducing product innovations into economic models cannot
but erode the foundation for using pure market transactions as a norm.

3.2.2 Product innovations and transaction costs

One alternative conception of the process of information exchange is the
transaction cost approach presented by Oliver E. Williamson (1975). What are
the implications of product innovations if we take this approach as our point
of departure? According to Williamson, markets characterized by small numbers, uncertainty, limited rationality and opportunistic behaviour will tend to
become hierarchies. High transaction costs will induce vertical integration.

A market where product innovations were frequent would certainly involve
fundamental uncertainty at both sides of the market. The uncertainty would
emanate not from the external conditions for the transaction but from qualitative change in the commodity itself. It would also imply what Williamson
refers to as 'informational impactedness'. This would be rooted in asymmet-
rical distribution of information. The innovating unit would, typically, have
much more, and more certain, information about the use-value characteristics
of the new product than the potential user.

In the Williamson framework, as in the neoclassical world, we would expect product innovations to be exceptional. We would expect them to become internalized and transformed into process innovations through vertical integration. It is, of course, quite difficult to measure in a precise manner, the proportion of innovative activities directed towards product innovations. One of the few systematic innovation data banks is the one developed at the Science Policy Research Unit, Sussex University. Among more than 2,000 important postwar innovations reported in Pavitt (1984), more than a half had been developed for outside firms (Ibid. p. 348). Organisation for Economic Co-operation and Development (OECD) data on the allocation of R&D activities confirm that product innovation is as important a phenomenon as process innovation in the OECD area.

Thus neither standard microeconomics nor the transaction cost approach is easily reconciled with the stylized facts of a modern industrial economy. In order to explain the actual importance of product innovations, we must take a closer look at the (assumed) market-hierarchy dichotomy.

3.2.3 The organized market as solution

If all transactions in the real world were taking place either in 'pure markets' or in 'pure organizations', innovative activities would be less frequent than they are and would mainly take the form of process innovations. The fact that product innovations are frequent in the real world demonstrates that most real markets are 'organized markets' rather than pure markets. The actually observed relative efficiency of the capitalist system in terms of innovative behaviour can only be explained by the fact that the invisible hand of the pure market economy has been replaced by bastard forms, combining organization elements with market elements.[1]

The organized market is characterized by transactions between formally independent units and by a flow of information on volume and price. But it also involves relationships of an organizational type. Those relationships might involve flows of qualitative information and direct cooperation. They might take a hierarchical form, reflecting that one party dominates the other, by means of financial power or of a superior scientific and technical competence. As we shall see, a purely hierarchical relationship will, however, often prove insufficient. Mutual trust and mutually respected codes of behaviour will normally be necessary in order to overcome the uncertainty involved.

3.2.4 User–producer interaction in the process of innovation

We shall now take a closer look at the specific forms of user–producer interaction in relation to the process of innovation. The producer will have a strong incentive to monitor what is going on in user units. First, process innovations within user units might be appropriated by producers or represent a potential competitive threat. Second, product innovations at the user level may imply new demands for process equipment. Third, the knowledge produced by learning by using can only be transformed into new products if the producers have a direct contact with users. Fourth, bottlenecks and technological inter-dependencies, observed within user units, will represent potential markets for the innovating producer. Finally, the producer might be interested in monitoring the competence and learning potential of users in order to estimate their respective capability to adopt new products.

The user, on the other hand, needs information about new products, and this information involves not only awareness but also quite specific information about how new use value characteristics relate to her/his specific needs. When new user needs develop, for example, when bottleneck problems occur, the user might be compelled to involve a producer in the analysis and solution of the problem. This can only be done successfully if the user has a detailed knowledge about the competence and reliability of different producers.

When complex and specialized equipment is developed and sold to users, there will be a need for *direct cooperation* during the process of innovation. The cooperation is not a single act but takes place at different stages of the process (Rothwell and Gardiner 1985). First, the user may present the producer with specific needs to be fulfilled by the new product. Second, the producer might install it and start it up in cooperation with the user. At this stage, the producer might offer specific training to the user. After the product has been adopted, there might follow a period where the producer would have obligations regarding repair and updating of the equipment.[2]

The uncertainty involved in this kind of transaction will be considerable. Not only is the user unit buying a product with unknown characteristics, it is also buying the cooperation of an external party for a future period. It should be obvious that the room for an opportunistic producer to cheat is considerable. Conversely, this implies that 'trustworthiness' becomes a decisive parameter of competition. If a user has a choice between a producer known for low price and technically advanced products, but having a weak record in terms of moral performance, and one well known for trustworthiness, the first will be passed by. This implies limits to opportunistic behaviour. These limits are reinforced when users pool their information about the reliability of different producers.

The exchange of information between user and producer also involves uncertainty and room for cheating and disloyal behaviour. The users must disclose their needs to the producer in order to get workable solutions. The producer unit has an interest in disclosing the full capacity of its product and in giving the users insight into its technical competence as a potential co-operator. Nevertheless, in both cases, a full disclosure might be abused by the other party. Information might be spilled to competitors, and each party may invade the market of the other party. Again, the abuse can only be restrained if codes of behaviour and mutual trust form an element of the relationship. Without any such restraints, transaction costs would become prohibitive and vertical integration would become a necessary outcome.

3.2.5 What determines the strength of the elements of organization?

The element of organization might be quite weak in certain markets. If the product is simple with slow changes in its use-value characteristics and the expenditure for its procurement forms a negligible part of the user's budget, the market might become quite 'pure'. When its use-value characteristics are complex, rapidly changing and the product is expensive, the element of organization will be strong. The former type of goods will typically be developed by the producer alone and bought 'off the shelf', while the latter will be developed in an interaction between the user and producer, and the act of exchange will involve direct cooperation and exchange of qualitative information.

3.2.6 The flow of information

In markets where element of organization is strong, the flow of information might be analysed in terms parallel to those applied in the theoretical analysis of organizations. Here we shall use elements from a conceptual framework developed by Kenneth Arrow (1974).

The flow of information can only take place if there are channels of information through which the message can pass. Further, a code of information is necessary in order to make the transmission of messages effective. The establishment of channels of information may, according to Arrow, be regarded as parallel to a process of investment in physical capital. It is a time-consuming process involving costs. The development of a common code is also time consuming and involves learning. The more the code is used in transmitting information, the more effective it becomes. 'Learning by interacting' increases the effectiveness of a given set of channels and codes of information.

3.2.7 The selectivity of user–producer interaction

The organizational element will not link every single producer to every single user – here we disregard pure monopolistic and pure monopsonistic situations.

Normally, each producer will have a close interaction with a subset of all potential users and each user will be attached to only one, or a small subset of all potential producers. This selectivity reflects the need to develop noneconomic relationships of hierarchy and mutual trust. It also reflects the need to develop effective channels and codes of information.

3.2.8 User–producer relationships in time

It takes time to develop selective relationships involving elements of hierarchy and mutual trust. It also takes time to develop effective channels and codes of information. Once those relationships have become established, it will not be costless to sever the connections. Inertia, reflecting a combination of a general resistance to change and risk aversion with rational motives, will reinforce existing user–producer relationships. Ceteris paribus, the user unit will prefer to trust a producer known from its own experience rather than getting involved with a new producer. The investment in information channels and codes will be lost if the old relationships are severed, and new investment in the creation of new relationships will be required. Therefore user–producer relationships will tend to become enduring and resistant to change. Only if the costs of continuing the existing relationships are apparent or the economic incentives offered by new relationships are substantial will a reorganization of the markets take place.

3.2.9 User–producer relationships in space

The user–producer relationship is defined in 'economic space' coupling units, close to each other, in an input–output system. The selective user–producer relationships will involve units more or less distant from each other in geographical and cultural space.

The importance of distance will vary with the type of innovative activity involved. When the technology is standardized and reasonably stable, the information exchanged may be translated into standard codes and long-distance transmission of information can take place and involve low costs. Here, user–producer relationships involving units located far away from each other might be effective.

When the technology is complex and ever changing, a short distance might be important for the competitiveness of both users and producers. Here, the information codes must be flexible and complex and a common cultural background might be important in order to establish tacit codes of conduct and to facilitate the decoding of the complex messages exchanged. The need for a short distance will be reinforced when user needs are complex and ever changing.

When the technology changes rapidly and radically – when a new technological paradigm (for a discussion and a definition, see Dosi 1982) develops – the need for proximity in terms of geography and culture becomes even more important. A new technological paradigm will imply that established norms and standards become obsolete and that old codes of information cannot transmit the characteristics of innovative activities. In the absence of generally accepted standards and codes able to transmit information, face-to-face contact and a common cultural background might become of decisive importance for the information exchange.

3.2.10 Vertical integration as a means of overcoming geographical and cultural distance

The development of transnational capital and vertically integrated firms operating all over the world reflects that 'organizational proximity' may overcome geographical and cultural distance. However, vertical integration may have its price. It tends to exclude integrated units from the interaction with producer units and user units outside the integrated firm. Such independent firms will tend to guard themselves against an open information exchange with a vertically integrated unit. As users, they risk getting less efficient technology than their integrated counterpart and competitor. As producers, they fear that the know-how built into their product innovations will become expropriated by the integrated user and transferred to an integrated competing producer.

In addition, the vertically integrated units may prove to be more rigid and less susceptible to new technological opportunities and new user needs than the parties operating in an organized market. The tendency towards vertical integration is strong, but there are also countertendencies at work. The trade-off between saved transaction costs and the losses in terms of more narrow interaction with external parties will differ between different parts of the economy. It will, among other things, reflect the state of the technology and the character of the process of innovation.

3.2.11 User and producer characteristics and the innovative potential of interaction

Not all user–producer relationships promote innovative activities. Being closely linked to conservative users with weak technical competence might be a disadvantage for a producer and vice versa. The innovativeness and the competences of users and producers are important qualities that might stimulate the other party. The degree of standardization among users might also be important. Being dependent on a set of users with diversified needs might make it difficult for the producer to accumulate experience and to exploit scale economies.

The effectiveness of the user–producer relationships grows with time. As a subset of users and producers accumulates more experience from interaction, the elements of hierarchy and mutual trust are strengthened and the exchange of information becomes more open. The code of information becomes more effective in transmitting complex messages related to the process of innovation. As we shall see below, this 'effectiveness' does not, however, guarantee *efficiency* if the criterion is user satisfaction at a low cost. The negative side is growing inertia and resistance to change.

3.2.12 Unsatisfactory innovations

Traditional welfare economics tends to disregard innovative activities. It analyses the allocation of a given set of use values with given characteristics. Neither are the concepts used in welfare economics applicable to a normative analysis of the process of innovation. There is, for instance, no point in asking how actual innovations deviate from 'an optimum'. The characteristics and usefulness of innovations not yet conceived are not known and therefore there are no well-defined points of reference for such an analysis.

In certain instances it might, however, be possible to demonstrate how innovative activities and technological trajectories deviate systematically from user needs. We might label such innovations as being 'unsatisfactory', when deviations neither can be ascribed to a lack of technical opportunities nor to an unwillingness among users to pay the costs for adaptation to the user needs.

When the user–producer relationships are characterized by a strong dominance of producers in terms of financial strength and technological competence, such deviations become more likely. In the field of consumer goods, the producer dominance is accentuated. The producer organizes both the process of innovation and most of the information exchange with users. In this field we should expect 'unsatisfactory innovations' to be frequent (Freeman 1982, 202ff).

Patterns of dominance and hierarchy might also be found when the user is a professional organization. If a few big firms produce scientifically based, complex and systemic products for a great number of small, independent user units – each with low technical and scientific competence – the producers will dominate the process of innovation and the likelihood of unsatisfactory innovations becomes high. In a study of the Danish dairy industry, such a pattern, resulting in 'hyper automation', was found to characterize the relationships between producers and users of dairy equipment (Lundvall et al. 1983).

In such situations coordination among users might develop and resources might be pooled in order to develop their competence. Such coordination will often be more difficult to make efficient when the users are consumers than when they are professional units. Government regulation or government support to user organizations might be necessary in order to rectify an unsatisfactory trajectory in consumer technology.

Another background for unsatisfactory innovations might be inertia in user–producer relationships and the level of 'effectiveness' of already established channels and codes of information. In a historical period characterized by the development and introduction of basic radical innovations, the rigidity of the existing set of user–producer relationships tends to become manifest. A basic radical innovation will often be produced by a new sector with weak forward linkages. The potential users of the innovation will be found in most parts of the economy, and those users will have backward linkages to producers having little experience and competence in relation to the new technology. Existing user–producer networks will prove to be tenacious, and it will take considerable time for a new network to become established. During such a period of transition, productivity might be stagnating while new technological opportunities seem to flourish.

Here, the problem is not only the specific unsatisfactory technical innovations but rather a general 'mismatch' in the whole economy. Christopher Freeman and Carlota Perez (1986) have discussed how a 'technological revolution', based on information technology, might provoke mismatch problems related not only to capital and labour but also to the existing socioeconomic institutional set-up. The rigidity of user–producer relationships might be regarded as one important aspect of this last type of mismatch. It is important because it has its roots in the very core of the market system. Policy strategies, putting all the emphasis on flexibility through market regulation and minimizing the role of government in the process of adjustment, seem to be somewhat off the point when rigidities are produced and reproduced within and by the markets themselves.

3.2.13 Is innovation induced by supply or by demand?

One classical dispute in innovation theory refers to the role of demand and supply in determining the rate and direction of the process of innovations (Mowery and Rosenberg 1979; Freeman 1982, 211). The user–producer approach puts this question in a new perspective. On the one hand, it demonstrates that demand does play an important role in the process of innovation. On the other hand, it puts more emphasis on the *quality of demand* than on demand as a quantitative variable. The very substantial user expenditure channelled into the demand for private transportation has not resulted in radical product innovations in the automobile industry. Conversely, very competent and demanding users have provoked radical innovations in areas where the volume of expenditure has been miniscule. The role of users in relation to the development of new scientific instruments is illustrative in this respect.

Individual innovations might appear unrelated to user needs, such as innovations emanating from science. In the second part of this chapter, it will be argued that even science has its users and that many innovations, appearing as purely supply-determined, have their roots in a user–producer interaction placed early in the chain of innovation. In this perspective, *general* statements about the role of 'demand' and 'supply' do not seem very relevant.

3.2.14 Some implications for industrial and technology policy

The fact that technology is influenced by the demand side has been used to argue for a *laissez-faire* technology policy. If demand is provoking the innovations called for, there is no need for state intervention. Those arguing that the supply side plays the dominating role will often recommend government support to R&D activities and education, combined with an active labour market policy.

The implications of a user–producer approach are somewhat more complex. First, technology policy should not only take into account the competence and innovativeness of units placed early in the chain of innovation. The lack of competence of users and the tendency of producers to dominate the process of innovation might be as serious a problem as a lack of competence on the producer side. Even when the state itself acts as a user, one will often find that the competence will be too weak, and this might result in 'unsatisfactory innovations'. Two Danish case studies, looking into the role of local government as user of waste-water technology and office technology, demonstrated how a lack of local user competence had a negative effect on the technological systems developed and used (Gregersen 1984; Brændgaard et al. 1984).

Second, government may intervene, directly or indirectly, in relation to the establishment and restructuring of patterns of user–producer relationships. In a period characterized by gradual technological change and incremental innovations, a national government might sustain national and international user–producer linkages that already exist. It might also support the establishment of specific organizations intermediating between groups of users and groups of producers, pooling information and thereby stimulating the production and diffusion of innovations.

In a period characterized by radical innovations and a shift in technological paradigm, the task of government becomes vastly more complex and important. In such a period, there is a need for a transformation of the existing network of user–producer relationships. The inertia originating in the organized markets will at the national level be supported by the political power of strong interest groups closely associated with the prevailing structure. The difficult task for government will be to stimulate the renewal, or severance, of well-established user–producer relationships and the establishment of new relationships.

3.2.15 Standard microeconomics and the user–producer approach

Our results can now be confronted with the microeconomic theory presented in standard textbooks. We make the following observations:

- The element of organization will be different, in terms of content and strength, between different markets, and it will change over time. Some markets will be more susceptible to an analysis based on the concepts of optimizing agents acting at arm's-length distance than others. This raises doubt about the intentions to construct one single model of micro-behaviour, assumed to be generally valid for all markets, a problem discussed by Kornai (1971, 207ff).
- The standard approach will be most relevant when technological opportunities are limited and user needs remain constant. When product innovations are continuously provoked by changing technological opportunities and user needs, it is no longer meaningful to assume optimizing behaviour. 'Short run' decisions, by producers to become involved in certain lines of innovating activities, and by users to choose among new products, will be characterized by fundamental uncertainty, as will, a fortiori, 'long run' decisions, referring to the establishment of (and investment in) new relationships and information channels.
- Standard microeconomics regards technological change as an exogenous process and its outcome as technological 'progress', indicating growing efficiency. In organized markets the existing set of user–producer relationships may produce technological trajectories, deviating systematically from what is 'satisfactory', even when users and producers act according to profit motives.
- In standard microeconomics, changes in relative prices will influence the decisions taken by users and producers automatically and instantaneously. A world characterized by organized markets will be sluggish in this respect. The existing set of user–producer relationships and the continuous qualitative change in products will reduce the responsiveness to changes in relative prices.

3.3 National Systems of Innovation

In the first part of this chapter, we found that the microeconomic framework, as presented in standard textbooks, is not easily reconciled with the stylized facts of the modern economy. A highly developed vertical division of labour, when combined with ubiquitous innovative activities, implies that most markets will be 'organized markets' rather than pure markets. In this second and final part, we shall sketch some of the implications of this micro-approach for the national and international level. Elements of a model of a national system of innovation will be introduced.

The subdisciplines in economics, most relevant in this context, are theories of economic growth and international trade. Standard growth models are developed under the assumption of a closed economy. This is a natural assumption in so far as the models regard new technology as falling 'as manna from heaven' and as equally accessible for all actors, sectors, regions and nations. Standard foreign trade theory assumes labour and capital to be perfectly immobile and commodities to be perfectly mobile across national borders. It has the assumption of a perfectly free and mobile technology in common with standard growth theory.

This last assumption is at odds with what can be observed in the real world where some countries establish themselves as technological leaders, generally or in specific technologies, while others tend to lag behind. According to the user–producer approach, geographical and cultural distance is a factor that may impede the interaction between users and producers. This might contribute to an explanation of why different national systems display different patterns of development.

3.3.1 The nation as a framework for user–producer interaction

The tendency towards internationalization of trade, capital and production has been strong during the postwar period. Some would even argue that nations tend to become obsolete as economic subjects. But this process of internationalization has not wiped out idiosyncratic national patterns of specialization in production and international trade. The fact that Denmark is strongly specialized in dairy machinery, Sweden in metal-working and wood-cutting technology and Norway in fishery technology cannot be explained by the general factor endowments in these countries. Rather, we should look for the explanation in the close interaction between producers of such machinery and a competent and demanding domestic-user sector (Andersen et al. 1981).

Interaction between users and producers belonging to the same national system may work more efficiently for several reasons. Short geographical distance is part of the explanation; more important may be a common language and the cultural proximity. It is thus interesting to note that firms in the Nordic countries tend to regard all the Nordic countries as their 'home market'. This might reflect that those nations have very much in common in terms of culture and social organization (Dalum and Fagerberg 1986).

Another factor of importance is, of course, national government. The role of government in relation to the process of innovation has been seriously underestimated according to recent historical studies (Yakushiji 1986). Besides more direct interventions in relation to specific innovations, government imposes standards and regulations making domestic interaction more efficient. In important instances the state intervenes directly in the network and supports existing user–producer relationships.

The fact that national economies have idiosyncratic technological capabilities reflects that international transfer of technology is neither costless nor instantaneous. Some parts of knowledge can be embodied in the traded commodities while others are embodied in the labour force. The limited mobility of labour across national borders can partly explain why technology is not easily transferred internationally. The structure of the national systems of production and innovation is a product of a historical process, and it cannot be transferred as easily as 'factors of production'. It might be here that we find the most fundamental restriction to international learning and international transfer of technology.

The importance of nations as frameworks for user–producer interaction does not rule out transnational interaction. In some industries and technologies, the required scale of the R&D effort is so enormous that not even the biggest of the transnational firms can afford to go alone when developing a new product. This is the case for civil aircrafts manufacturing, space technology and nuclear power. Here, the pattern of user–producer interaction transcends national borders. But even in these areas, national interests related to international competitiveness and military goals put certain limits to the actual cooperation taking place, according to case studies (OECD 1986).

Applying a user–producer perspective to international relations brings forward the structural interdependency, characterizing the process of innovation within and between nations. On this background we shall sketch the outlines of 'a national system of innovation'. Earlier research involving international comparisons of innovative capabilities has demonstrated important international differences at the micro level in terms of management strategies and firm behaviour, sometimes taking into account differences in the environment of firms, financial institutions and labour relations, for example. Such studies, useful as they are, might underplay the importance of the structure of the full system of innovation, however. When the process of innovation is regarded as the outcome of a complex interaction, it is obvious that the whole system must be more than a sum of its parts.

The concept of the national system of innovation will be developed step by step, using earlier contributions on systems of production and on the division of labour within systems of innovation as some of its elements.

3.4 National Systems of Production

While Anglo-Saxon industrial economics tends to regard national economies as 'a bunch of industrial sectors', the French tradition has been more oriented towards the systemic interdependence between different parts of the economy. Verticals of production or *filières*, that encompass all stages of production from raw materials to final products, are important units of analysis in this tradition (de Bandt and Humber 1985). A broader concept also bringing public agencies and financial institutions into the analysis, industrial subsystems or *mesosystemes industriels*, has been developed and proposed as the units most adequate for analysis and for industrial policy (de Bandt 1985).

An even more ambitious approach, presented by some French Marxists and inspired by the work of Francois Perroux, defines 'the national system of production' as unit of analysis. The national industrial system is divided into a small number of sections, defined by the economic function of the output and by its sector of use (investment goods, semi-manufactured goods and consumer goods) (GRESI 1975). Some of the contributions in this tradition assume the section producing investment goods for the production of investment goods (machine tool industry) to be strategic for economic growth and development. National systems, having a strong position in this area, will tend to have a strong international competitiveness and vice versa. The national system of production is thus not assumed to be a closed system. On the contrary, it is the specific degree and form of openness that determines the specific dynamics of each national system of production.

3.4.1 Production and innovation

In order to judge the relevance of this model, it is necessary to look into the relationship between the process of production and the process of innovation. These processes differ in important respects but they are obviously mutually interdependent.

Production is a repetitive process where routines tend to develop. The flows of goods and services between different subsystems can, if use value characteristics remain constant, easily be quantified in terms of value and volume. The process of innovation might be continuous and cumulative, but it will always have a unique element stressing the importance of creativity, as opposed to routine decision-making. The flows between the subsystems will be complex and systemic information will be difficult to translate into quantitative terms.

The interdependence between production and innovation goes both ways. On the one hand, learning taking place in production – as 'learning by doing' or as 'learning by using' – forms an important input into the process of innovation. 'Learning by interacting' will typically take place between parties linked together by flows of goods and services originating from production (this is a prerequisite for user–producer relationships to become enduring and selective). On the other hand, the process of innovation might be the single most important factor restructuring the system of production by introducing new sectors, breaking down the old linkages and establishing new ones in the system of production.

This interdependency between production and innovation makes it legitimate to take the national system of production as point of departure for defining a system of innovation. But the division of labour in the system of innovation is not just a reflection of the division of labour in the system of production. Some parts of the production system will be more active in terms of innovations, while others primarily will be users of innovations developed by others.

3.4.2 The vertical division of labour in the national system of innovation

Most innovation studies focusing on vertical interaction have put the emphasis on the division of labour in the process of innovation. The pioneering studies of the sector producing scientific instruments, made by von Hippel (1976), demonstrated that process innovations were often developed by the sector itself. Even when independent producers were involved, users played an important active part in the process of innovation.

Pavitt (1984) presents a taxonomy referring to different types of industries according to their respective role in the process of innovation. Using a database for important UK innovations, containing information of origin and address of each innovation, three different types of sectors were identified: supplier-dominated sector, production-intensive sector and science-based sector. This taxonomy and the further subdivisions made are extremely useful in defining the division of labour within the national system of innovation.

3.4.3 Flows and stocks in the national system of innovation

Earlier we pointed out that the flows within the system of innovation take the form of complex and systemic information – messages difficult to translate into quantities. This is also true for the stocks of the system. Knowledge, scientific as well as know-how and tacit knowledge, is difficult to measure. Other important 'stocks' may be the inventiveness and creativity of individuals and organizations, and those are even more difficult to assess in quantitative terms.

In standard economics there is a tendency to define scientific analysis as synonymous with the establishment of quantitative and mathematical models. If we accepted this dictum, important aspects of the national system of innovation would be regarded as being outside the realm of economics science. As pointed out by Georgescu-Roegen (1971, 316ff), this ideal of science is not uncontroversial, however. It reflects an epistemology imported from Newtonian physics. Georgescu-Roegen demonstrates that 'dialectical concepts' – along with what he refers to as 'arithmomorphic' concepts – must be a part of any science analysing change.

Further, there have been different attempts to develop a quantitative analysis of the flows within national systems of innovation. As a matter of fact, the already mentioned study by Pavitt (1984) may be regarded as a quantitative approach using the number of 'important UK innovations' as the unit of account. Another interesting contribution in this field is 'Inter-industry technology flows in the United States' (Scherer 1982). Here a detailed input–output matrix for the US industrial system is developed on the basis of information gathered on patenting and R&D activities. In both of these papers, it is the industrial system that is at the centre of analysis. This is natural in so far as most innovations emanate within this system. But when we look at the system of innovation from a user–producer perspective, it becomes interesting to take a closer look at the interfaces between industry and the academic community and at the interfaces between industry and some of the 'end users' of industrial innovations – workers, consumers and the public sector.

In Nelson (1986) the division of labour and performance of the US systems of innovation is discussed. It is demonstrated that universities and other public institutions involved in the production of science are important parts of this system, acting in a way which makes them complementary to the innovative activities going on in the private sector. It is obvious that any model of a national system of innovation must take into account the interaction between universities and industry.

3.4.4 Science and technology in a user–producer perspective

In the first part of this chapter we focused mainly on the interaction between firms producing goods and services. The user–producer perspective might, however, be applied to early stages in the chain of innovation from basic research to applied research and developmental activities. It is almost built into the definition of 'basic research' (as nonapplied), that it should take place without any specific purpose or address. This picture is too simple, however. Even pure science, as mathematics and logics, has its users, and the agenda of science will often be determined by users in applied science. Also in this area, the innovativeness and competence of users may influence the rate and direction of scientific discovery. In a case study referring to Bell Telephone Laboratories, Nelson (1962) has demonstrated the close interaction between basic and applied research.

What separates pure science from technology is primarily the institutional framework. Science will typically be produced in universities according to an academic 'mode of behaviour', while technology primarily will be produced in private firms according to a profit-oriented 'mode of behaviour'. The academic mode will typically be characterized by nonpecuniary incentives – with the 'search for excellence' as a strong motive power (sometimes combined with curiosity and an urge to understand what is going on). The output of science will be widely dispersed because the worldwide diffusion of research results is a precondition for recognition of excellence (David 1984). This mode implies a different culture from the one predominant in profit-oriented firms. Norms, values and incentives are different as well as the language and the codes of information used in the two spheres.

It is not surprising that the link between universities and industry has become a political issue. The growing recognition of the role of science in relation to technology and production has made it a national priority to strengthen this link. The symbolic effect of Silicon Valley characterized by a close interaction between 'excellent' universities and hi-tech firms in different parts of the world has given the debate further impetus. In most OECD countries the establishment of 'science parks' and 'technopolises' has become an important part of industrial policy.

The efforts made to integrate and subordinate academic activities in relation to industry may not be costless, however. If the academic mode of production is undermined and replaced by a profit-oriented mode, where pecuniary incentives become more important and where secrecy regarding the output becomes more frequent, the academic mode may lose one of its principal merits – its tradition for worldwide diffusion of knowledge. In the field of biotechnology this process seems already to have reached a critical level (Chesnais 1986). National systems of innovation may temporarily become strengthened when universities become subordinated to industry. In the long run, the production and worldwide distribution of knowledge may be weakened.

3.4.5 Introducing the final users of technology into the system

The classical actors studied in innovation studies are individual entrepreneurs and the R&D laboratories of big firms. Secondary parts may be played by scientists and policymakers. The user–producer approach points to the fact that 'final users' in terms of workers, consumers and the public sector may have a role to play in relation to innovation.

The fact that workers and consumers tend to be absent from the scene in most innovation studies reflects, to a certain degree, the reality of a modern industrial system. Both in planned and market economies, the process of innovation tends to become a professionalized activity and workers and consumers tend to become passive beneficiaries or victims in relation to new technology rather than subjects taking active part in the process of innovation. It is, however, not self-evident that such a division of labour is 'natural' and appropriate. Active and competent final users might enhance the innovative capability of a national system of innovation.

Further, the actual participation of 'final users' may be underrated in the literature on innovation. Workers play an important part in the daily learning process taking place in production and many incremental innovations may be the product of skilled workers' improvements on the process equipment. Where workers are directly involved in the process of innovation, the outcome in terms of productivity and efficiency might be more satisfactory than when they are excluded. Some studies of the Japanese experience seem to point in this direction.

Among consumers, we find some interesting examples in the user clubs established in relation to specific brands of personal computers. Here, private consumers act as professional users developing new software in an interaction with producers of hardware and software. However, for most consumer goods, the interaction is organized exclusively by producers gathering information about, and manipulating, consumer needs. An interesting theoretical contribution giving consumer learning an important role in the overall development of the national economy is Pasinetti (1981) who maintains that the learning of new needs is of crucial importance for the maintenance of full employment. When productivity is growing and demand for existing consumer goods becomes satisfied, the learning of new needs of consumers is a necessary condition for avoiding 'technological unemployment'.

We have already pointed out the importance of public sector as a final user in relation to technology policy. The most comprehensive and important historical example might be the military industrial complexes in the United States and the Soviet Union. In both these cases, the state has acted as a competent and very demanding user on a very big scale. Through long-term contracts, radically new and advanced products have been developed. In the Scandinavian countries, there is a growing debate on the possibilities of building 'welfare-industrial complexes' oriented towards the fulfilment of social needs in relation to energy, housing, environment, transport and the health service. Such complexes might, if the public sector acts as a competent user with a long-term perspective, be as effective as 'warfare-industrial complexes' in provoking new technology. There is no reason to believe that the positive impact on the well-being of citizens should be less.

3.4.6 Social innovation as the basis for technical innovation

In a period characterized by radical change in the technological basis of the economy, established organizational and institutional patterns might prove to be important obstacles to the exploitation of the full potential of new technology. In such a period, social innovations might become more important for the wealth of nations than technical innovations. The Gorbatchev drive for social change and democratization in Soviet Union might be seen in this light. In the capitalist countries the focus is still narrowly oriented, either towards the manipulation of financial variables or towards an 'acceleration of technological progress'. Institutional change, strengthening the competence and the power of final users, might be one of the social innovations that can give national systems of innovation a stronger position in the world economy. It would also imply that unsatisfactory innovations became less frequent.

The need for social innovations and institutional change is even more urgent at the global level. The enormous and growing gaps between rich and poor countries reflect that the international transmission of knowledge and technology is not working as assumed by standard economic theory. In so far as specific technological capabilities are rooted in national networks of user–producer relationships, 'technology transfer' can only solve part of the problem, however. There is a need for strengthening the whole national system of innovation, including science, industry and final users in the poor countries.

3.5 Conclusion

This chapter introduces the concept of user–producer interaction and the national systems of innovation to meet the theoretical challenge of understanding the systemic interactions and dynamics that take place at different levels of economic systems.

It starts from the stylized fact that ubiquitous innovation takes place in an economic system with a highly developed vertical division of labour. On this basis, we show that there is a need to revise some basic elements in neoclassical economics. In a system with pure markets and with arm's length and anonymous relationships between producers and users, there would be little innovation.

A key element in a dynamic economic is the organized market where users and producers interact and build lasting relationships. This micro perspective is then applied at a more aggregate level such as on the relationship between science and technology and between university and industry. It is argued that whenever new knowledge is produced, there is a need for feedback from the users of the knowledge to those engaged in producing it. National systems differ not only in terms of their production specialization but also in terms of how institutions link users and producers of knowledge in the system.

The analysis of user–producer interaction and product innovation has been presented as the micro-foundation of new understanding of national innovation systems.

Notes

1 Williamson, in his most recent work, recognizes that most transactions take place in organized markets. The dichotomy between pure markets and pure hierarchies is sub- stituted by a scale where those two forms represent the extreme points. It is now argued that most transactions take place 'in the middle range' of such a scale (Williamson 1985, 83). Still his analysis tends largely to neglect the process of innovation per se as a fac- tor reinforcing vertical integration and organized markets. Recent contributions by Japanese economists (Imai and Itami 1984) do take into account technical innovation as a factor affecting the pattern of organized markets, but their focus is primarily manage- ment strategies rather than the implications for economic theory.

2 Adam Smith recognized the significance of this separation, presenting it as an impor- tant source of wealth and productivity growth: 'All the improvements in machinery, however, have by no means been the inventions of those who had occasion to use the machines. Many improvements have been made by the business of a peculiar trade' (1776, 8).

References

Amann, R. and J. Cooper. (eds.) 1982. *Industrial Innovation in the Soviet Union*. New Haven, CT: Yale University Press.

Andersen, E. S., B. Dalum and G. Villumsen. 1981. 'The Importance of the Home Market for the Technological Development and the Export Specialization of Manufacturing Industry'. In *Technical Innovation and National Economic Performance*, IKE seminar. Aalborg: Aalborg University Press.

Arrow, K. J.. 1974. *The Limits of Organization*. New York: W.W. Norton & Company.

Bandt J. de. 1985. 'French Industrial Policies: Successes and Failures'. In *A Competitive Future for Europe?*, Congress Report, Rotterdam.

Bandt, J. de and M. Humbert. 1985. '*La mesodynamique industrieille*', in *Cahiers du CERNEA*, Nanterre.

Brændgaard A., B. Gregersen, B.-A. Lundvall, N. Maarbjerg-Oiesen and I. Aaen. 1984. *Besparelser eller beskæftigelse: en undersøgelse af danske kommuners anvendelse af EDB og ETB*. Aalborg: Aalborg University Press.

Carter, A. P. 1986. 'Diffusion from an Input-Output Perspective'. Paper presented at the Conference on Innovation Diffusion, Venice, March.

Chesnais, F. 1986. 'Some Notes on Technological Cumulativeness: The Appropriation of Technology and Technological Progressiveness in Concentrated Market Structures', Paper presented at the Conference on Innovation Diffusion, Venice, March.

Dalum, B. and J. Fagerberg. 1986. 'Diffusion of Technology, Economic Growth and Intra-Industry Trade: The Case of the Nordic Countries'. Paper presented at the Second Knoellinger Seminar, Aabo, April, mimeo.

David, P. 1984. 'On the Perilous Economics of Modern Science'. Paper presented at the TIP Workshop, Stanford University, August, mimeo.

Dosi, G. 1982. 'Technological Paradigms and Technological Trajectories: A Suggested Interpretation of the Determinants and Directions of Technical Change'. *Research Policy* 11, no. 3: 147–62.

Eaton, W. O. 1985. *The Economic Institutions of Capitalism: Firms, Markets, Relational Contracting.* New York: Praeger.

Freeman, C. 1982. *The Economics of Industrial Innovation.* London: Frances Pinter.

Freeman, C. and C. Perez. 1986. 'The Diffusion of technological Innovations and Changes of Techno-Economic Paradigm'. Paper presented at the Conference on Innovation Diffusion, Venice, March.

Georgescu-Roegen, N. 1971. *The Entropy Law and the Economic Process.* Cambridge MA: Harvard University Press.

Gregersen, B. 1984. *Det miljoindustrielle kompleks: teknologispredning og Beskæftigelse.* Aalborg: Aalborg University Press.

GRESI (Groupe de reflexions pour les strategies industrielles). 1975. 'La Division Internationale de travail', Etudes de politique industriel no. 9, Ministere de lindustrie et de la Recherche, Paris.

Imai, K. and H. Itami. 1984. 'Interpenetration of organization and market: Japan's firm and market in comparison with the US'. *International Journal of Industrial Organisation* 2 no. 4: 285–310.

Kornai, J. 1971. *Anti-equilibrium.* Amsterdam: North Holland.

Lundvall, B.-Å. 1985. *Product Innovation and User-Producer Interaction.* Aalborg: Aalborg University Press.

Lundvall B.-Å., N. Maarbjerg-Olesen and I. Aaen. 1983. *Det landbrugsindustrielle kompleks: teknologiudvikling, konkurrenceevne og beskæftigelse.* Aalborg: Aalborg University Press.

Mowery, D. and N. Rosenberg. 1979. 'The Influence of Market Demand upon Innovation: A Critical Review of Some Recent Empirical Studies'. *Research Policy* 8, no. 2: 102–53.

Nathan, R. 1982. *Inside the Black Box: Technology and Economics.* Cambridge: Cambridge University Press.

Nelson, R. R. (ed.). 1962. 'The Link between Science and Invention: The Case of the Transistor'. In *National Bureau of Economic Research, The Rate and Direction of Inventive Activity.* Princeton, NJ: Princeton University Press. (pp. 549–84).

———. 1986. 'The Generation and Utilization of Technology: A Cross-Industry Analysis'. Paper presented at the Conference on Innovation Diffusion, Venice, March.

OECD. 1983. 'Report on the Results of the Workshop on Research, Technology and Regional Policy', DSTI/SPR, 83.117.

———. 1986. 'Technical Cooperation Agreements between Firms: Some Initial Data and Analysis', DSTI/SPR/86.20, May.

Pasinetti, L. 1981. *Structural Change and Economic Growth*. Cambridge: Cambridge University Press.

Pavitt, K. 1984. 'Sectoral Patterns of Technical Change: Towards a Taxonomy and a Theory'. *Research Policy* 13, no. 6: 343–73.

Rosenberg, N. 1976. *Perspectives on Technology*. Cambridge: Cambridge University Press.

Rothwell, R. and P. Gardiner. 1985. 'Invention, Innovation, Re-Innovation and the Role of the User: A Case Study of British Hovercraft Development'. *Technovation* 3, no. 4: 167–86.

Scherer, P. M. 1982. 'Inter-industry Technology Flows in the United States'. *Research Policy* 11, no. 4: 227–45.

Smith, A. 1776/1910. *An Inquiry into the Nature and Causes of the Wealth of Nations*. Darlington: J. M. Dent & Sons.

Von Hippel, E. 1976. 'The Dominant Role of Users in the Scientific Instruments Innovation Process'. *Research Policy* 5, no. 3: 212–39.

Williamson, O. E. 1975. *Markets and Hierarchies: Analysis and Antitrust Implications*. New York: Free Press.

Williamson, O. E. 1985. *The Economic Institutions of Capitalism*. New York: Free Press.

Yakushiji, T. 1986. 'Technological Emulation and Industrial Development'. Paper presented to the Conference on Innovation Diffusion, Venice, March.

Chapter 4

NATIONAL SYSTEMS OF INNOVATION: TOWARDS A THEORY OF INNOVATION AND INTERACTIVE LEARNING

Bengt-Åke Lundvall

4.1 Introduction

Theories in the social sciences may be regarded as 'focusing devices'. Any specific theory brings forward and exposes some aspects of the real world, leaving others in obscurity. That is why a long-lasting hegemony of one single theoretical tradition is damaging, both in terms of understanding and policy-making. In the field of economics, the dominating neoclassical paradigm puts its analytical focus on concepts such as scarcity, allocation and exchange in a static context. Even if these concepts reflect important phenomena in the real world, they only bring forward some aspects of the economic system. One aim of this book is to demonstrate the need for an alternative and supplementary focusing device that puts interactive learning and innovation at the centre of analysis.

Through more than a decade, a group of economists at Aalborg University working on a research program on Innovation, Knowledge and Economic Dynamics – the IKE group – has worked together studying industrial development and international competitiveness from such a perspective. This book presents results from this work in relation to one specific subject: national systems of innovation.[1]

Our choice of perspective and subject is based on two sets of assumptions. First, it is assumed that the most fundamental resource in the modern economy is knowledge and accordingly that the most important process is learning. The fact that knowledge differs in crucial respects from other resources in the economy makes standard economics less relevant and motivates efforts to develop an alternative paradigm.[2]

Second, it is assumed that learning is predominantly an interactive, and therefore a socially embedded, process that cannot be understood without taking into consideration its institutional and cultural context. Specifically, it is assumed that the historical establishment and development of the modern nation state was a necessary prerequisite for the acceleration of the process of learning, which propelled the process of industrialization during the last centuries. Finally, it is recognized that the traditional role of nation states in supporting learning processes is now challenged by the process of internationalization and globalization.

These ideas are reflected in the overall structure of the book, which is divided into three main parts. The first part presents the theoretical framework, the second part analyses the most important elements of the system of innovation and the third part is devoted to the opening of national systems through internationalization and globalization. This introductory chapter presents basic definitions, theoretical starting points, a road map for the book as a whole and finally references to other attempts to analyse national systems of innovation.

4.2 National Systems of Innovation

4.2.1 A first definition

According to Boulding (1985), the broadest possible definition of a system is 'anything that is not chaos'. Somewhat more specifically, a system is constituted by a number of elements and by the relationships between these elements. It follows that a system of innovation is constituted by elements and relationships that interact in the production, diffusion and use of new and economically useful knowledge and that a national system encompasses elements and relationships, either located or rooted inside the borders of a nation state.[3]

Using the terminology of Boulding, it is obvious that the national system of innovation is a *social* system. A central activity in the system of innovation is learning, and learning is a social activity that involves interaction between people. It is also a *dynamic* system, characterized by both positive feedback and reproduction. Often the elements of the system of innovation either reinforce each other in promoting processes of learning and innovation or, conversely, combine into constellations blocking such processes. Cumulative causation and virtuous and vicious circles are characteristics of systems and subsystems of innovation. Another important aspect of innovation system relates to the reproduction of knowledge of individuals or collective agents.

4.2.2 Nation states and national systems

The concept of national systems of innovation presumes the existence of nation states, and this phenomenon has two dimensions: the national–cultural and the political. The ideal 'abstract nation state' is the one where the two dimensions coincide, that is, where all individuals belonging to a nation – defined by cultural, ethnical and linguistic characteristics – are gathered into one single geographical space controlled by one central state authority (without foreign nationalities).

It is difficult to find any nation states, in this strict sense, in the real world. Countries differ both in the degrees of cultural homogeneity and political centralization. In some cases it is not even clear where to locate the borders of a 'national' system of innovation. This might be true both for 'multinational' states such as Belgium, Canada and Switzerland and for single-national but federal states such as Germany. At the extreme, a country might be solely constituted by a joint foreign policy with little in common in terms of institutional set up and culture. In such cases, the concept of a 'national' system of innovation would be of little relevance.

Most of the contributors to this book have their roots in a minority of small countries, which may be characterized as culturally homogeneous and socioeconomically coherent systems (Sweden, Denmark and Norway). This gives a certain bias to our world outlook (it should do so according to our basic understanding where theoretical conceptualization is assumed to be culturally bound). However, it may be argued that it is quite useful, analytically, to use concepts that are archetypes rather than 'averages'. In order to bring out sharply the limits and consequences of globalization and regionalization, it is useful at least as a starting point, to assume that countries are homogeneous in political and cultural terms.

4.2.3 National systems, globalization and regionalization

Readers might ask why we are focusing on the *national* level, in an era where many analysts point to an accelerating process of internationalization and globalization characterized by multinational firms, loosening their relations to their home countries and entering into alliances with foreign firms. This process might actually be most advanced when it comes to the production of new knowledge and innovations in science-based technologies such as biotechnology, pharmaceuticals and electronics.

At the same time, a growing number of social scientists – often inspired by new sets of ideas labelled as 'flexible specialization', 'networking' and 'post-Fordism' – have argued that regional production systems, industrial districts and technological districts are becoming increasingly important. Some authors analyse these two tendencies as interconnected and mutually reinforcing (Storper 1991a; Camagni 1990 and also Porter 1990). They assume that globalization and international specialization have their roots in the strengthening of specialized technological districts and regional networks.

Both globalization and regionalization might be interpreted as processes that weaken the coherence and importance of national systems. In this book, we do not deny the validity of these trends. Actually, we think that they make it even more pertinent to understand the role and implications of national systems of innovation, both historically and in the present era.

First, we believe that national systems still play an important role in supporting and directing the processes of innovation and learning. The uncertainties involved in innovation and the importance of learning imply that the process calls for a complex communication between the parties involved. This will especially be the case when the knowledge exchanged is tacit and difficult to codify. When the parties involved originate in the same national environment – sharing its norms and culturally based system of interpretation – interactive learning and innovation will be easier to develop.

However, it must be recognized that important elements of the process of innovation tend to become transnational and global rather than national, and here the trend will be most important in science-based areas where the communication is easier to formalize and codify. Some of the big corporations are weakening their ties to their home countries while beginning to spread their innovative activities and to 'source' different national systems of innovation. These changes are important as they challenge the traditional role of national systems of innovation, but they do not make it less important to understand how national systems work.

When an old institutional order is threatened and a new one is beginning to develop, it becomes critically important to understand the basic mechanisms of the old order. Without such an understanding, the costs of transformation might become unnecessarily high. More specifically, the process of far-reaching European integration may run into serious problems if it does not take into account the complex interaction between institutions and economic structure in promoting innovation at the national level.

Behind the analysis lies also, as mentioned earlier, the hypothesis that the modern nation states in the Western world – not necessarily the new states in the former colonies – have worked as 'engines of growth'. They were constituted and shaped into their present form in a period characterized by a rapid economic transformation, including the massive movement of labour from agriculture to industrial production. Their social institutions and state policies have supported such a transformation as well as the new institutions aiming directly at economic wealth creation through innovation have been established in the course of the last century and have become integral parts of national systems of production.

From what has been said, it is obvious that national systems of innovation are open and heterogeneous systems. Processes of innovation transcend national borders and sometimes they are local rather than national. Actually this has always been the case for most national systems. The rapid industrialization and modernization of European countries, starting more than 100 years ago, was closely connected with an opening up of the national economies in terms of foreign trade, capital import and import of foreign ideas and experts, and already at that time the international specialization was often reflected in a regional specialization within the countries.

4.2.4 Public policy and national systems of innovation

As pointed out at the very beginning of this introduction, one main purpose of this book is to contribute to a theoretical understanding of interactive learning and innovation. However, the concept 'national systems of innovation' may also be useful when it comes to inspire public policies at the national and the international level.

First, in order to determine what governments should do in order to promote innovation, it is useful to know the specific systemic context in which a national government intervenes. Otherwise, government policies might either reproduce weaknesses of the national system or introduce mechanisms incompatible with the basic logic of the system.

Second, in the increasingly serious international conflicts, about which countries are paying for (the United States) and respectively appropriating benefits from (Japan) the investment in science and development of new technology, it is important to understand how different and very diverse national systems work. This is a point made by experts close to the General Agreement on Tariffs and Trade (GATT) negotiations (Ostry 1990).

Third, in a world characterized by a radical shift in techno-economic foundations, the ability of national systems to successfully cope with change and to exploit new technical opportunities seems to be quite divergent (Freeman and Perez 1988). Learning from the experience of foreign systems in this respect might be facilitated if the workings of the respective national systems as a whole are properly understood. Strategies based on naive copying may be avoided and institutional learning across national borders might be stimulated. Not least, the development in Eastern Europe points to a strong need to develop a realistic understanding of the workings of 'real market economies' in relation to innovation.

Actually, the concept 'national systems of innovation' has already entered the vocabulary of policymakers at the national and the international level. An ambitious effort to understand the importance of technology for economic change was launched by OECD in 1988 as the 'Technology/Economy programme' (TEP). When the outcome of this programme was summed up in Montreal in 1991, the concept of 'national systems of innovation' was given a prominent place in the conclusions.

It was pointed out that the assignment of proper roles for respectively the government and the private sector in enhancing technological capabilities should build on a better understanding of national systems of innovation. Moreover, it was concluded that the growing international conflicts, regarding the global sharing of burdens, and benefits emanating from development and use of new technology might be kept within reasonable limits only if the parties get a better understanding of the diversity of the National Innovation Systems (NSIs) (OECD – Canada 1991). The fact that the concept has already entered the everyday vocabulary of policymakers makes it even more important to give the NSI concept an analytical basis.

4.2.5 Performance of national systems of innovation

In order to design policies relevant for national system of innovation, it is necessary to agree on which should be the 'desiderata' of the system (Kornai 1971, 214). From the standpoint of general equilibrium theory, the main performance dimension refers to the more or less efficient allocation of scarce and given resources. A more dynamic version would point to the adaptability of the system. A Keynesian perspective would emphasize the degree of utilization of existing resources and especially of the labour force.

At this general level, we would like to propose that the most relevant performance indicators of national system of innovation should reflect the efficiency and effectiveness in producing, diffusing and exploiting economically useful knowledge. Such indicators are not well developed today. One of the classical measures for comparing different national systems is R&D expenditure as a proportion of GDP. There are two obvious problems with this indicator. First, it reflects only an input effort and does not say anything about what comes out of the effort. Second, R&D expenditure is only one kind of relevant input to the process of innovation; learning in connection with routine activities may be more important than R&D.

The output measures used are more recently developed and include patents (Pavitt and Patel 1988), the proportion of new products in sales (Kristensen and Lundvall 1991) and the proportion of hi-tech products in foreign trade (Dalum et al. 1988). Each one of these indicators has its own specific weaknesses, and it is wise to combine them in order to get a more satisfactory picture of the performance of a national system. A common weakness is that these measures do not take into account the diffusion of process technology and in order to get a more complete picture, indicators for diffusion should be taken into account (Edquist and Jakobsson 1988).

Technical progress is not regarded as a goal in itself. The main reason why national governments engage in innovation policy is the assumption that innovation is a key element in national economic growth. Different indicators of economic growth (national income or consumption per capita) are relevant when it comes to comparing the systems. But such indicators will reflect factors that have little to do with innovation, and more importantly, they give little insight into how innovation takes place in different countries. One interesting observation is that different systems may develop different modes of innovation while still following parallel growth paths.[4] Bringing together several different specific innovation indicators helps characterizing the specific national mode of innovation.

4.2.6 The normative dimension

The choice of performance criteria and of the respective weights to be assigned to these criteria is fundamentally a normative decision. One of the most developed attempts to come to grips with implicit and explicit value judgements in economic analysis is by Myrdal (1968). He argues that as a minimum requirement, economists should make their value premises explicit. Further, Myrdal actually presents a method for bringing value premises into the analysis of national economies. While studying problems of the poor Asian countries, he chooses to accept the set of value premises predominating among the national establishments in the countries studied – the ideal of modernization.

Given the lack of alternatives, it is tempting to use a similar approach to national systems of innovation. To identify the ambitions and goals of national governments in the area of innovation is apparently quite easy. The public discourse is dominated by references to the international competitiveness of the national economy and to national economic growth. There seems to be a broad social acceptance in the national establishment that these are the main goals. However, this is not the only relevant level to be taken into account.

Another level of analysis refers to international organizations of the rich countries such as the European Union and OECD. Politicians and experts at this level are more oriented towards strengthening economic growth in their respective region and towards avoiding international conflicts within the community of countries they represent.

Finally, there is a global level of analysis with a rather weak representation in organizational terms such as the UN organizations, global environmentalist organizations, etc. At this level, it becomes more obvious to experts and politicians that the long-term survival of the global economy is dependent on ecological sustainability and on a reduction of the extreme social inequality at the global level.

We do not find it proper to adopt the set of value premises of any single one of these three levels, however. On the one hand, we consider national policies and goals relating to innovativeness and competitiveness to be legitimate to a certain degree. The pursuit of such goals has been an important motor behind the dramatic increase in economic wealth in the OECD area and in some newly industrialized countries in Asia. Additionally, policies designed to strengthen the system of innovation are less of 'beggar-thy-neighbour' character than exchange rate or incomes policies.

On the other hand, we realize that some forms of national science and technology policy may actually be zero-sum games and that there is a growing number of examples of unpleasant trade-offs between short-term national economic growth and long-term global sustainability (in terms of environment, natural resources, etc.). The national context tends to become too narrow when it comes to solving problems such as global inequality and sustainability. The value premises of the national establishment must be confronted with these broader long-term concerns.

This is one reason why we welcome the development and strengthening of organizations and agencies operating at the international and global level. However, as already pointed out, it might be premature to dismantle the nation states and the national systems of innovation. The ongoing process of innovation changes the social conditions of citizens and regions – some for the better and some for the worse. The most important role of the nation state in this context has been to compensate the weak and to put some restraint on the strong. Without the formation of new agencies capable of realizing such a 'social dimension', a process of internationalization and globalization, which undermines national systems of innovation, might result in a long-term social and political crisis rather than in creative destruction.

4.3 Towards a Theory

4.3.1 Innovation as a cumulative process

In the models of standard economics, innovations appear as extraordinary events, coming from the outside, which temporarily disturb the general equilibrium. After a process of adjustment, reflecting the work of the price mechanism, a new state of equilibrium is established. This approach might have been adequate in preindustrial societies where innovations seemed to occur as rare and exogenous events. In modern capitalism, however, innovation is a fundamental and inherent phenomenon; the long-term competitiveness of firms and national economies reflects their innovative capability. Moreover, firms must engage in activities that aim at innovation just in order to hold their ground.

One of our starting points is that innovation is a ubiquitous phenomenon in the modern economy. In practically all parts of the economy, and at all times, we expect to find ongoing processes of learning, searching and exploring that result in new products, new techniques, new forms of organization and new markets. In some parts of the economy, these activities might be slow, gradual and incremental, but they will still be there if we take a closer look.

The first step in recognizing innovation as a ubiquitous phenomenon is to focus on its gradual and cumulative aspects. Such a perspective gives rise to simple hypotheses about the dependence of future innovations on those that took place in the past. In this context, an innovation may be regarded as a new use of preexisting possibilities and components. Here, Schumpeter's choice of terminology, where 'innovations' and 'new combinations' are used as synonyms, is enlightening. Almost all innovations reflect elements of already existing knowledge combined in new ways.

This is, however, not to say that a step towards a new combination is always of the same character. Sometimes an innovation might be inevitable; the new combination might be easy to find and to realize. In other cases, it might take an enormous intellectual effort or an extremely creative mind to identify a potential new combination. And sometimes the process of innovation results in radical breaks with the past, making a substantial part of accumulated knowledge obsolete. Another of Schumpeter's concepts, 'creative destruction', points to this discontinuity, and it might be applied not only to the structure of production but also to the structure of knowledge.

Nevertheless, we will put some emphasis on the ubiquitous and cumulative character of innovation. In such a perspective, the distinction made in innovation theory between invention, innovation and diffusion as three separate stages necessarily becomes blurred. We also understand why it is difficult to date invention and innovation in time, and why an innovation does not stay the same throughout its diffusion. Innovation appears now, not primarily as a single event, but rather *as a process*.

A second starting point is that interactive learning and collective entrepreneurship are fundamental to the process of innovation. In his early work on the theory of economic development, Schumpeter pointed to entrepreneurs who act individually as the most important economic agents bringing innovations into the economic system (Schumpeter 1934). Later he revised his theoretical scheme, however, by giving a critical role to the collective work in R&D laboratories (Schumpeter 1942). In a sense, through introducing systems of innovation, we take this trajectory from individual towards collective entrepreneurship a further step ahead.

We will argue that the most important forms of learning may fundamentally be regarded as interactive processes and that together the economic structure and the institutional set up form the framework for, and strongly affect, the processes of interactive learning sometimes resulting in innovations. In the chapters to follow, this general point will be illustrated at different levels of analysis.

4.3.2 Learning and the structure of production

One of the most important institutional innovations in the last century was the establishment of R&D laboratories in the big private firms (Freeman 1982). Scientific activities and technical change have been brought closer together becoming increasingly interdependent activities, and today the capability to innovate cannot be assessed in isolation from efforts in science, research and development. However, here we will insist on the fact that not all important inputs to the process of innovation emanate from science and R&D efforts. We thus assume that learning takes place in connection with routine activities in production, distribution and consumption, and produces important inputs to the process of innovation. The everyday experiences of workers, production engineers and sales representatives influence the *agenda* determining the direction of innovative efforts as they *produce knowledge and insights* forming crucial inputs to the process of innovation.

When bottleneck problems are met and registered in production or in the use of a product, the agendas of producers change, affecting the direction of their innovation efforts. Everyday experience also increases technical knowledge and gives ideas about in which direction solutions should be looked for. Such activities involve learning by doing – increasing the efficiency of production operations (Arrow 1962), learning by using – increasing the efficiency of the use of complex systems (Rosenberg 1982) and learning by interacting – involving users and producers in an interaction resulting in product innovations (Lundvall 1988).

If innovation reflects learning and if learning partially emanates from routine activities, innovation must be *rooted in the prevailing economic structure*. The areas where technical advance will take place will primarily be those where a firm, or a national economy, is already engaged in routine activities.[5]

4.3.3 Learning and the institutional set-up

The institutional set-up (of a specific firm, a constellation of firms, or a nation) is the second important dimension of the system of innovation. Institutions provide agents and collectives with guideposts for action. In a world characterized by innovative activities, uncertainty will be an important aspect of economic life. Institutions make it possible for economic systems to survive and act in an uncertain world. Institutions may be routines guiding everyday actions in production, distribution and consumption, but they may also be guideposts for change. In this context, we may regard technological trajectories and paradigms, which focus the innovative activities of scientists, engineers and technicians as one special kind of institution.[6]

One of the fundamental characteristics of institutions is their relative stability over time. They arise because in a changing and uncertain world, agents and organizations need guidance and institutions make life more manageable and comfortable (not necessarily more efficient in any sense of this term) for them.

4.3.4 Product innovation and user–producer interaction

One way to illustrate how the structure of production and the institutional set-up together affect the rate and direction of innovation is to focus on product innovations and their roots in the interaction between producers and users. First, at the micro level, the structure of production defines sets of user–producer relationships, which condition the scope and direction of the process of innovation. Second, the institutional form, which characterizes these relationships and especially the elements of organization in these markets, reflects the characteristics of the process of innovation. Third, the institutional set-up, once established, will affect the rate and direction of innovation. Fourth, one interesting dimension of user–producer relationships can be shown to be distance in cultural and geographical space.

4.3.5 Learning, searching and exploring[7]

Above, we have indicated the importance of learning rooted in routine activities. But of course, economic agents and organizations also consciously invest time and resources in expanding their technical knowledge. *Searching* is another important activity, creating inputs to the system of innovation.

Organizations normally learning only from routine activities of production and distribution might engage in search activities under certain extreme circumstances. When the survival of the organization is threatened, its members become engaged in what might be called 'desperate search'. This kind of search might begin as local search, looking for alternatives (in terms of products, processes, markets, etc.) close to the ones already well known to the organization and only if it is impossible to find any satisfactory solutions in this area, expanding search to more distant alternatives.[8]

However, desperate search is not always very efficient. Especially when technology is science based, complex and changing, it becomes attractive to establish special departments permanently engaged in searching activities. Divisions with searching as their special mission might be departments for market analysis as well as R&D departments and laboratories.

Searching which takes place in academic or science-oriented organizations, outside the private firms, brings forward another kind of raw material for the process of innovation. We call this kind of search 'exploring'. The most important difference between exploring and searching is that 'exploring' is less goal-oriented than profit-oriented search. If we take a closer look at scientific activities, we shall however often find that they too have a specific aim and direction. Even if the paradigms and trajectories, which determine the aims and directions of basic science, develop more according to their own internal logic and are less responsive to changes in economic parameters than innovations in private firms, the producers of basic science will, to a certain extent, be oriented towards users outside the realm of pure science. The direction of research in mathematics and logic may, for example, reflect new needs developed by computer scientists and software experts.

Exploring, because of its weaker goal orientation, will sometimes result in outcomes neither foreseen nor looked for by profit-oriented organizations. This adds to technological change a dimension of dynamism and radical change, extremely important in the long run. Exploring will sometimes result in breaks in cumulative paths and create the basis for new technological paradigms.

4.3.6 Incremental versus radical innovations

If innovation is rooted in learning, and learning in routine activities, we might expect all innovative activities to be incremental, and it would be rather simple to predict the direction of technical change. But we must take into account the fundamentally uncertain and disruptive character of the process of innovation. As mentioned earlier, uncertainty rules in the process of scientific activities and these activities produce, from time to time, results which were neither anticipated nor looked for. Uncertainty also rules regarding the economic impact of an innovation. A new product might fail either for technical reasons or because it does not successfully address potential user needs. Conversely, a product originally addressed towards the needs of a small subset of users might later prove to be a commercial success applicable in very substantial parts of the economy.

When distinguishing between incremental and radical innovations, we may refer primarily either to the technical or to the economic dimension. On the one hand, some innovations, incremental in technical terms, may have a crucial impact on the economy. This will be true for a small technical change solving a bottleneck problem of strategic importance (the introduction of vehicles with inflated rubber wheels in agriculture did not represent any radical technical break, but it had a dramatic impact on the productivity of this sector). On the other hand, an innovation very radical in technical terms and signalling a new technological paradigm, might for technical reasons, be premature and have a very limited impact on the economy (it took the Babbage version of the computer, obviously a radical innovation in technical terms, more than a century before it had any economic impact at all). It follows that many radical innovations will be radical only in one of the two dimensions while remaining incremental in the other dimension.

For these reasons, we assume that the process of innovation is neither totally accidental nor totally predetermined by the economic structure and the institutional set-up. The analysis of systems of innovation helps us to understand and explain why technology develops in a certain direction and at a certain rate, but a strong element of randomness will always remain.

4.3.7 Defining the NSI – the role of theory and history

From what has been said, it follows that we may make a distinction between a system of innovation in the narrow sense and a system of innovation in the broad sense. The narrow definition would include organizations and institutions involved in searching and exploring, such as R&D departments, technological institutes and universities. The broad definition that follows from the theoretical perspective presented above includes all parts and aspects of the economic structure and the institutional set-up affecting learning as well as searching and exploring – the production system, the marketing system and the system of finance present themselves as subsystems in which learning takes place.

Determining in detail which subsystems and social institutions should be included, or excluded, in the analysis of the system is a task involving historical analysis as well as theoretical considerations.

In different historical periods, different parts of the economic system or different interfaces between subsystems may play a more or less important role in the process of innovation. In the early British industrialization, new technology reflected primarily the learning inside firms that developed and tested new production equipment, either developed in-house or in cooperation with artisans from small workshops. The development of the new industries of chemistry and electricity at the end of the eighteenth century changed the location of the innovation nexus and brought it closer to the R&D laboratories of big firms.

Today, it seems as if the crucial interfaces of systems of innovation have shifted again. Radical innovations in information technology, which are themselves science based, have put the focus on the coupling of routine-based learning to searching and R&D. 'The factory as a laboratory' formula reflects these new trends. At the same time, however, more and more innovative activities have to draw on quite different and separate sets of generic knowledge (biotechnology, microelectronics, new materials) making the process of science-based innovation even more costly and complex.

However, the theoretical perspective is also important. The broad definition of the system used in this book reflects the importance attached to interactive learning as a basis for innovation. Alternatively, a 'linear model of technical change' – where technical innovations were assumed to follow mechanically from scientific efforts and from research efforts inside firms – would define the system of innovation much more narrowly and identify it with the R&D system.

On this background, it should be obvious that a definition of the system of innovation must, to a certain degree, be kept open and flexible regarding which subsystems should be included and which processes should be studied. It also follows that we cannot insist on one single approach to the national system of innovation as the only legitimate one. Different theoretical perspectives bring forward different aspects of the system.

4.4 The Elements of the System

In the real world, the state and the public sector are rooted in national states and their geographical sphere of influence is defined by national borders. The focus on *national* systems reflects the fact that national economies differ regarding the structure of the production system and regarding the general institutional set-up. Specifically, we assume that basic differences in historical experience, language and culture will be reflected in national idiosyncrasies in:

- Internal organization of firms
- Inter-firm relationships
- Role of the public sector
- Institutional set-up of the financial sector
- R&D intensity and R&D organization

International differences in these elements are important for the working of the system as a whole, but the relationships between the elements are just as important. For example both the organization and strategies of the public sector, including its responsibility for education and R&D, and the financial sector will affect the way firms organize and form networks. The other way around, the historical specialization of firms and networks of firms will be reflected in the public infrastructure of education and R&D.

First, we assume that the internal organization of private firms is one important aspect of the system of innovation. Most innovations are developed by firms and many innovation studies have demonstrated that the organization of the flow of information and of the learning process is important and affects the innovative capability of the firm. The interaction between different departments engaged in, respectively, sales, production and R&D is one important aspect of the organization, which is attracting a growing interest in comparative innovation studies.

However, we also assume that inter-firm relationships are important in structuring the system of innovation. In standard economics, these relationships are assumed to be characterized by competition and by pure markets. Focusing on innovation makes it clear that cooperation between firms is a necessary supplement to competition, and one form of cooperation is user–producer interaction. In an increasing number of knowledge-intensive industries, other forms of inter-firm cooperation tend to become increasingly important such as network relationships and industrial districts including informal exchange of technical know-how.

The public sector plays an important role in the process of innovation. It is involved in direct support of science and development, and its regulations and standards influence the rate and direction of innovation. Moreover, it is the single most important user of innovations developed in the private sector and may act as a more or less competent user of innovations.

The connection between the financial system and the process of innovation was strongly emphasized earlier by Schumpeter and recently there has been a growing public interest in the enabling role of the financial system in regards to innovation. As already noted, the process of innovation is closely connected to the R&D system, its resources, competencies and organization.

Missing among these elements is the national education and training system. For different reasons, this extremely important element of the national system of innovation has not been given its proper treatment in this book. There are big differences between countries in their formal and informal education and training systems, which affect their innovative capabilities. This refers to the quantitative investment in education, the enrolment in science and engineering, the investment in training of skilled workers, etc. Other differences are qualitative and also relate to the social norms and values reproduced by the system and to the degree of egalitarianism versus elitism in the society. An important task for future research is to integrate both education and training systems with innovation systems in one single analytical framework.[9]

4.5 Opening the System

As pointed out, we do not assume the process of innovation to be exclusively localized inside national borders. On the contrary, we recognize that the process of innovation has increasingly become multinational and transnational reflecting, for example, R&D cooperation between big firms based in different nations. In four of the chapters in *National Systems of Innovation: Toward a Theory of Innovation and Interactive Learning* (Lundvall 1992), we analysed how national systems of innovation are open and increasingly becoming wide open.

In 'Export Specialisation, Structural Competitiveness and National Systems of Innovation' (Dalum 1992), some important structural features of national systems of innovation are characterized by data on export specialization. The long-term development patterns of specialization were analysed in terms of industry life cycles; distinctly different patterns country by country were found. The specialization patterns were revealed in relation to structural competitiveness and in this context the strategic role of the engineering sector is emphasized.

Fagerberg (1992) focuses on one branch of trade theory with special relevance for the analysis of national systems of innovation: the home market theory. The relative importance of linkages between export specialization in user and producer industries are tested econometrically. This chapter and the one by Dalum (1992) are focused on trade patterns (arm's length trade) and do not take into account foreign direct investment and multinational enterprises.

Andersen and Brændgaard (1992) present an analysis of economic integration from an evolutionary perspective and study what might be regarded as an embryonic transnational system of innovation. The empirical case relates to the specialization and competitiveness of the European Community in information technology and refers to some of the political efforts to strengthen the European Community in this field in relation to Japan and United States.

While these three chapters mentioned above focus on internationalization in the form of international trade and specialization, Chesnais (1992) brought foreign direct investment and multinational capital into the picture. It describes and analyses how the process of internationalization has entered a new phase of globalization, which fundamentally changes the role of national systems of innovation. Chesnais shows that the new tendencies challenge the relative autonomy of national systems and weaken their coherence but also give a new and even more important role to public policy.

4.6 Alternative Approaches and Methods

4.6.1 Introduction

As pointed out, the definition of the national system of innovation is dependent on the theoretical approach, and therefore it is useful to see how different authors have used the concept and to relate the approach of this book to these alternatives.[10]

4.6.1.1 Friedrich List

The first systematic and theoretically based attempt to focus on national systems of innovation goes back to Friedrich List (1841/1959). His contribution is also interesting because it is developed as an explicit alternative to Adam Smith and his contemporary followers. List makes a distinction between Adam Smith's 'cosmopolitan' approach, which puts the focus on exchange and allocation, and his own national perspective focusing on the development of productive forces. We think that this is a fruitful and interesting distinction.

The only element of List's quite complex and rich – sometimes somewhat confusing – analysis still left in modern economics is his argument for protection of 'infant industries'. His analysis went much further, however, indicating the need for governmental responsibility for education and training and for developing an infrastructure supporting industrial development. Actually, he sketched some of the most important elements of the national system of innovation.

4.6.1.2 Christopher Freeman

The first explicit use of the concept national systems of innovation may be the one in Freeman's (1987) book on Japan. Here the concept refers both to the nation-specific organization of subsystems and to the interaction between subsystems. The organization of R&D and of production in firms, the inter-firm relationships and the role of government and MITI[11] are at the centre of the analysis, which is both historical and based on modern innovation theory.

4.6.1.3 Richard Nelson

Almost at the same time, Nelson presented studies of the US system (1987, 1988). The focus of the analysis was on the combined public and private character of technology and the role of government, universities and private firms respectively in the production of new technology. It was shown that different industrial sectors use different methods to appropriate the benefits from their innovations.

The approaches of the two authors differ in two important respects. First, while the focus in Nelson's work is on the production of knowledge and innovation and on the innovation system in the narrow sense, Freeman focuses on the interaction between the production system and the process of innovation. Second, while Freeman applies a combination of organization and innovation theory – which organizational forms are most conducive to the development and efficient use of new technology? – Nelson's main theoretical tool is related to law and economics – how well can different institutional set-ups take into account and solve the private/public dilemma of information and technical innovation?

The approach of this book is closest to Freeman's because we focus on organizational matters as related to processes of learning, but we also recognize the importance of institutional factors of the kind brought forward by Nelson's work in this area. If one should point to one specific dimension that characterizes our approach, it would be the emphasis put on interactive learning anchored in the production structure and in the linkage pattern of the system of production.

4.6.1.4 Michael Porter

The book by Michael Porter (1990) may be read as a work on national systems of innovation. Porter points to four different determinants affecting the competitiveness of a national industry: Firm strategy, factor conditions, demand conditions and supporting industries.

Actually, Porter refers to the constellation of determinants as a system (p. 75), and he argues that the level at which this system works most strongly is national (and local) rather than international and global. Our approach is akin to Porter's in some respects but different in others. One might say that the basic elements overlap but their ordering is different.

The main focus in this book is on explaining learning and innovation and this corresponds to the creation of qualitatively new 'factor conditions'. We regard the economic structure (including 'demand conditions' and 'supporting industries') as one important determinant affecting these processes. The second fundamental determinant of processes of learning is the institutional set-up and this includes 'firm strategy' – including modes of cooperation as well as competition.

The most important difference between our approach and Porter's may be the level of analysis. While Porter tends to present national systems as environments to single industries involved in international competition, our focus is on the working of the national system in its own right.[12]

4.6.1.5 Different methods to analyse national systems of innovation

Most discussions of national systems of innovation have been connected to one single or to a comparison of a few specific country cases. In *National Systems of Innovation; A Comparative Study* (Nelson 1993), 14 different country-specific case studies are presented. The strength of his approach is that the stories told may reflect the complex historical interplay of social, institutional and cultural factors in shaping current systems (Edquist and Lundvall 1993). The weakness might be the lack of a common and explicit theoretical basis and the fact that the elements brought into the analysis are idiosyncratic reflecting the special interests of each author.

In *National Systems of Innovation: Toward a Theory of Innovation and Interactive Learning* (Lundvall 1992), we do not recount any specific case stories even if we refer to relevant cases in order to illustrate some general points. Instead we have tried to present a theoretical perspective that might be used in the case studies and to discuss some of the most important subsystems in the system of innovation. The price we have to pay for choosing this more general approach is a loss in terms of historical richness, especially when it comes to the social and cultural dimensions.

This is the reason why we believe that together this book, Nelson (1993) and Porter (1990) may give a good starting point for future work on national systems of innovation.

Notes

1 The IKE group had through the last decade (1980s) cooperated with Christopher Freeman from Science Policy Research Unit, Sussex University; Jan Fagerberg from the Institute of Foreign Affairs, Oslo and Francois Chesnais, University of Paris and OECD. Previous contributions from the IKE group on national systems of innovation are to be found in Lundvall (1988), Andersen and Lundvall (1988) and Johnson and Lundvall (1991).

2 Knowledge does not decrease in value when used. On the contrary, its use increases its value (i.e., knowledge is not scarce in the same sense as other natural resources and technical artefacts). Some elements of knowledge may be transferred, easily, between economic agents, while others are tacit and embodied in individual, or collective, agents. Knowledge is not easily transacted in markets and not easily privately appropriated. In spite of attempts to find institutional solutions to the problem (patent laws, etc.), property rights to knowledge are not easily defined. When it comes to knowledge, market failure is the rule rather than the exception.

3 This implies, for example, that a foreign-owned firm will be part of two different national systems – its home country and its host country.
4 For the case of Denmark versus Sweden, see Edquist and Lundvall (1993). A number of different European countries are compared in Bruno et al. (1991).
5 One specific illustration of this general phenomenon is that countries strongly specialized in exports of, for example, agriculture and food products will also be strongly specialized in machinery for agriculture and food industry. The explanation of this pattern is that export-oriented users often are both competent and demanding and that the feedback of knowledge from the users forms a critical input to the innovation process of producers of specialized machinery (Andersen et al. 1981b).
6 In this context, we use the concepts *technological trajectories* and *paradigms* in the sense they were introduced in Dosi (1982). For a discussion of different uses of these concepts see Dosi (1988a, 223–228).
7 The distinction between 'learning' and 'searching/exploring' may seem somewhat awkward; in everyday language, 'searching/exploring' will result in 'learning'. The terminology chosen in this chapter reflects our wish both to distinguish clearly between and to combine two different perspectives – structuralist oriented (learning) and action oriented (searching/exploring). This combined perspective has much in common with recent developments in social theory such as structuration theory (Giddens 1984).
8 This corresponds to the central behavioural assumption in the evolutionary model of economic growth developed by Nelson and Winter (1982).
9 The OECD publication 'New Technologies in the 1990s' represents a step towards such an integration (OECD 1988).
10 For an overlapping but more detailed discussion, see McKelvey (1991) who compares some of the recent literature on national systems of innovation.
11 Ministry of International Trade and Industry is currently known as Ministry of Economy, Trade and Industry (METI).
12 One problem with Porter's approach (1992), is that it is unclear how he moves from the analyses of cases, at the industry level to his conclusions, which refer to national systems as a whole.

References

Andersen, E. S. and A. Brændgaard. 1992. 'Integration, Innovation and Evolution'. In *National Systems of Innovation: Toward a Theory of Innovation and Interactive Learning*, edited by B.-Å. Lundvall. London and London: Pinter Publishers.

Andersen, E. S. and B.-Å. Lundvall. 1988. 'Small National Systems of Innovation Facing Technological Revolutions – an Interpretative Framework'. In *Small Countries Facing the Technological Revolution*, edited by C. Freeman and B.-Å. Lundvall. London and New York: Pinter Publishers.

Andersen, E. S., B. Dalum and G. Villumsen. 1981b. 'The Importance of the Home Market for Technological Development and the Export Specialization of Manufacturing Industry'. In *Technological Innovation and National Economic Performance*, edited by C. Freeman. Aalborg: Aalborg University Press.

Arrow, K. J. 1962. 'The Economic Implications of Learning by Doing'. *Review of Economic Studies* 29, no. 80: 155–73.

Bent, D., J. Björn and B.-Å. Lundvall. 1992. 'Public Policy in the Learning Society'. In *National Systems of Innovation: Toward a Theory of Innovation and Interactive Learning*, edited by B. Å. Lundvall. London and New York: Anthem Press.

Boulding, K. E. 1985. *The World as a Total System*. Beverly Hills: Sage Publications.

Bruno, S., P. Cohendet, F. Desmartin, P. Llerena and A. Sorge. 1991. *Modes of Usage and Diffusion of New Technologies and New Knowledge, A Synthesis Report. FOP 227, Protective Dossier 1, Commission of the European Communities, Brussels*.

Camagni, R. P. (ed.). 1990. 'Local Milieu, Uncertainty and Innovation Networks: Towards a New Dynamic Theory of Economic Space'. In *Innovation Networks: The Spatial Perspective*. London: Belhaven-Pinter.

Chesnais, F. 1992. 'National Systems of Innovation, Foreign Direct Investment and the Operations of Multinational Enterprises'. In *National Systems of Innovation: Toward a Theory of Innovation and Interactive Learning*, edited by B.-Å. Lundvall. London and New York: Anthem Press.

Dalum, B. 1992. 'Export Specialisation, Structural Competitiveness and National Systems of Innovation'. In *National Systems of Innovation: Toward a Theory of Innovation and Interactive Learning*, edited by B.-Å. Lundvall. London and New York: Anthem Press.

Dalum, B., J. Fagerberg and U. Jørgensen. 1988. 'Small Open Economies in the World Market for Electronics: The Case of the Nordic Countries'. in *Small Countries Facing the Technological Revolution*, edited by C. Freeman and B.-Å. Lundvall. London and New York: Pinter Publishers.

Dosi, G. 1982. 'Technological Paradigms and Technological Trajectories: A Suggested Interpretation of the Determinants and Directions of Technical Change'. *Research Policy* 11, no. 3: 147–62.

———. 1988a. 'The Nature of the Innovative Process'. In *Technical Change and Economic Theory*, edited by G. Dosi et al. London: Pinter Publishers.

Edquist, C. and S. Jakobsson. 1988. *Flexible Automation – the Global Diffusion of New Technology in the Engineering Industry*. Oxford: Blackwell.

Edquist, C. and B.-Å. Lundvall. 1993. 'Comparing the Danish and Swedish Systems of Innovation'. In *National Systems of Innovations: A Comparative Study*, edited by R. R. Nelson. Oxford: Oxford University Press.

Fagerberg, J. 1992. 'The Home Market Hypothesis Reexamined: The Impact of Domestic User-Producer Interaction on Export Specialisation'. In *National Systems of Innovation: Toward a Theory of Innovation and Interactive Learning*, edited by B.-Å. Lundvall, London and New York: Anthem Press.

Freeman, C. 1982. *The Economics of Industrial Innovation*. London: Pinter Publishers.

———. 1987. *Technology and Economic Performance: Lessons from Japan*. London: Pinter Publishers.

Freeman, C. and C. Perez. 1988. 'Structural Crisis of Adjustment: Business Cycles and Investment Behaviour'. In *Technical Change and Economic Theory*, edited by G. Dosi et al. London: Pinter Publishers.

Giddens, A. 1984. *The Constitution of Society*. Cambridge: Polity Press.

Johnson, B. and B.-Å. Lundvall. 1991. 'Flexibility and Institutional Learning'. In *The Politics of Flexibility*, edited by B. Jessop et al. Aldershot: Edward Elgar.

Kornai, J. 1971. *Anti-equilibrium*. Amsterdam: North Holland.

Kristensen, A. and B.-Å. Lundvall. 1991. *Den Nordiske Innovationsundersøgelse*. København: Industri–og Handelsstyrelsen.

List, F. (1841/1959). *Das Nationale System der Politischen Oekonomie*. Basel: Kyklos-Verlag.

Lundvall, B.-Å. 1988. 'Innovation as an Interactive Process – from User-Producer Interaction to the National System of Innovation'. In *Technical Change and Economic Theory*, edited by G. Dosi et al. London: Pinter Publishers.

McKelvey, M. 1991. 'How Do National Systems of Innovation Differ? A Critical Analysis of Porter, Freeman, Lundvall and Nelson'. In *Rethinking Economics: Markets, Technology and Economic Evolution*, edited by G. Hodgson and E. Screpanti. London: Edward Elgar.

Myrdal, G. 1968. *Asian Drama*. New York: Pantheon.

Nelson, R. R. 1987. *Understanding Technical Change as an Evolutionary Process*. Amsterdam: North Holland.

———. 1988, 'Institutions Supporting Technical Change in the United States'. In *Technology and Economic Theory*, edited by G. Dosi et al. London: Pinter Publishers.

———. 1993. *National Systems of Innovation; A Comparative Study*. Oxford: Oxford University Press.

Nelson, R. R. and S. G. Winter. 1982. *An Evolutionary Theory of Economic Change*. Cambridge, MA: Belknap Press of Harvard University Press.

OECD – Canada. 1991. *Summary of Discussions, the Conference on Technology and the Global Economy*, February 1991, Montreal.

OECD. 1988. *New Technologies in the 1990s, A Socioeconomic Strategy* (The Sundqvist Report), Paris.

Ostry, S. 1990. 'Governments and Corporations in a Shrinking World: Trade and Innovation Policies'. New York: Council on Foreign Relations Press.

Patel, P. and K. Pavitt. 1988. *The International Distribution and Determinants of Technological Activities*, Brighton, SPRU, University of Sussex, September, mimeo.

Porter, M. E. 1990. *The Competitive Advantage of Nations*. London: Macmillan.

Rosenberg, N. 1982. *Inside the Black Box: Technology and Economics*. Cambridge: Cambridge University Press.

Schumpeter, J. A. 1934. *The Theory of Economic Development: An Inquiry into Profits, Capital, Credit, Interest and the Business Cycle*. London: Oxford University Press.

———. 1942. *Capitalism, Socialism and Democracy*. London: Unwin, 1987.

Storper, M. 1991. *Production Organisation, Technological Learning and International Trade*, mimeo.

Chapter 5

THE LEARNING ECONOMY

Bengt-Åke Lundvall and Björn Johnson

Our juxtaposition of the extreme X-society and the extreme Y-society should have demonstrated fully that such purely competitive or purely planned societies never have and never will exist. But this is not all: we have also tried to show that both these types of societies are incomprehensible as logical constructs. (Akerman 1936, 141; our translation)

5.1 Introduction

One of the most fundamental and recurring discourses in political economy has concerned how society should be instituted in terms of self-organized markets versus conscious government regulations, intervention and planning. In this chapter we join this discourse from a quite specific and original perspective. If we take it seriously that knowledge *is* the most fundamental resource in our contemporary economy and that learning is therefore the most important process, what are the implications for the institutional set-up of the economy? And what are the implications for economic theory? What are the consequences for the plan / market discourse?

The institutional set-up of modern capitalism may be analysed from two perspectives: what *is* and what *should be*. In this chapter we primarily present reflections on what *is* from the perspective of how it affects the use of knowledge and learning. Starting from assumptions regarding the character of knowledge, learning and innovation, we end up by supporting the stance of the Swedish institutionalist economist Johan Åkerman quoted above. The learning economy is, and must be, 'a mixed economy', and it is mixed in a much more fundamental sense than normally assumed.

We cannot totally avoid the discussion of what 'should be', however. Specifically we conclude that many of the most common arguments for and against the free market are either mistaken or one sided. There is actually a need to reopen the old discourse on a totally new basis: How does the market mechanism allocate knowledge and how does it affect learning? This is especially interesting in a period characterized by post-Fordism in the West and by postsocialism in the East. The need for open mindedness about how to organize the economy is greater than ever, while adherents to mainstream economics seem to believe that the breakdown of socialism marked the final victory of pure capitalist principles.

This chapter represents an effort to develop concepts in relation to learning processes in the economy. It is inspired by and based on both theoretical and empirical research about the relation between technical and economic change conducted at the Department of Business Studies at the University of Aalborg in Denmark. In particular, research about the introduction of microelectronics-based production methods and products into the economy have convinced the authors of the central role that interactive learning and new combinations of knowledge play in the process of economic change. We, therefore, need to develop a conceptual framework to give knowledge and learning the central roles that they deserve in the analysis of economic change. This chapter is a modest step in that direction.

5.2 The Knowledge-Intensive Economy

In a sense knowledge has always been a crucial resource in the economy. The natural resources and the pure, physical, human effort put very strict limits on how much and what can be produced and consumed. In addition, the so-called primitive economies have relied on the know-how of producers and consumers in order to make a living possible in adverse and difficult environments. Knowledge was layered in traditions and routines passed on from generation to generation and learning led to increased know-how and made population growth possible.

The most important consequence of the advent of industrialization was not that it involved the use of knowledge but rather that it made learning a much more fundamental and strategic process than before. While inventions and innovations did develop and diffuse in, for example, feudal Europe, the process was marginal, slow and uneven. During the period of industrialization, learning and innovation became a ubiquitous process. While most people in traditional societies could live their whole life on the basis of a rather narrow and constant set of skills used in environments with rather constant characteristics, this is no longer the case in the industrial economy.

The early industrialization process had an ambiguous effect on skills. On the one hand, it increased the demand for skill-intensive mechanical engineering for constructing machinery. On the other hand, the workers using the machinery were often characterized by low and narrow skills. But technical change became the order of the day both for engineers and workers, and in all kinds of enterprises, demand for skills in management and coordination increased. The Fordist paradigm, which is a caricature of the development of some core industries in the first half of this century, may be regarded as an attempt not only to harvest the benefits of scale economies but also as an attempt by management to reduce their dependency on the skills of workers.

5.3 Knowledge Intensity and Learning in the Post-Fordist Era

The post-Fordist era has brought into being new constellations of knowledge and learning into the economy. These may be related to three interconnected phenomena. The first relates to the development of the information, computer and telecommunication technologies (ICT), the second to the movement towards flexible specialization and the third to changes in the process of innovation.

ICT has drastically reduced the costs of handling, storing and moving information. The gathering of data, however, is still expensive even if the new technologies make it possible to reduce these costs in the future, for instance, through interactive information networks. What is even more costly is the competence to use the relevant data in an efficient way. Information flows are becoming so rich that the main problem has become how, where and when to dip into these flows.

Flexible specialization is a model or 'ideal type' of what is going on in parts of the industrial system today. The flexibility refers to the possibility to adapt, rapidly and with small costs, to changes in demand and to other external changes. In the short term, it refers to minor changes in the products. In the long term, it may be related to the capability to develop product innovations to meet new user needs. The most fundamental aspect of flexible specialization may be that it signals some limits to both economies of scale and to the possibilities of increasing the division of labour in the narrow sense. In this era specialization goes hand in hand with communication and cooperation between workers, departments, firms and even competitors. All parts of the organization become involved in cooperation and many parts are also involved in external communication and cooperation. One consequence is that knowing how to do things in isolation is not the decisive type of knowledge any more. Knowing how to communicate and cooperate becomes much more important than before.

Finally, the process of innovation has changed in important respects. Continuing, incremental innovation has become a necessity for the survival of firms. This process emanates from interactive learning taking place at a great number of interfaces inside and outside the firm. This is true also for many applications of information technology, where the need to cooperate closely with specialized users is important in developing useful new systems or machinery.

At the same time important parts of industry (computers, nuclear technology, aviation, automobiles etc.) are confronted by a steep increase in the costs connected to the development of a new product or system. They are also confronted with an increase in the diversity of knowledge sources, which must be mobilized in any successful innovation process. When this is combined with shorter product life cycles, a series of implications follows. First, it becomes crucial to develop organizational forms, which increase the learning ability of the firm; this includes the opening up of horizontal communication at all levels of the firm. Second, it makes it necessary to enter into cooperation and alliances with other firms, both in order to share the financial risks and gain access to a more diversified knowledge base.

These changes affect the demand for knowledge in different ways. First, there is a growing need for a broader participation in learning processes. Swift and efficient innovation processes must involve all layers in the firm. Second, multi-skilling and networking skills become of crucial importance. Third, the capability to learn and to apply learning to the processes of production and sales becomes the most important dimension for the viability of the modern firm. Management skills become related to the establishment of routines and rules, which stimulate interactive learning.

This is why we regard the contemporary first-world capitalist economies not only as knowledge-based economies but also as 'learning economies'. In a way all economies are learning economies, in the sense that economic life always forms a basis for some processes of interactive learning, which results in the production and introduction of new knowledge. But in the modern learning economy, technical and organizational change has become increasingly endogenous. Learning processes have been institutionalized and feedback loops for knowledge accumulation have been built in such a way that the economy as a whole, including both its production and consumption spheres, is 'learning by doing' and 'learning by using'.

In the learning economy the organizational modes of firms are increasingly chosen in order to enhance learning capabilities; networking with other firms, horizontal communication patterns and frequent movements of people between posts and departments are becoming more and more important. The firms of the learning economy are to a large extent 'learning organizations'.

In a world of learning economies the specialization of firms and countries becomes increasingly important for economic performance. Some areas of production and consumption are characterized by steep learning curves, rap-idly falling costs and growing markets. This may be the case for a broad set of ICT areas but also for niches in more traditional product areas. The learning economy is a dynamic concept; it involves the capability to learn and to expand the knowledge base. It refers not only to the importance of science and technology systems – universities, research organizations, in-house R&D departments and so on – but also to the learning implications of the economic structure, the organizational forms and the institutional set-up.

Even if all economies are in some sense learning economies, the concept refers first of all to the ICT-related techno-economic paradigm of the post-Fordist period. It is through the combination of widespread ICT, flexible specialization and innovation as a crucial means of competition in the new techno-economic paradigm that the learning economy gets firmly established. Firms start to learn how to learn.

Of course, different countries are not equally successful in coping with the challenges of the new techno-economic paradigm. Thus, it is well known and much discussed that the Japanese system of innovation (Freeman 1987) has some characteristics that are important in relation to interactive learn-ing. It has been observed, for example, that many Japanese corporations rely heavily on participatory communication and cooperation between workers and employers. Japanese markets are also said to be organized to a higher degree than in the United States and Western Europe. Loyalty and voice seem to be relatively important and government intervention plays an important role in promoting interaction and cooperation. It has been suggested, however, that this is not primarily a Japanese cultural phenom-enon but rather a rational response by competing firms to their changing environment (Aoki 1990). In this sense Japanese firms have simply been the first to introduce elements of a new techno-economic paradigm of univer-sal relevance.

The concept of the learning economy refers to an ideal type, and of course the learning economies of the real world are very different from each other. A large part of economic learning is in the form of learning from abroad. Technologies, as well as organizational forms and institutions are borrowed from other countries. In relation to this, there are important dif-ferences between 'front' learners and 'catching-up' learners. But there may be other differences as well; especially when it comes to organizational forms and institutional set-ups, it is not easy to identify best practice. An interna-tional diversity of institutions and organizational forms may be an impor-tant part of the environment of the learning economy (Dalum et al. 1992).

5.4 What Is Economic Knowledge?

It is a risky enterprise to enter a discussion of how to define knowledge and learning. These concepts touch on areas where many scientific disciplines have important things to say and what can be contributed by economists is not necessarily the most interesting. But, if what we have said above is only partially true, economists have no choice but to enter this discussion. Knowledge is a crucial economic resource.

We think that it is useful to make distinctions between different kinds of knowledge. We suggest that economically relevant knowledge can be grouped into four broad categories: know-what, know-why, know-who (when and where) and know-how. These categories refer to the possibilities to carry through transactions with economically relevant knowledge and to combine pieces of knowledge in new ways. Such a taxonomy should make it easier to analyse the institutional set-up of the learning economy.

Know-what refers to the knowledge about 'facts'. How many people live in New York, what are the ingredients in pancakes and when was the battle of Waterloo are examples of this kind of knowledge. Here knowledge is close to what is normally called information – it can be broken down into bits. An extremely developed ability to know-what may be profitable in TV shows, but generally its relevance has been diminished by the information revolution. Still there are complex areas where experts must have a lot of this kind of knowledge in order to fulfil their jobs – practitioners of law and medicine belong to this category. It is interesting to note that many of these experts will, typically, work in independent, specialized consulting firms.

Know-why refers to scientific knowledge of principles and laws of motion in nature, in the human mind and in society. This kind of knowledge has been extremely important for technological development in certain areas such as, for example, in the chemical and electric/electronic industries. To have access to this kind of knowledge will often make advances in technology more rapid and reduce the frequency of errors in procedures of trial and error. Today, however, experts on innovation emphasize that the coupling between basic science and technological advance is much less direct than assumed by the public and policymakers. Again, the production and reproduction of know-why is to an important degree organized in specialized organizations such as, for example, universities; firms, which need access to this kind of knowledge, have to interact with these organizations.

Know-who refers to specific and selective social relations. It is not a question of knowing that person A is the director of firm B – this we would include in know-what – but to know who knows what and can do what and to have social relations to those who know relevant things. The rather peculiar know-who form of knowledge is introduced here because innovation is basically an interactive process. To know key persons and to be integrated in knowledge intensive networks may be more important to the success in innovation than knowing basic scientific principles.

The interactive and cumulative character of the innovation process also makes know-when and know-where important categories of knowledge. In the learning economy, which continuously introduces novelty, questions about time and space are of strategic importance for successful innovation. When and where are there good chances to introduce and diffuse innovations? Since know-when and know-where are closely related to know-who, they will in the following be treated as belonging to the same category. Basically they refer to concrete and economically useful knowledge about markets.

Know-how refers to skills (i.e., the capability to do different kinds of things). It might relate to production activities but also to many other activities in the economic sphere, including management, research and consumption.

It might be useful to reflect on these four kinds of knowledge and how they relate to fundamental economic concepts. From a transactional point of view there are important differences between them. The first two categories, which include very different elements from trivial information to the understanding of the laws of nuclear physics, have certain common features. Databases can be precisely described and copied by others. The growing number of expert systems demonstrates that the *know-what* type of knowledge of experts is also becoming reproducible. The same is true for normal science (as distinguished from science in a process of paradigmatic change). The observed differences between know-what and know-why in terms of public access and reproducibility may simply be a question of convention. While access to databases and expert knowledge is often given only after a pecuniary compensation, science is widely published and scientific knowledge is only kept private in very specific circumstances (for example biotechnology is one area where academic research has become regarded as a private commodity).

The privatization of both these kinds of knowledge involves, of course, all the classical problems pertaining to information as a commodity. Information cannot be transacted as an ideal private commodity, and the transaction costs are often very high. The buyers will know little about the value of information without having access to it, and if they get access to it, there is no longer any reason to pay for it. The transfer of property rights is problematic because normally the seller keeps the knowledge sold. Finally, it is very difficult to make sure that the knowledge once sold is not duplicated by the buyer and sold to other potential customers. This is a problem for software companies and video producers, but it reflects a much broader set of problems.

Also, the information is unevenly distributed between buyer and seller. This asymmetry, which is actually the basis for the transaction, gives the seller opportunities to exploit the buyer. As a reaction to this case of market failure, a complex set of formal and informal institutions have developed in this area.

According to the original transaction cost approach, we should expect vertical integration to take place, but on the contrary, these are areas where expertise is often concentrated in independent units (Williamson 1975). This may reflect the fact that the scale and learning effects are so important that they compensate for high transaction costs. Know-what and know-why in a complex and changing area may be so demanding that it takes cooperation in specialized teams and frequent confrontations with many different situations to develop and keep up with the knowledge.

An interesting point made by Elam (1993) is that information, because of the market failures connected to it, may be used as a gift. When it proves impossible to appropriate a specific piece of knowledge, which might be useful for another party, it is given away. But there are seldom completely free gifts. Strings are attached and without it being stated in any contract, it is expected that the donor may be repaid with relevant knowledge sometime in the future. This kind of 'gossiping' is obviously an important activity not only at coffee parties but in clubs and in professional societies as well. It does not only refer to the private life of colleagues, but involves technical information central for innovation processes as well.

Information as a gift may also be part of establishing social relationships in terms of respect, trust and friendships. It is obvious that this kind of information exchange is not something that can be managed from the top of the firm. Management may try to establish some ground rules and a more or less open atmosphere in the organization, but any attempt to regulate such processes in any detail would make them lose their original meaning. Even if strings are attached, information given as a gift should not be interpreted as being purely instrumental. We all know of gifts which everyone knows are purely instrumental, and we also know that such gifts mean little when it comes to developing and deepening social relationships. Therefore, as a minimum, it is necessary that at least one of the parties involved regards the gift as more than purely instrumental.

Know-who (when and where) and know-how differ from the kinds of knowledge discussed above. None of them can be easily translated into codes understandable by other agents, and therefore they are not commodities in the normal sense. In modern Western society conventions dictate that the know-who kind of knowledge should not be regarded as something which may be bought on the market. But there are instances of markets for this kind of knowledge, for example, different forms of corruption, where a payment to a person in a hierarchy may be necessary in order to get in touch with someone at a higher level. What you get for your money is not very valuable, however.

As Arrow has pointed out, you cannot buy trust, and if you could buy it, it would be of little value (1971). There might be a gift element involved: I introduce this important person to you and later you introduce me to one of your influential friends. But again, if such social games become too cynical, they tend to lose their intrinsic value for the parties involved.

Know-how is at the very centre of the economic process. What makes the economy grow are new combinations in the forms of new methods and new products and, in a sense, knowing how to do and change things is more difficult to learn, than it is to learn about facts and science. Often this kind of knowledge cannot be transformed into codes understandable by others; often you cannot even describe for yourself how you do things. This is not true for all activities however. In the processing industries, much of the know-how is science based and well understood.

Parts of the know-how can be sold as patents and other parts as turnkey plants, but important parts remain tacit and cannot be removed from their human and social context. To a certain degree the labour market is a market for know-how. Firms may compete in recruiting persons with specific know-how. The problem here is that know-how and tacit knowledge is often specific and related to its original context. One might say that important elements of tacit knowledge are collective rather than individual. Here, takeovers and mergers may be regarded as attempts to gain access to tacit knowledge and know-how.

In this case the market fails for two different reasons. The parts of know-how that are general, explicit and codifiable will give rise to the same kinds of market failures as discussed earlier. The parts that are specific, tacit and impossible to codify cannot be transacted on the market without taking over parts or the whole of the organization in which the knowledge is embedded. Again, there are strong theoretical grounds for vertical integration but the actual pattern shows that vertical integration is not taking place in most of these cases. Instead, we get different kinds of organized markets, for example, durable user–producer relationships and network relationships. One reason for the high frequency of these kinds of relationship might be that they give access to know-how, which is at the middle of the scale between tacitness and codifiability and between specificity and generality.

In the learning economy, all different categories of knowledge are combined in the innovation process. If we regard innovation as 'the craft of combination' (Elam 1993) and the entrepreneur, individual or collective, as the wielder of this craft, then entrepreneurial knowledge consists of know-what, know-why, know-how and, to a considerable extent, of know-who, when and where. Since all these forms of knowledge have transactional peculiarities, the pure market does not constitute a proper institutional set-up. Thus, the institutional characteristic of the learning economy becomes a crucial question.

5.5 Is Knowledge a Scarce Resource?

Scarcity, in the sense that resources are limited in relation to needs and wants, is at the very foundation of economics. If there were no scarcity or if the economy were not able to continuously create and recreate needs and wants, the allocation of resources would be of little interest. Innovations might be done for the fun of it, but they would not be important for the well-being of society. Knowledge is an interesting resource in this context. While one should restrict the use of most resources because they diminish in use value when used, this is not true for most forms of knowledge. The exchange value of knowledge may be reduced if it is used in a way that gives other people access to it, but even that is not necessarily true. Teaching people to drive a car and to use a computer may be the only way to stimulate the demand for more teaching in these areas. Learning increases the appetite for knowledge and vice versa. There is an important difference between commodities like materials and energy, on the one hand, and knowledge, on the other. While materials and energy are used up in the production process, knowledge is increased. Production is a source of different kinds of learning and even if a certain amount of 'forgetting' (loss of knowledge) is an aspect of production too, the economy can be organized so as to stimulate the growth of knowledge.

Of course, the knowledge we have at any specific point in time is scarce in the sense that we, as collectives and individuals, know very little of all there is to know. It is a good idea to economize with knowledge and use it as sensibly as possible. But this is not the traditional economic problem of fully employing the available resources. In a sense, there is always too much knowledge around, stored in different ways, which is more or less accessible. The problem often becomes one of knowing which sources of knowledge to draw on and which sources not to use. Again, this could be thought of as a question of transaction costs.

At other times, it is a problem of fitting relevant pieces of knowledge to each other in order to make them more productive. New pieces of knowledge do not automatically fit with older pieces; knowledge can easily become obsolete without necessarily actually ceasing to be knowledge.

Much knowledge is, for different reasons, not put to use. Consumer preferences and consumer habits may not be in favour of it. Prices may not stimulate it. Organizational forms and management routines may not be adapted to it. Product standards may lag behind. Much scientific knowledge has not been transformed into working technologies and some technologies are not put to active use or are not diffusing. A lot of technical knowledge may not become ingrained into the economy in the forms of norms, routines, standards and habits; it has not been institutionalized.

If the existence of large amounts of unused resources means that these resources are abundant, then knowledge is abundant. Maybe we could say that knowledge is abundant but the ability to use it is scarce. This has important implications for how to allocate it. We should, for example, use it more than would be called for by a myopic calculation, and we should pay a lot of attention to how the stock of knowledge changes and how its different elements fit with each other.

5.6 Interactive Learning

We might say that the stock of knowledge is affected by two flows. The one that increases knowledge we might call learning, and the one that reduces it, we might call forgetting. In addition we have to recognize that knowledge deteriorates when not used (forgetting by not doing), which means that it has to be maintained by a process we might call remembering. These three activities – learning, forgetting and remembering – in the change of knowledge are central processes in the learning economy. It is not obvious, however, what constitutes rational choice in this context, since every change in knowledge changes the basis on which rational calculations must rest. When we discuss changes in knowledge, it is more relevant to think in terms of communicative and interactive processes rather than in terms of rational choice with given resources at specific points of time.

Almost all learning is interactive, but it may be useful to take into account that there are different kinds of learning that involve different degrees of social interaction (Johnson 1992). Undoubtedly there is some simple, individual and isolated imprinting of immediate experiences on the memory, but this is certainly not the most important form of learning. There is also rote learning (i.e., you learn by repetition, but you do not necessarily have to understand what you are doing). This usually includes observing and learning from other people and thus involves more human interaction than simple imprinting. A lot of learning is done by feedback, which involves still more interaction. We do try or say something and get a response from other people, which tells us something about our first action and so on. Finally there is systematic and organized searching for new knowledge, for example, in universities, research institutes and R&D departments; it involves intense and complex forms of interaction. Technical change often requires dialogue or conversation (i.e., sequences of exchanges of information and knowledge between different people in different departments and at different levels, within firms and between firms). The more technically or scientifically advanced the innovations, the more complicated the communication processes they usually require.

It is a fundamental feature of the learning economy that it gradually develops its capability to learn. Modern firms often search systematically and in organized ways for new knowledge to be used in production as new processes or new products. This searching is restricted and channelled in different ways. First, to the extent that technical change is a rent-seeking activity under competition, searching will always be conducted under some degree of concealment so that the results from learning in one firm are not immediately accessible by other firms. Second, the specific combination of skills, education, knowledge and experience that characterizes the personnel of the R&D department of a firm will influence the innovation process including the problems formulated, the methods chosen and the solutions sought. Third, because of the particular technological opportunities and bottlenecks of the firm's product area, the searching is likely to follow specific technological trajectories (Dosi 1988). Fourth, the dominant 'techno-economic paradigm' influences learning and searching at all levels in society (Freeman and Perez 1988). The habits of thought created by the dominant paradigm instruct researchers in how to pose their problems and choose their methods, and they also hint at possible solutions.

Knowledge is also gained from economic activities, which are *not* explicitly or primarily aimed at its generation. Learning is often connected, for example, to the routine procurement, production and sales activities of the firm and to normal communication between firms. It is, then, rather a byproduct of activities organized with other aims in mind.

The distinction between intentional learning (education, training, R&D, market research) and learning as a byproduct of routine economic activities (learning by doing, by using and by interacting in relation to normal production and marketing activities by firms) is important in the learning economy. We might call the first kind 'learning by searching', and the second kind 'learning by producing'. Learning by searching and learning by producing are not, however, mutually exclusive activities. They are interdependent, and there are many mixed forms in between. On the one hand, routinized searching is certainly a possibility in modern production, especially in production areas where technological trajectories are well established. Habits of thought are important elements in research. On the other hand, repetitive production activities can be consciously and systematically monitored and controlled in order to stimulate innovations. They can be organized in ways that increase the learning potential.

5.7 Remembering and Forgetting

Since human knowledge does not exist all by itself but is coded into the central nervous system of human beings, it may easily and quickly get lost. Knowledge can be stored in many ways, however. Usually we presume, for both institutional and epistemological reasons, that learning is cumulative so that the stock of knowledge is increasing over time. This need not be the case, however. Maintaining the knowledge requires continuous reinvestments in both human and physical capital. Economic knowledge, which is not actively used deteriorates and context-dependent knowledge can be destroyed quite quickly, for example, by closing down a department or an organization. Knowledge is thus changed both by learning and by forgetting.

In fact, forgetting is neither rare nor unimportant. Knowledge which is not institutionally supported and does not fit into a cultural context tends to be forgotten (Douglas 1987). Sometimes knowledge is destroyed very quickly and veritable bursts of forgetting have occurred several times in history, as for example through the demise of great cultures. In fact, every change of scientific or techno-economic paradigm involves massive losses of knowledge.

The positive role of forgetting in the development of new knowledge has probably been underestimated. The enormous power of habits of thought in the economy constitutes a permanent risk for blocking potentially fertile learning processes. It may be argued that some kind of creative destruction of knowledge is necessary in order to make it possible for radical innovations to diffuse throughout the economy. Old habits of thought, routines and patterns of cooperation, within as well as between firms, have to be changed. Forgetting is an essential and integrated part of learning even if it is not always easy to separate ex ante between creative forgetting and just forgetting.

Economic development can be looked on as an unfolding sequence of transformations going on at many levels of aggregation. Termination of existing activities is often a prerequisite for the development of new ones, not only at the firm level in the form of bankruptcies and births of new firms but also within firms. Departments are closed down. Production of specific commodities and the use of certain processes are stopped, and so on. Closing down of activities is thus a normal and integrated part of economic development.

5.8 Learning in Pure and Mixed Economies

Since learning is interactive, it is affected by the institutional set up of the economy. Institutions are here defined as the sets of habits, routines, norms and laws that regulate the relationships between people and thus shape human interaction and learning (Johnson 1992). In the next sections we will discuss the institutional preconditions for the learning economy. The learning economy is neither a pure market economy nor a pure planned economy; it is a mixed economy in the fundamental sense of the term.

One way to illustrate the limits of the pure market economy as environment for learning and innovation is to focus on how different institutional settings affect product innovations. In mainstream theoretical models of production and growth, technical change is assumed to be reflected in changes in technical coefficients. Implicitly all innovations are assumed to be process rather than product innovations. Macroeconomic growth is often analysed in models describing either a one-commodity world or proportional growth in all sectors. But this is rather misleading; economic growth could not be sustained in any of these worlds. What keeps demand growing is the development of radically new products and change in the composition of aggregate demand as incomes grow. It is obvious that neither national economies nor private firms could survive competition if they did not introduce new products. Gradually, the demand for any specific product will stagnate, and increases in productivity through process innovations will, at best, delay the time when firms and nations have to introduce new products in order to survive.

Thus, there are good reasons for putting product innovations at the centre of the analysis. How will such a change in perspective affect our understanding of firms and markets as environments for learning and innovation? Will perfect competition and pure markets – the ideal institutional set up for allocation of given resources – be ideal also, when it comes to bringing forward new ideas and materializing them into new products adapted to the needs of potential users?

Scientists who develop new instruments for their own use, in order to be able to pursue a specific experiment in the laboratory, know better than anyone else which needs the instruments should address and satisfy. They will also have a better insight into the new use-value characteristics of the resulting innovation than anyone else. Here insights about needs and technical opportunities are combined in one single person.

The R&D laboratory engaged in the development of new process equipment and the production department in the same firm are in a more difficult situation. A reciprocal flow of qualitative information, with regard to technical opportunities and user needs, must connect the two departments. How to efficiently organize this relationship is not a simple matter.

But the problem of organizing coordination and exchange of qualitative information will be even more difficult when the innovating producer and the potential user belong to two different organizations linked only by a pure market relation. Therefore, it seems paradoxical that such a large proportion of innovative activities (measured both as input and as output) aims at or results in product innovations (Pavitt 1984). How can the producer know the needs of potential users when markets separate users from producers? How can the potential user gain information about the specific characteristics of a new product?

It is obvious that product innovations would be rare and accidental if markets were characterized simply by anonymous relationships between producers and users. Producers would have difficulties in observing new user needs and users would lack qualitative information as to the characteristics of the new products. It is also evident that there would be very little learning going on within the firms; at least not when firms are pictured as in standard neoclassical theory (i.e., as technical input–output relationships). There is not much room for novelty-generating or novelty-utilizing communication and interaction in a production function. Although the pure market is presented as an ideal norm in the neoclassical analysis of allocation, it represents an institutional set-up that is hostile to innovation.

The extreme organizational alternative to the pure market in economic theory is the pure hierarchy (the centrally planned economy can be thought of as a hierarchy of hierarchies) in which prices play no role at all and all communication is in terms of simple messages up and clear orders down. From the discussion above of the character of economic knowledge and learning, it follows that such organizations would be effective innovation brakes. The communication in a pure hierarchy is too restricted and simple to constitute the main substance in complicated interactive learning processes. New combinations of different pieces of knowledge are rare in pure hierarchies, and these would also have difficulties in utilizing unexpected novelty.

In a purely planned economy, there would be problems with both process innovations and product innovations. It is true that users and producers would not necessarily have any difficulties to meet, in a way they would be members of the same organization, but the simple character of their communication and interaction would prevent advanced learning. Simple learning by doing and learning by using might exist, and learning by searching might be effective in special basic research organizations separated from production, but innovation would not be a ubiquitous process.

5.9 The Organized Market as Institutional Response

Paradoxically, product innovations are not rare in the real world. Why? The simple answer is that most markets are not pure markets characterized by anonymous relationships between buyers and sellers. Most markets involve an element of mutual exchange of qualitative information and sometimes direct cooperation between users and producers in the process of innovation. The relative importance of product innovations indicates that most markets are organized markets, which allow for interactive learning. This implies that modern economies are 'mixed' in a fundamental sense. Not only does the private sector coexist with a large public sector but the relative success of the market economies in terms of technical progress reflects not the purity of the markets but rather their impurities.

The basic function of the user–producer relationships, in relation to product innovations, is to communicate information about both technological opportunities and user needs. Sometimes, the relationships between users and producers will involve direct cooperation. For example, a user might invite a producer to take part in solving a specific problem within the organization. Cooperation might take place at different stages – while defining the problem, developing the solution or introducing it in the user organization.

User–producer relationships will often involve elements of power and hierarchy and the direction of innovations will reflect the dominance of one of the parties. But in most user–producer relationships, we find other social elements beside hierarchy and dominance. Without a certain degree of commitment, loyalty, mutual respect of each other's autonomy and mutual trust, transaction costs would become prohibitively high and vertical integration would take place.

It follows from what has been said that user–producer relationships tend to be durable and selective. It takes time to develop efficient codes and channels of information. This might be even more so when it comes to establishing relationships of commitment, trust and common codes of conduct. In order to obtain communication economies, the number of producers and users connected must be limited, and this implies that user–producer relationships must be selective, connecting to each other relevant subsets of all potential users and producers.

The main reason why markets tend to become organized, therefore, is that they support innovative activities. It follows that the intensity and the character of user–producer relationships might be very different in different parts of the economy. In parts where product technology remains almost constant, the relationships might become close to the ideal of the pure market. In other areas, a high degree of complexity and radical change in technologies might result in a complete and formal vertical integration. But in between these two extremes, we should expect to find the vast majority of markets, each one including varying elements of organization.

5.10 Benefits and Costs of Organized Markets

What, then, are the relative advantages of organized markets as compared to the pure market and the pure hierarchy? Here, it might be useful to repeat an argument put forward by Arrow (1974). The formation of an organization might be regarded as a process involving both growing efficiency and growing inflexibility. The positive effect from an extension of the organization is that communication is likely to become more efficient through the development of common codes and channels of information. The negative aspect of bringing more and more activities into organizations is that the activities get 'locked in' within a network of communication codes and channels, difficult to adjust when faced with radical change in the environment. The organized market might be regarded as a compromise, taking into account both the advantages of acting collectively – in our context, primarily, to stimulate learning by interacting – and the costs of rigidity. The organized market represents a degree of rigidity necessary to produce innovations, but a rigidity of a lower degree than the one represented by complete integration.

We must also take into account how vertical integration affects the participation of integrated units in interactive learning taking place outside the pair of integrated units. Integrating a producer will give a user more direct access to technological know-how and at the same time, the integrated producer will get more direct access to knowledge about the changing needs of this particular user.

But the price paid for these intimate relationships might be high in the long run. Users and producers not integrated will be reluctant to give away sensitive information to the pair of integrated units. Nonintegrated users will be reluctant to surrender information about their strategic bottleneck problems to a producer integrated with a competitor. And nonintegrated producers will be unwilling to give away their most advanced technical knowhow to a user unit integrated with a competing producer.

As a result, interactive learning becomes specialized and limited in scope. Thus, there is a trade-off between the short-term advantages of a closer interaction between the integrated units and the long-term costs of their isolation from the broader process of interactive learning involving several formally independent users and producers. The informal solution of the organized market is less exclusive in this respect and keeps open a more diversified network for interactive learning. Firms may prefer relatively high communication and transaction costs in the organized market rather than join a pure hierarchy locking them into a more narrowly defined space for interactive learning.

We have used the user–producer relationship to illustrate the idea of an organized market. It should be underlined, however, that the informally organized markets of the learning economy can take many forms. The heart of the matter is interactive learning by creative combinations of knowledge. In the learning economy these interactions are not only going on in the science and technology system but also on much more anonymous and mundane levels.

Let us take an example. A few years ago a small furniture producing firm (about 30 employees) in Jutland, Denmark, with considerable success introduced a new work bench specially designed for repair and service work on television sets, hi-fi equipment, personal computers and so on. It was constructed of a dust-repelling material, which also prevents interference from static electricity. It had a very practical size and form and was equipped with a handy set of shelves and drawers and had, generally speaking, an attractive design. This work bench can be taken as an example of a kind of everyday incremental innovation which a surviving furniture industry has to be able to repeat over and over again. At the same time, it is a result of a rather sophisticated process of interactive learning. It started at a furniture exhibition. The firm was approached by some people from an autonomous repair and service department within a major Danish firm in the consumer electronics industry. They had for a long time been looking for a better work bench and had some specific ideas as to what properties it should have. A furniture architecture firm, which previously had cooperated with the furniture producer, was contacted and a project group was set up. This group soon discovered that they needed to consult experts on material technology from the Danish technological service system, a state-sponsored body. After a series of meetings between the four parties, a prototype of the new work bench was constructed, tested and introduced onto the market. The whole process took less than a year. This is not a big thing. It is just a small example of what goes on within a bewildering diversity of interactive learning activities in the learning economy. It is very important for the dynamic efficiency of the economy, but it still waits to be systematically observed and analysed by scholars.

5.11 Government Intervention in the Learning Economy

Is there also a role of government involvement in the learning economy? In fact, not only general equilibrium theory but also economic theories, which treat the economy as a process rather than as an equilibrium system, are predominantly sceptical as to the possibilities of planning, learning and innovation processes. In connection with the learning economy, the general equilibrium framework becomes rather empty. A modern definition of general equilibrium says that it is a situation in which no signals are generated, which can cause agents to change their theories or policies. This is a situation where nothing happens, where nothing can change the situation. All kinds of learning have ceased.

There is, for example, the 'Austrian' argument that the market is a very effective discovery process, the results of which cannot be improved by policymakers. The significance of the market is that it coordinates the use of widely dispersed knowledge, and during this process, through competitive entrepreneurial entry and intervention, discovers new possibilities. In Hayek's words, the market 'turns out to be a more efficient mechanism for digesting dispersed information than any man has deliberately designed' (1975).

Such arguments warn against intervening in subtle processes whose future directions and results we know very little about. In a 'kaleidic society' (Shackle 1972), where unexpected novelty is sooner or later bound to disintegrate, change and rearrange existing patterns into new ones, economic policy is an uncertain affair. The market process of discovery is necessarily decentralized, subtle and surprising. Any attempt to centralize it risks destroying it, so it seems.

But there is still room for economic policy in relation to long-term economic development and growth. First, the evolution of knowledge is not only accidental in its character. It is also cumulative and often developing along 'trajectories', which may remain quite stable for long periods. This perspective makes it clear that the role of policy might be twofold. It might either stimulate the progress along the prevailing trajectories – and this is what industrial policies often end up doing – or it may take on the more demanding task of making it easier for agents to shift from one trajectory to another.

First, the cumulativeness and path dependency of innovation highlights the risks of lock-in within technological and institutional cul-de-sacs. In such a context, there is a need for economic policy to keep options open and to stimulate and protect technological and institutional diversity which can be done through the educational system, the research system, the system of technological service and so on.

Second, there is no such thing as an unregulated market. Markets are always embedded in institutions. For example, we have demonstrated that markets characterized by product innovation are 'organized markets', even if they are not organized by the government. There are no strong reasons to believe, however, that politically determined rules – for example, rules for environmental protection today or rules against child labour during the Industrial Revolution – necessarily harm market discovery processes more than they stimulate them. It is not at all obvious that a government-supported technological service system, for example, will hamper entrepreneurial action.

Third, the impossibility of acquiring any certain knowledge about the future state of the world does not mean, for example, that safeguards against risks and incentive mechanisms for stimulating learning cannot be designed. After all, the fact that you do not know tomorrow's weather is a poor argument against building some form of weather proofing on your house today.

In addition, the argument that unregulated market processes are invincible mechanisms for discovering new knowledge does not distinguish clearly enough between knowledge and learning. The Austrian argument is mostly about coordinating already existing but dispersed knowledge and about discovering persistently emerging imbalances between revenues, costs and wants, knowledge about changing market conditions, unused opportunities, 'which things or services are wanted and how urgently they are wanted' (Hayek 1978). It shares with the neoclassical tradition the focus on the allocation of scarce resources. In this sense, the Austrian learning process *is* subordinated to the allocation process. It has not much to do with institutional, organizational and technological learning. In fact, it has nothing to do with innovation or learning. Analysis of the learning economy calls for a completely fresh approach.

In the perspective of this chapter, the role of government in the learning economy becomes one of supporting learning processes and sometimes processes of forgetting. It has important roles to play in relation to the following topics, at least:

• The means to learn
• The incentives to learn
• The capability to learn
• The access to relevant knowledge
• Learning to forget

5.12 The Means to Learn

The most important and obvious way public policy can strengthen the capability to learn and to innovate is through investing in education and training and through continuously renewing the form and content of these activities. Education policy is not just a question of the quantity of government funding. The ability of the education and training system to adapt to new social and technological developments is extremely important in the present era. The increasingly systemic character of new technologies, where old borders between technical and scientific disciplines are broken down, makes it necessary to review the traditional departmentalized organization of academic training and research.

5.13 The Incentives to Learn

Incentives to engage in learning may be of a pecuniary kind. At the level of the individual, systems of salaries and wages and income taxes may be designed to promote learning and creative efforts. At the level of the firm, patent laws and tax rules, including depreciation allowances for investment in tangible and intangible resources, may affect learning activities and efforts.

The importance of pecuniary incentives may be overstated, however. In the present period, individual entrepreneurship plays a more limited role than it has done and 'collective entrepreneurship' has become much more important. The cooperation and interaction between departments within the firm as well as between firms in industrial networks has become an important source of innovation. The public sector has a role to play as a professional user interacting with private firms and government programmes supporting projects of cooperation; networks between firms may help to establish a more efficient communication between parties otherwise reluctant to cooperate. Individualized pecuniary incentive systems will hamper processes of interactive learning if they reinforce instrumental rationality, weaken the capability to engage in open communication with other parties and foster opportunism, making all kinds of cooperation burdened by high transaction costs.

5.14 The Capability to Learn

The firm's capability to learn reflects the way it is organized. The movement away from tall hierarchies with vertical flows of information towards more flat organizations with horizontal flows of information is one aspect of the learning economy. Other elements relate to the circulation of personnel between departments and functions and the broad definition of jobs. One obvious way for government to promote organizational change in this direction would be to study systematically how domestic firms advance in this area and then to diffuse information about experiences made by 'lead firms' to laggards and give financial support to organizational innovations and experimenting. This is the content of government-inspired 'Best Practice' programmes.

5.15 Access to Relevant Knowledge

Old and new scientific results may be inputs to the process of learning and innovation at different stages. Here, access to universities and technical institutes is of importance. One of the main problems in this context is communication between industry and university. Big science-based firms in fine chemistry, biotechnology and electronics sectors, for example, might be well prepared to communicate with universities knowing their codes and their culture, while smaller engineering firms may have great difficulties in this respect. When there are 'bridging' problems, agents affecting links between knowledge producers and knowledge users may be established by government. Public and semi-public technological service institutions and libraries are also important in this connection.

Another kind of knowledge source is the informal, not codified and more or less tacit knowledge accumulated through learning inside firms. One of the reasons why firms establish network relationships is that these relationships give access to such knowledge. Network formation may be stimulated by government programmes supporting projects of cooperation.

5.16 Learning to Forget

One important aspect of the learning economy is its capacity to preserve and store knowledge. Again, government agencies may play a role together with private consultants and institutes. But in a learning economy it is also important to be able to forget, both in the literal meaning and in a broader sense. For the individual, the interpretation of forgetting relates to the abandoning of obsolete skills and professional expertise. Within firms it is a question of having mechanisms to put an end to outmoded activities, projects and products. Between firms it is a question of having a mechanism that helps to distinguish the firms with a future from those with no learning capability. The most apparent mechanism in this context is the market, But in some countries, for example, Japan and South Korea, the state has also played an important role in the closing down of ailing industries.

For all kinds of forgetting, people are burdened with the costs of change. These may be very unevenly distributed and may provoke resistance. One obvious way to support 'creative forgetting' is a system of redistribution that compensates the victims of change and makes it easier for them to move ahead into more promising activities. This will typically involve different kinds of social security arrangements, active labour market and retraining policies.

The need for and role of state intervention will differ dramatically between nations. But fundamentally, in addition to providing the means to learn by public investment in education and training, the role will be one of stimulating creativity and the generation of novelty, preserving knowledge and keeping technological options open and dispersing the personal and social costs of change (Dalum et al. 1992). Since learning is interactive and partly emanates from routine activities in production and consumption, government intervention should in general be oriented primarily at shaping the overall structure of production and the institutional set-up so that these promote self-organized learning and thereby reduce the need for fine tuning and detailed intervention into the economy.

5.17 Concluding Remarks

In this chapter, we have taken up the classical 'market versus state intervention' discourse from the perspective of the learning economy. We have disregarded the traditional discussion of efficient allocation of given scarce resources of capital, labour and land and concentrated on the development and allocation of the rather peculiar but crucial resource of knowledge. We have argued that knowledge is not scarce in the usual sense. We have discussed how it is changed by the social processes of learning, remembering and forgetting. Furthermore, we have discussed innovation as an interactive, ubiquitous process of introducing new knowledge into the economy and treated innovations as the results of learning.

Our conclusion is that the learning economy is neither a pure market economy nor a pure planned economy. Such economies would not learn very much, if they could exist and survive at all. The learning economy is, and has to be, a mixed economy in a very fundamental sense. In such economies (despite some influential arguments to the contrary), there are important roles for the public sector and for different kinds of policy. In the learning economy, very basic economic institutions such as firms and markets are mixed. Markets are embedded in habits, rules and norms and are organized for the communication and exchange of qualitative, nonprice type of information. Firms show a diversity of different organizational forms, which influence communication between different persons and departments. Its continually changing institutional set-up forms the environment for interactive learning-by-producing and learning-by-searching processes, which are the main mechanism for recombining and introducing new knowledge in the economy. Thus it is mixed in the sense that it displays a rich mix of organizational forms between the extremes of market and hierarchy.

If this picture is only a little bit true, if knowledge is the crucial resource and learning the most important process in the modern economy, we are, as economists, in trouble. We need a new theoretical orientation since the models of pure market economies in mainstream economics are not very helpful in understanding the critical features of the learning economy.

References

Akerman, J. 1936. *Ekonomisk Kausalitet ('Economic Causality')*. Lund: Gleerups forlag.

Aoki, M. 1990. 'The Participatory Generation of Information Rents and the Theory of the Firm'. In *The Firm as a Nexus of Treaties*, edited by M. Aoki, B. Gustafsson and O. Williamson. London: Sage Publications.

Arrow, K. 1962. 'The Economic Implications of Learning by Doing'. *Review of Economic Studies* 29, no. 80: 155–73.

———. 1971. 'Political and Economic Evaluation of Social Effects and Externalities'. In *Frontiers a Quantitative Economics*, edited by M. lnrrilligator. Amsterdam: North Holland.

———. 1973. *Information and Economic Behaviour*. Stockholm: Federation of Swedish Industries.

———. 1974. *The Limits of Organisation*. New York: W. W. Norton & Company.

Dalum, B., B. Johnson and B.-Å. Lundvall. 1992. 'Public Policy in the Learning Society'. In *National Systems of Innovation*, edited by B.-Å. Lundvall. London: Pinter.

Dosi, G. 1988. 'Sources, Procedures and Microeconomic Effects of Innovation'. *Journal of Economic Literature* 26, no. 3.

Douglas, M. 1987. *How Institutions Think*. London: Routledge.

Elam, M. 1993. *Innovation as the Craft of Combination, Department of Technology and Social Change*. Sweden: Linkoping University.

Freeman, C. 1987. *Technology and Economic Performance, Lessons from Japan*. London: Pinter.

Freeman, C. and Perez, C. 1988. 'Structural Crises Of Adjustment, Business Cycles and Investment Behaviour'. In *Technical Change and Economic Theory*. G. Dosi, C. Freeman, R.. Nelson, G. Silverberg and L. Soete. London: Pinter.

Hayek, F. A. 1975. *The Pretence of Knowledge. Nobel Memorial Lecture*. Stockholm: Les Prix Nobel en 1974.

———. 1978. 'Competition as a Discovery Procedure'. In *New Studies in Philosophy, Politics, Economics and the History of Ideas*, edited by F. A. Hayek. Chicago, IL: University of Chicago Press.

Johnson, B. 1992. 'Institutional Learning'. In *National Systems of Innovation*, edited by B.-Å. Lundvall. London: Pinter.

Kirzner, M. I. (ed.). 1978. 'Government Regulation and the Market Discovery Process'. In *Perils of Regulation: A Market Process Approach. Law and Economics Centre Occasional Papers*. University of Miami, School of Law.

Lundvall, B.-Å. 1985. *Product Innovation and User-Producer Interaction*. Aalborg: Aalborg University Press.

Lundvall, B.-Å. (ed.). 1992. *National Systems of Innovation*. London: Pinter Publishers.

Pavitt, K. 1984. 'Sectoral Patterns of Technical Change: Towards a Taxonomy and a Theory'. *Research Policy* 13.

Shackle, G. L. S. 1972. *Epistemics and Economics: A Critique of Economic Doctrines*. Cambridge: Cambridge University Press.

Part III
ECONOMICS OF KNOWLEDGE AND LEARNING

Chapter 6

FROM THE ECONOMICS OF KNOWLEDGE TO THE LEARNING ECONOMY

Bengt-Åke Lundvall

6.1 Introduction

In this chapter we present a conceptual framework to analyse knowledge and learning from an economic perspective. The starting point is the assumption that we are in a knowledge-based economy, but we conclude by proposing that it is more adequate to characterize the current era as 'a learning economy'. Crucial issues analysed here are distinctions between private/public, local/global and tacit/codified knowledge. While appearing 'academic' at first sight, these distinctions have important implications both for innovation policy and for the management of innovation and knowledge at the level of the firm.

It has become commonplace among policymakers to refer to the current period as characterized by a knowledge-based economy, and increasingly it is emphasized that the most promising strategy for economic growth is one aiming at strengthening the knowledge base of the economy.[1] This discourse raises a number of unresolved analytical issues. What constitutes the knowledge base? At what level can we locate and define a knowledge base? What are the specificities of local- and sector-specific knowledge bases? How stable is the knowledge base? In order to approach an answer to these questions, three different themes are introduced: first, basic concepts related to knowledge and learning; second, the contribution of economic analysis to the understanding of the production, mediation and use of knowledge; and third, new economic trends and the formation of a learning economy.

6.2 A Terminology of Knowledge

6.2.1 Is knowledge a public or a private good?

Sidney Winter concluded his seminal paper on knowledge and management strategy by pointing out that there is 'a paucity of language' and 'a serious dearth of appropriate terminology and conceptual schemes' for analysing the role of knowledge in the economy (1987). Since then, the number of relevant publications has grown immensely but little headway has been made in terms of a terminology acceptable to all. There is little agreement on questions such as: What is the meaning of knowledge and knowledge production? What separations and distinctions between different kinds of knowledge are most useful for understanding the interaction between learning, knowledge and economic development?

Knowledge and information appear in economic models in two different contexts. The most fundamental assumption of standard microeconomics is that the economic system is based on *rational choices made by individual agents*. Thus, *how much and what kind of information* agents have about the world in which they operate and their *ability to process the information* are crucial issues.

The other major perspective is one in which knowledge is regarded as an *asset*. Here, knowledge may appear both as an input (competence) and output (innovation) in the production process. Under certain circumstances, it can be privately owned and/or bought and sold in the market as a commodity. The economics of knowledge is to a high degree about specifying the conditions for knowledge to appear as 'a normal commodity' (i.e., as something similar to a producible and reproducible tangible product).

In what follows, attention is on knowledge in this latter sense. In analysing knowledge as an asset, its properties in terms of transferability across time, space and people is central. This issue is at the core of two different strands of economic debate. One is the public/private dimension of knowledge and the role of government in knowledge production; the second is the formation of industrial districts and the local character of knowledge.

Is knowledge a private or a public good? In economic theory, the properties that give a good the attribute of 'public' are the following:

a) Its benefits can be enjoyed by many users concurrently as well as sequentially without being diminished
b) It is costly for the provider to exclude unauthorized users

One reason for the interest in this issue is that it is crucial for defining the role of government in knowledge production. If knowledge is a public good that can be accessed by anyone, there is no incentive for rational private agents to invest in its production. If it is less costly to imitate than to produce new knowledge, the social rate of return would be higher than the private rate of return and again, private agents would invest too little. In Nelson's article 'The Simple Economics of Basic Economic Research' (1959) and Arrow's 'Economic Welfare and the Allocation of Resources for Invention' (1962b), classical contributions demonstrated that, in such situations, there is a basis for government policy either to subsidize or to take charge directly of the production of knowledge. Public funding of schools and universities, as well as of generic technologies, has been motivated by this kind of reasoning, which also brings to the fore the protection of knowledge, for instance by patent systems.

In a sense, this fundamental problem remains at the core of the economics of knowledge production. However, another strand of thought, which has roots far back in the history of economic theory, has become more strongly represented in the debate in the last decades. It is the question of how to share knowledge that is difficult to mediate. Marshall (1923) was concerned to explain the real-world phenomenon of *industrial district*: why is it that certain specialized industries are located in certain regions and why do they remain competitive for long historical periods. His principal explanation was that knowledge was localized in the region and rooted both in the local labour force as well as in local institutions and organizations. This perspective with its focus on localized knowledge has, in the light of the Silicon Valley phenomenon, resurfaced strongly among industrial and regional economists over the last decades. Correspondingly, the management literature has seen a growing interest in the promotion of 'knowledge sharing' within and between firms.

These two perspectives, while seemingly opposed in their contrasting emphasis on protection and sharing of knowledge, raise the same fundamental questions. Is knowledge public or private? Can it or can it not be transferred? Is the consent of the producer needed for the mediation to be successful or can knowledge be copied against the will of the producer? How difficult is it to transfer knowledge, and what are the transfer mechanisms? Is it possible to change the form of knowledge so that it gets easier (or more difficult) to mediate? How important is the broader sociocultural context for the transferability of knowledge? One reason for the distinctions between different kinds of knowledge proposed below is that they help sort out these questions.

Responding to these questions is also a way of specifying what constitutes the knowledge base of the economy. If knowledge was completely public, it would be meaningful to speak of one common knowledge base for the whole economy, and there would be a strong need for coordinating investments in knowledge production at the global level. Conversely, if knowledge was completely individual and private, there would be no common knowledge base at all, and investment in knowledge production could be left to the individuals themselves. As we shall see, reality is complex and most knowledge is neither completely public nor completely private. The knowledge base is fragmented and may best be illustrated as constituted by a number of semi-public 'pools' to which access is shared regionally, professionally and through networking.

6.2.2 Four different kinds of knowledge

Knowledge is divided here into four categories, which in fact have ancient roots (Lundvall and Johnson 1994).[2]

- Know-what
- Know-why
- Know-how
- Know-who

Know-what refers to knowledge about 'facts'. How many people live in New York, what the ingredients in pancakes are, and when the battle of Waterloo took place are examples of this kind of knowledge. Here knowledge is close to what is normally called information; it can be broken down into bits and communicated as data.

Know-why refers to knowledge about principles and laws of motion in nature, in the human mind and in society. This kind of knowledge has been extremely important for technological development in certain science-based areas such as the chemical and electric/electronic industries. Access to this kind of knowledge will often make advances in technology more rapid and reduce the frequency of errors in procedures involving trial and error.

Know-how refers to skills (i.e., the ability to do something). It may be related to the skills of artisans and production workers, but actually it plays a key role in all important economic activities. The businessmen judging the market prospects for a new product or the personnel managers selecting and training staff use their know-how. It would also be misleading to characterize know-how as practical rather than theoretical. One of the most interesting and profound analyses of the role and formation of know-how is actually about scientists' need for skill formation and personal knowledge (Polanyi 1958/1978). Even finding solutions to complex mathematical problems is based on intuition and on skills related to pattern recognition, which are rooted in experience-based learning rather than on the mechanical carrying out of a series of distinct logical operations (Ziman 1979, 101–102).

Know-how is a kind of knowledge developed and kept within the borders of an individual firm or a single research team. As the complexity of the knowledge base increases, however, cooperation between organizations tends to develop. One of the most important reasons for industrial networks to form is the need for firms to be able to share and combine elements of know-how. Similar networks may, for the same reasons, be formed between research teams and laboratories.

This is one reason why *know-who* becomes increasingly important. The general trend towards a more composite knowledge base with new products typically combining many technologies, each of which is rooted in several different scientific disciplines, makes access to many different sources of knowledge more essential (Pavitt 1998). Know-who involves information about who knows what and who knows what to do. But it also involves the social ability to cooperate and communicate with different kinds of people and experts.

6.2.3 How public or private are the four kinds of knowledge?

The public or private character of these kinds of knowledge differs both in terms of degree and form. Databases can bring together 'know-what' in a more or less user-friendly form. Information technology extends enormously the information potentially at the disposal of individual agents, although the information still has to be found and selected what is relevant. The effectiveness of search engines developed in connection with the Internet is highly relevant in this context as this helps to specify how accessible the data actually are. Even with the most recent advances in this area, access to this kind of knowledge is still far from perfect (Shapiro and Varian 1999). Even today, the most effective medium for obtaining pertinent facts may be through the 'know-who' channel (i.e., contacting an outstanding expert in the field to obtain directions on where to look for a specific piece of information.

Scientific work aims at producing theoretical models of the type *know-why*, and some of this work is placed in the public domain. Academics have strong incentives to publish and make their results accessible. The Internet offers new possibilities for speedy electronic publishing. Open and public access is of course a misnomer, in that it often takes enormous investments in learning before the information has any meaning. Again know-who, directed towards academia can help the amateur obtain a 'translation' into something more comprehensible.

This is one strong motivation for companies' presence in academic environments and sometimes even engaging in basic research. Some big companies contribute to basic research and they tend to take over functions of 'technical universities' (Eliasson 2000). But at the same time, the close connections between academic science and the exploitation of new ideas by business in fields such as biotechnology tend to undermine the open exchange that has characterized academic knowledge production.

To gain access to scientific know-why, it is necessary, under all circumstances, to pursue R&D activities and to invest in science. This is true for individuals and regions as well as for firms. There is much less completely free 'spill-over' available than assumed in standard economics; absorptive capacity will reflect historical investment in R&D (Cohen and Levinthal 1990).

In fields characterized by intense technological competition, technical solutions are often ahead of academic know-why. Technology can solve problems or perform functions without a clear understanding of why it works. Here, knowledge is more know-how than know-why.

Know-how is the kind of knowledge with the most limited public access and for which mediation is the most complex. The basic problem is the difficulty of separating the competence to act from the person or organization that acts. The outstanding expert – cook, violinist, manager – may write a book explaining how to do things, but what is done by the amateur on the basis of that explanation is of course less perfect than what the expert would produce. Attempts to use information technology to develop expert systems show that it is difficult and costly to transform expert skills into information that can be used by others. It has also been demonstrated that the transformation always involves changes in the content of expert knowledge (Hatchuel and Weil 1995). This is true of an individual's skills and competence, of professional skills and a team's competence.

Eliasson (1996) has illustrated the limits of using management information systems as a substitute for management skills by pointing out the strategic failures of IBM and other big ICT firms. Know-how is never a completely public good and normally firms get access to it only by hiring experts or merging with companies with the knowledge they want.

Know-who refers to a combination of information and social relationships. Telephone books that list professions as well as databases that list producers of certain goods and services are in the public domain and can, in principle, be accessed by anyone. In the economic sphere, however, it is extremely important to obtain quite specialized competencies and to find the most reliable experts, hence the enormous importance of good personal relationships with key persons one can trust. These social and personal relationships are by definition not public. They cannot be transferred and more specifically, they cannot be bought or sold on the market. As pointed out by Arrow (1971), 'You cannot buy trust and, if you could, it would have no value whatsoever'.

However, the social context may support to a greater or lesser degree, the formation of know-who knowledge, while the cultural context determines the form it takes. When characterizing national business systems, Whitley emphasizes factors having to do with trust and the capacity to build extra-family collective loyalties (1996, 51). This is also an important aspect of the concept of social capital (Woolcock 1998). In situations where technology is character-ized by rapid change or where the knowledge base is not well documented, it is necessary to meet face to face from time to time in order to first to define and then to solve problems.

6.2.4 Most knowledge is neither strictly public nor strictly private

It is clear from what precedes that very little knowledge is 'perfectly pub-lic'. Even information of the know-what type may be impossible to access for those not connected to the right telecommunications or social networks. Moreover, at the current stage of development of information technology access for those who are connected remains limited. And while scientific and other types of complex knowledge may be perfectly accessible in principle for effective access, the user must have invested in building absorptive capacity. Know-how is never fully transferable since how a person does things reflects that individual's personality (even organizations have a 'personality' in this sense).

However, little economically useful knowledge is completely private in the long run. Tricks of the trade are shared within the profession. Know-how can be taught and learnt in interaction between the master and the apprentice. New technological knowledge may be costly to imitate, but when it is much more efficient than the old, there are several ways to obtain it. Even when the possessor of private knowledge does not want to share it with others, there are ways to obtain it such as reverse engineering, which involves taking products apart to find out how to produce them. If necessary, private agents will engage in intelligence activities aimed at getting access to competitors' secrets.

Different parts of economic theory handle this mixed situation differently. Underlying much of the neoclassical theory of production and economic growth is the simplifying assumption that there is a global bank of blueprints from which anybody can get a copy to be used for starting up production. This ignores the fact that skilled agents can only use most accessible knowledge and that skills differ and are not easily transformed into blueprints.

The resource base theory of the firm takes the opposite view and assumes that the competence of the firm determines the directions in which it expands its activities (Penrose 1959/1995). It is the specificity of the knowledge base that determines the specific pattern of economic growth. However, actually, this model implies an even more dynamic perspective characterized by con-tinuous creation of new competencies within the firm, and it points towards the need to develop 'learning organizations'. Otherwise, imitation and innova-tions in competing firms would, sooner or later, erode the firm's competencies.

In real-life firms will have to engage simultaneously in copying well-known routines from others, exploiting internal capabilities and engaging in building new ones. This is what makes management a difficult art and why firms cannot be reduced to maximizing algorithms in the way they are presented in standard textbooks based on neoclassical economics.

6.2.5 On tacitness and codification of knowledge

There is currently a lively debate among economists about the role of tacitness in knowledge (Cowan et al. 2000; Johnson et al. 2002). The reason for the interest is, of course, that tacitness relates to the transferability and to the public character of knowledge. It has been assumed that the more knowledge is tacit, the more difficult it is to share it between people, firms and regions. Specifically, markets might fail and other mediation mechanisms would have to be given more attention.

Tacit knowledge is knowledge that has not been documented and made explicit by the one who uses and controls it. The fact that a certain piece of knowledge is tacit does not rule out the possibility of making it explicit if incentives to do so are strong enough. To make this clear, it is useful to distinguish between tacit knowledge that can be made explicit – tacit for lack of incentives – and knowledge that cannot be made explicit – tacit by nature (Cowan et al. 2000).

Knowledge about the state of the world can, to a certain extent, be made explicit. Know-what can be entered into databases and know-why can be made explicit in theorems. Skills embodied in persons and competencies embodied in organizations can only be documented to a much more limited degree. There are 'natural' limits to how far it is possible to make 'know-how' explicit; only approximations are possible. This is why outstanding experts whose activities are based on their unique know-how and firms whose activities are based on unique competencies and permanent innovation may earn extra rents for long periods.

An important issue in this context is how much effort should be made to 'codify' knowledge. Only those with access to the code can access knowledge written down in a code. Two parties can share the knowledge or one party can sell the knowledge to another. Codified knowledge is potentially shared knowledge while noncodified knowledge remains individual, at least until it can be learnt in direct interaction with the possessor. Sectors where the knowledge base is dominated by noncodified but potentially codifiable knowledge may be sectors where systematic progress towards more efficient practices is difficult. Economists have used education as a typical example of a production process characterized by tacit techniques (Murnane and Nelson 1984).

OECD (2000) presents a unique attempt to compare the production, diffusion and use of knowledge across some important sectors – health and education among them.

The debate on codification has been complicated by the fact that two different meanings of 'codes' have been alluded to. Some are explicit and available in the form of textbooks, manuals, formulas and organizational diagrams. Other 'codes' have developed spontaneously as a means of communication within or between organizations (Arrow 1974). The latter are implicit and no individual in the organization may be able to give a full description. The issue concerning to what extent such implicit codes can be transformed into explicit ones is important. It is well known that organizational diagrams and management information systems lose some of the complexity and richness that characterize real existing social systems. If these codes could be made explicit, they could be made available to external parties, and mediation of knowledge would become less difficult. Another reason for making implicit codes explicit could be that, in some instances, codification might make it easier to formulate and realize strategies of change.[3]

What has just been considered as important attributes of knowledge (public/private, codified/tacit) suggests that there may be marked differences among various sectors with regard to their knowledge base. Some science-intensive sectors base their activities mainly on codified knowledge, while others operate and compete mainly on the basis of unstructured and experience-based implicit knowledge. But there are no pure cases. Even in the most strongly science-based sectors, tacit knowledge will be a key element in their competitive position, and conversely, it is difficult to find firms in the OECD area that can avoid completely the need to codify. Accounting and reporting to tax authorities requires a minimum in this respect and the wide diffusion of computers both contributes to and reflects the trend among firms towards operating on the basis of codified knowledge (information).

6.3 An Economic Perspective on the Production, Mediation and Use of Knowledge

6.3.1 What is produced when firms produce knowledge?

Most authors using the concept of knowledge creation and knowledge production refer to technological knowledge and technical innovation as the outputs of the process (Antonelli 1999; Nonaka and Takeuchi 1995). In the new growth theory, the output of the R&D sector is viewed either as a blueprint for a new production process that is more efficient than the previous one assuming that it can be protected by private property instruments such as patents, or as a production of new semi-manufactured goods that cannot easily be copied by competitors (Verspagen 1992, 29–30).

A striking characteristic of knowledge production resulting in innovation is the fact that knowledge, in terms of skills and competencies, is the most important input. In this sense, it recalls a 'corn economy' in which corn and labour produce corn. But it differs from such an economy in one important respect. While the corn used to produce corn disappears in the process, *skills and competencies improve with use*. Important characteristics of knowledge reflect that its elements are not scarce in the traditional sense: the more skills and competencies are used, the more they develop. This points to knowledge production as a process of joint production in which innovation is one kind of output and the learning and skill enhancement that takes place in the process is another.

6.3.2 Innovation as one major outcome of knowledge production

There are two reasons for regarding innovation as an interesting outcome of knowledge production. One is that innovation represents, by definition, something new and therefore adds to existing knowledge. The second is that innovation is, again by definition, knowledge that is in demand. (Innovation is defined as an invention that has been introduced in the market, and it thus represents knowledge that has proven its relevance for the market economy.)

On the other hand, it is important to note that innovation, as Schumpeter emphasized, is part of a process of 'creative destruction'. An innovation may open up new markets and create the basis for new firms and jobs but it will, at the same time, close down some old markets and some firms and jobs will disappear. This has a parallel in the impact on the stock of knowledge used in the market economy. Moral depreciation of intellectual capital is the other side of innovation. For instance, the know-how necessary to produce mechanical office equipment and the competencies of firms engaged in their production became obsolete when semiconductors and computers were introduced.

There are important sectoral differences in knowledge production. Such differences are reflected in the character, the mode and the outcome of the innovation process. The taxonomy developed by Keith Pavitt (1984) represents an important effort to capture these differences systematically. By analysing 2,000 important technical innovations in the United Kingdom, Pavitt defined four categories of firms and sectors. First, there are *supply-dominated* sectors (e.g., clothing, furniture) in which firms develop few important innovations on their own but obtain some from other firms. Second, there are *scale-intensive* sectors (e.g., food, cement), which focus their innovation activities on developing more efficient process technology. Third, there are *specialized suppliers* (e.g., engineering, software, instruments), and these carry out frequent product innovations, often in collaboration with customers. Finally, there are *science-based producers* (e.g., chemical industry, biotechnology, electronics) that develop new products as well as processes in close collaboration with universities.

For a long time, knowledge production/innovation processes were largely considered as the province of the fourth category; still there is a bias in this direction, often in combination with a linear view that assumes that new scientific results are the first step in the process, technological invention the second step and the introduction of innovations as new processes or products the third. There is now a rich body of empirical and historical work that shows that this is the exception rather than the rule (Rothwell 1977; von Hippel 1988; Lundvall 1988). Of all scientific advances, very few are immediately transformed into innovations, and *vice versa*, innovations very seldom reflect recent scientific breakthroughs. It is nonetheless true that knowledge production/innovation processes are facilitated by science in various ways, although normally it is old rather than new scientific results that support the innovation process. Kline and Rosenberg (1986) have reviewed the complex interaction between science and technology throughout the innovation process.

The recent models of innovation emphasize that knowledge production/innovation is an interactive process in which firms interact with customers, suppliers and knowledge institutions. Empirical analysis shows that firms seldom innovate alone.[4]

6.3.3 Competence as the other major outcome of knowledge production

The change from a linear to an interactive view of innovation and knowledge production has also been a way to connect innovation and the further development of competence. As now understood, the innovation process may be described as a process of *interactive learning* in which those involved increase their competence while engaging in the innovation process.

In economics, there have been various approaches to competence building and learning. One important contribution is Arrow's analysis of 'learning by doing' (Arrow 1962a) in which he demonstrated that the efficiency of a production unit engaged in producing complex systems (aeroplane frames) grew with the number of units already produced and argued that this reflected experience-based learning.[5] Later, Rosenberg (1982) introduced 'learning by using' to explain why efficiency in using complex systems increased over time (the users were airline companies introducing new models). The concept of 'learning by interacting' points to how interaction between producers and users in innovation enhances the competence of both (Lundvall 1985, 1988)

In most of the contributions mentioned above, learning is regarded as the unintended outcome of processes with a different aim than learning and increasing competence. Learning is seen as a side effect of processes of production, use, marketing or innovation. An interesting new development that refers to learning as an instrumental process is the growing attention given to 'learning organizations' (Senge 1990). The basic idea is that the way an organization is structured and the routines followed will have a major effect on the rate of learning that takes place. The appropriate institutional structures may improve or speed up knowledge production in terms of competence building based on daily activities.

The move towards learning organizations is reflected in changes both in the firm's internal organization and in inter-firm relationships. Within firms, the accelerating rate of change makes multilevel hierarchies and strict borders between functions inefficient. It makes decentralization of responsibility to lower level employees and formation of multifunctional teams a necessity. This is reflected in the increasing demand for workers willing to learn, and at the same time skilful, flexible, cooperative and willing to shoulder responsibility. Inter-firm relationships with suppliers, customers and competitors become more selective and more intense. 'Know-who' becomes increasingly important in an economy that combines a complex knowledge base and a highly developed, rapidly changing specialization.

Apart from these organizational changes, there is growing emphasis on making employees and teams of employees more aware of the fact that they are engaged in learning. It has been suggested that second-loop learning (i.e., a process in which the crucial element is that agents reflect on what has been learnt and on how to design the learning process) is more efficient than simply relying on the impact of experience (Argyris and Schön 1978).

It is much more difficult to capture, empirically, competence building through learning than innovation. Competence is primarily revealed in practice and sometimes in no other way. This may become a problem as experience-based learning and competence become increasingly important for the competitiveness of workers, firms and regions. Tomlinson (1999) has made an interesting and original attempt to map sector differences in competence building through experience. Using UK labour market survey data, he shows that learning is more intensive and extensive at the top than at the bottom of organizations. His data also indicate that learning is more important in sectors characterized by frequent innovation. When it comes to the development of indicators, this is the most difficult but perhaps also the most important area.

These measurement problems reflect the general state of economic analysis in this field. While economists have made substantial contributions to the economics of innovation, their contribution to understanding competence building is much more modest. With scholars such as Christopher Freeman, Richard R. Nelson and Nathan Rosenberg as entrepreneurs and spiritual leaders, there has been a massive effort to understand the process of innovation in relation to economic theory (Dosi et al. 1988) and in a historical and empirical perspective, including the development of statistical indicators. There is no parallel for knowledge production as learning and competence building. On this aspect of knowledge production, sociologists, psychologists and anthropologists have more to offer economists in terms of systematic insights than vice versa (see, for instance, Kolb 1984).

6.3.4 Production of knowledge as a separate activity or as a byproduct of regular routine activities: A differentiation which is becoming blurred

It is useful to separate two different perspectives on the process of knowledge production, which are not mutually exclusive but which can be found, in more or less pure form, in the literature on innovation systems and the information society. They are also reflected in attempts to measure the relative importance of knowledge in the economy and in theoretical models such as models of economic growth.

On the one hand, one might look for *a separate sector* in charge of producing new knowledge or handling and distributing information. Such a sector could involve universities, technical institutes and government S&T policies, as well as R&D functions in firms. Here, the production of knowledge would take place as a deliberate activity, outside the realm of production. On the other hand, one might regard the creation and diffusion of knowledge as rooted in and emanating from routine activities in economic life, such as learning by doing, by using and by interacting. Here, the production of knowledge would take place as a byproduct of ordinary economic activities through learning by doing or learning by using.

Another important distinction already touched upon is between 'offline' and 'online' learning activities. Above we referred to the growing focus on establishing learning organizations. Another related new trend is the emergence of a form of learning qualified as 'experimental'. This form of learning taking place 'online' (i.e., during the process of producing the good or providing the service) involves experimenting during the production process. By doing so, one creates new options and variety. This form of learning is based on a strategy whereby experimentation allows for collecting data, on the basis of which the best strategy for future activities is chosen.

With the emergence of experimental learning and learning organizations, the feedback and reciprocal links that tie 'online' learning process and in-house R&D together become crucial. One issue here is determining the extent to which the knowledge produced 'by doing' is valued. It might be a problem that management rarely considers routine activities as activities that produce knowledge, although different national systems differ markedly in this respect. The establishment of feedback loops requires effective recognition, identification and valorization of the knowledge produced through the learning process.

6.3.5 Mediation of knowledge

While the production of knowledge is important for the overall dynamics of the global economy in the long run, the greatest economic impact comes from broadening the use of knowledge in the economy. This is reflected in public efforts to increase the diffusion of innovations as well as in training and education aimed at the formation of skills and competencies. How can different aspects of knowledge be mediated? The natural starting point for an economic analysis is to see under what conditions the market can mediate knowledge.

Some of the difficulties in mediating knowledge through the market have already been indicated. Tacit knowledge in the form of know-how or an implicit code or competence cannot be separated from the person or organization containing it. This is what von Hippel (1994) calls 'sticky data'. In this case, mediation may take the form of the purchase by a customer of the services of the person or the firm rather than the competence itself.

Carriers of such knowledge may have a problem demonstrating the quality of their competence to potential buyers, and buyers may have a problem locating the best offers in terms of quality. Reference from key customers, which can be shown as evidence to potential customers, is one strategy used by firms operating in this kind of market.

This form of mediation and the problems it involves tend to take on growing economic importance. The increasing specialization in the production of knowledge makes mediation more crucial for the system as a whole. This is reflected in the fact that knowledge-intensive business services, a sector directly engaged in the production and sale of knowledge, are among the most rapidly growing sectors in OECD countries. Consultancy firms, accountancy firms and financial firms have taken over the role of 'strategic sector' historically played by the sector producing machinery, summarizing and generalizing experiences from local learning and delivering embodied and disembodied knowledge to a broad set of users. This is confirmed by econometric studies demonstrating a close correlation between the input of these kinds of services and productivity growth in user sectors (Tomlinson 2001).

A second way to mediate this kind of knowledge is to engage in a process of interactive learning with the carrier of the knowledge. This may be a conscious choice, for example, when an apprentice enters into a contract with a master, or it may be a side effect of cooperation between people and organizations to solve shared problems. A third way to obtain this kind of knowledge is to hire experts as employees or take over the organization controlling the knowledge.

Even when knowledge is explicit and can be separated from its carrier, there are problems with using the market as a mediator, which Kenneth Arrow in particular has worked to define. One is for the customer to determine the value of the information before the transaction has taken place; a user wants to know something in advance about the knowledge and the seller does not want to give information away for free. Another is the difficulty for the seller to restrict the use of the information once it has been sold and, vice versa, the difficulty for the buyer to restrict its further distribution by the seller.

Despite these difficulties, a large and growing amount of knowledge is the object of transactions in something that looks like a market (there is a buyer, a seller and a price). One reason why markets work is that formal and informal institutions – including legal protection in terms of patents, licenses and copyright – support transactions. Reputation mechanisms lower the risk for entering into contractual relationships. An even more fundamental reason is that many markets for knowledge transactions are not pure but rather organized markets. Long-term relationships with elements of experience-based trust often play a major role in knowledge markets (Lundvall 1985, 1988).

So far, the discussion has been limited to the mediation of what economists call disembodied knowledge. Substantial flows of knowledge are built into products. Scientific instruments and computers embody a great deal of knowledge, and users with sufficient competence can perform very advanced operations with this kind of equipment. Mediation of knowledge via embodied technology is sometimes combined with a transfer of disembodied knowledge. For example, suppliers of complex process equipment may offer training to the personnel of the customer organization.

Finally, knowledge can be mediated in several other informal ways. One way to overcome market limitations is for professionals belonging to separate and sometimes even competing organizations to exchange pieces of knowledge on a barter basis (Carter 1989).

6.4 Towards the Learning Economy

Many indicators show that there has been a shift in economic development in the direction of a more important role for knowledge production and learning. This section looks at some of these changes and the issues they raise for the knowledge base of the education system.

Moses Abramowitz and Paul David (1996) have demonstrated that this century has been characterized by increasing knowledge intensity in the production system. The OECD's structural analysis of industrial development supports their conclusion. It has been shown that the sectors that use knowledge inputs such as R&D and skilled labour most intensively grow most rapidly. At the same time, the skill profile is on an upward trend in almost all sectors. In most OECD countries, in terms of employment and value added, the most rapidly growing sector is knowledge-intensive business services (OECD 1998, 48–55).

These observations have led more and more analysts to characterize the new economy as 'knowledge based', and there is in fact little doubt about a relative shift in the demand for labour towards more skilled workers (OECD 1994). However, this perspective may underestimate the destructive aspects of innovation and change. In an alternative interpretation of the change in the composition of the labour force, Anne P. Carter (1994) pointed out that the main function of most nonproduction workers is to introduce or cope with change. The rising proportion of nonproduction workers may thus be taken as the expression both of the growing cost of change and of acceleration in the rate of change.

Acceleration in the rate of change implies that knowledge and skills are more exposed to rapid moral depreciation. Therefore, the increase in the stock of knowledge may be less dramatic than it appears. An alternative hypothesis is that we are moving into a learning economy where the success of individuals, firms, regions and countries will reflect, more than anything else, their ability to learn. The speeding up of change reflects the rapid diffusion of information technology, the widening of the global marketplace with the inclusion of new strong competitors and deregulation of and less stability in markets (Drucker 1993; Lundvall and Johnson 1994; Archibugi and Lundvall 2001).

In this context, learning is defined as a process, the core of which is the acquisition of competence and skills that allow the learning individual to be more successful in reaching individual goals or those of his/her organization. It will also involve a change in context of meaning and purpose for the individual and affect his/her existing knowledge. This corresponds closely to what is commonly meant by learning and to what experts on learning, who are not economists, understand by the concept (Kolb 1984). It is also the kind of learning most crucial to economic success. At the same time, it differs from some definitions of learning in standard economic theory where it is synonymous either with 'information acquisition' or treated as a black-box phenomenon assumed to be reflected in productivity growth.

6.5 Conclusion

It may be argued that, in a sense, all economic theory is about information and knowledge. Problems of coordination have been at the core of economic theory since Adam Smith. Individual agents make choices independently on the basis of information offered by the market. Important differences between economic models and theories reflect differences in the assumptions made about what agents know and about the degree to which they learn anything from what they do. This separates neoclassical economics from Austrian economics: the former takes fully informed agents as the reference whereas the latter emphasizes ignorance as the starting point for learning (von Hayek). It also separates those who assume hyperrationality and rationality from those who assume limited rationality (Herbert A. Simon).

Modern economics is more than ever aware of the importance of knowledge and learning. New growth theory and new trade theory assume a strong link between the increase in knowledge base and the rate of productivity growth. Austrian economists treat learning as a fundamental process in the analysis of market transactions. Over the last decades we have witnessed many new contributions related to institutional economics and the economics of innovation. In these new fields, knowledge and learning play a pivotal role in economic development. New theories of the firm focus on building capabilities and competencies. The management literature has made the concept of 'learning organizations' central for theoretical developments and especially for practitioners.

However, in almost all of these contributions, the understanding of knowledge and learning remains narrow. In theories that form the core of standard economics, it is assumed that rational agents make choices on the basis of a given amount of information. The only kind of learning allowed for is agents' access to new bodies of information. The most recent developments within standard economics are contradictory and ambivalent in this respect. On the one hand, new growth theory and new trade theory focus on the importance of investments in education and research. On the other hand, some of the most fashionable developments in macroeconomics assume rational expectations and general equilibrium frameworks, thus operating with even more extreme assumptions leaving no room for learning by agents.

Recent developments outside standard economics have been less constrained in these respects. Research on the economics of institutional and technical change has resulted in many new insights. Institutional economics, evolutionary economics, socioeconomic research, industrial dynamics and the economics of innovation have typically developed in close interaction with historical and empirical research programmes. This is why we know much more than before about how innovation takes place in different parts of the economy now than we did 20 years ago.

When it comes to the other aspect of knowledge production (i.e., competence building and learning), it is only recently that research has begun to address important questions about who learns what and how learning takes place in the context of economic development. In this area, economists have a lot to learn from other disciplines and not least from education specialists who have developed a more systematic and empirically based understanding of learning (Kolb 1984). This reflects the fact that when economists begin to focus on learning, they face issues for which their traditional toolbox is insufficient. Scholars in philosophy, psychology, education, anthropology and other disciplines have illuminated different aspects of these issues. The increasing division of labour in the production of knowledge – useful as it might have been for the rapid advances within special fields – has had as a major negative consequence the lack of a deep and systematic understanding of the complex process of knowledge creation and learning.

In this chapter I have used a broad definition of economics as a reference platform, but at the same time, I have broadened the perspective to include perspectives from other disciplines whenever an understanding of the real-world phenomena requires it. One of the major conclusions is that it is not meaningful to pretend that economic performance can be explained without bringing into the analysis social relationships and organizational structures. The innovation literature has been instrumental in opening up the black box of technical change; now the time has come to open up the black box of social interaction through focus on how learning takes place in the real world.

Notes

1 OECD has pursued several analytical activities along these lines (Foray and Lundvall 1996; OECD 1996). The Portuguese chairmanship for the EU Ministerial Council for the first half of 2000 was pursued under the theme of 'a Europe based on knowledge and innovation'.

2 Knowledge has been at the centre of analytical interest from the very beginning of civilization. Aristotle distinguished between: *Epistèmè*: knowledge that is universal and theoretical; *Technè*: knowledge that is instrumental, context specific and practice related; *Phronesis*: Knowledge that is normative, experience based, context specific and related to common sense: 'practical wisdom'. At least two of our categories have roots that go back to these three intellectual virtues; know-why is similar to *epistèmè* and know-how to *technè*. But the correspondence is imperfect since we will follow Polanyi and argue that

scientific activities always involve a combination of know-how and know-why. Aristotle's third category, *phronesis*, which relates to the ethical dimension, will be reflected in what is to be said about the need for a social and ethical dimension in economic analysis and about the importance of trust in the context of learning.

3 For two different perspectives on the limits and the usefulness of codification, see Cowan et al. (2000) and Johnson et al. (2002)

4 This is also the background for developing a systemic approach to knowledge production (Freeman 1987; Lundvall 1992; Nelson 1993; Edquist 1997). Innovation systems may be defined as regional or national or as sector or technology specific. The common idea is that the specificities of knowledge production reflect unique combinations of technological specialization and institutional structure. In national systems, the education and training system and the institutional set up of labour markets are among the most important factors explaining national patterns and modes of innovation.

5 A more recent analysis of learning by doing focuses on how confronting new problems in the production process triggers searching and learning, which imply interaction between several parties as they seek solutions (von Hippel and Tyre 1995).

References

Abramowitz, M. and P. David. 1996. 'Technological Change and the Rise of Intangible Investments: The US Economy's Growth Path in the Twentieth Century'. In *Employment and Growth in the Knowledge Based Economy*, edited by D. Foray and B.-Å. Lundvall. Paris: OECD.

Antonelli, C. 1999. *The Micro-Dynamics of Technological Change*. London: Routledge.

Archibugi, D. and B.-Å. Lundvall (eds.). 2001. *The Globalizing Learning Economy*, Oxford: Oxford University Press.

Argyris, C. and D. Schon. 1978. *Organizational Learning*. Reading, MA: Addison-Wesley.

Arrow, K. J. 1962a. 'The Economic Implications of Learning by Doing'. *Review of Economic Studies* 29, no. 80.

———. 1962b. 'Economic Welfare and the Allocation of Resources for Invention'. In *The Rate and Direction of Inventive Activity: Economic and Social Factors*, edited by R. R. Nelson. Princeton, NJ: Princeton University Press.

———. 1971. 'Political and Economic Evaluation of Social Effects and Externalities'. In *Frontiers of Quantitative Economics*, edited by M. Intrilligator. North Holland.

———. 1974. *The Limits of Organisation*. New York: W.W. Norton and Co.

Carter, A. P. 1989. 'Know-how Trading as Economic Exchange'. *Research Policy* 18, no. 3.

———. 1994. 'Production Workers, Meta Investment and the Pace of Change'. Paper prepared for the meetings of the International J. A. Schumpeter Society, Munster, August.

Cohen, W. M. and D.A. Levinthal. 1990. 'Absorptive Capacity: A New Perspective on Learning and Innovation'. *Administrative Science Quarterly* 35: 128–52.

Cowan, R., P. A. David and D. Foray. 2000. 'The Explicit Economics of Knowledge Codification and Tacitness'. *Industrial and Corporate Change* 9: 211–53.

Dosi, G. *et al.* (eds.). *Technology and Economic Theory*. London: Pinter Publishers.

Drucker, P. 1993. *The Post-Capitalist Society*. Oxford: Butterworth Heinemann.

Edquist, C. (ed.). 1997. *Systems of Innovation: Technologies, Institutions and Organizations*. London: Pinter Publishers.

Eliasson, G. 1996. *Firm Objectives, Controls and Organization*. Netherlands: Kluwer Academic Publishers.

———. (2000) 'Industrial Policy, Competence Blocs and the Role of Science in Economic Development'. *Journal of Evolutionary Economics* 10: 217–41.

Foray, D. and B.-Å. Lundvall (eds.). 1996. 'The Knowledge-based Economy: From the Economics of Knowledge to the Learning Economy'. In *Employment and Growth in the Knowledge-based Economy*. Paris: OECD Documents.

Freeman, C. 1987. *Technology Policy and Economic Policy: Lessons from Japan*, London, Pinter.

Hatchuel, A. and B. Weil. 1995. *Experts in Organisations*. Berlin:Walter de Gruyter.

Johnson, B., E. Lorenz and B.-Å. Lundvall. 2002. 'Why All This Fuss about Codified and Tacit Knowledge?'. *Industrial and Corporate Change* 11, no. 2: 245–62.

Kline, S. J. and N. Rosenberg. 1986. 'An Overview of Innovation'. In *The positive Sum Game*, edited by R. Landau and N. Rosenberg. Washington DC: National Academy Press.

Kolb, D. A. 1984. *Experiential Learning*. Englewood Cliffs, NJ: Prentice Hall.

Lundvall, B.-Å. 1985. *Product Innovation and User-Producer Interaction*. Aalborg: Aalborg University Press.

———. 1988. 'Innovation as an Interactive Process – From User–Producer Interaction to the National System of Innovation'. In *Technical Change and Economic Theory*, edited by G. Dosi et al. London: Pinter Publishers.

———. (ed.). 1992. *National Systems of Innovation: Towards a Theory of Innovation and Interactive Learning*. London: Pinter Publishers.

Lundvall, B.-Å and B. Johnson, 1994. 'The Learning Economy'. *Journal of Industry Studies* 1, no. 2: 23–42.

Marshall, A. P. 1923. *Industry and Trade*. London: Macmillan.

Maskell, P. and A. Malmberg. 1999. 'Localised Learning and Industrial Competitiveness'. *Cambridge Journal of Economics* 23, no. 2: 167–185.

Murnane, R. J. and R. R. Nelson, 1984. 'Production and Innovation When Techniques Are Tacit'. *Journal of Economic Behaviour and Organization* 5, no. 3–4: 353–73.

Nelson, R. R. 1959. 'The Simple Economics of Basic Economic Research'. *Journal of Political Economy* 67: 323–48.

———. 1993. *National Innovation Systems: A Comparative Analysis*. Oxford: Oxford University Press.

Nonaka, I. and H. Takeuchi. 1995. *The Knowledge Creating Company*. Oxford: Oxford University Press.

OECD. 1994. *The OECD Jobs Study*. Paris: OECD.

———. 1996. *Transitions to Learning Economies and Societies*. Paris: OECD.

———. 1998. *Employment Outlook*. Paris: OECD.

———. 2000. *Knowledge Management in the Learning Society*. Paris: OECD.

Pavitt, K. 1984. 'Sectoral Patterns of Technical Change: Towards a Taxonomy'. *Research Policy* 13: 343–73.

———. 1998. 'Technologies, Products and Organisation in the Innovating Firm: What Adam Smith Tells Us and Joseph Schumpeter Doesn't'. Paper presented at the DRUID 1998 Summer Conference, Bornhom, June 9–11.

Penrose, E. 1959/1995. *The Theory of the Growth of the Firm*. Oxford: Oxford University Press.

Polanyi, M. 1958/1978. *Personal Knowledge*. London: Routledge & Kegan.

Rosenberg, N. 1982. *Inside the Black Box: Technology And Economics*. Cambridge: Cambridge University Press.

Rothwell, R. 1977. 'The Characteristics of Successful Innovators and Technically Progressive Firms'. *R&D Management* 7, no 3: 191–206.

Senge, P. 1990. *The Fifth Discipline: The Art and Practice of Learning.* New York: Doubleday.

Shapiro, C. and H. R. Varian. 1999. *Information Rules: A Strategic Guide to the Network Economy.* Boston: Harvard Business School Press.

Simon, H. A. 1955. 'A Behavioral Model of Rational Choice', *Quarterly Journal of Economics* 69: 99–118.

Tomlinson, M. 1999. 'The Learning Economy and Embodied Knowledge Flows in Great Britain'. *Journal of Evolutionary Economics* 9, no. 4: 431–51.

———. 2001. 'A New Role for Business Services in Economic Growth. In *The Globalizing Learning Economy, Guildford and King's Lynn,* edited by D. Archibugi and B.-Å. Lundvall. Oxford: Oxford University Press.

Verspagen, B. 1992. *Uneven Growth between Interdependent Economies.* Maastricht: Faculty of Economics and Business Administration.

von Hayek, F. A. 1945. 'The Use of Knowledge in Society'. *American Economic Review* 35, no. 4: 519–530.

Von Hippel, E. 1988. *The Sources of Innovation.* New York and Oxford: Oxford University Press.

———. 1994. 'Sticky Information and the Locus of Problem Solving: Implications for Innovation'. *Management Science* 40: 429–39.

Von Hippel E. and M. Tyre. 1995. 'How Learning by Doing Is Done: Problem Identification and Novel Process Equipment', *Research Policy* 24, no. 5.

Whitley, R. 1996. 'The Social Construction of Economic Actors: Institutions and Types of Firm in Europe and Other Market Economies'. In *The Changing European Firm,* edited by R. Whitley. London: Routledge.

Winter, S. 1987. 'Knowledge and Competence as Strategic Assets'. In *The Competitive Challenge: Strategy for Industrial Innovation and Renewal,* edited by D. Teece. Cambridge, MA: Ballinger Publishing Company.

Woolcock, M. 1998. 'Social Capital and Economic Development: Toward a Theoretical Synthesis and Policy Framework'. *Theory and Society* 27, no. 2: 151–207.

Ziman, J. 1979. *Reliable Knowledge.* Cambridge: Cambridge University Press.

Chapter 7

FORMS OF KNOWLEDGE AND MODES OF INNOVATION

Morten Berg Jensen, Björn Johnson, Edward Lorenz and
Bengt-Åke Lundvall

7.1 Introduction

This chapter is about the tension between two ideal type modes of learning and innovation. One mode is based on the production and use of codified scientific and technical knowledge namely Science, Technology and Innovation (STI) mode, while the other one is an experience-based mode of learning through Doing, Using and Interacting (DUI-mode). At the level of the firm, this tension may be seen in the need to reconcile knowledge management strategies prescribing the use of Information and Communication Technologies (ICT) as tools for codifying and sharing knowledge with strategies emphasizing the role played by informal communication and communities of practice in mobilizing tacit knowledge for problem solving and learning.

The tension between the STI- and DUI-modes corresponds to two different approaches to national innovation systems: One perspective focusing on the role of formal processes of R&D that produce explicit and codified knowledge and another perspective focusing on the learning from informal interaction within and between organizations resulting in competence building often with tacit elements.

There is, of course, an important body of empirical and historical work showing that both these modes of learning and innovation play a role in most sectors, the role being different depending on the sector characteristics as well as the strategy of the firm (Von Hippel 1976; Rothwell 1977; Rosenberg 1982; Pavitt 1984). Recent models of innovation emphasize that innovation is an interactive process in which firms interact both with customers and suppliers and with knowledge institutions (Freeman 1986; Kline and Rosenberg 1986; Lundvall 1988; Vinding 2002).

Despite the broad acceptance of this literature, there remains a bias among scholars and policymakers to consider innovation processes largely as aspects connected to formal processes of R&D, especially in the science-based industries. At the policy level, this can be seen in the emphasis on benchmarking variables related to STI and in the focus on instruments such as tax subsidies to R&D, the training of scientists in high-tech fields such as ICT, bio and nanotechnology and strengthening the linkages between firms and universities in these specific fields. At the level of scholarly research, there is a tendency to expect that the increasing reliance on science and technology in the 'knowledge-based economy' will enhance the role played by formal processes of R&D requiring personnel with formal science and technology qualifications. And the vast majority of quantitative survey based studies of innovation simply have little to say about the relation of DUI-mode learning to innovative performance.[1]

In what follows we argue that by focusing the analysis on the frameworks and structures that promote learning within and across organizations, it is both possible to develop meaningful measures of DUI-mode learning and to demonstrate that firms can promote such learning through particular practices and policies. Utilizing data from a project on the Danish innovation system in comparative perspective (the DISKO-project (see Lundvall 2002 for a report from the project), we present what we believe to be the first quantitative survey based analysis of the way the two modes of learning contribute to innovative performance. Our empirical results not only show that the two modes of learning are practiced with different intensities in different firms but also that firms combining them are more innovative.

In sections 7.2 and 7.3 we develop definitions of the two modes of learning and show how they are connected to different types of knowledge. Section 7.4 explores the relations between the two modes, pointing to factors that encourage firms to adopt mixed strategies combining the two modes rather than relying predominately on one mode or the other. Section 7.5 develops the empirical indicators of the modes and explores econometrically the relation between their use and innovative performance for a representative sample of Danish firms. Section 7.6 relates the two modes of learning to innovation system research and points to important policy implications.

7.2 What Is Knowledge?

7.2.1 Explicit versus implicit knowledge

The two learning modes presented and analysed in this chapter relate to different types of knowledge. Thinking about knowledge seems to have resulted in a number of two-sided distinctions (dichotomies). We have already mentioned the distinction between tacit and codified knowledge (or rather between tacit and codified elements of knowledge) on which there is now a vast literature and a lively debate (Cowan et al. 2001; Johnson et al. 2002). One way to make knowledge explicit is to write it down. Knowledge that can be written down may be passed on to others and be absorbed by those who can read and understand the specific language. But absorbing such knowledge is seldom automatic – the idea of effortless 'knowledge transfer' is normally misleading and a 'prepared mind' helps a lot when it comes to absorbing codified knowledge. Furthermore, often knowledge can be partially but not totally written down as for example in the typical 'book of instruction'. In order to understand messages about the world, you need to have some prior knowledge about it. In order to implement 'recipes' about how to manage and change the world, you will often need to have prior skills and competences. Scientific texts give meaning only to other scientists and manuals may prove useful only to highly skilled workers. This implies that codified knowledge that stands alone is not economically useful.

7.2.2 Local versus global knowledge

Codification and efforts to make explicit what is implicit may be seen as one important way to enhance the capacity to share knowledge in society. But to codify knowledge does not necessarily make it more accessible to others. Using a 'secret code' is a way to establish the opposite effect. In his seminal article from 1974, Kenneth Arrow uses the concept 'codes of information' with reference to more efficient means of communication inside an organization to the exclusion of outsiders. Lundvall (1988) drew on Arrow's insight in arguing that establishing common codes provides a basis for efficient local communication between users and producers in the context of product innovation.

Neither is codification the only way to generalize knowledge. Education and training systems generalize knowledge and 'embody' knowledge in people. Machinery producers may embody general knowledge in technical systems and knowledge intensive business service firms may deliver disembodied general knowledge to customers as standard solutions. The mobility of workers is another important mechanism for spreading experience-based knowledge.[2] From the point of view of the whole economy, the transformation of local knowledge into global knowledge is of great interest.

Actually in economic practice, it is seldom a question of working with knowledge that is either tacit or codified. The zone in between and the complementarities between the tacit and codified elements of knowledge are often what matters most (Nonaka and Takeuchi 1995). The same is true for the distinction between local and global knowledge. When we make the distinction between the two modes of innovation and relate this to the different forms of knowledge, this should be kept in mind. What is referred to are two 'ideal types' that appear in a much more mixed form in real life.

7.2.3 From know-what to know-who

The dichotomies mentioned above have played an important role in the discussion of the concept of knowledge in business and economics, and they have contributed to a better understanding of its intricacy. They, in turn, can be linked to a somewhat more elaborate set of distinctions developed by Lundvall and Johnson (1994) that are useful for understanding the different channels and mechanisms through which learning of different types of knowledge takes place.

* Know-what
* Know-why
* Know-how
* Know-who

Learning these four types of knowledge tends to take place in different ways and through different channels. While important aspects of know-what and know-why may be obtained through reading books, attending lectures and accessing databases, the other two categories are more rooted in practical experience. Written manuals may be helpful but in order to use them, some prior basic skills in the field of application are usually needed. The STI-mode gives high priority to the production of 'know-why' while the DUI-mode typically will produce 'know-how' and 'know-who'. However, at the same time, very specialized 'know-what' is often a prerequisite for operating in a science-based learning mode.

Know-how will typically be learnt in apprenticeship relations where the apprentice follows his master, studies his 'body language' as well as his spoken language and relies on his authority (Polanyi 1958/1978, 53 et passim). Know-how is what characterizes a skilled worker and an artisan, but it is also something that distinguishes the first-rate from the average manager and scientist.

Know-who is also learnt in social practice, and some of it is learnt in specialized education environments. Communities of engineers and experts are kept together through reunions, conferences and professional societies, etc. giving the participant access to discussion of experiences and information bartering with professional colleagues (Carter 1989). It also develops through day-to-day dealings with customers, subcontractors and independent institutes.

Relational learning may contribute both to common codes of information and to social bonds of friendship.

7.3 Forms of Knowledge and Modes of Learning

7.3.1 The STI-mode

The different types of knowledge may be related to differences in the two modes of learning and innovation that we have identified. It will be easier to bring out these relationships if we start by recognizing that technologies should be 'understood as involving both a body of practice, manifest in the artefacts and techniques that are produced and used, and a body of understanding which supports, surrounds and rationalizes the former' (Nelson 2004, 457). Some of this understanding takes the form of empirical-based generalizations made explicit by practitioners about what works and what constitutes reliable problem-solving methods. Although this kind of know-how may be specific to particular firms, much of it is more generalized knowledge common to wider professional or technical communities who work within the same technological fields.

However, as Nelson (1993, 2004) and others have observed[3] over the twentieth century, most powerful technologies have come to be connected to and supported by different fields of science. One of the stylized facts emerging from the research on the relation between science and technology is that in most areas, the results of scientific research are not directly useful for technological advance.[4] Rather, the contribution of science is usually more indirect. General scientific understanding both 'illuminates how artefacts and techniques employed work', thus providing guidance and clues for their further development, and provides 'powerful ways of experimenting and testing new departures' (Nelson 2004, 458).[5] For example, as Pavitt (2005, 92) has observed, advances in computing and simulation methods can reduce the costs of search in technological advancement by making it possible to explore virtually alternative technical configurations.

Thus, as Brooks (1994, 478) notes, technology should be seen as incorporating generic understanding (know-why), which makes it seem like science. Yet it is the understanding pertaining to particular artefacts and techniques that distinguishes technology from science. The STI-mode of innovation most obviously refers to the way firms use and further develop this body of science-like understanding in the context of their innovative activities. Over the twentieth century, and still today, a major source for the development of this knowledge about artefacts and techniques has been the R&D laboratories of large industrial firms (Mowery and Oxley 1995; Chandler 1977).

The emphasis placed here on the way STI uses and further develops explicit and global know-why and know-what should not be taken to imply an insignificant role for locally embedded tacit knowledge. For instance, scientists operating at the frontier of their fields in the R&D departments of large firms need to combine their know-why insights with know-how when making experiments and interpreting results, and specific R&D projects will often be triggered by practice, for example, problems with new products, processes and user needs. We will still define it as predominantly STI because almost immediately attempts will be made to restate the problem in an explicit and codified form. The R&D department will start going through its earlier work, looking for pieces of codified knowledge, as well as looking for insights that can be drawn from outside sources. In order to communicate with scientists and scientific institutions outside, it will be necessary to make knowledge explicit and translate the problem into a formal scientific code. In the empirical section of the chapter, we use R&D activities and collaboration with scientists attached to universities and research institute as indicators of the STI-mode.

All through the process, documenting results in a codified form remains important. It is not sufficient that a single scientist keeps results in his own memory as tacit knowledge. Often the project involves teamwork and modularization where single results are used as building blocks for other members in the team. At the end of the process – if it is successful – a transfer of the results within the organization or across organizational borders will call for documentation as well. In the case that an application is made for a patent, the documentation needs to be made in a techno-scientific language that allows the patenting authority to judge the originality of the innovation.

This means that, on balance, the STI-mode of learning even if it starts from a local problem will make use of 'global' knowledge all the way through and ideally, it will end up with 'potentially global knowledge' (i.e., knowledge that could be used widely if it were not protected by intellectual property rights). In terms of knowledge management it corresponds well to a strategy of knowledge sharing through wide access to codified knowledge inside the firm. The generalization of the knowledge in the form of a patent and the use of licenses will make it disembodied at least when compared to what comes out of the DUI-mode of innovation.[6]

7.3.2 The DUI-mode

While scientific understandings have increasingly come to illuminate and support technological practice, it is still the case that 'much of practice in most fields remains only partially understood and much of engineering design practice involves solutions to problems that professional engineers have learned "work" without any particularly sophisticated under-standing of why' (Nelson 2004, 458). This provides the first hint as to why the DUI-mode is crucial to successful innovation. This kind of knowledge, regardless of the extent to which it is ultimately codified, is acquired for the most part on the job as employees face ongoing changes that confront them with new problems. Finding solutions to these problems enhances the skills and know-how of the employees and extends their repertoires. Some of the problems are specific while others are generic. Therefore learning may result in both specific and general competencies for the operator. When the process is complex – a good example is the learning by using of new models of air-planes – it will involve interaction within and between teams, and it may result in new shared routines for the organization. As the whole organization gets more insight into the actual working of the system, it might find more efficient ways to organize work and solve problems as they pop up. This is the kind of case that Rosenberg (1982) uses to illustrate learning by using.

Both learning by doing and using normally also involve interaction between people and departments. In particular, an important result coming out of empirical surveys on the innovation process is that successful innovation depends on the development of links and communication between the design department and production and sale (Rothwell 1977). These links are typically informal and serve to transmit the tacit elements that contribute to making successful designs that can be produced and that respond to user demands. As Lundvall (1992) and others have shown, these links extend beyond the bound-aries of the firm to connect relatively small specialized machinery producers and business service providers with their mostly larger clients.

As the above discussion implies, the DUI-mode of learning most obviously refers to know-how and know-who, which is tacit and often highly localized. While this kind of learning may occur as an unintended byproduct of the firm's design, production and marketing activities, the point we want to make here is that the DUI-mode can be intentionally fostered by building struc-tures and relationships, which enhance and utilize learning by doing, using and interacting. In particular, organizational practices such as project teams, problem-solving groups, and job and task rotation, which promote learning and knowledge exchange, can contribute positively to innovation performance.

There is a vast business literature on 'high performance work systems' that examines the relation of such organizational practices to enterprise productiv-ity and financial performance in general (see, for example, Becker and Huselid 1998; Osterman 1994, 2000; Ramsay et al. 2000; Wood 1999). One of the most interesting empirical results based on the statistical analysis of national or international survey data is that there is a positive relation between the organi-zational practices identified in this high performance literature and successful product innovation (Laursen and Foss 2003; Lorenz et al. 2004; Lorenz and Valeyre 2006; Lundvall and Nielsen 1999; Michie and Sheenan 1999).

Since this experience-based learning results in 'local' knowledge, we should not expect it to have any radical impact on the growth of the whole economy. To lift knowledge out of its local context, to generalize it and to make it global, there are different mechanisms including learning by interacting, which we regard as part of the DUI-mode of learning (Christensen and Lundvall 2004). For the economy as a whole, *a specific sector* may become the one that – through its engagement in processes of interactive learning with a diverse set of users – generalizes local knowledge and diffuses it widely in the economy.

Historically, as Rosenberg (1976) has shown, machinery production consti- tuted a strategic sector. Machinery producers addressed many different users and gathered knowledge about their needs and about the performance of dif- ferent technical solutions. In this way, they developed more global and efficient solutions on the basis of local knowledge and learning. Today, we may see similar specialization and technological convergence with respect to informa- tion technology (Pavitt 2005) and to the role played by *knowledge intensive business service* (KIBS) providers. For the single manufacturing firm, it is attractive to outsource certain service functions to specialized KIBS firms. The KIBS firm will address several customers and help them to solve their problems in a well- defined field. This gives access to many different processes of local learning taking place under diverse conditions. The KIBS firm will be able to transform this diversity of experiences into more global and more efficient solutions.

7.4 The Need for a New Empirical Approach

The importance of both STI- and DUI-mode learning for innovation per- formance is well documented in both the theoretical and the qualitative case study literature on innovation. Yet, when one turns to policy analysis and pre- scription as well as to the quantitative survey-based studies, which often serve to support and justify policy, we would contend there is a clear bias to consider innovation processes largely as aspects connected to formal scientific and tech- nical knowledge and to formal processes of R&D.

At the European level, this kind of bias can be most easily seen by exam- ining the empirical measures used and the supporting research undertaken for EU-sponsored benchmarking exercises, such as Trendchart.[7] Trendchart's annual ranking of the innovative performance of EU member nations is based largely on conventional S&T measures such as R&D expenditures, patenting, the share of the population with tertiary education, the weight of S&E graduates in the workforce, ICT expenditures and the importance of venture capital. None of the 22 individual measures that are used to construct the 2004 'summary innovation index' for EU member countries are designed to capture organizational aspects linked to informal processes of learning by using, doing and interacting.

A Trendchart workshop focusing on the extent of an 'innovation gap' between the EU and the United States is representative of the survey-based research supporting such innovation benchmarking exercises. It is notable that the scoping paper for the workshop explains the gap exclusively in terms of R&D expenditures, patenting and the importance of tertiary education.[8]

Of course it can be argued with some justification that this sort of bias in policy and quantitative research reflects the kinds of quantitative measures that are available for comparative research. There now exist internationally harmonized data on R&D, patenting, the development of S&T human resources, ICT expenditures and innovation expenditures more generally, whereas at present there are no harmonized data that could be used to construct measures of learning by doing and using. We would contend, though, that these limitations of the data simply reflect the same bias at a deeper level. The ongoing development of harmonized S&T indicators over the postwar period has resulted from political initiatives at the EU and international levels. The lack of DUI measures reflects political priorities and decision-making rather than any inevitable state of affairs.

A final argument seeking to justify the existing bias in quantitative measures is that organizational change and learning processes linked to DUI-mode learning are simply too complex to capture with survey-based methods. While we would agree that the multi-dimensional and multi-level nature of these informal learning dynamics creates problems for measurement that go beyond those confronted in measuring R&D and the development of human resources for science and technology, we firmly believe that these can be surmounted. In what follows we propose a set of indicators for DUI-mode learning, and we show that the DUI-mode when combined with the STI-mode serves to improve innovation performance.

7.5 Empirical Analysis

7.5.1 Illustrating empirically how DUI- and STI-learning promote innovation

In what follows we will show that the probability of successful product innovation increases when the firm has organized itself in such a way that it promotes DUI-learning. We will also show that firms that establish a stronger science base will be more innovative than the rest. But the most significant and important result is that firms using mixed strategies – that combine organizational forms promoting learning with R&D-efforts and cooperation with researchers at knowledge institutions – are much more innovative than the rest. *It is the firm that combines a strong version of the STI-mode with a strong version of the DUI-mode that excels in product innovation.*

The empirical analysis is based on a survey addressed to all Danish firms in the private sector – not including agriculture – with 25 or more employees, supplemented with a stratified proportional sample of firms with 20–25 employees. Selected firms received 6,991 questionnaires. This survey collected information from management. In total, 2,007 usable responses from management have been collected and integrated in a cross-sectional data set. This makes the overall response rate of the survey 29 per cent. A closer response analysis broken down on industries and size shows acceptable variations on response rates here, and nonrespondent information on some of the potential dependent variables together with comparison to other surveys does not indicate unacceptable bias.

The survey, which was carried out in 2001, was supplemented in 2004 by additional questions designed to obtain further information on STI-mode learning processes. The sampling frame in the 2004 survey was the 1,688 firms from the 2001 survey, which were still alive according to the information held by Statistics Denmark. However, of these 1,688 firms, 45 were unreachable, which left us with a sampling frame of 1,643 firms. Of these firms, 1,141 answered the second questionnaire, resulting in an impressive response rate for the second questionnaire of almost 70 per cent. The subsequent analysis of the response rates indicates no unacceptable variation within size and industry.

Finally, we have access to register data, allowing us to determine the workforce composition for the relevant firms. As the latent class analysis requires answers to all the questions considered in the analysis, the number of firms available for undertaking this analysis (see Table 7.2) is reduced to 692.

Obtaining a meaningful quantitative measure of innovation and innovative behaviour on the basis of information collected in firms belonging to industries with very different conditions is not unproblematic. The phenomenon that firms refer to may vary in relation to conditions and configurations. Our data indicate that for the most part we are confronted with incremental qualitative change rather than radical change when we ask the firms whether they, during the period of 1998–2000, have introduced new products or services to the market. Three-fourths of the innovations introduced within the period 1998–2000 were already known at the national as well as international markets. Thirteen per cent of the firms have introduced at least one innovation new to the national market, although already existing in the world markets. A small group of firms (6%) have introduced at least one innovation that is new both to the national and the world market.

7.5.2 Developing indicators of STI- and DUI-mode learning

Two of the three measures we used to capture STI-mode learning are standard measures used to benchmark science and technology development in innovation policy studies: expenditures on R&D and the employment of personnel with third-level degrees in science or technology. Although of recognized importance, the third measure – cooperation with researchers attached to universities or research institutes – is less commonly used in policy studies due to the lack of survey data.

For DUI-mode learning, the choice of measures is based on a reading of two complementary literatures that deal with the characteristics of 'learning organizations': the 'high performance work system' literature referred to above (Clegg et al. 1996; Dertoutzos et al. 1989; Gittleman et al. 1998; Osterman 1994, 2000; Ramsay et al. 2000; Truss 2001; Wood 1999) and the literature dealing with the relation between organizational design and innovation (Burns and Stalker 1961; Mintzberg 1979; Lam 2005). Both of these literatures draw a distinction between relatively bureaucratic or rigid organizations and those with a greater capacity for learning and innovative response, though the latter has tended to develop somewhat more elaborate typologies of organizational forms. The 'high performance' literature focuses on the diffusion of specific organizational practices and arrangements that enhance the firm's capacity for responding to changes in markets and technology. These include practices designed to increase employees' involvement in problem solving and decision-making such as autonomous teams, problem-solving groups and systems for collecting employee suggestions. The first four of our six indicators of DUI-mode learning measure whether or not the firm makes use of the core high-performance work practices.

A similar contrast between rigid and adaptable organizations can be seen in Burns and Stalker's (1961) distinction between 'mechanistic' and 'organic' organizations, or in Mintzberg's (1979) distinction between the 'machine bureaucracy' and the 'operating adhocracy'. Lam (2005) also distinguishes between rigid and flexible organizations while making a further distinction between two relatively flexible organizational forms that support learning and innovation: the 'operating adhocracy' and the 'J-form'. The term J-form is used because its archetypical features are best illustrated by the 'Japanese-type' organization discussed in the work of Aoki (1988) and Nonaka and Takeuchi (1995). In order to capture the difference between relatively hierarchical and rigid organizations, on the one hand, and the more flexible and decentralized structure of learning organizations, on the other, we included a measure of the extent to which functions are integrated and a measure of the extent to which demarcations are softened (Table 7.1).[9]

Table 7.1 Indicators of DUI- and STI-mode learning

Indicators

DUI-mode learning

Interdisciplinary workgroups	1 if the firm makes some use of interdisciplinary groups, 0 otherwise
Quality circles	1 if the firm makes some use of quality circles, 0 otherwise
Systems for collecting proposals	1 if the firm makes some use of systems for collective proposals, 0 otherwise
Autonomous groups	1 if the firm makes some use of autonomous groups, 0 otherwise
Integration of functions	1 if the firm makes some use of integration of functions, 0 otherwise
Softened demarcations	1 if demarcations between employee groupings have become more indistinct or invisible during 1998–2000, 0 if they are unchanged or have become more distinct
Cooperation with customers	1 if the firm has developed closer cooperation with customers during 1998–2000 to a high extent, 0 if to a small or medium extent or not at all

STI-mode learning

Expenditures on R&D as share of total revenue	1 if the firm's expenditures on R&D are positive, 0 otherwise
Cooperation with researchers	1 if the firm cooperates with researches attached to universities or scientific institutes rarely, occasionally, frequently or always, 0 if it never engages in these forms of cooperation
Indicator for workforce composition	Register data indicating whether a firm employs scientifically trained personnel.[10] 1 if the firm employs scientifically trained personal, 0 otherwise

In order to find out how the different DUI measures are combined with the capacity to handle scientific and codified knowledge, we have pursued a clustering across firms using latent-class analysis. Latent-class analysis can be seen as an alternative to the more familiar cluster analysis methods (e.g., methods based on proximity measures of the observations. For an elaborate review, see e.g., Hagenaars and McCutcheon (2003)). The latent-class analysis is able to cope with data that are measured on a nominal or ordinal measurement scale. In addition the technique is based on a statistical model such that the goodness-of-fit of the model can be measured and tested. The outcome of the latent-class analysis consists of the conditional probabilities for implementing a particular practice given that the firm is from a particular cluster. Moreover, it is possible to estimate the cluster membership given a firm has implemented a particular set of practices. The latter is used in the logistic analysis further ahead. Table 7.2 presents the results as they come out when the 4-cluster solution is used and in Appendix 2 the goodness-of-fit of the model is shown together with the results of an alternative 5-cluster solution. The percentage figures presented in Table 7.2 show the probability that a firm in a particular cluster is characterized by a practice or policy.

The first cluster is a static or low-learning cluster. It brings together firms that neither have highly developed forms of organizations that support DUI-learning nor engage in activities that indicate a strong capacity to absorb and use codified knowledge. The low-learning cluster encompasses firms that do not spend on R&D nor cooperate with researchers. The latter may be explained by the fact that these firms have a low probability of employing scientifically trained personnel.

The second cluster, which we refer to as the STI cluster, encompasses about 10 per cent of the firms. Firms belonging to the STI cluster have activities that indicate a strong capacity to absorb and use codified knowledge. However, the firms in the STI cluster have rarely implemented organizational characteristics typical for the learning organizations. The STI cluster includes firms that have established the STI-mode without combining it with the DUI-mode.

The third cluster, which we refer to as the DUI cluster, brings together about one-third of the firms in a group that is characterized by an over-average development of organizational characteristics typical for the learning organization but without activities that indicate a strong capacity to absorb and use codified knowledge. The firms in this cluster have a low probability of employing scientifically trained personnel and their cooperation with researchers attached to universities or research institutes is below average. This cluster includes firms that have introduced elements of the DUI-mode but are weak in terms of using the STI-mode.

The fourth cluster includes firms using mixed strategies that combine the DUI and STI modes. It includes one-fifth of the firms and these firms tend to combine the characteristics indicating a strong capacity for informal experience-based learning with activities that indicate a strong capacity to absorb and use codified knowledge.

These outcomes of the latent class analysis are interesting. They indicate that quite a number of firms that operate in economic activities where scientific and codified knowledge are important have also adopted organizational

Table 7.2 Clustering of 692 Danish firms based on latent class analysis: probability that a firm will be characterized by a policy/practice according to cluster

	Low-Learning Cluster	STI Cluster	DUI Cluster	DUI/STI Cluster	All Firms
Makes use of interdisciplinary workgroups	0.1155	0.0143	0.5448	0.9888	0.3960
Makes use of quality circles	0.0159	0.2670	0.5054	0.5483	0.2890
Makes use of systems for proposals	0.1481	0.3554	0.6253	0.5757	0.3931
Makes use of autonomous groups	0.2145	0.4427	0.5320	0.6139	0.4090
Makes use of integration of functions	0.1346	0.2254	0.5545	0.6392	0.3642
Demarcations more indistinct/invisible	0.2709	0.4879	0.5671	0.6256	0.4494
Ccoperation with customers high	0.2582	0.4292	0.5512	0.4970	0.4090
R&D expenditures positive	0.1002	0.9875	0.2977	0.8742	0.4017
Ccoperation with researchers positive	0.1088	0.8586	0.2195	0.9550	0.3829
Employs scientifically trained personnel	0.0854	0.3544	0.1091	0.6826	0.2341
Percentage distribution of firms across clusters	0.4050	0.1099	0.2974	0.1877	1.0000

practices designed to promote knowledge exchange, problem solving and learning among their employees (DUI/STI cluster). But there are also a number of firms in the STI cluster where knowledge flows exist between the firm and external partners with over 95 per cent spending on R&D and more than 85 per cent cooperating with researchers, but where there is little evidence of the practices designed to promote employee learning and problem solving. Finally, the share of firms belonging to the DUI cluster is quite high. Hence there exists a significant group of firms that might well be transformed so as to acquire the characteristics of the combined DUI/STI cluster. Below we present evidence that indicates that such a transformation might stimulate innovation.

Table 7.3 shows the frequency distribution of the different clusters by firm size, industry, group ownership and production. It is clear that the different clusters are distributed unevenly across industry, size and ownership. In terms of size, it is not surprising to find that relative to the population average the smallest firm size category is overrepresented in the low-learning cluster. The other result that stands out is the marked overrepresentation of the 100 and over employee size category in the combined STI/DUI cluster. The mid-range 50–99 employee category is somewhat overrepresented in the stand alone STI and DUI clusters. In terms of sector, it is not surprising to find that construction, trade and other services are underrepresented in the STI and DUI/STI clusters given the relatively low levels of R&D expenditure that characterize these sectors. Foreign groups tend to be overrepresented in the STI and DUI/STI clusters suggesting that they are characterized by relatively high levels of R&D and relatively well-developed links with universities or research institutes. Single firms, on the other hand, tend to be underrepresented in these two clusters. The frequency distribution of the standard and customized product categories across the clusters tends to conform to the population averages with the exception that the standard product category is slightly overrepresented in the STI cluster.

In order to examine the effect of the learning modes on the firm innovative performance, we use logistic regression analysis as reported in Table 7.4. The dependent variable for this exercise is whether or not the firm has introduced to the market a new product or service (P/S innovation) over the last three years. The independent variables in the Model 1 specification are binary variables indicating whether or not the firm belongs to a particular cluster. In the Model 2 specification, we include control variables to account for the effects of industry, firm size, ownership structure and whether the firm produces customized or standard products.

Table 7.3 The frequency of the three clusters by firm size, sector, group ownership and production type (per cent horizontal)

Variables	Low-Learning Cluster	STI Cluster	DUI Cluster	DUI/STI Cluster	N
Less than 50 employees	0.5605	0.0855	0.2566	0.0973	339
50–99 employees	0.3314	0.1775	0.3018	0.1893	169
100 and more employees	0.2457	0.1257	0.2686	0.3600	175
Manufacturing, high tech	0.2231	0.2645	0.2314	0.2810	121
Manufacturing, low tech	0.3522	0.1321	0.2893	0.2264	159
Construction	0.6139	0.0495	0.2574	0.0792	101
Trade	0.5780	0.0462	0.3064	0.0694	173
Business service	0.2727	0.0909	0.2576	0.3788	66
Other services	0.6512	0.0465	0.2791	0.0233	43
Danish group	0.4073	0.1371	0.2460	0.2097	248
Foreign group	0.2903	0.1694	0.2903	0.2500	124
Single firm	0.4890	0.0789	0.2776	0.1546	317
Standard product	0.3574	0.1687	0.2851	0.1888	249
Customized product	0.4518	0.0871	0.2635	0.1976	425
All firms	0.4249	0.1171	0.2673	0.1908	692

Table 7.4 Logistic regression of learning clusters on product/service innovation

Variables	Model 1 (without controls)		Model 2 (with controls)	
	Odds ratio estimate	Coefficient estimate	Odds ratio estimate	Coefficient estimate
STI cluster	3.529	1.2611**	2.355	0.8564**
DUI cluster	2.487	0.9109**	2.218	0.7967**
DUI/STI cluster	7.843	2.0596**	5.064	1.6222**
Business services			1.433	0.3599
Construction			0.491	−0.7120*
Manufacturing (high tech)			1.805	0.5905*
Manufacturing (low tech)			1.250	0.2229
Other services			0.747	−0.2923
100 and more employees			1.757	0.5635*
50–99 employees			0.862	−0.1481
Danish group			0.859	−0.1524
Single firm			0.521	−0.6526*
Customized product			1.378	0.3203
Pseudo R^2	0.1247	0.1247	0.1775	0.1775
N	692	692	692	692

Note: ** = significant at the .01 level; * = significant at the .05 level.

Using the static or low-learning cluster as benchmark, the Model 1 results without controls show that the probability of introducing a new product or service to the market for firms belonging to the DUI cluster is more than twice as high, while for the STI cluster the probability is more than three times. The difference is significant for both clusters. We find an almost eight times as high a chance of P/S innovation for the combined DUI/STI cluster firms, and here the difference is also highly significant.[11]

When we add the control variables to account for the effects of size, sector, ownership and product type (Model 2), the difference observed in the probability of P/S innovation between the STI and DUI clusters disappears. For firms grouped in the combined DUI/STI cluster, the probability of innovating decreases substantially to approximately five times as high as for those grouped in the low-learning cluster. In the case of the STI cluster, the difference between the Model 1 and Model 2 results can most plausibly be accounted for by this cluster's overrepresentation in the high-tech sector, which has a positive and significant impact on the probability of innovation, and its underrepresentation in the construction and single-firm categories both of which have negative and significant impacts on the probability of innovation. For the combined DUI/STI cluster, the decrease in the size of the odds ratio estimate in the Model 2 results can similarly be explained by this cluster's overrepresentation in the high-tech category and its underrepresentation in construction. A further factor is the overrepresentation of the DUI/STI cluster in the 100 and over employee firm size category, which has a positive impact on the probability of innovation.

Overall, the results of the logistic analysis show that adopting DUI-mode enhancing practices and policies tends to increase firm innovative performance. Further, they support the view that firms adopting mixed strategies combining the two modes tend to perform better than those relying predominately on one mode or the other.

7.6 Conclusion: Implications for Innovation Analysis and Policy

Our empirical analysis indicates the existence in the Danish economy of both DUI and STI firms. The indication is a bit stronger for the STI-mode, but we can also discern a group of firms that have introduced DUI-mode practices without connecting strongly to external research and without engaging in R&D.

One of the areas where the explicit distinction between the two modes of learning may be of special interest is the study of innovation systems (Freeman 1987; Lundvall 1992; Nelson 1993; Edquist 1997). One common assumption behind the idea of innovation systems is that elements of knowledge important for economic performance are localized and not easily moved from one place to another. It is obvious that in a fictive neoclassical world where knowledge was identical to information and where society was populated with perfectly rational agents, each with unlimited access to information, national innovation systems would be a completely unnecessary construct. In this sense, there is an implicit assumption that some of the learning in a system of innovation takes place in the DUI-mode.

Further, recognizing and analysing the coexistence, coevolution and synergies between the DUI- and STI-modes more systematically may represent progress in innovation theory. It might correspond to how the 'innovation as an interactive process' perspective overcame the traditional split between those who argued that supply-side factors were most important and those arguing that demand factors determine the rate and direction of innovation.

In this respect, it is important to note that the two modes of learning and innovation, though present to a greater or lesser degree, do not exclude each other. Actually, elements of both are present in all business activities in sectors where innovation is an option. Any strategy to promote innovation needs to take both of these sources of innovation into account. While the STI-mode may be of marginal importance in some informally organized businesses the firms that use the STI-mode most intensely will be highly dependent on the successful organization of the DUI-mode.

Our cluster analysis indicates that many firms that are involved in STI learning have established organizational elements related to the DUI-mode. They will operate in sectors where there is supply-driven and sometimes radical change in products and processes. To cope with these changes, the need for learning by doing, using and interacting will be strongly felt. Likewise for firms in traditional sectors, it is no longer sufficient to base competitiveness on know-how and DUI-learning. Firms that connect more systematically to sources of codified knowledge may be able to find new solutions and develop new products that make them more competitive. Moreover, the cluster analysis shows that what really improves innovation performance is using mixed strategies that combine strong versions of the two modes.[12]

It also shows that the two modes of learning coexist and can be made to complement each other, which doesn't necessarily mean that they are always in harmony with each other. Sometimes there may be contradictions between them, which have to be tackled before potential benefits could be reaped. The STI-mode calls for codification and for codes that are general while the DUI-mode tends to thrive on the basis of implicit and local codes. It is a major task for knowledge management to make strong versions of the two modes work together in promoting knowledge creation and innovation.

Our results strongly suggest that firms with an exclusive focus on developing their science and technology base are foregoing important gains that could be reaped by adopting practices and measures designed to promote informal learning by using and doing. This has major implications for benchmarking innovation systems and for innovation policy. As we have observed in the current European 'innovation scoreboard', there is a strong bias towards indicators that reflect the STI-mode while those referring to the DUI-mode are absent. Our results clearly point to the need to develop harmonized indicators of the DUI-mode to arrive at an adequate understanding of the bases for differences in innovative performance.

Correspondingly, it also implies the need for a realignment of policy objectives and priorities given the tendency to develop innovation policy with a one-sided focus on promoting the science base of high-technology firms. Equally, it suggests that too little attention is being given to policies that serve to strengthen linkages to sources of codified knowledge for firms operating in traditional manufacturing sectors and services more generally.

Thinking in terms of the two modes and their evolution in the learning economy may also have implications for wider aspects of public policy and institution building. Education may prepare students to work with specialized global codes in the different disciplines as well as involve them in learning to develop and use local codes through problem-based learning. The design of intellectual property rights and of labour contracts might need to strike a balance between the two modes. Organizing innovation policy and distributing responsibility between, for instance, ministries of education, science, industry and economic affairs needs to balance the two modes in innovation policy.

It is our contention that applying the STI- and DUI-modes of learning to innovation systems and to analyse how they coevolve is a way to clarify and further develop this concept. This is true not only for national systems but also for sectoral, technological and regional systems (Breschi and Malerba 1997; Carlsson and Jacobsson 1997; Maskell and Malmberg 1997). Our empirical analysis demonstrates, not surprisingly, that the modes are applied with different weights in different sectors, and this implies that regional specialization and clustering will also make them appear differently in geographical space.

Of course in the context of this chapter, we can only hint at these possible consequences of our framework. Our main objective has been to demonstrate the usefulness of the conceptual distinction between the DUI- and STI-modes of learning and to demonstrate that these concepts can be made operational. If we have succeeded at that task, we are confident that future research will take up the wider implications for institution building in the learning economy.

Appendix 1 The Questions Used and the Original Coding in the Questionnaire

Table A7.1 The questions used in the survey

	Original coding in the questionnaire			N	Coding used in his chapter		N
	Yes	No	Don't know		Yes	No	
Does the firm make use of some of the following ways of planning the work and paying the employees?							
Interdisciplinary workgroups	38.12%	59.47%	2.41%	1907	39.60%	60.40%	692
Quality circles/groups (Formal delegation of quality control)	28.14%	68.03%	3.83%	1905	28.90%	71.10%	692
Systems for collecting proposals from employees	37.79%	59.07%	3.14%	1913	39.31%	60.69%	692
Autonomous groups	41.35%	56.36%	2.29%	1925	40.90%	59.10%	692
Integration of functions (e.g., sales, production)	33.63%	59.41%	6.96%	1897	36.42%	63.58%	692
How have the demarcations between the employee groupings within production/service (main field) developed during 1998–2000? Are they	More distinct	More indistinct	Invisible during the period	Invisible before the period	Remain unchanged	Only one occupational group in production/service	More indistinct + Invisible during the period + Invisible before the period	More distinct + Remain unchanged

Table A7.1 (*cont.*)

	Original coding in the questionnaire	N	Coding used in his chapter	N
To which extent has the firm developed a closer co-operation with the following actors during 1998–2000? Customers	5.98% High extent; 30.57% Some extent; 2.10% Small extent; 3.27% Not at all; 45.71% Don't know; 12.37% Not relevant	1956	44.94% High extent; 55.06% Some extent + Small extent + Not at all	692
How large a share of total revenue did expenditure on R&D constitute	39.75% 0%; 46.77% 0–2%; 8.35% 3–5%; 2.65% 6–15%; 0.87% Above 15%; 1.63% Don't know	1965	40.90% 0%; 59.10% 0–2% + 3–5% + 6–15% + Above 15%	692
How often does the firm cooperate with researchers attached to universities of scientific institutes	59.17% Never; 20.00% Rarely; 7.93% Occasionally; 3.69% Frequently; 1.47% Always; 7.74% Don't know	1085	59.83% Rarely + Occasionally + Frequently + Always; 40.17% Never	692
	63.41% Never; 19.46% Rarely; 10.85% Occasionally; 3.41% Frequently; 0.72% Always; 2.15% Don't know	1115	61.71% Rarely + Occasionally + Frequently + Always; 38.29% Never	692

Appendix 2 The Goodness of Fit of the Model

Table A7.2 Summary statistics from the latent class analysis

Solution	BIC(L^2)	AIC(L^2)	p-value
2-cluster	−3471.06	−515.788	0
3-cluster	−3491.35	−527.002	0.502
4-cluster	−3535.77	−503.201	0.288
5-cluster	−3396.10	−513.462	0.432

The choice between the various solutions is determined by the fit of the model to the data, the Bayesian information criteria (BIC), the Akaike information criteria (AIC) and the interpretability.

To examine the fit of the model, we test the null hypothesis, which states that each model fits the data whereas the alternative hypothesis states that the model involved does not fit the data. The test is a standard chi-squared test, well known from the analysis of contingency tables. From Table A7.2, we see that a 3-cluster, 4-cluster as well as a 5-cluster solution all fit the data as the p-values are well above 0.1.

With respect to the information criteria, we have a mixed pattern. From the literature it is well known that that the BIC criteria is too conservative with respect to the number of classes, whereas the AIC is known to be too liberal (see e.g., McLachlan and Peel (2000)). Therefore we have chosen to report both. We see that the BIC points towards a 5-cluster solution, whereas AIC indicates that a 4-cluster solution is the most appropriate. Thus, the information criteria do not unequivocally identify the most appropriate solution.

Therefore the interpretability becomes the decisive criteria. In Table A7.3, we have reported the 5-cluster solution. It is possible to identify a low learning, a STI, a DUI and a STI/DUI cluster in the 5-cluster solution. However, the fifth cluster is a mixture of cluster 3 and 4 (DUI/STI and STI). All things considered, we decided to use the 4-cluster solution, which will be the premise for the analysis.

Table A7.3 The five-cluster solution

	Cluster 1 (DUI)	Cluster 2 (Low)	Cluster 3 (DUI/STI)	Cluster 4 (STI)	Cluster 5 3 and 4
Makes use of int. discip. workgroups	0.5454	0.1156	0.9913	0.1072	0.0103
Makes use of quality circles	0.4909	0.0253	0.5560	0.0124	0.3387
Makes use of systems for proposals	0.6254	0.1913	0.5762	0.0096	0.4491
Makes use of autonomous groups	0.5244	0.2609	0.6198	0.0713	0.5723
Makes use of integration of functions	0.5557	0.1511	0.6456	0.0833	0.2450
Demarcations more indistinct/invisible	0.5602	0.3017	0.6301	0.1864	0.5811
Cooperation with customers high	0.5492	0.2497	0.4969	0.2718	0.4840
R&D expenditures positive	0.3196	0.0061	0.8811	0.4700	0.9930
Cooperation with researchers positive	0.2378	0.0250	0.9616	0.4168	0.9082
Employs scientifically trained personal	0.1274	0.0362	0.6900	0.2589	0.3202
Percentage distribution of firms across clusters	0.3079	0.3018	0.1803	0.1261	0.0840

Notes

1 This bias is similar to the 'S&T perspective that gives too much weight to S&T indicators, especially R&D spending, for understanding technological innovation as discussed by Laestadius (1998). On the basis of in-depth case studies from the pulp and paper sector in Sweden, he argues that this bias has implied a relative neglect of innovation in, for example, mechanical technologies and other low- and medium-tech areas. Furthermore, development costs in these areas are often underreported and/or accounted as other types of costs. It turns out that R&D data only have a weak relation to what is actually going on in the sector. We share Laestadius view that such a bias exists in both theory and policymaking. Our methodology differs from Laestadius's, however, in that we use quantitative survey data. Our focus is also a bit different since we concentrate on types of learning rather than on technologies.

2 For example, in the early industrialization of Sweden, the use of synthetic dyestuff in textiles was learnt through immigration of skilled labour from Germany. The electrification of Sweden was based upon headhunting of Scandinavians that had migrated to the United States and worked in that country's electric industry (Fridlund 1999).

3 See Pavitt (2005) and Brooks (1994).

4 The notable exceptions are the fields of biotechnology and ICT software, where university research often results in inventions with direct industrial applications. See Mansfield (1991) and Pavitt and Steinmueller (2001).

5 See Price (1984) for a classic statement.

6 There are several caveats to this ideal type of STI-mode of learning. R&D may be oriented to solve very local problems, and the results may be kept secret by other means than patents. The most talented scientists will in spite of documentation be carriers of 'personal knowledge' that cannot be easily substituted. There are stories about the Swedish Company ASEA – now part of Asea Brown Bowery – that an important reason that major breakthroughs were made in strong current technology was a lack of documentation and control that made it possible to have private projects in the desk drawer. And finally the patenting may be seen as the tip of the iceberg and as a signal that a lot of tacit knowledge is hidden under the surface.

7 See http://www.trendchart.org/

8 See http://trendchart.cordis.lu/ws_paper.cfm?ID=9. While this is obviously not the place to survey the vast amount of literature to be found on the Trendchart website, we would contend that the STI bias will be evident to anyone who takes the time to browse through it.

9 In Appendix 1 the exact formulation of the questions and the distribution of the answers can be found.

10 Scientifically trained personnel include bachelors, master and PhD students within the natural sciences, as well as civil engineers.

11 There may, of course, be reverse causality involved in these results in the sense that firms that succeed in innovating are better able and motivated to introduce DUI organizational traits and invest in R&D. This sort of problem, however, applies for any study that relies on cross-sectional data. What we show here is simply that some sets of firm characteristics are good predictors of innovative performance.

12 These results are consistent with the presence of complementarities between the sets of practices making up the two modes but are not sufficient to demonstrate such complementarity. Demonstrating complementarity between the two modes would require showing that using to a greater extent the practices making up one mode increases the

returns from using to a greater extent the practices making up the other. For a useful discussion of the different statistical approaches that have been used to test for the presence of complementarity among a group of variables, see Galia et al. (2004, 1191–92).

References

Aoki, M. 1988. *Information, Incentives and Bargaining Structure in the Japanese Economy.* Cambridge: Cambridge University Press.

Arrow, K. J. 1974. *The Limits of Organization.* New York: W. W. Norton.

Becker, B. and B. Huselid. 1998. 'High-Performance Work Systems and Firm Performance: A Synthesis of Research and Managerial Implications'. In *Research in Personnel and Human Resources,* edited by G. Ferris. Vol. 16, 53–102. Greenwick, CT: JAI Press.

Breschi, S. and F. Malerba. 1997. 'Sectoral Innovation Systems'. In *Systems of Innovation: Technologies, Institutions and Organizations,* edited by C. Edquist. London: Pinter Publishers.

Brooks, H. 1994. 'The Relationship between Science and Technology'. *Research Policy* 23: 477–86.

Burns, T. and G. M. Stalker. 1961. *The Management of Innovation.* London: Tavistock.

Carlsson, B. and S. Jacobsson. 1997. 'Diversity Creation and Technological Systems: A Technology Policy Perspective'. In *Systems of Innovation: Technologies, Institutions and Organizations,* edited by C. Edquist. London: Pinter Publishers.

Carter, A. P. 1989. 'Know-how Trading as Economic Exchange'. *Research Policy* 18: 155–163.

Chandler, A. D. 1977. *The Visible Hand: The Managerial Revolution in American Business.* Cambridge, MA: Belknap Press.

Christensen J. L. and B.-Å. Lundvall (eds.). 2004. *Product Innovation, Interactive Learning and Economic Performance.* Amsterdam: Elsevier Ltd.

Clegg, C., C. Axtell, L. Damodaran, B. Farby, R. Hull, R. Lloyd-Jones, J. Nicholls, R. Sell, C. Tomlinson, A. Ainger, and T. Stewart. 1996. 'The Performance of Information Technology and the Role of Human and Organisational Factors'. Report to the ESRC, UK.

Cowan, M., P. David, and D. Foray. 2001. '*The Explicit Economics of Knowledge Codification and Tacitness.' Industrial and Corporate Change* 9: 211–53.

Dertoutzos, M. L., R. K. Lester and R. M. Solow. 1989. *Made in America.* Cambridge, MA: MIT Press.

Edquist, C. (ed.). 1997. *Systems of Innovation: Technologies, Institutions and Organizations.* London: Pinter Publishers.

Freeman, C. 1986, *The Economics of Industrial Innovation.* London: Pinter Publishers.

———. 1987. *Technology Policy and Economic Performance: Lessons from Japan.* London: Pinter Publishers.

Fridlund, M. 1999. *Den gemensamma utvecklingen. Staten, storföretaget och samarbetet kring den svenska elkraftstekniken.* Stockholm: Symposion.

Galia, F. and D. Legros. 2004. 'Complementarities between Obstacles to Innovation: Evidence from France'. *Research Policy* 33: 1185–99.

Gittleman, M., M. Horrigan and M. Joyce. 1998. 'Flexible' Workplace Practices: Evidence from a nationally Representative Survey'. *Industrial and Labour Relations Review* 52: 99–115.

Hagenaars, J. A. and A. L. McCutcheon (ed.). 2003. *Applied Latent Class Analysis.* Cambridge: Cambridge University Press.

Johnson B., E. Lorenz and B.-Å. Lundvall. 2002. 'Why All This Fuss about Codified and Tacit Knowledge'. *Industrial and Corporate Change* 11: 245–62.

Kline, S. J. and N. Rosenberg. 1986. 'An Overview of Innovation'. In *The Positive Sum Game*, edited by R. Landau and N. Rosenberg. Washington DC: National Academy Press.

Laestadius, S. 1998. 'The Relevance of Science and Technology Indicators: The Case of Pulp and Paper'. *Research Policy* 27: 385–95.

Lam, A. 2005. 'Organizational Innovation'. In *Handbook of Innovation*, edited by J. Fagerberg, D. Mowery and R. Nelson. Oxford: Oxford University Press.

Laursen, K. and N. Foss. 2003. 'New HRM Practices, Complementarities, and the Impact on Innovation Performance'. *Cambridge Journal of Economics* 27: 243–63.

Lorenz, E. and A. Valeyre. 2006. 'Organisational Forms and Innovative Performance: A Comparison of the EU-15'. In *How Europe's Economies Learn: Coordinating Competing Models*, edited by E. Lorenz and B.-Å. Lundvall (eds.). Oxford: Oxford University Press.

Lorenz, E., F. Wilkinson and J. Michie. 2004. 'HRM Complementarities and Innovative Performance in French and British Industry'. In *Product Innovation, Interactive Learning and Economic Performance*, edited by J. L. Christensen and B.-Å. Lundvall. Amsterdam: Elsevier Ltd.

Lundvall, B.-Å. 1988. 'Innovation as an Interactive Process: From User-Producer Interaction to the National Innovation Systems'. In *Technology and Economic Theory*, edited by G. Dosi, C. Freeman, R. R. Nelson, G. Silverberg and L. Soete. London: Pinter Publishers.

———. (ed.). 1992. *National Systems of Innovation: Towards a Theory of Innovation and Interactive Learning*. London: Pinter Publishers.

———. 2002. *Innovation, Growth and Social Cohesion: The Danish Model*. London: Elgar Publishers.

Lundvall, B.-Å. and B. Johnson. 1994. 'The Learning Economy'. *Journal of Industry Studies* 1: 23–42.

Lundvall, B.-Å. and P. Nielsen. 1999. 'Competition and Transformation in the Learning Economy – Illustrated by the Danish Case'. *Revue d'Economie Industrielle* 88: 67–90.

Mansfield, E. 1991. 'Academic Research and Industrial Innovation', *Research Policy*, 20: 1–12.

Maskell, P. and A. Malmberg. 1997. 'Towards an Explanation of Regional Specialization and Industry Agglomeration'. *European Planning Studies* 5: 25–41.

McLachlan, G. and D. Peel. 2000. *Finite Mixture Models*. New York: Wiley.

Michie, J. and M. Sheehan. 1999. 'HRM Practices, R&D Expenditure and Innovative Investment: Evidence from the UK's 1990 Workplace Industrial Relations Survey'. *Industrial and Corporate Change* 8: 211–234.

Mintzberg, H. 1979. *The Structuring of Organisation*. Engelwood Cliffs, NJ: Princeton University Press.

Mowery, D. C. and J. E. Oxley. 1995. 'Inward Technology Transfer and Competitiveness: The Role of National Innovation Systems'. *Cambridge Journal of Economics* 19: 67–93.

Nelson, R. R. 2004. 'The Market Economy and the Scientific Commons'. *Research Policy* 33: 455–71.

———. (ed.). 1993. *National Systems of Innovations: A Comparative Analysis*. Oxford: Oxford University Press.

Nonaka, I. and H. Takeuchi. 1995. *The Knowledge Creating Company*. Oxford: Oxford University Press.

Osterman, P. 1994. 'How Common Is Workplace Transformation and Who Adopts It?' *Industrial and Labor Relations Review* 47: 173–88.

————. 2000. 'Work Reorganization in an Era of Restructuring: Trends in Diffusion and Effects on Employee Welfare'. *Industrial and Labor Relations Review* 53: 179–96.

Pavitt, K. 1984. 'Sectoral Patterns of Technical Change: Towards a Taxonomy and a Theory'. *Research Policy* 13: 343–73.

————. 2005. 'Innovation Processes'. In *Handbook of Innovation*, edited by J. Fagerberg, D. Mowery and R. Nelson, 86–114. Oxford: Oxford University Press.

Pavitt, K. and E. Steinmuller. 2001. 'Technology in Corporate Strategy: Change, Continuity and Information Revolution'. In *Handbook of Strategy and Management*, edited by A. Pettigrew, H. Thompson and R. Whitington. London: Sage.

Polanyi, M. 1958/1978. *Personal Knowledge*. Routledge and Kegan Paul: London.

Price, D. de S. 1984. 'The Science/Technology Relationship, the Craft of Experimental Science, and Policy for the Improvement of High Technology Innovations'. *Research Policy* 13: 3–20.

Ramsay, H., D. Scholarios and B. Harley. 2000. 'Employees and High-Performance Work Systems, Testing inside the Black Box'. *British Journal of Industrial Relation* 38, 501–31.

Rosenberg, N. 1976. 'Technological Change in the Machine Tool Industry, 1840–1910'. In *Perspectives on Technology*. Cambridge: Cambridge University Press.

————. 1982. 'Inside the Black Box: Technology and Economics'. Cambridge: Cambridge University Press.

Rothwell, R. 1977. 'The Characteristics of Successful Innovators and Technically Progressive Firms'. *R&D Management* 7: 191–206.

Truss, C. 2001. 'Complexities and Controversies in Linking HRM with Organisational Outcomes'. *Journal of Management Studies* 38: 1121–49.

Vinding, A. L. 2002. 'Absorptive Capacity and Innovative Performance: A Human Capital Approach'. PhD dissertation, Department of Business Studies. Aalborg: Aalborg University.

Von Hippel, E. 1976. 'The Dominant Role of Users in the Scientific Instrument Innovation Process'. *Research Policy* 5: 212–39.

Wood, S. 1999. 'Getting the Measure of the Transformed High-Performance Organisation'. *British Journal of Industrial Relations* 37, no. 3: 391–417.

Chapter 8

HOW EUROPE'S ECONOMIES LEARN: A COMPARISON OF WORK ORGANIZATION AND INNOVATION MODE FOR THE EU-15

Anthony Arundel, Edward Lorenz, Bengt-Åke Lundvall and Antoine Valeyre

8.1 Introduction

The innovation literature has long recognized the role of research and development (R&D) and skilled scientists and engineers in successful innovation in science-based sectors. More recent works within the national innovation systems perspective highlighted the importance of other factors to successful innovation, particularly in low- and medium-technology sectors, where formal R&D frequently plays a secondary role. These other factors include interactions with suppliers and customers, other forms of 'open innovation' and feedback mechanisms from the market. These interactions frequently form within localized networks creating unique innovation systems at the regional or national level (Lundvall 1988; Nelson 1993).

Both innovation strategies based on science and on interactive networks require learning in order to develop competences and to be able to rapidly exploit external and internal change. In such a 'learning economy', the speed of the innovation process is a critical factor in economic performance. Using Danish data, Jensen et al. (2007) show that innovation performance is significantly enhanced when firms combine science-based learning with experience-based learning. One possibility is that how firms organize the production and distribution of responsibilities among their workforce could have a significant effect on learning and hence on innovative capabilities.

Some of the early contributions to the innovation literature evaluated the effect of organizational structures on the success of innovation. The Sappho study pointed to the importance of interactions between different divisions of the same firm (Rothwell 1972). Indirectly, Kline and Rosenberg's (1986) 'chain-link' model of innovation points to the importance of feedback loops and interactions between agents within the same organization but operating at different stages of the innovation process. Freeman's (1987) analysis of the Japanese innovation system partly explained the success of Japanese innovation performance by the specific organizational characteristics of Japanese firms, while Gjerding (1992) looked at the role of organizational change in national innovation systems. More recently, there have been several systematic attempts to evaluate the effect of specific modes of work organization on national innovation performance (Lundvall 2002; Lam 2005; Lam and Lundvall 2006; Lorenz and Valeyre 2006).

Work organization could influence innovation performance through two main mechanisms[1]. First, forms of work organization that stimulate interaction among agents with a diverse set of experiences and competences could be more creative, leading to the development of original ideas for new products and processes. Second, work organization forms that delegate responsibility for problem solving to a wide range of employees could be more successful both in upgrading the competences of workers and in transforming ideas into new products and processes.

Despite a growing acceptance of the importance of work organization to innovation, only a few studies have used quantitative survey methods to explore the link between organizational environments and learning and innovation (Laursen and Foss 2003; Nielsen and Lundvall 2006; Jensen et al. 2007). There is a need to further explore the linkages between workplace organization and the dynamics of innovation at the level of the firm as well as at the level of sectoral, regional and national innovation systems. This partly requires indicators that capture how material and human resources, such as R&D and skilled scientists and engineers, are used within the firm and whether or not the organization of work promotes innovation. This could occur through forms of work organization that encourage responsibility and further development of the knowledge and skills of employees.

This chapter uses quantitative survey data at the national level to assess the effect of different analytical concepts of work organization on innovative capabilities. The chapter develops a set of aggregate indicators to explore, at the level of national innovation systems, the relation between innovation and the organization of work. The indicators are constructed from the results of two European surveys. Indicators on the organization of work are obtained from the third European Survey of Working Conditions in 2000 carried out at the level of occupied persons. Indicators on national innovative capabilities are obtained from the third Community Innovation Survey (CIS-3) conducted in 2001 but covering innovation activities of enterprises between 1998 and 2000. The survey data on working conditions are used to develop what we believe to be the first EU-wide mapping of the adoption of different types of work organization. The innovation survey data are used to develop a typology of innovation at the firm level and to calculate the distribution of these innovation types within each of 14 EU countries for which data are available.

The chapter is structured as follows. Section 8.2 describes the variables to characterize work organization in the 15 countries of the European Union and presents the results of a factor analysis and a hierarchical clustering used to construct a typology of forms of work organization. Section 8.3 examines differences in the relative importance of these forms across the EU, controlling for the effects of sector, firm size and occupational category. Section 8.4 presents the data used to construct a typology of firm level innovative capabilities or innovation modes, based on the work of Arundel and Hollanders (2005) in cooperation with Eurostat.[2] Section 8.5 combines the two sets of results to examine, at the national level, the relationship between the forms of work organization adopted in a nation and the distribution of firm level innovation capabilities. The concluding section considers some of the main implications of the research for European policy.

8.2 Measuring Forms of Work Organization in the European Union[3]

In order to map the forms of work organization adopted by firms across the European Union, we draw on the results of the third European Survey of Working Conditions undertaken by the European Foundation for the Improvement of Living and Working Conditions.[4] The survey questionnaire was directed to approximately 1,500 active persons in each country with the exception of Luxembourg with only 500 respondents. The total survey population is 21,703 persons, of which 17,910 are salaried employees. The survey methodology is based on a 'random walk' multistage random sampling method involving face-to-face interviews undertaken at the respondents' principal residence. In order to provide comparable data to the Community Innovation Survey (CIS), which is limited to industrial and service firms in the private sector, the analysis is based on the responses of 8,081 salaried employees working in industry or service sector firms with at least 10 employees. This excludes employees in agriculture and fishing, public administration and social security, education, health and social work and private domestic employees.

It is important to emphasize that the use of employee level data allows us to capture the prevalence of different forms of work organization within private sector establishments in the EU. However, we are unable to determine the prevalence of particular types of firms or organizational structures. This means that our results allow for the obvious possibility that multiple forms of work organization are in use within the same establishment. We return to the implications of this point in section 8.5 on the relationship between different forms of work organization and modes of innovation.

The choice of variables for the analysis is based on a reading of two complementary literatures that address the relation between the forms of work organization used by firms and the way they learn and innovate: the 'high performance work system' literature dealing with the diffusion of Japanese-style organizational practices in the United States and Europe (Dertouzos et al. 1989; Gittleman et al. 1998; Osterman 1994, 2000; Ramsay et al. 2000; Truss 2001; Wood 1999) and the literature dealing with the relation between organizational design and innovation (Burns and Stalker 1961; Lam 2005; Lam and Lundvall 2006; Mintzberg 1979, 1983). The 'high performance' literature focuses on the diffusion of specific organizational practices and arrangements that are seen as enhancing the firm's capacity for making incremental improvements to the efficiency of its work processes and the quality of its products and services. These include practices designed to increase employee involvement in problem solving and operational decision making such as teams, problem-solving groups and employee responsibility for quality control. Many of the practices identified in this literature were innovations developed by large Japanese automobile and electronics firms in the 1970s and 1980s. Some authors refer specifically to the diffusion of the 'lean production' model associated with Toyota (Womack et al. 1990; MacDuffie and Pil 1997). The diffusion of these Japanese style organizational practices is thought to have contributed to the progressive transformation of more hierarchically structured firms that relied on Taylor's principles of task specialization and a clear distinction between the work of conception and execution.

The distinction between hierarchical and flexible or 'transformed' work organization developed in the 'high performance' literature can also be seen in Burns and Stalkers's (1961) classic distinction between 'bureaucratic' and 'organic' organizations. Mintzberg (1983), within the context of a broad distinction between bureaucratic and organic organizations, develops a more complex typology of organizational forms. He identifies two types of organic organization with a high capacity for adaptation: the operating adhocracy and the simple organization. The forms of work organization and types of work practices that characterize these two organic forms are quite different. The simple form relies on direct supervision by one individual (typically a manager) and a classic example of this type of organization is the small entrepreneurial firm. Adhocracies rely on mutual adjustment in which employees coordinate their own work by communicating informally with each other. Various liaison devices such as project teams and task forces are used to facilitate the process of mutual adjustment. Work autonomy is low in the simple organization and high in the adhocracy.

In contrast to these 'organic' forms, Mintzberg identifies two basic bureaucratic forms with a limited capacity for adaptation and innovation: the machine bureaucracy and the professional bureaucracy.[5] The key characteristic of work organization in the former is the standardization of jobs and tasks through the use of formal job descriptions and rules imposed by management. Thus there is a high degree of centralization and limited employee discretion over how work is carried out or over the pace of work. In the professional bureaucracy, on the other hand, centralization is low and behaviour is regulated and standardized through the acquisition of standardized skills and the internalization of professional norms and standards of conduct. As a result, operating procedures are stable and routinized despite considerable autonomy in work.

Lam (2005) synthesizes and extends these two literatures by contrasting two ideal organizational forms that support different styles of learning and innovation: the 'operating adhocracy' and the 'J-form'.[6] She observes that the operating adhocracy relies on the expertise of individual professionals and uses temporary project structures to creatively combine the knowledge of these experts. High levels of discretion in work provide scope for exploring new knowledge, creating a superior capacity for radical innovation. Compared to the operating adhocracy, the J-form is a relatively bureaucratic form that relies on formal team structures and rules of job rotation to embed knowledge within the collective organization. Stable job careers within internal labour markets provide incentives for members to commit themselves to the goals of continuous product and process improvement. Consequently, the J-form tends to excel at incremental innovation.

In summary, both the high performance and the organizational design literatures identify different organizational archetypes and posit a relationship between how a firm organizes work and its innovative style and capacity. In order to identify the prevalence of specific types of work organization, we use the Working Conditions survey data to construct 15 binary variables that cover work responsibilities and tasks and then use cluster analysis to identify four main types of work organization. The 15 binary variables are presented in Table 8.1.[7]

The first four variables measure the use of the core work practices identified in the high performance literature: teamwork, job rotation, employee responsibility for quality control and precise quality norms. Two of these

Table 8.1 Variables for work organization and tasks

	Per cent of employees affected
Teamwork	64.2
Job rotation	48.9
Responsibility for quality control	72.6
Quality norms	74.4
Problem-solving activities	79.3
Learning new things at work	71.4
Complexity of tasks	56.7
Discretion in fixing work methods	61.7
Discretion in setting work pace	63.6
Horizontal constraints on work pace	53.1
Hierarchical constraints on work pace	38.9
Norm-based constraints on work pace	38.7
Automatic constraints on work pace	26.7
Monotony of tasks	42.4
Repetitiveness of tasks	24.9
N	*8081*

Source: Third Working Conditions survey, European Foundation for the Improvement of Living and Working Conditions.

variables capture whether employees engage in learning and problem solving, characteristics of both adhocracies and the J-form. One question captures whether work tasks are complex or not and is relevant to the operating adhocracy.

Work discretion, a characteristic of adhocracies, is measured by two variables that capture whether employees are able to choose or change their work methods and their pace of work. Four variables measure different constraints on employee discretion in setting their pace of work: 'automatic' constraints on work pace, which is linked to the rate at which equipment is operated or a product is displaced in the production flow; 'hierarchical' constraints linked to the direct control, which is exercised by one's immediate superiors; 'norm-based' constraints on work pace linked to the setting of quantitative production norms; and 'horizontal' constraints linked to how one person's work rate is dependent on the work of their colleagues. Hierarchical and automatic constraints are classic characteristics of Taylorist work settings, while norm-based constraints characterize both Taylorism and the Japanese forms of work organization. The horizontal constraints variable provides a measure of whether work is carried out collectively rather than individually. Finally, the two variables measuring task repetitiveness and task monotony capture typical features of Taylorist work settings.

8.2.1 Variety in European organizational practice

In order to assign employees to distinct categories or groups, we use factor analysis[8] to identify the underlying associations that exist among the 15 variables described in Table 8.1. We then use the factor scores or the coordinates of the observations on all 15 factors as a basis for clustering individuals into distinct groups of work systems, using Ward's hierarchical clustering method. This method identifies four basic systems of work organization as presented in Table 8.2.[9] The four clusters capture forms of work organization that are characteristic of several of the main organizational forms discussed in the literature: 'Discretionary learning', which corresponds to work organization in the notion of an adhocracy; 'Lean production' or the J-form organization; the hierarchically structured Taylorist form; and the 'Traditional' organization based on a simple management structure.

The first cluster, which accounts for 39 per cent of the employees,[10] is distinctive for the way high levels of autonomy in work are combined with high levels of learning, problem solving and task complexity. There is a below-average prevalence of the variables measuring constraints on work pace, monotony and repetitiveness. The use of team work is near the average, while less than half of the employees in this cluster participate in job rotation, which points to the importance of horizontal job specialization. The forms of work organization in this cluster correspond rather closely to those found in adhoc-racies and due to the combined importance of work discretion and learning we refer to this cluster as the 'discretionary learning' form.

The second cluster accounts for 28 per cent of the employees. Compared to the first cluster, work organization is characterized by low levels of employee discretion in setting work pace and methods. The use of job rotation and teamwork, on the other hand, are much higher than in the first cluster, and work effort is more constrained by quantitative production norms and by the collective nature of work organization. The use of quality norms is the highest of the four clusters and the use of employee responsibility for quality control is considerably above the average level for the population as a whole. These features point to a more structured or bureaucratic style of organizational learning that corresponds rather closely to the characteristics of the Japanese or 'lean production' model associated with the work of MacDuffie and Krafcik (1992) and Womack et al. (1990). This cluster also has the highest prevalence of repetitive tasks, possibly due to codified production methods.

Table 8.2 Work organization clusters

Variable	Per cent of employees by work organization cluster reporting each variable				
	Discretionary learning	Lean production	Taylorism	Traditional organization	Average
Teamwork	64.3	84.2	70.1	33.4	64.2
Job rotation	44.0	70.5	53.2	27.5	48.9
Quality norms	78.1	94.0	81.1	36.1	74.4
Responsibility for quality control	86.4	88.7	46.7	38.9	72.6
Problem-solving activities	95.4	98.0	5.7	68.7	79.3
Learning new things in work	93.9	81.7	42.0	29.7	71.4
Complexity of tasks	79.8	64.7	23.8	19.2	56.7
Discretion in fixing work methods	89.1	51.8	17.7	46.5	61.7
Discretion in setting work rate	87.5	52.2	27.3	52.7	63.6
Horizontal constraints on work rate	43.6	80.3	66.1	27.8	53.1
Hierarchical constraints on work rate	19.6	64.4	66.5	26.7	38.9
Norm-based constraints on work rate	21.2	75.5	56.3	14.7	38.7
Automatic constraints on work rate	5.4	59.8	56.9	7.2	26.7
Monotony of tasks	19.5	65.8	65.6	43.9	42.4
Repetitiveness of tasks	12.8	41.9	37.1	19.2	24.9
Total share of employees	*39%*	*28%*	*14%*	*19%*	

Source: Third Working Conditions survey, European Foundation for the Improvement of Living and Working Conditions.

The third class, which groups 14 per cent of the employees, corresponds in most respects to a classic characterization of Taylorism. The work situation is in most respects the opposite of that found in the first cluster, with low discretion and low level of learning and problem solving. Interestingly, three of the core work practices associated with the lean-production model – teams, job rotation and quality norms – are somewhat overrepresented in this cluster implying that these practices are highly imperfect measures of a transition to new forms of work organization characterized by high levels of learning and problem solving. The characteristics of this cluster draw attention to the importance of what some authors have referred to as 'flexible Taylorism' (Boyer and Durand 1993; Cézard et al. 1992; Linhart 1994).

The fourth cluster groups 19 per cent of the employees. All the variables are underrepresented with the exception of monotony in work, which is close to the average. The frequency of the two variables measuring learning and task complexity is the lowest among the four types of work organization, while at the same time there are few constraints on the work rate. As shown below, the sectoral breakdown suggests that this class consists of traditional forms of work organization based on informal and noncodified systems.

8.3 How Europe's Economies Work and Learn

The cluster analysis identifies three forms of work organization whose features correspond rather closely to the forms of work organization found, respectively, in adhocracies, J-form organizations and machine bureaucracies or Taylorist firms. As the figures in Table 8.3 show, the discretionary learning form of work organization is especially prevalent in several service sectors, notably business services, banks and insurance and in the gas, electricity and water utilities. As one would anticipate, the lean model of production is more developed in the manufacturing sector, notably in the production of transport equipment, electronics and electrical production, wood and paper products and printing and publishing. The Taylorist form is notably present in textiles, clothing and leather products, food processing, wood and paper products and transport equipment, while underrepresented in the service sectors. The traditional organizational form is found principally in the services, notably land transport, personal services, hotels and restaurants, post and telecommunications and wholesale and retail trade.

Table 8.4 links the four types of work organization by occupational category. As one would expect, the discretionary learning form of work organization is especially a characteristic of the work of managers, professionals and

Table 8.3 Forms of work organization by sector of activity

	Per cent of employees by sector in each organizational class				
	Discretionary learning	Lean production	Taylorism	Traditional organization	Total
Mining and quarrying	42.4	41.5	3.4	12.7	100.0
Food processing	18.4	34.9	24.6	22.1	100.0
Textiles, garments, leather products	27.2	25.9	30.2	16.8	100.0
Wood and paper products	27.6	40.7	23.9	7.8	100.0
Publishing and printing	31.1	43.8	14.1	11.0	100.0
Chemicals and plastics	34.7	34.1	21.9	9.2	100.0
Metal products and mechanical engineering	31.8	35.7	19.8	12.7	100.0
Electrical engineering and electronics	41.5	38.5	8.6	11.4	100.0
Transport Equipment	28.1	38.7	23.2	10.0	100.0
Other industrial production	50.9	22.1	18.4	8.5	100.0
Electricity, gas and water	58.5	19.4	6.2	15.8	100.0
Construction	40.9	31.4	10.6	17.1	100.0
Wholesale and retail trade	41.5	20.4	11.7	26.4	100.0
Hotels and restaurants	29.7	25.8	16.6	27.9	100.0
Land transport	26.3	24.0	10.2	39.5	100.0
Other transport	39.2	36.1	5.0	19.7	100.0

Post and telecommunications	38.1	27.1	7.7	27.1	100.0
Financial services	58.1	21.5	3.4	16.9	100.0
Business services	57.6	18.7	6.9	16.7	100.0
Personal services	39.7	18.9	7.6	33.8	100.0
Average	39.1	28.2	13.6	19.1	100.0

Source: Third Working Conditions survey. European Foundation for the Improvement of Living and Working Conditions.

Table 8.4 Forms of work organization by occupational category

	Per cent of employees by occupational category in each organizational class				
	Discretionary learning	Lean production	Taylorism	Traditional organization	Total
Managers	69.1	24.7	0.2	6.0	100.0
Engineers and professionals	75.9	14.0	5.2	4.9	100.0
Technicians	61.0	24.6	2.4	12.0	100.0
Clerks	43.2	21.9	9.4	25.5	100.0
Service, shop and market sales persons	30.3	21.4	12.4	35.9	100.0
Craft and related trades	34.2	38.5	16.5	10.8	100.0
Machine operators and assemblers	15.7	37.7	24.3	22.3	100.0
Unskilled trades	14.8	23.9	26.7	34.5	100.0
Average	39.1	28.2	13.6	19.1	100.0

Source: Third Working Conditions survey. European Foundation for the Improvement of Living and Working Conditions.

technicians, while the lean form of work organization primarily characterizes the work of employees in craft and related trades and machine operators and assemblers. The Taylorist form is most frequent among machine operators and the unskilled trades. Finally, the traditional form is most prevalent among service workers and shop and market sales persons.

Establishment size is only weakly correlated with the different organizational models. The learning form of work organization is slightly underrepresented in the medium-size category of establishments (100 to 249 employees). The lean and Taylorist forms increase with establishment size (>250 employees) while the reverse tendency can be observed for the traditional forms of work organization.

In combination, Tables 8.2, 8.3 and 8.4 gives us a better idea of what the different clusters represent. Discretionary learning refers to jobs where a lot of responsibility is allocated to the employees who are expected to solve problems on their own. The business services sector is a typical example where many jobs continuously deal with new and complex problems. Although some of the tasks take place in a team, teamwork is not seen as imposing narrow constraints on the work. In this category, teamwork may involve brainstorming by professional experts as much as collectively solving narrowly defined problems.

Lean production also involves problem solving and learning but here the problems are more narrowly defined and the scale of possible solutions less broad. The work is highly constrained, and it is often repetitive and monotonous. The extensive use of management techniques such as job rotation (between similar tasks within the same division) and team work may be seen as attempts to overcome the limits of Taylorist production and to create some degree of active participation of production workers and sales staff in order to limit labour turnover and absenteeism.

Taylorism is distinctive for low levels of learning and for the virtual absence of problem-solving activity. The work is highly constrained and monotonous. It may be seen as the old-style factory work where the tasks to solve are narrowly defined and repetitive. It is a kind of work where the required qualifications are limited and the worker can easily be substituted by another worker or by a machine. In the era of globalization, this category of work is interesting because it can be easily outsourced to low-wage countries.

Traditional organization involves even less complex problems. It is more individualistic than all the other categories and less monotonous than lean production and Taylorism. It includes traditional service jobs. Many of those involve a direct and indirect interaction with local customers, and they may therefore be less footloose than the Taylorist jobs.

8.3.1 National effects on the diffusion of organizational practice

Table 8.5 shows that there are wide differences in the importance of the four forms of work organization across European nations. The discretionary learning form of work organization is most prevalent in the Netherlands, the Nordic countries and to a lesser extent Germany and Austria, while it is the least prevalent in Ireland and the Southern European nations. The lean model is most in evidence in the United Kingdom, Ireland and Spain and to a lesser extent in France, while it is less developed in the Nordic countries or in Germany, Austria and the Netherlands. The Taylorist form of work organization shows almost the reverse trend compared to the discretionary learning forms, being most frequent in the Southern European nations and in Ireland. Finally, the traditional form of work organization is most prevalent in Greece and Italy and to a lesser extent in Germany, Sweden, Belgium, Spain and Portugal.

As shown in Tables 8.3 and 8.4, each form of work organization tends to be associated with particular sectors and occupational categories. This raises the question of what part of the variation in the importance of these forms across EU nations can be accounted for by the nation's specific industrial and occupational structure or by other unexplained national factors, such as sociocultural attitudes on the part of management and workers, historical developments and the rate at which new organizational forms are adopted by firms. In order to determine the importance of 'national factors', we use logit regression analysis to provide estimates of the impact of national effects on the relative likelihood of adopting the different types of work organization (See Table 8.6). Germany, the most populous nation within the EU, is the reference case for the estimates of national effects. In each case the dependent variable is a binary variable measuring whether or not the individual is subject to the particular form of work organization. On the left side of Table 8.6 (columns 1 through 4), there is only one independent variable for the country where the employee works, with Germany as the reference category. Thus column 1 gives the likelihood that employees are subject to the 'discretionary learning' form of work organization in each country relative to the German case.

On the right side of Table 8.6 (columns 5 through 8), the independent variables include nationality plus three control variables for each employee's sector of work, the establishment size, and occupational category. The respective reference categories for the estimates are the vehicle sector – firms with 10 to 49 employees – and the occupational category of machine operator and assembler.[11]

As the column 1 results show, the country where the employee works has a significant impact on the relative likelihood of discretionary learning forms of employment. Compared to the German case, for which the use of the discretionary learning form of work organization is near the 15-country weighted

Table 8.5 National differences in forms of work organization

Per cent of employees by country in each organizational class

	Discretionary learning	Lean production	Taylorist organization	Traditional organization	Total
Belgium	38.9	25.1	13.9	22.1	100.0
Denmark	60.0	21.9	6.8	11.3	100.0
Germany	44.3	19.6	14.3	21.9	100.0
Greece	18.7	25.6	28.0	27.7	100.0
Italy	30.0	23.6	20.9	25.4	100.0
Spain	20.1	38.8	18.5	22.5	100.0
France	38.0	33.3	11.1	17.7	100.0
Ireland	24.0	37.8	20.7	17.6	100.0
Luxembourg	42.8	25.4	11.9	20.0	100.0
Netherlands	64.0	17.2	5.3	13.5	100.0
Portugal	26.1	28.1	23.0	22.8	100.0
United Kingdom	34.8	40.6	10.9	13.7	100.0
Finland	47.8	27.6	12.5	12.1	100.0
Sweden	52.6	18.5	7.1	21.7	100.0
Austria	47.5	21.5	13.1	18.0	100.0
EU-15	39.1	28.2	13.6	19.1	100.0

Source: Third Working Condition survey. European Foundation for the Improvement of Living and Working Conditions.

Table 8.6 Logit estimates of national effects on organizational practice

	Logit estimates without structural controls				Logit estimates with structural controls			
	1	2	3	4	5	6	7	8
	Discretionary learning organization	*Lean organization*	Taylorism	Traditional organization	*Discretionary learning organization*	*Lean organization*	Taylorism	Traditional organization
Belgium	−0.22	0.32	−0.03	0.01	−0.23	0.42*	−0.11	−0.09
Denmark	0.63**	0.14	−0.82**	−0.79**	0.79**	0.29	−0.86**	−1.06**
Greece	−1.24**	0.35	0.85**	0.31	−1.33**	0.42	0.84**	0.12
Italy	−0.61**	0.24*	0.46**	0.20*	−0.51**	0.20	0.33**	0.16
Spain	−1.15**	0.96**	0.31*	0.04	−1.15**	1.08**	0.06	−0.17
France	−0.26*	0.72**	−0.29*	−0.27**	−0.32**	0.84**	−0.33**	−0.38**
Ireland	−0.92**	0.91**	0.45	−0.27	−1.11**	1.14**	0.47	−0.50
Luxembourg	−0.06	0.33	−0.21	−0.11	−0.17	0.42	0.00	−0.20
Netherlands	0.81**	−0.16	−1.10**	−0.59**	0.79**	0.02	−0.94**	−0.74**
Portugal	−0.81**	0.47**	0.58**	0.05	−0.78**	0.51**	0.44*	−0.01
UK	−0.40**	1.03**	−0.31**	−0.56**	−0.68**	1.32**	−0.24*	−0.72**
Finland	0.14	0.45*	−0.15	−0.71*	−0.01	0.63**	−0.07	−0.78*
Sweden	0.33*	−0.07	−0.77**	−0.01	0.22	0.06	−0.68*	0.00
Austria	0.13	0.12	−0.10	−0.24	0.33	0.14	−0.26	−0.43*

Note: * = significant at 5%, **: significant at 1%, Reference country: Germany.

Source: Third European Survey of Working Conditions. European Foundation for the Improvement of Living and Working Conditions.

average (see Table 8.5), there are three countries where the discretionary learning model is more frequent: Sweden, the Netherlands and Denmark. There are no significant differences in the use of discretionary learning in four countries: Belgium, Luxembourg, Finland and Austria. This work form is less frequent in the remaining seven countries. Column 5 indicates that these results are robust after controlling for the effect of firm size, industry structure and occupation, with the exception of Sweden, for which the coefficient estimate though still positive is no longer significant.

Column 2 of Table 8.6 presents the estimates of national effects on the likelihood of using the lean form without controls. Compared to Germany, where the use of the lean model is relatively low in relation to the 15-country weighted average (see Table 8.5), Spain, France, Ireland, Finland, the United Kingdom and Portugal display a relatively high propensity to use lean production methods. The coefficients are especially high for the United Kingdom, Ireland and Spain, and they increase slightly and remain significant when structural controls are included.

Overall, the results show that the large national differences in the prevalence of different forms of work organization are not due to national differences in the distribution of firm size, industry and occupation. Instead, unexplained national factors that could be due to historically inherited management-worker relations or attitudes to organizational innovation strongly influence national differences in the use of different sets of organizational practices.

In so far as the organizational practices adopted by firms can influence their ability to develop and profit from innovation, the results in Table 8.6 suggest that the large differences within the European Union in national innovative performance[12] might reflect national differences in the distribution of different types of work organization, particularly the use of discretionary learning forms that enhance the opportunities for learning. This possibility is explored in sections 8.4 and 8.5.

8.4 Measuring Differences in Innovation Mode

Economists and business scholars frequently measure innovation by R&D expenditures or by the number of patents applied for or granted. The weaknesses of these measures are well known. R&D doesn't necessarily result in the development of new products or processes and many innovative firms do not perform R&D. A large fraction of innovations are not patented and the importance of patenting varies according to sector. Furthermore, R&D and patents entirely fail to capture innovation that occurs through diffusion processes, such as when a firm purchases innovative production equipment or product components from other firms. The Community Innovation Surveys (CIS) were in part designed to respond to these limitations by providing survey-based estimates of the percentage of manufacturing firms and selected service sector firms[13] that have developed or introduced a new product or process over a three-year time period. However, the CIS estimates of the percentage of innovative firms are based on a very broad definition of innovation ranging from intensive in-house R&D that results in new-to-market products or processes to minimal effort to introduce manufacturing equipment purchased from a supplier. Consequently, a broad all-encompassing definition where a distinction is made between 'innovative firms' and 'non-innovative firms' is both misleading in international comparisons and fails to provide a clear picture of the structure of innovation capabilities within individual countries.

In order to overcome these limitations, we draw on a taxonomy developed by Arundel and Hollanders (2005), in collaboration with Paul Crowley of Eurostat, in order to classify all innovative CIS respondent firms into three mutually exclusive innovation modes that capture different methods of innovating, plus a fourth group for noninnovators.[14] The classification method uses two main criteria: the level of novelty of the firm's innovations and the creative effort that the firm expends on in-house innovative activities. The three innovation modes are as follows:

Lead innovators: For these firms, creative in-house innovative activities form an important part of the firm's strategy. All firms have introduced at least one product or process innovation developed at least partly in-house, performed R&D at least on an occasional basis and have introduced a new-to-market innovation. These firms are also likely sources of innovations that are later adopted or imitated by other firms.

Technology modifiers: These firms primarily innovate through modifying technology developed by other firms or institutions. None of them perform R&D on either an occasional or continuous basis. Many firms that are essentially process innovators that innovate through in-house production engineering will fall within this group.

Technology adopters: These firms do not develop innovations in-house, with all innovations acquired from external sources. An example is the purchase of new production machinery.

Table 8.7 presents the distribution of firms according to innovation mode for 14 EU nations for which the necessary data are available and also includes the percentage of firms that did not innovate. The results are weighted to reflect the distribution of all firms within the industry and service sectors covered by CIS-3. The results show that Finland, Germany, Sweden and Luxembourg have the highest percentage of firms in the lead category of innovators, while Germany, Luxembourg and Austria have the highest percentages of firms that

Table 8.7 Distribution of innovation modes in 14 EU member nations, 1998–2000

	Leaders	Modifiers	Adopters	Noninnovators	Total
Belgium	20	16	14	50	100
Denmark	19	11	14	56	100
Germany	25	25	11	39	100
Greece	13	5	10	72	100
Italy	18	15	4	64	100
Spain	8	5	19	67	100
France	20	10	11	59	100
Luxembourg	24	20	4	52	100
Netherlands	22	16	8	55	100
Portugal	18	16	13	54	100
United Kingdom	11	5	16	68	100
Finland	29	10	3	55	100
Sweden	25	14	8	53	100
Austria	20	20	9	51	100

Source: Third Community Innovation Survey (CIS).

are technology modifiers. In Spain, Greece and the United Kingdom over 80 per cent of firms are either adopters or noninnovators.

8.5 The Relation between Organizational Practice and Innovation Mode

As our introductory discussion pointed out, much of the discussion in the organizational behaviour literature on the relation between organization and innovation focuses on whether or not particular organizational designs are better suited for undertaking radical or incremental innovations. Radical innovations can be defined as innovations that transform existing markets or industries and on which many incremental innovations are developed. For example, Lam (2005) and Lam and Lundvall (2006) argue that Mintzberg's (1979, 1983) 'operating adhocracy' form of organization, which relies on networks of professional experts and the creation of ad hoc project teams, is especially adapted to developing novel or radical innovations characteristic of new emerging technologies. The firms of Silicon Valley provide good examples of this organizational form (Bahrami and Evans 2000; Saxenian 1996). In contrast, it is widely asserted in the literature on the Japanese firm that its organizational design is especially suited for progressive or incremental improvements in product quality and design (Aoki 1990; Coriat 1991; Womack et al. 1990). The Japanese organization relies on firm-specific knowledge that is embedded in the firm's organizational routines and relatively stable team structures for continuous product and process improvement.

Since the business practices and forms of work organization captured in our discretionary learning and lean clusters correspond rather closely to those that characterize the 'operating adhocracy' and the 'Japanese-firm', this literature led us to anticipate differences in the relative frequency of radical and incremental innovations in a nation depending on the relative prevalence of the discretionary learning and lean forms of work organization. Developing empirical indicators to identify radical and incremental modes of innovation is problematic, however. Survey manuals, such as the Oslo Manual that provide the basis of the CIS questions, do not propose guidelines for how to measure radical innovations. This makes it difficult to bring survey-based evidence to bear on the various propositions developed in the organizational literature.

Our typology of innovation modes captures a different but related distinction in the nature of innovation by distinguishing between firms that have developed in-house, 'new-to-market' product or process innovations (lead innovators) versus firms that have only introduced 'new to firm' innovations that were partly or entirely developed outside the firm (technology modifiers and technology adopters). This distinction is not identical to the difference between radical and incremental innovations, since not all 'new-to-market' innovations will have major transformative impacts on markets or industries. However, there are large differences along the continuum between lead innovators and technology adopters in each firm's capacity to explore new knowledge, which is conceptually similar (although on a different scale) to the difference between radical and incremental innovations.

In order to provide evidence that bears on the proposed link between organizational practices and innovation modes, in this section we start by presenting a series of scatter plot diagrams showing, for all sectors, the correlations between the frequency of the four innovation modes and the frequency of the discretionary learning, lean and Taylorist forms of work organization for the 14 EU nations for which data are available. We then present separate sets of correlations for manufacturing and for services.[15]

Figure 8.1 presents the results of this exercise for the discretionary learning (DL) form of work organization. The main result is that there is a positive correlation between discretionary learning and the frequency of the two innovation modes for which the levels of novelty and creative in-house effort are the highest, the lead innovators and modifiers, while there is a negative correlation between discretionary learning and the frequency of noninnovators.

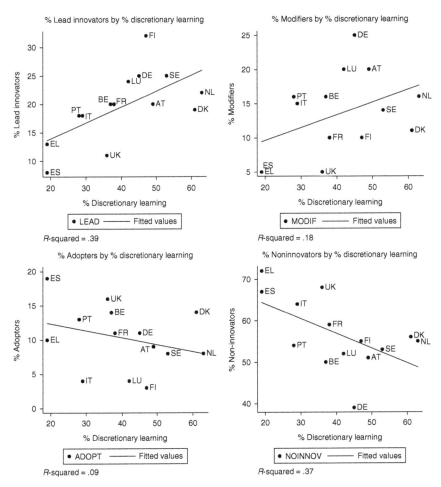

Figure 8.1 Correlations between innovation modes and discretionary learning, all sectors

Furthermore, the strongest positive correlation is between lead innovators and discretionary learning, with an R^2 of 0.39.[16]

Figure 8.2 presents the same analysis using the frequency of the lean form of work organization. The results tend to go in the opposite direction of those for discretionary learning. Thus they show a negative correlation between the frequency of the lean form and the frequency of the two innovation modes, which depend on in-house creative effort for innovation, and a positive correlation with the frequency of adopters and noninnovators.[17]

Figure 8.3 shows that the frequency of the Taylorist forms of work organization is negatively correlated with the frequency of lead innovators and positively correlated with the frequency of noninnovators. The correlations are relatively weak, though, and are not significant at the .10 level.

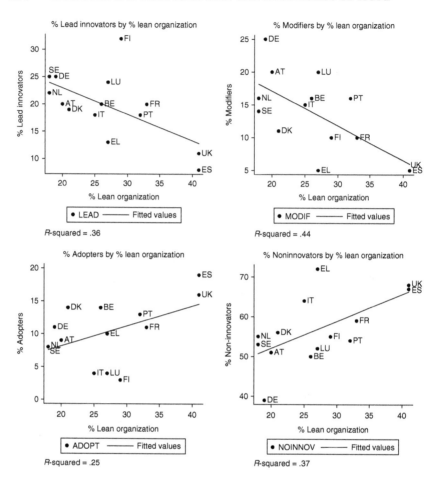

Figure 8.2 Correlations between innovation modes and lean organization, all sectors

These results provide support for the view that there are systemic links between the way work is organized in a nation and the distribution of different innovation modes.[18] More specifically, the positive correlation between discretionary learning and the frequency of lead innovators provides support for the hypothesis developed in the qualitative literature that the forms of work organization characteristic of operating adhocracies support the exploration of new knowledge that is needed for creative, in-house innovative activities that can lead to the development of new-to-market innovations and possibly radical innovations.

The results, however, are unexpected in two respects. First, while the negative correlation between the frequency of Taylorism and lead innovators and

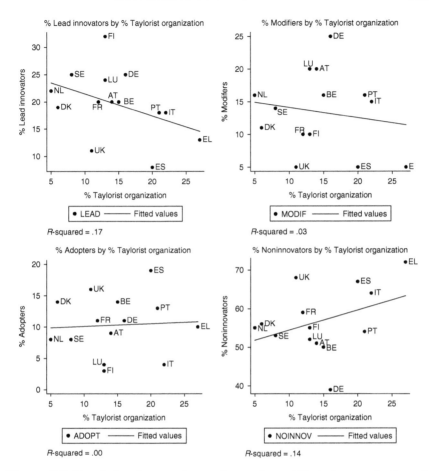

Figure 8.3 Correlations between innovation modes and Taylorist organization, all sectors

the positive correlation between Taylorism and noninnovators are consistent with the ideas developed in the organizational design literature; the correlations are relatively weak compared to those observed for the discretionary learning and lean forms of work organization. One possible explanation for this is that our employee level data is picking up that some innovating firms use Taylorist work organization for production operations while discretionary learning is practised in more knowledge-intensive activities. If this were the case, there would be little reason to expect variations in its use to be strongly correlated with innovation mode. This possibility is further explored below in the section comparing manufacturing and services.

Second, while the negative correlations shown in Figure 8.2 between the lean forms of work organization and the frequency of the lead innovators are consistent with our reading of the organizational design literature, the negative correlation with the frequency of modifiers is not. Based on the Japanese experience, we expected the frequency of the lean forms to be positively correlated with the prevalence of technology modifiers, which are dominated by innovation based on minor incremental improvements. Furthermore, the results in Table 8.2 show that employees subject to the lean forms of work organization report above average rates of problem solving and learning. Nevertheless, the negative correlation with the frequency of technology modifiers is the highest observed (R^2 value of 0.44) while the lean forms are positively correlated with the prevalence of firms that either do not innovate or only innovate through adopting new technology. Firms grouped in this latter category do not need to invest very much in exploring new knowledge in order to innovate.[19]

The lack of a positive correlation between the lean form of work organization and the prevalence of modifiers could be due to limitations with the data. However, an alternative possibility is that the lean model could have been adopted by European firms as a more efficient alternative to Taylorism, without adopting the Japanese emphasis on the delegation of decision-making responsibility to shop-floor employees. Under these conditions, the problem solving and learning tasks reported by employees subject to lean organization could be severely limited by the high prevalence of reported constraints (see Table 8.2), limiting opportunities to suggest or implement incremental improvements.[20] This interpretation finds support in the fact that monotonous and repetitive work is as frequent or even more frequent in the lean production category than it is in Taylorist work form. If true, such restrictions on lean organizational forms could explain part of an innovation performance gap between Europe and Japan.

8.6 Differences between Manufacturing and Services

The relationships observed at the level of national aggregates could be the outcome of contradictory patterns in different parts of the economy. Due to access limitations to the CIS data, we were unable to conduct detailed analyses at the sector level,[21] but it is possible to divide the economy into two main sectors – services and manufacturing. Below we present a series of scatter plot diagrams showing, for manufacturing and services separately, the correlations between the frequency of the four innovation modes and the frequency of the discretionary learning, lean and Taylorist forms of work organization. This analysis is interesting since it will also allow us to determine in a preliminary manner whether the observed relations between forms of work organization and modes of innovation display sector specificities.

Figure 8.4 presents the correlations between the frequency of discretionary learning and the innovation modes. In both manufacturing and services, the

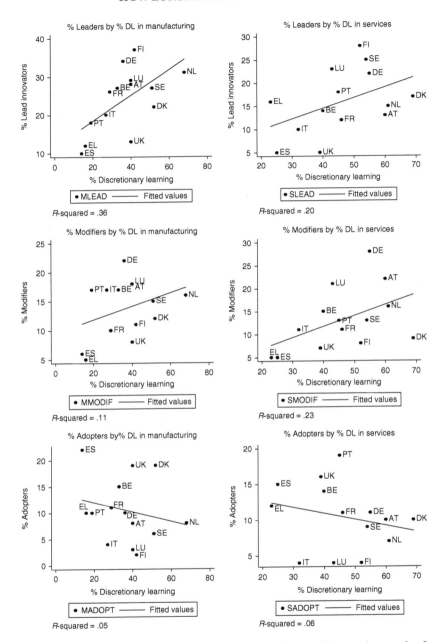

Figure 8.4 Correlations between discretionary learning and innovation modes for manufacturing and for services

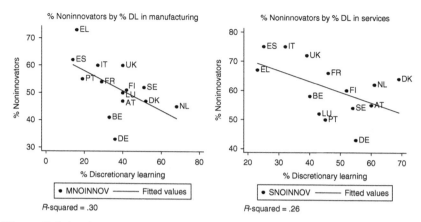

Figure 8.4. (*cont.*)

frequency of discretionary learning varies between a low of about 20 per cent and a high of about 70 per cent. The frequency of lead innovators tends to be somewhat higher in manufacturing than in services and the frequency of noninnovators somewhat lower.

The relations between the frequency of discretionary learning and the frequency of the innovation modes that are observed for all sectors combined are for the most part reproduced for manufacturing and for services separately, though the positive correlation with lead innovators is somewhat higher for manufacturing. The results support the basic conclusion about the positive relation between the use of discretionary learning and firms' capacities for knowledge exploration and innovation.

Figure 8.5 presents scatter plot diagrams showing the correlations between the frequency of use of lean organization and the innovation modes. Manufacturing and services exhibit some noticeable differences, with services displaying stronger negative correlations between the frequency of lean organization and the frequencies of both lead innovators and modifiers, and a stronger positive correlation between the frequency of lean organization and the frequency of noninnovators. The results suggest that while the lean forms of work organization are poorly suited to the requirements of knowledge exploration and innovation in general, this is especially the case for services. One possible explanation for this pertains to the coverage of CIS-3, which excludes retailing, hotels and restaurants and personal services and so is relatively weighted to the more knowledge-intensive service sectors such as business and financial services. Some of the defining characteristics of lean work organization, such as strong hierarchical and norm-based constraints on work pace, may be especially unsuited to the dynamics of knowledge exploration and innovation in these service sectors.

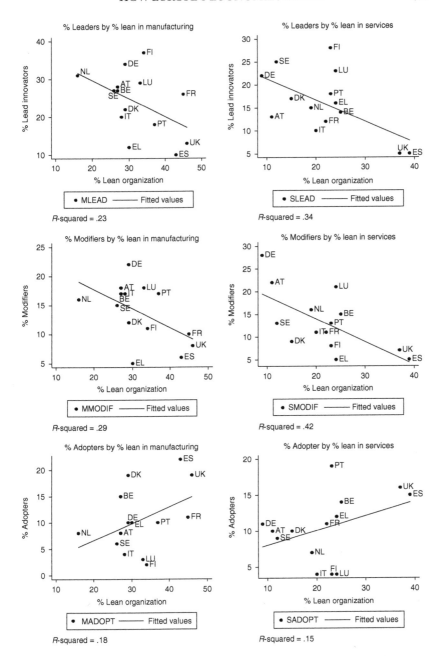

Figure 8.5 Correlations between innovation modes and lean organization for manufacturing and services

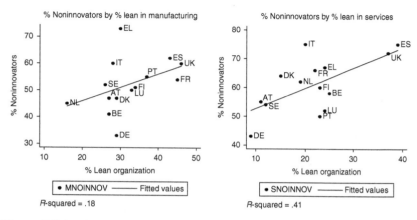

Figure 8.5 (*cont.*)

Figure 8.6 shows the correlations between the frequency of Taylorist forms of work organization and the innovation modes. The differences between manufacturing and services are even more striking than for the case of the lean forms of work organization. While there is no obvious relation between the frequency of Taylorism and the frequency of the innovation modes for services, there is a statistically significant negative correlation between the frequency of Taylorism and the frequency of lead innovators and a comparably strong positive correlation between Taylorism and the frequency of noninnovators. This difference between manufacturing and services might be accounted for along the lines suggested above. Although the frequency of use of Taylorist methods of work organization varies considerably across EU nations, it is relatively low in the service sectors with an average frequency of less than 9 per cent. This low frequency of use of Taylorism could simply reflect the fact that within the service sectors under consideration, Taylorist work methods are primarily used for ancillary operations within firms that are predominately organized according to either the discretionary learning or lean principles of work organization. Under these circumstances, there would be little reason to expect that variations in the use of Taylorism would be sharply correlated with the frequency of each innovation mode. A fuller treatment of this question would require access to disaggregated data.

8.7 Conclusion

This chapter develops a set of EU-wide aggregate measures that are used to explore, at the level of the national innovation system, the relation between innovation and the organization of work. Although our data can only show correlations rather than causality and are aggregated at the national level, they

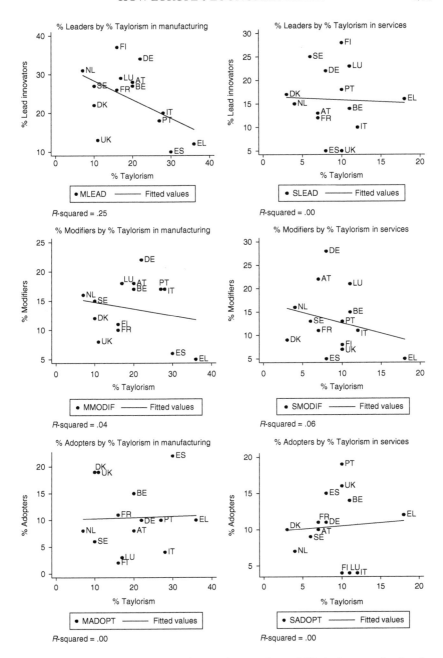

Figure 8.6 Correlations between innovation modes and Taylorist organization for manufacturing and services

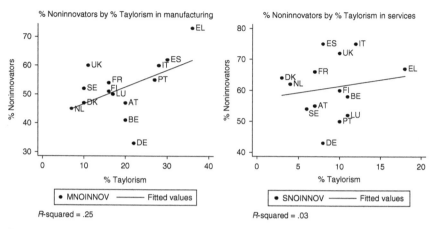

Figure 8.6 *(cont.)*

support the view that the way work is organized is highly nation-specific and that it coevolves with an equally highly nation-specific distribution of different modes of innovation.

Before going further in terms of conclusions, we need to introduce some caveats. Both the dataset behind the work organization analysis and the dataset behind the pattern of innovation modes are from surveys pursued in parallel in the EU-15: in the first case addressed to employees and in the second to management. There are obvious problems with interpreting survey data emanating from different countries. Different responses to the same question may reflect national 'cultural' differences rather than real existing differences. For instance the big gap in the share of innovative firms between Germany and the United Kingdom calls for closer scrutiny. Another issue is if the substantial differences, both in terms of work organization and innovation modes, between the two Nordic countries of Denmark and Finland are real or reflect different attitudes among employees and managers. Finding new ways to 'triangulate' results of national surveys with the aim to make them more reliable – for instance by combining detailed case studies with testing questionnaire responses in different countries – is a major challenge. Until we get more reliable methods, we must work on the assumption that the observed national differences are either real or that the cultural biases equally affect the responses from employees and from managers. With this in mind, we will point to what we see as the main findings and their implications for future research, indicator work and public policy.

A first major finding is that in nations where work is organized to support high levels of discretion in solving complex problems, firms tend to be more active in terms of innovations developed through their own in-house creative efforts. In countries where learning and problem solving on the job are constrained and little discretion is left to the employee, firms tend to engage in a supplier-dominated innovation strategy. Their technological renewal depends more on the absorption of innovations developed elsewhere. The negative correlation between 'lean production' and 'modifier innovation' raises important questions about how successful European firms have been able to make the J-form of organization support innovation. Our analysis gives rise to new hypotheses on how management techniques such as job rotation and teamwork are related to innovation. They point to a need to develop analytical concepts that can link workplace organization and the dynamics of innovation at the level of the firm.

Second, the results indicate that learning and interaction within the organizations and at workplaces are at least as important for innovation performance as learning through interactions with external agents. Therefore, in order to understand national systems of innovation, it is necessary to bring the organization of work into the analysis. Early conceptions of national innovation systems were built on an analysis of interactive learning between producers and users. Now the analysis needs to be founded also on an understanding of how people interact and learn at the workplace in different national economies.

A third implication is that the indicators for innovation need to do more than capture material inputs such as R&D expenditures and human capital inputs, such as the quality of the available pool of skills based on the number of years of education. Indicators also need to capture how these material and human resources are used and whether or not the work environment promotes the further development of the knowledge and skills of employees. One step towards more adequately addressing the relation between organization and innovation is to gather and analyse complementary firm-level data on both innovation modes and organizational forms. One option is to develop better indicators of organizational innovation and practices in future CIS surveys, as proposed by the third revision of the Oslo Manual in 2005. The CIS could respond to some of the limitations inherent in relying on the employee-level data of the European Survey on Working Conditions by supplying establishment-level data on the way knowledge flows and knowledge sharing are organized within firms and how they relate to other aspects of corporate strategy.

Fourth, some tentative policy implications may be drawn from the analysis. Though based on simple correlations that cannot establish a causal relation, our results suggest that European policy efforts to improve innovation performance as part of the revised Lisbon strategy need to take a close look at the effects of organizational practices on innovation. The bottleneck to improving the innovative capabilities of European firms might not be low levels of R&D expenditures, but the widespread presence of working environments that are unable to provide a fertile atmosphere for innovation. If this is the case, European policy should make a major effort to develop policy instruments that could stimulate the adoption of 'pro-innovation' organizational practice, particularly in countries with poor innovative performance.

Finally, a striking result is that there are fundamental differences between the countries with respect to both in how work is organized and in how firms innovate. These differences remain after controlling for differences in industrial structure. It is a major challenge for future research to understand the underlying 'unexplained' national factors that influence firms' organizational (work organization) choices as well as their innovation performance. Preliminary analysis suggests that some specific variables reflecting institutional differences among the countries are quite strongly correlated with the prevalence of discretionary learning (levels of trust, labour market and welfare-state characteristics as well as frequency of vocational training). We have chosen not to introduce these issues here since it would require a thorough analysis of the role of institutions in shaping national systems of innovation. Such an analysis is a major challenge for future research.

We hope our results will widen the debate and stimulate further theoretical work and comparative research exploring the links between organizational forms, innovative performance and the institutional context within Europe.

Appendix 1 Organizational Variables Used in Factor Analysis

Variable		Mean
Teamwork	1 if your job involves doing all or part of your work in a team, 0 otherwise	64.2
Job rotation	1 if your job involves rotating tasks between yourself and colleagues, 0 otherwise	48.9
Quality norms	1 if your main paid job involves meeting precise quality standards, 0 otherwise	74.4
Discretion in fixing work methods	1 if you are able to choose or change your methods of work, 0 otherwise	61.7
Discretion in setting work pace	1 if you are able to choose or change your pace of work, 0 otherwise	63.6
Horizontal constraints on work pace	1 if on the whole your pace of work is dependent on the work of your colleagues, 0 otherwise	53.1
Hierarchical constraints on work pace	1 if on the whole your pace of work is dependent on the direct control of your boss, 0 otherwise	38.9
Norm-based constraints on work pace	1 if on the whole your pace of work is dependent on the numerical production targets, 0 otherwise	38.7
Automatic constraints on work pace	1 if on the whole your pace of work is dependent on the automatic speed of a machine or movement of a product, 0 otherwise	26.7
Employee responsibility for quality control	1 if the employee's main paid job involves assessing him or herself the quality of his or her own work, 0 otherwise	72.6
Employee problem solving	1 if your job involves solving unforeseen problems on your own, 0 otherwise	79.3
Learning new things	1 if your job involves learning new things on your own, 0 otherwise	71.4
Task Complexity	1 if your job involves complex tasks, 0 otherwise	56.7
Task monotony	1 if your job involves monotonous tasks, 0 otherwise	42.4
Task repetitiveness	1 if your work involves short repetitive tasks of less than one minute, 0 otherwise	24.9

Appendix 2 Graphical Representation of Factor Analysis – 15 Organizational Variables

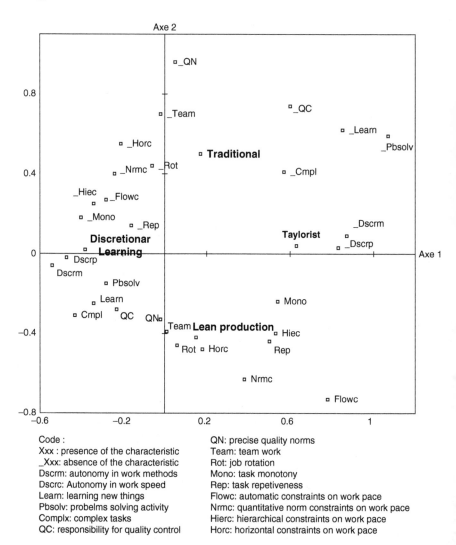

Figure A8.1 Forms of work organization

The figure above presents graphically the first two axes or factors of the multiple correspondence analysis (MCA). The first factor or axis, accounting for 18% of the inertia or chi-squared statistic, distinguishes between Taylorist and 'post-Taylorist' organizational forms. Thus on one side of the axis we find the variables measuring autonomy, learning, problem-solving and task complexity and to a lesser degree quality management, while on the other side we find the variables measuring monotony and the various factors constraining work pace, notably those linked to the automatic speed of equipment or flow of products and to the use of quantitative production norms. The second factor or axis, accounting for 15% of the chi-squared statistic, is structured by two groups of variables characteristic of the lean production model: first, the use of teams and job rotation, which are associated with the importance of horizontal constraints on work pace, and second, those variables measuring the use of quality management techniques, which are associated with what we have called 'automatic' and 'norm-based' constraints. The third factor, which accounts for 8 per cent of the chi-squared statistic, is also structured by these two groups of variables. However, it brings into relief the distinction between, on the one hand, those organizational settings characterized by team work, job rotation and horizontal interdependence in work, and, on the other hand, those organizational settings where the use of quality norms, automatic and quantitative norm-based constraints on work pace are important. The second and third axes of the analysis demonstrate that the simple dichotomy between Taylorist and lean organizational methods is not sufficient for capturing the organizational variety that exists across European nations.

The projection of the centre of gravity of the four organizational clusters coming out of the hierarchical classification analysis (see Table 8.2) onto the graphic representation of the first two factors of the MCA shows that the four clusters correspond to the quite different working conditions. The discretionary learning cluster is located to the east of the graph, the lean cluster to the south, the Taylorist cluster to the west and the traditional cluster to the north.

Notes

1 We ignore here the effect of organizational forms that provide financial or other incentives to employees to innovate.

2 Results for the United Kingdom were provided by the Department of Trade and Industry and results for Denmark by the Danish Centre for Studies in Research and Research Policy.

3 This section draws extensively from Lorenz and Valeyre (2005).

4 The initial findings of the survey are presented in a European Foundation report by D. Merllié and P. Paoli [2001].

5 Mintzberg also refers to a third bureaucratic form, the 'divisionalized' form. Unlike the other four configurations, he describes it as a partial structure superimposed on others (i.e. divisions); each of which is driven towards the machine bureaucracy.

6 The term J-form is used because its archetypical practices and forms of work organization are best illustrated by the 'Japanese-type' organization discussed in the work of Aoki (1988) and Nonaka and Takeuchi (1995).

7 For the questions and coding used to construct the measures on which the statistical analysis is based, see Appendix 1.

8 The factor analysis method used here is multiple correspondence analysis (MCA), which is especially suitable for the analysis of categorical variables. Unlike principal components analysis where the total variance is decomposed along the principal factors or components, in multiple correspondence analysis the total variation of the data matrix is measured by the usual chi-squared statistic for row-column independence, and it is the chi-squared statistic that is decomposed along the principal factors. It is common to refer to the percentage of the 'inertia' accounted for by a factor. Inertia is defined as the value of the chi-squared statistic of the original data matrix divided by the grand total of the number of observations. (See J. P. Benzecri (1973); Greenacre (1993, 24–31)).

9 For a graphical presentation of the positions of the centres of gravity for the clusters on the first two factors of the MCA, see Appendix 2.

10 The percentages are weighted.

11 A third model, which included controls of age, gender and a measure of the importance of further education received by the employee, gave substantially the same results. The only differences were that working in Austria becomes a significant predictor of the likelihood of working under the discretionary learning forms; working in Portugal is no longer a significant predictor of the likelihood of working under the lean forms, and working in Finland or Austria is no longer significant negative predictor of the likelihood of working under the traditional forms.

12 As an example, the 2005 European Innovation Scoreboard finds a 2.5 fold difference between the best and worst EU-15 member states on the Summary Innovation Index.

13 CIS-3 did not include firms in several sectors covered in the Third Working Conditions Survey: construction (NACE 45) and several service sectors: retail trade (NACE 52), automobile trade and repair (NACE 50), hotels and restaurants (NACE 55), some business services (NACE 74.1 and NACE 74.4 to 74.8) and personal services (NACE 90 to 93). However CIS-3 did include wholesale trade (NACE 51). The main effect is that the CIS innovation modes data will underestimate the percentage of firms with traditional forms of work organization (see below, pp.).

14 Data are available for all EU member nations in 2000 with the exception of Ireland. The original Arundel, Hollanders and Crowley classification makes a further distinction between lead innovators that make continuous use of R&D and are active on national or international markets and lead innovators that make only occasional use of R&D and/or are only active on local or regional markets. Since our interest is the relation between forms of work organization and the capacity for creative in-house development of novel products or processes regardless of R&D expenditures or the scope of markets, we have merged these two categories into a single 'lead innovator' group. For full details on the methodology for innovation modes, see Annex B of the Trend Chart document 'EXIS: An Exploratory Approach to Innovation Scoreboards' available at http://trendchart.cordis.lu/scoreboards/scoreboard2004/pdf/EXIS.pdf).

15 In order to calculate the correlations on the basis of survey samples, which are harmonized to the fullest extent possible, firms from construction (NACE 45), hotels and restaurants (NACE 55) and personal services (NACE 90 to 93) have been excluded from the Working Conditions Survey sample.

16 The correlations between the frequency of discretionary learning and the frequencies of lead innovators and noninnovators are significant at the .05 level.

17 All these correlations are significant at the .05 level or better with the exception of the positive correlation between lean and the frequency of adopters, which is significant at the .10 level.

18 The innovation modes are only weakly correlated with the frequency of the traditional forms of work organization (R-squared less than .10 in all cases).

19 Some investment in learning will nevertheless be required, both to select the new technology to adopt and to adapt employee skills and competences to its use.

20 The vast literature on the transfer of Japanese management practices by Japanese multinationals to their affiliates located in Europe and the United States and during the 1980s and 1990s provides evidence relevant to this issue. Most of this literature argues that Japanese management practices are modified in the process of transfer resulting in hybrid organizational forms combining elements of work organization and HRM practices characteristic of the host country. See Kenney and Florida 1993; Liker et al. 1992; Oliver and Wilkinson 1992. For evidence on the limited delegation of decision-making authority to shop-floor personnel in Japanese transplants located in the United Kingdom, see Lorenz (2000); Doeringer et al. (2003).

21 Access to CIS-3 data was restricted, with the results for innovation mode calculated in-house by Eurostat and by national statistical offices at our request. Both lacked the resources to conduct detailed analyses at a highly disaggregated sector level. Since then, the micro CIS-3 data for some countries can by analysed by researchers on site at Eurostat, but unfortunately the micro data for most of the original EU-15 countries are still unavailable.

References

Amable, B. R., R. Barré and R. Boyer. 1997. *Les systèmes d'innovation à l'ère de la globalisation*. Paris: Economica.

Aoki, M. 1990. *Information, Incentives and Bargaining in the Japanese Firm*. Cambridge: Cambridge University Press.

Arundel, A. and H. Hollanders. 2005. EXIS: An Exploratory Approach to Innovation Scoreboards. http://trendchart.cordis.lu/scoreboards/scoreboard2004/pdf/EXIS. pdf, March.

Bahrami, H., and S. Evans. 2000. Flexible Recycling and High-technology Entrepreneurship. In *Understanding Silicon Valley*, ed. M. Kenney, pp. 165–89. Stanford, CA: Stanford University Press.

Benzecri, J.-P. 1973. 'L'analyse des données', Vol. 2. Paris: Dunod.

Boyer, R. and J.-P. Durand. 1993. 'L'après fordisme'. Paris: Syros.

Burns, T. E. and G. M. Stalker. 1961. *The Management of Innovations*. London: Tavistock Publications.

Cézard M., F. Dussert and M. Gollac. 1992. 'Taylor va au marché. Organisation du travail et informatique'. *Travail et Emploi*, no. 54: 4–19.

Coriat, B. 1991. *Penser à l'envers: travail et organisation dans l'entreprise japonaise*. Paris: Christian Bourgois.

Coutrot, T. 1998. *L'entreprise néolibérale, nouvelle utopie capitaliste?* Paris. La Découverte.

Dertoutzos, M. L., R. K. Lester and R. M. Solow. 1989. Made in America. Cambridge, MA: MIT Press.

Doeringer, P., E. Lorenz, and D. Terkla. 2003. 'National Hybrids: How Japanese Multinationals Transfer Workplace Practices to Other Countries'. *Cambridge Journal of Economics 7*: 265–86.

Freeman, C. 1987. *Technology Policy and Economic Performance: Lessons from Japan*. London: Pinter Publishers.

Freyssenet, M. 1995. 'La 'production réflexive': une alternative à la 'production de masse' et à la 'production au plus juste?' *Sociologie du Travail* 7, no. 3: 365–89.

Gittleman, M., M. Horrigan and M. Joyce. 1998. 'Flexible' Workplace Practices: Evidence from a nationally Representative Survey'. *Industrial and Labour Relations Review* 52, no. 1: 99–119.

Gjerding, A. N. 1992. 'Work Organisation and the Innovation Design Dilemma'. In *National Systems of Innovation: Towards a Theory of Innovation and Interactive Learning*, edited by B.-Å. Lundvall, 95–115. London: Pinter.

Greenacre, M. J. 1993. *Correspondence Analysis in Practice*. New York: Academic Press.

Hall, P. and D. Soskice. 2001. *Varieties of Capitalism*. Oxford: Oxford University Press.

Ichiniowski, C., K. Shaw. and G. Prennushi. 1997. 'The Effects of Human Resource Management Policies on Productivity: A Study of Steel Finishing Lines', *American Economic Review* 17, no. 1.

Jensen, M., B. Johnson, E. Lorenz and B.-Å. Lundvall. 2007. 'Forms of Knowledge, Modes of Innovation and Innovation Systems'. *Research Policy* 36: 680–93.

Kenney, M. and R. Florida. 1993. *Beyond Mass Production: The Japanese system and its transfer to the US*. New York, Oxford University Press.

Kline, S. J. and N. Rosenberg. 1986. 'An Overview of Innovation'. In R. Landau and N. Rosenberg. *The Positive Sum Game*. Washington DC: National Academy Press.

Knack, S. and P. Keefer. 1997. 'Does Social Capital Have an Economic Payoff? A Cross-Country Investigation', *Quarterly Journal of Economics* 112: 1251–88.

La Porta, R., F. Lopez-de-Salanes, A. Shleifer. and R. Vishny. 1997. 'Trust in Large Organizations'. *American Economic Review Paper and Proceedings* 87: 333–38.

Lam, A. 2005. 'Organizational Innovation'. In *Handbook of Innovation*, edited by J. Fagerberg, D. Mowery and R. Nelson. Oxford: Oxford University Press.

Lam, A., and B.-Å. Lundvall. 2006. 'The Learning Organisation and National Systems of Competence Building and Innovation'. In *How Europe's Economies Learn: Coordinating Competing Models*, edited by E. Lorenz and B.-Å. Lundvall. Oxford: Oxford University Press.

Laursen, K., and N. Foss. 2003. 'New Human Resource Management Practices, Complementarities and the Impact on Innovation Performance'. *Cambridge Journal of Economics* 27: 243–65.

Liker, J., W. Fruin, and P. Adler. (eds.). 1992. *Remade in America: Transplanting and Transforming Japanese Management Systems*. Oxford: Oxford University Press.

Linhart, D. 1994. *La modernisation des entreprises*. Paris: La Découverte.

Lorenz, E., 2000. 'Societal Effects and the Transfer of Business Practices to Britain and France'. In *Embedding Organisatons: Societal Effects of Actors, Organisatons and Socioeconomic Context*, edited by M. Maurice and A. Sorge. Amsterdam: John Benjamins.

Lorenz, E., and A. Valeyre. 2006. 'Organisational Forms and Innovative Performance'. In *How Europe's Economies Learn: Coordinating Competing Models*, edited by E. Lorenz and B.-Å. Lundvall, 140–61. Oxford: Oxford University Press.

Lundvall, B.-Å. 1988. 'Innovation as an Interactive Process: From User-Producer Interaction to the National Innovation Systems'. In *Technology and Economic Theory*, edited by G. Dosi, C. Freeman, R. R. Nelson, G. Silverberg, and L. Soete. London. Pinter Publishers.

———. 2002. *Innovation, Growth and Social Cohesion: The Danish Model*. Cheltenham: Edward Elgar.

MacDuffie, J. P. and J. Krafcik. 1992. 'Interacting Technology and Human Resources For High Performance Manufacturing: Evidence From the International Auto Industry'.

In *Transforming Organisations*, edited by T. Kochan and M. Useem. New York: Oxford University Press.

MacDuffie, J. P. and F. Pil. 1997. 'Changes in Auto Industry Employment Practices: An International Overview'. In *After Lean Production*, edited by K. Thomas, R. Lansbury, and J.-P. MacDuffie, 9–42. Ithaca, NY: Cornell University Press.

Merllié, D. and P. Paoli. 2001. Third European Survey on Working Conditions (2000). Luxembourg: Office for official publications of the European communities, 2001.

Mintzberg, H. 1979. *The Structuring of Organisation*. Engelwood Cliffs, NJ: Princeton University Press.

———. 1983. *Structure in Fives. Designing Effective Organizations*. Englewood-Cliffs, NJ: Prentice Hall.

Nelson, R. R. (ed.). 1993. *National Innovation Systems: A Comparative Analysis*. Oxford: Oxford University Press.

Nielsen, P. and B.-Å. Lundvall. 2006. 'Learning Organisations and Industrial Relations: How the Danish Economy Learns'. In *How Europe's Economies Learn: Coordinating Competing Models*, edited by E. Lorenz and B.-Å. Lundvall. Oxford: Oxford University Press.

Nonaka, I. and H. Takeuchi. 1995. *The Knowledge Creating Company*. Oxford: Oxford University Press.

Oliver, N. and B. Wilkinson. 1992. *The Japanisation of the British Economy*. London: Blackwell.

Osterman, P. 1994. 'How Common Is Workplace Transformation and Who Adopts It?' *Industrial and Labor Relations Review* 47: 173–88.

———. 2000. 'Work Reorganization in an Era of Restructuring: Trends in Diffusion and Effects on Employee Welfare'. *Industrial and Labor Relations Review* 53: 179–96.

Ramsay, H., D. Scholarios and B. Harley. 2000. 'Employees and High-Performance Work Systems, Testing inside the Black Box'. *British Journal of Industrial Relation* 38, no. 4: 501–31.

Rothwell, R. 1972. 'Factors for Success in Industrial Innovations: Project SAPPHO – A Comparative Study of Success and Failure in Industrial Innovation'. In *Science Policy Research Unit*. Brighton: University of Sussex.

Saxenian, A. L. 1996. *Regional Advantage: Culture and Competition in Silicon Valley and Route 128*. Cambridge, MA: Harvard University Press.

Truss, C. 2001. 'Complexities and Controversies in Linking HRM with Organisational Outcomes'. *Journal of Management Studies* 38, no. 8: 1120–49.

Womack J. P., D. T. Jones and D. Roos. 1990. *The Machine That Changed the World*. New York: Rawson Associates.

Wood, S. 1999. 'Getting the Measure of the Transformed High-Performance Organisation'. *British Journal of Industrial Relations* 37, no. 3: 391–417.

Zak, P. and S. Knack. 1998. 'Trust and Growth'. IRIS Center Working Paper No. 219.

Chapter 9

POSTSCRIPT: INNOVATION SYSTEM RESEARCH; WHERE IT CAME FROM AND WHERE IT MIGHT GO

Bengt-Åke Lundvall

9.1 Introduction

When the first edition of this book[1] was published in 1992, the concept of 'national innovation system' was known only by a handful of scholars and policymakers. Over a period of 15 years, there has been a rapid and wide diffusion of the concept. Giving 'Google' the text strings 'national innovation system(s)' and 'national system(s) of innovation' you end up with almost one million references. Going through the references, you find that most of them are recent and that many of them are related to innovation policy efforts at the national level while others refer to new contributions in social science.

Using Google Scholar (May 2007), we find that more than 2,000 scientific publications have referred to the different editions of Lundvall (1992). Economists, business economists, economic historians, sociologists, political scientists and especially economic geographers have utilized the concept to explain and understand phenomena related to innovation and competence building.[2]

In this chapter we argue that during the process of diffusion there has been a *distortion* of the concept as compared to the original versions as developed by Christopher Freeman and the IKE group in Aalborg. Often policymakers and scholars have applied a narrow understanding of the concept and this has given rise to so-called 'innovation paradoxes', which leave significant elements of innovation-based economic performance unexplained.

Such a bias is reflected in studies of innovation that focus on science-based innovation and on the *formal* technological infrastructure and in policies aiming almost exclusively at stimulating R&D efforts in hi-tech sectors.

Without a broad definition of the national innovation system encompassing individual, organizational and interorganizational learning, it is impossible to establish the link from innovation to economic growth. A double focus is needed where attention is given not only to the science infrastructure but also to institutions/organizations that support *competence building* in labour markets, education and working life. This is especially important in the current era of the *globalizing learning economy* (Lundvall and Johnson 1994; Lundvall and Borras 1998; Archibugi and Lundvall 2001).

We see one major reason for this distortion in the uncomfortable coexistence in international organizations such as OECD and the European Commission of the innovation system approach and the much more narrow understanding of innovation emanating from standard economics (Eparvier 2005). Evolutionary processes of learning where agents are transformed and become more diverse in terms of what they know and what they know how to do are not reconcilable with the rational 'representative agents' that populate the neoclassical world (Dosi 1999). Actually, we regard the neglect of 'learning as competence building' as the principal weakness of standard economics and the narrow definitions of innovation systems as reflecting a negative spillover from this misdirected abstraction.

Both 'Mode 2 knowledge production' (Gibbons et al. 1994) and the 'Triple Helix' approach focus on science and the role of universities in innovation. When they present themselves or are applied by policymakers, not as analysing a subsystem within but as full-blown alternatives to the innovation system approach (Etzkowitz and Leydesdorff 1995; Etzkowitz; Leydesdorff 2000), these approaches contribute to the distortion. These perspectives capture processes linking science and technology to innovation; below we refer to this as *STI learning*. The fact that science and codified knowledge become increasingly important for more and more firms in different industries – including the so-called low-tech ones – *does not imply that experience-based learning and tacit knowledge have become less important* for innovation. To bring innovations, including science-based innovations to the market, organizational learning, industrial networks as well as employee participation and competence building are more important than ever. We refer to these processes as *DUI learning*.

Section 9.2 takes a brief look at how the concept National System of Innovation (NSI) came about and developed on the general background of the history of innovation research.[3] Section 9.3 confronts the theoretical foundations of the concept with standard economics; section 9.4 defines analytical challenges. Section 9.5 relates the concept to economic development, inequality and sustainability. The chapter ends with the concluding section 9.6. As mentioned, the literature on innovation systems has grown exponentially over the last 15 years, and what follows does not aim at a full and fair survey of the literature. The issues raised and the sources cited reflect my own priorities.

9.2 A Concept with Roots Far Back in History

9.2.1 Milestones in the development of the innovation system concept

Basic ideas behind the concept 'national systems of innovation' go back to Friedrich List (1841).[4] His concept of 'national systems of production' took into account a wide set of national institutions including those engaged in education and training as well as infrastructure such as networks for transportation of people and commodities (Freeman 1995a). To the best of my knowledge, the first written contribution that used the concept 'national system of innovation' was the unpublished paper by Christopher Freeman from 1982 that he produced for the OECD expert group on Science, Technology and Competitiveness (Freeman 1982, 18).[5] Here he takes Friedrich List as one central point of reference.

Box 9.1 Regional, Sectoral, Technological and Corporate Systems

Over the last decade several new concepts representing the systemic perspective on innovation have been developed. The literature on 'regional systems of innovation' has grown rapidly since the middle of the 1990s (Cooke 1996; Maskell and Malmberg 1997). Bo Carlsson with colleagues from Sweden developed the concept 'technological systems' in the beginning of the 1990s (Carlsson and Stankiewitz 1991). Franco Malerba with colleagues from Italy has developed the concept of 'sectoral systems of innovation' (Breschi and Malerba 1997). Ove Granstrand has proposed the 'corporate innovation system' as a perspective. Some of the crucial ideas inherent in the innovation system concept such as vertical interaction and innovation as an interactive process are central also in the literature on industrial clusters by Porter and colleagues.

Of these different perspectives, the regional system approach is the one that resembles most the original versions of the national system of innovation. It has in common with the NSI approach that it uses the fact that some knowledge is local and tacit to explain that innovation systems are localized. Also, both approaches attempt to explain economic performance of geographical entities. The corporate system perspective may also have economic performance at focus at the level of the single enterprise.

The other perspectives aim at explaining the innovation process in relation to specific technologies and sectors. The analysis of technological systems has been especially useful in analysing how new technologies emerge. The sectoral system approach is unique among the different approaches in not defining as analytical object a vertically integrated system. The approach may be seen as the outcome of a cross fertilization between industrial and innovation economics.

In the beginning of the 1980s, the idea of a national system of innovation was immanent in the work of several economists studying innovation. Richard R. Nelson together with other US scholars had compared technology policy and institutions in the high-tech field in the United States with Japan and Europe (Nelson 1984). Science Policy Research Unit (SPRU) at Sussex University pursued several studies comparing industrial development in Germany and the United Kingdom covering, for instance, differences in the management of innovation, work practices and engineering education.

The idea of a national system of innovation was immanent also in the research program pursued by the IKE group at Aalborg University.[6] In several working papers and publications from the first half of the 1980s, we referred to 'the innovative capability of the national system of production'. The handier 'innovation system' appears for the first time in *Product Innovation and User-Producer Interaction* (Lundvall 1985) but without the adjective 'national'. Again, it was Christopher Freeman who brought the modern version of the full concept 'national innovation system' into the literature. He did so in 1987 in his book on innovation and innovation policy in Japan (Freeman 1987).

When Freeman collaborated with Nelson and Lundvall in the project on technical change and economic theory supported by the International Federation of Institutes for Advanced Study (IFIAS), the outcome was a book (Dosi et al. 1988) with a section having several chapters on 'national systems of innovation' (Freeman 1988; Lundvall 1988; Nelson 1988). After that followed three major edited volumes on the subject (Lundvall 1992; Nelson 1993; Edquist 1997).[7]

The innovation system concept may be regarded as a practical tool for designing innovation policy, but it might also be seen as a synthesis of analytical results produced by scholars working on understanding innovation. In this section, we give a brief review of the history of innovation research with focus on how different generations of economists have contributed to the modern understanding of innovation systems.

9.2.2 Innovation research starting with Adam Smith

The idea that innovation matters for economic development is present in the work of the classical economists. Innovation plays an important role in the introduction to Adam Smith's classical work on the *Wealth of Nations*. It is especially interesting to note that he identifies and distinguishes *two different modes of innovation* (see Box 9.2).

Box 9.2 Adam Smith on Innovation and Modes of Learning

Adam Smith (1776, 8) on the DUI-mode of learning:

A great part of the machines made use of in those manufactures in which labour is most subdivided, were originally the invention of common workmen, who, being each of them employed in some very simple operation, naturally turned their thoughts towards finding out easier and readier methods of performing it. Whoever has been much accustomed to visit such manufactures, must frequently have been shown very pretty machines, which were the inventions of such workmen, in order to facilitate and quicken their own particular part of the work. In the first fire engines, a boy was constantly employed to open and shut alternately the communication between the boiler and the cylinder, according as the piston either ascended or descended. One of those boys, who loved to play with his companions, observed that, by tying a string from the handle of the valve which opened this communication to another part of the machine, the valve would open and shut without his assistance, and leave him at liberty to divert himself with his play-fellows. One of the greatest improvements that has been made upon this machine, since it was first invented, was in this manner the discovery of a boy who wanted to save his own labour.

Adam Smith (1776, 9) on the STI-mode of learning:

All the improvements in machinery, however, have by no means been the inventions of those who had occasion to use the machines. Many improvements have been made by the ingenuity of the makers of the machines, when to make them became the business of a peculiar trade; and some by that of those who are called philosophers, or men of speculation, whose trade it is not to do anything, but to observe everything, and who, upon that account, are often capable of combining together the powers of the most distant and dissimilar objects. In the progress of society, philosophy or speculation becomes, like every other employment, the principal or sole trade and occupation of a particular class of citizens. Like every other employment, too, it is subdivided into a great number of different branches, each of which affords occupation to a peculiar tribe or class of philosophers; and this subdivision of employment in philosophy, as well as in every other business, improves dexterity, and saves time. Each individual becomes more expert in his own peculiar branch, more work is done upon the whole, and the quantity of science is considerably increased by it.'

The first mode is experience based, and I will refer to it as the DUI-mode – learning by doing, using and interacting. The other mode refers to science-based research processes and I will refer to it as the STI-mode – science is seen as the first step towards technology and innovation. In this chapter, we will argue that this distinction is fundamental when it comes to analysing modern innovation systems and also when it comes to designing management strategy as well as public policy.[8]

9.2.3 Friedrich List on the need for an active state to build innovation systems

While Adam Smith was propagating free trade and a liberal economy, the German economist Friedrich List disagreed. He characterized Adam Smith's theory as 'cosmopolitan' and argued that if followed by other countries, it would just confirm and reinforce the dominance of the British Empire in the world economy (Reinert 1999).

He argued that for countries such as Germany, trying to 'catch up' with the leading economy, there was a need for government intervention. List presented a broad agenda for government in the building of infrastructure that could contribute to technical advance. It is interesting to note that he referred to 'mental capital' as the most important kind of capital. He argued that the wealth of nations more than anything else reflected '*the accumulation of all discoveries, inventions, improvements, perfections and exertions of all generations which have lived before us*' (Freeman 1995a, 6).

9.2.4 Karl Marx on technological progress

The historical parts of *Das Kapital* give deep insights into how new technologies shape the economy and society. The basic assumption in his historical analysis that new productive forces may get into conflict with 'production relations' is a useful guideline for how to study innovation systems. At the micro level this corresponds to the fact that radically new technologies cannot flourish in firms 'locked in' into old organizational forms and competence sets. At the aggregate level it corresponds to the need to transform societal institutions, competences and organizations in order to reap the benefits of technological revolutions.[9]

Marx is a pioneer also when it comes to emphasizing the importance both of 'science as a force of production' and 'technological competition' where firms need to engage in innovation in order to gain markets and reduce costs. Many of his insights on the role of science and technology in relation to the economy are very advanced for his time (Rosenberg 1976).

9.2.5 Marshall's contribution

Marshall (1919, 1920) is known as one of the founding fathers of modern neoclassical economics. He was also the one who introduced the concept 'the representative firm' – a concept that has contributed to the lack of understanding of economic development in modern neoclassical economics. But as documented by Metcalfe in a different reading, he may be seen as contributing not only to evolutionary understanding of industrial dynamics in general but also to the idea of a national system of innovation (Metcalfe 2006, 17). He links innovation to management competences, brings the wider institutional setting in terms of different types of research laboratories into the analysis and recognizes that the overall system and mode of innovation may differ across national borders (19).

Marshall's focus on incremental innovation – rather than on the radical innovations as emphasized by Schumpeter – may be seen as an important inspiration for modern innovation research. As will be argued below, any attempt to link innovation to economic growth and development not only needs to capture radical and incremental innovations but also the ongoing processes of imitation and learning (Arocena and Sutz 2000a).

As with Adam Smith it is possible to discern two types of mechanisms for the advancement of knowledge and technology and in the case of Marshall they are linked to two types of 'innovation systems'. One refers to industrial districts where the focus in on experience-based learning (DUI) and the other refers to the national system of research (STI).

Marshall is unique in being a potential source of inspiration both for mainstream and evolutionary economics. This reflects his ambition to develop a theory that explains fluctuations in supply and demand with a theory that explains economic development. His method to try to combine the short-term static analysis and the evolutionary development where innovation takes place and agents become more competent is to introduce the distinction between short period, long period and secular period. Metcalfe argues that this should be seen primarily as an attempt to link order and change.

While the national innovation system approach assumes innovation to be a ubiquitous and ongoing process, not to be relegated to 'the secular period', it also operates with a distinction between order and change. It assumes that for national economies there are systemic features in terms of economic structures and relationships as well as institutions that represent continuity and order, and that form the environment for innovation processes where technical knowledge and the competence of individuals and organizations change.

9.2.6 Joseph Schumpeter as the grandfather of modern innovation theory

Joseph Schumpeter is generally seen as the founder of modern innovation research and many scholars who work on innovation would accept to be classified as neo-Schumpeterian.[10]

In *Theory of Economic Development* (Schumpeter 1934), innovation is seen as the major mechanism behind economic dynamics. The dynamo of the system is the individual entrepreneur who introduces innovations in markets and creates new enterprises. After the pioneers follow imitators and gradually the profits created by the original wave of innovation are eroded.

In *Capitalism, Socialism and Democracy* (Schumpeter 1942), the innovation mechanism is quite different. Here the major source of innovation is not the brave individual entrepreneur but the big company with experts working together in R&D teams searching for new technological solutions. The distinction between the two ways to present the motor of innovation has led scholars to refer to *Schumpeter Mark I* and *Schumpeter Mark II*.

We can use some of Schumpeter's ideas to inspire our analysis of innovation systems. First, we might note the important role of imitation. The overall performance of an innovation system will reflect not only the pioneers but also the capability of followers. Second, we might revise his analytical scheme and regard the total population of firms in a system as including both Mark I and Mark II firms. We may characterize a specific national system as being more or less dominated by one type or the other.

But at one very important point, Schumpeter's ideas deviate from the basic insights behind the innovation system concept. Schumpeter took an extreme position assuming *that the demand side would simply adjust to the supply side.*[11] It is true that he defines the opening of new markets as one kind of innovation. But in general, consumers and users are assumed to be ready to absorb whatever new innovation is brought to them by entrepreneurs or firms. Actually, it might be argued that the innovation system perspective came out of a criticism of Schumpeter's relative neglect of the demand side.

Schmookler (1966) opened the debate with taking almost the opposite view of Schumpeter. He used a host of empirical data on inventions as well as from secondary sources to demonstrate that inventions and innovations tend to flourish in areas where demand is strong and growing. One important outcome of the ensuing debate was *a new perspective on innovation as reflecting the interplay between technology push and demand pull*. The critical debate of Schmookler's empirical results confirmed this new perspective (Mowery and Rosenberg 1979).

The 'chain-link model', where both supply push and demand pull are analysed in relation to scientific knowledge, may be seen as one contribution to the new perspective (Kline and Rosenberg 1986). The perspective on innovation as a process of interaction between producers and users may be seen as introducing its micro-foundation (Lundvall 1985).

9.2.7 Christopher Freeman as the father of modern innovation theory

Christopher Freeman played a key role in stimulating these new theoretical developments, especially in Europe.[12] In the early 1980s, his lectures to PhD students were on Schumpeter Mark I and Mark II and on the controversy between Schumpeter and Schmookler regarding the role of supply and demand in the innovation process.[13] His founding of SPRU at Sussex University in 1966 was a major step towards giving innovation studies a more permanent institutional foundation.

One important reference in his lectures in the beginning of the 1980s was to the *Sappho-study* organized at SPRU (Rothwell 1972, 1977). This study was simple but original in design. The research team located a number of innovation pairs – 'twins' in terms of major characteristics – where one of the two was a success, while the other a failure. The two innovations were then compared in terms of characteristics of the 'host' organization. The most important result was that the *interaction* between departments within the organization and interaction with external organization came out as the prerequisites for success in innovation. Innovations that took place in firms where divisions operated without interaction with each other and in firms that did not interact with suppliers, users and customers were less successful than the more interactive firms.[14]

Freeman pioneered the vision that innovation should be understood as an interactive process, not as a linear one where innovation automatically comes out of R&D efforts. As mentioned above, Freeman was also the pioneer when it came to introducing the concept of 'national system of innovation' (Freeman 1982/2004).

9.2.8 The flourishing 1980s

The 1980s was a period when innovation research became 'emancipated' and more ambitious also in confronting basic assumptions in standard economics. Important work took place in different areas both in Europe and in the United States. Dosi, Pavitt and Soete made important contributions to the role of innovation in relation to foreign trade (Dosi et al. 1990). Christopher Freeman and Soete analysed employment issues in relation to technical innovation (Freeman and Soete 1987). Giovanni Dosi established his hypothesis on shifts in technological paradigms (Dosi 1984).

Box 9.3 Different Perspectives on National Systems

Scholars, comparing national systems in terms of how they differ in qualitative terms and in terms of how they perform, have developed and made use of different perspectives. The analysis of the *national competitive advantage* by Michael Porter borrowed some ideas from the innovation system tradition – especially the importance of domestic demand and domestic user for product innovation. But he also added unique ideas about the positive impact of domestic competition on innovation in specific sectors of clusters.

Whitley's analysis of *national business systems* offers important inspiration for the analysis of innovation systems (Whitley 1994). The basic idea that match and mismatch between different elements of the system affect performance and that it is possible to develop a typology of national systems are in line with Freeman's comparison between the Japanese and the Anglo-Saxon systems. But Whitley's analysis is broader, and it introduces cultural and social dimensions in the analysis.

Similar intentions lay behind the concept of Social Systems of innovation (Amable et al. 1997). Recent work on the micro-organizational basis for learning by Lorenz and Valeyre indicates that the systemic features distinguishing the taxonomic categories are rooted in different types of micro-organizational structures.

In the United States, the Nelson and Winter's evolutionary economic approach to economic growth signalled a more ambitious agenda for innovation research (Nelson and Winter 1982). Rosenberg and Kline presented the chain-linked model (Kline and Rosenberg 1986). Freeman and Lundvall developed further ideas about innovation as an interactive process and innovation systems together with Richard Nelson.

Box 9.4 Does the Innovation System Have a Function?

Edquist (2005) argues that the NSI concept is vague and unclear and calls for making it a more rigorous, systematic and 'theory-like' concept. This is always a legitimate concern, but it is not obvious that the direction he recommends for the effort would bring us in this direction.

Edquist argues that the innovation system has 'as general function' to pursue innovation processes. His functionalist approach seems to emanate from a version of system theory as is practiced among engineers (Rickne

2000). *We would argue that social systems only have the functions that we assign to them.* In a normative perspective it could be argued that the function is 'to contribute to economic performance on the basis of processes of creation and diffusion of knowledge'. This would correspond to the normative focus of those who pioneered the NSI concept.

Edquist lists 10 *activities* (also referred to as 'functions' on p. 189) that should be studied in a systematic manner in terms of their respective 'causes and determinants'. The list encompasses quite disparate elements including, for instance, forms of knowledge creation and learning, organizational forms, market demand and public policy instruments.

The idea of studying separately each of the listed activities reminds us somewhat of Edward Denison's attempt to reduce the growth residual through growth accounting. We can see the listing of a number of 'activities' as being potentially useful as establishing a checklist for managers and policymakers (Rickne 2000). It might also be helpful when comparing market with nonmarket economies (Liu and White 2001).

But in terms of theoretical understanding, it represents a step backwards since much of what we already know about the innovation process is neglected. For instance, the distinction made between the three kinds of learning neglects that one of them (innovation) comes out of practising the other two (R&D and competence building) (Edquist 2005, 191–92). It is therefore not obvious how studying them separately would lead to more rigorous theory.

These different efforts merged in two different major projects. One was a major book project led by a team consisting of Dosi, Freeman, Nelson, Silverberg and Soete (1988). The other major project took place in the policy realm and was organized by the Directorate for Science Technology and Industry at OECD. Around 1988, Director Chabbal initiated the technology and economics program (TEP) with Francois Chesnais as project coordinator and intellectual dynamo of the project. The TEP report integrated many of the most advanced ideas developed among innovation scholars in the 1980s, and it gave innovation policy as well as innovation studies a new kind of legitimacy in all OECD countries (OECD 1992). The idea that innovation is an interactive process and that it is useful to analyse 'national innovation systems' was spread to policymakers.

While the TEP project gave legitimacy to the innovation system concept among policymakers, it did not result in a clean break with the linear model where innovation is seen as emanating more or less automatically from science. In international organizations, as in national governments, the strong position of expertise based on standard economics contributed to a narrow interpretation of the national system of innovation. Triple Helix and Mode 2 theories also tend to support a perspective where the DUI-mode of innovation is neglected.

9.2.9 Intentions behind the original conceptualization of national systems of innovation

As we have seen, the innovation system perspective integrates principal results from innovation research. For several of the protagonists of the concept, including Freeman and myself, it was seen not only as a tool to explain innovation but also as constituting an alternative analytical framework and a challenge to standard economics when it comes to explain competitiveness, economic growth and development. In the next section we compare the NSI perspective with the basic assumptions of standard economics.

Many recent contributions to innovation systems have different and in a sense more modest ambitions 'to explain innovation' by linking inputs in terms of investment in R&D to outputs in terms of patents or new products. They may emanate from scholars connected to technical universities and business schools and have as principal aim to give good advice to business managers or specialized government agencies. Other contributions, emanating from international economic organizations analysing national growth performance combine the system perspective with elements of neoclassical economics. Some even utilize production function techniques based on standard economics assumption, including agents acting on the basis of rational expectations. In this post scriptum, I will stick to the original ambitions when discussing how to study national systems of innovation.

9.3 National Innovation System as Analytical Focusing Device

The innovation system framework is in direct competition with standard economics when it comes to giving advice to policymakers. In this section we will try to present the core theoretical ideas behind the innovation system perspective and confront them with those of standard economics. Our main conclusion is that the neglect in standard economics of 'learning as competence building' is a major weakness that makes it less relevant for understanding innovation and dynamic economic performance, especially in the current era of the learning economy.

9.3.1 Theoretical elements entering into the innovation system concept

As indicated in the first section the national innovation system approach is grounded on empirical findings through the 1970s and 1980s, many of which emanated from scholars connected to SPRU. Of special importance were the Sappho study and the Pavitt taxonomy (Rothwell 1977; Pavitt 1984). The Sappho study demonstrated that interaction and feedbacks are crucial for the innovation performance of the firm while the Pavitt taxonomy helped to see how different sectors interact and play different roles as producers and users of innovation in the overall innovation system.

But, the concept also reflects deductive reasoning explaining the stylized facts observed in empirical studies. For instance, on reflection, it is obvious that product innovation could not thrive in an economy with 'pure markets' characterized by arm's length and anonymous relationships between the innovating producer and the potential user (Lundvall 1985; Lund-Vinding 2002; Christensen and Lundvall 2004).

Box 9.5 Is Innovation System a Theory?

Edquist has raised the question if innovation is 'a theory', and his response has been in the negative. In a sense it is obvious that 'innovation system' is a concept rather than 'a general theory'. It is certainly true that it does not specify *general* laws of cause and effect. But nonetheless this way of putting the question may lead to misleading conclusions for how to proceed with research and analytical work in relation to innovation systems.

One problem with posing and answering the question is that it is far from clear what should be meant with 'theory' in social science. As indicated in the earlier section, the innovation system perspective is built on a series of coherent assumptions. It is also true that most of these assumptions are rooted in systematic empirical work and that they can be tested as well as rejected by further empirical work. Using the perspective helps to see, understand and control phenomena that could not be seen, understood or controlled without using this (or a similar) concept. In this sense it does what theory is expected to do: it helps to organize and focus the analysis, it helps to foresee what is going to happen, it helps to explain what has happened and it helps to give basis for action.

The fact that different scholars work with different delimitations of the components of the system and with different focus on elements and relationships does not make the concept less theoretical or scientific. In this chapter, I will argue in favour of a 'broad definition of the NSI'. But this argument reflects a specific purpose – that is, to link innovation to economic performance at the national level. It is equally legitimate to pursue the analysis with a more narrow perspective – such as the one implicit in the triple helix approach – if, for instance, the purpose is to analyse international differences in the emergence of science-based technologies.

A more realistic and fertile approach for social science than the aim to develop general theory is to combine attempts to build general, valid and reliable knowledge about causalities with the insight that social science, by definition, always will remain historical. In such an endeavour, heuristic concepts and focusing devices such as national systems of innovation may play a major role since they offer a broad and flexible framework for organizing and interpreting case studies and comparative analyses (Mjøset 2001, 2002). To develop a 'general theory' of innovation systems that abstracts from time and space would therefore undermine the utility of the concept both as an analytical tool and as a policy tool (Shin 2004).

The only solution to the paradox that product innovations are quite frequent in the market economy is that most markets are not 'pure', rather they are 'organized' and include a mix of trust, loyalty and power relationships. To establish these durable relationships, it is necessary for the parties involved to invest in codes and channels of information – and to build 'social capital'. When it is realized that actual markets are mixed with organizational elements, it opens up the possibility that the elements of organization will differ between national and regional systems. This may be seen as constituting a micro-foundation for the innovation systems concept, and it was presented as such by Nelson in Dosi et al. (1988) and in *National Innovation Systems: A Comparative Analysis* (Nelson 1993).[15]

Evolutionary economics constitutes a general theoretical framework for the analysis of innovation systems. It is a key assumption in evolutionary economics that agents and organizational routines differ and that *diversity* is fundamental for the dynamics of the system. Innovation creates novelty and diversity in the system whereas competition has a double effect on diversity. On the one hand it stimulates efforts to innovate, and on the other hand it is a selection process that reduces diversity, while some routines are reproduced over time. In what follows, we will assume that *evolution in terms of what people and organizations know and in terms of how they learn is especially important for the dynamic performance of the national innovation system.*

9.3.2 Knowledge and learning

In the introduction to *National Innovation Systems: Towards a Theory of Innovation and Interactive Learning* (Lundvall 1992), I stated that 'the most fundamental resource in the modern economy is knowledge and, accordingly, the most important process is learning.' But at that time (1992), our use of the concepts of knowledge and learning were not at all well developed. Over the last

15 years, the attempts to get a better understanding of the knowledge-based economy and the learning economy have created a more satisfactory theoretical foundation for the understanding of innovation systems (see, for instance, Lundvall and Johnson 1994; OECD 2000; Foray 2004; Amin and Cohendet 2004).

The understanding has been developed using the basic distinctions between information and knowledge, between 'knowing about the world' and 'knowing how to change the world' and between knowledge that is explicit and codified versus knowledge that remains implicit and tacit (Johnson et al. 2002). In Lundvall and Johnson (1994), we introduced a distinction between know-what, know-why, know-how and know-who that has proved to be useful in understanding knowledge creation and learning in innovation systems. These distinctions are especially helpful when it comes to contrasting the theoretical micro-foundations of innovation systems with those of standard economics.

If neoclassical models include learning, it is understood either as getting access to more information about the world (know-what) or it is treated as a black-box phenomenon as in growth models assuming 'learning by doing'. The very fundamental fact that agents – individuals as well as firms – *are more or less competent* (in terms of know-how and know-why) and are *more or less integrated in knowledge-based networks* (know-who) is abstracted from – in order to keep the analysis simple – and based on 'representative firms' and agents. *This abstraction is most problematic in an economy where the distribution of competences becomes more and more uneven and the capability to learn tends to become the most important factor behind the economic success of people, organizations and regions* (Lundvall and Johnson 1994).

9.3.3 The theory behind innovation systems

As pointed out, List was critical to the exaggerated focus on allocation as opposed to knowledge creation and growth. Table 9.1 illustrates how the analytical framework connected to innovation systems relates to mainstream economic theory. The theoretical core of standard economic theory is about rational agents making choices to which well defined (but possibly risky) alternative outcomes are connected, and the focus of the analysis is on the allocation of scarce resources. As illustrated by Table 9.1 the emphasis is different in the innovation system approach.

The analysis of innovation systems is based on a two-dimensional shift of focus towards the combination of innovation and learning. While standard economics is preoccupied with specifying the institutional set-up that results in an optimal allocation of existing resources, we are concerned with how different institutional set-ups affect the creation of new resources. While

Table 9.1 The two-dimensional shift in perspective

	Allocation	Innovation
Rational choice	Standard neoclassical	Project management
Learning	Austrian economics	Innovation systems

standard economics analyses how agents make choices on the basis of given sets of information and competences, we are interested in how the knowledge – including both information about the world and know-how of agents – change in the economic process.

This double shift in perspective has implications for innovation policy. Just to take one example, a policy analysis of patent races where 'winner takes it all' will, as far as it neglects the learning and competence building that takes place during the race, end up with too restrictive conclusions regarding the role of government in stimulating R&D.

9.3.4 The NSI perspective is more complex – not less theoretical – than standard economics

What has been said obviously implies a more complex theory than standard neoclassical economics where it is assumed that all agents have equal access to technologies and are equally competent in developing and utilizing them. But it would be wrong to conclude that the theory behind innovation systems is 'less theoretical'.

Basically, the theory underlying innovation system analysis is about learning processes involving skilful but imperfectly rational agents and organizations. It assumes that organizations and agents have a capability to enhance their competences through searching and learning, that they do so in interaction with other agents and that this is reflected in innovation processes and outcomes in the form of innovations and new competences.

The methodological dictum within neoclassical economics that a theory should be both general and abstract sometimes takes Occam's razor too far leading to negligence of the concrete and historical. But the most important weakness of neoclassical theory is not that it is too abstract. *It is rather that it makes the wrong abstractions.* In a context where knowledge is the most important resource and learning the most important process, neoclassical theory tends to abstract from the very processes that make a difference in terms of the economic performance of firms and for the wealth of nations.

Processes of competence building and innovation are at the focal point in innovation system analysis. The focus is on how enduring relationships and patterns of dependence and interaction are established, evolve and dissolve as time goes by. New competences are built while old ones are destroyed. At each point of time, discernable patterns of collaboration and communication characterize the innovation system. But, of course, in the long run, these patterns change in a process of creative destruction of knowledge and relationships. A crucial normative issue is how such patterns affect the creation of new resources and to what degree they support learning among agents.

Box 9.6 Different Meanings of Learning

As any everyday concept, learning has several different connotations. In the literature on learning organizations, it is often referred to as *adaptation*: as a process where agents when confronted with new circumstances register and internalize the change and adapt their behaviour accordingly.

In education learning is seen as a process of *competence building*. It is assumed that new competences can be established through education and training and thereafter mobilized when coping with and mastering theoretical and practical problems.

In our analysis of innovation systems, we see learning as referring both to adaptation and competence building. And we emphasize that competence building takes place also on-the-job through learning by doing, learning by using and learning by interacting.

9.3.5 Standard economics favours narrow interpretation of innovation systems

Standard economics tends to stick to the idea that only quantitative as opposed to qualitative concepts can be accepted as scientific (Georgescu-Roegen 1971). One reason for the bias towards narrow interpretations of innovation systems is that it is much easier to develop quantitative analysis of R&D and patents than it is to measure organizational forms and outcomes of organizational learning.

Standard economics will typically focus on potential market failure and on choices to be made between different alternative uses of scarce resources. In the context of innovation policy, the concern will be, first, if public rates of return are higher that private rates and second, if the rate of return of public money is higher in investing in R&D than it would be in other areas of public investment.[16] The very idea that there might be organizational forms that are more efficient than the ones already in use cannot be reconciled with the basic analytical framework where it is assumed that agents, including firms, are equally rational and competent.

Standard economics will tend to see the market as the 'natural', if not optimal, framework of human interaction and economic transactions. This leads to biased conclusions when considering how to organize the economy (Nelson 2006). The concept 'market failure' reflects this bias since it indicates that other institutional set-ups should be considered only when it is obvious that the market cannot do the job.

9.4 Challenges for Innovation System Research

9.4.1 Causality in a systemic context

A major challenge for innovation system analysis is to avoid thinking in terms of mechanical models of causality and develop theory as well as analytical techniques that make it possible to study how different factors interact in a systemic context.

When studying national systems it is a specific challenge for statistical analysis that the 'population' (the number of nations) is so small and heterogeneous. Some statistical procedures will as first approximation look for causality patterns that are general for the whole population – for all national systems of innovation. Such procedures are sometimes used in empirical analysis of determinants of economic growth. We believe that other methods are more useful when it comes to studying national systems of innovation. These might include clustering procedures dividing the population into different 'subspecies' or 'families' with common characteristics (level of development, size, continental belonging, etc.), and then looking for patterns of interdependency for each of the different families and finally relating this to multidimensional indicators of economic performance.

It is, for instance, common to rank the United States at the top of performance together with the small Nordic countries. But it is also well known that the US system is fundamentally different from the small Nordic countries in terms of institutions and characteristics (population size, size of the public sector, degree of inequality, industrial structure and modes of innovation). Therefore, in spite of the fact that both categories of countries belong to the same species 'national systems of innovation', there is no reason to assume that the mechanism linking R&D effort to innovation and economic performance is the same in the two countries.

The idea that the aim of innovation research is to end up with general laws that can be applied equally in all national systems is mistaken. There are certain activities that can be linked to innovation and that link innovation to economic growth in all systems. But the mechanisms differ across different national systems. This is why theoretical work on national innovation systems cannot dispense from historical analysis.

9.4.2 Understanding knowledge and learning

One important challenge for innovation system analysis is to deepen the understanding of how different kinds of knowledge are created and used in the process of innovation. Some elements of knowledge are local and tacit, embodied in people and embedded in organizations. Other elements are global, explicit and can easily be transferred from one part of the world to another. Different sectors in the economy and in society make use of different mixes of local and global knowledge and in some areas, such as education and business consulting, it is especially difficult to codify the know-how that consultants and teachers make use of when they give advice and teach (OECD 2000).

To understand how learning takes place within organizations as well as in the interaction between organizations, it is a key to understand how systems of innovation work. While it is important to study national characteristics in terms of organizations that pursue R&D, it is equally important to understand national characteristics in terms of how firms interact with customers and to what degree different firms give employees access to competence building in connection with ongoing economic activities.

9.4.3 The coevolution of the division of labour, interaction and cooperation

As pointed out by Adam Smith, a fundamental process in economic development and economic growth is the deepening and extension of the division of labour. Specialization within and between organizations makes it possible to exploit scale economies and also to focus on competence building so that it can advance more rapidly.

As the horizontal and vertical division of labour evolves, it contributes to *diversity* and diversity feeds innovation. But the growing specialization also creates new barriers for communication and interaction. This is highly relevant because innovation is the outcome of combining knowledge located at different sites (and embodied in different experts) in a specialized innovation system. It is well documented that different departments (R&D, production, sales, etc.) within a firm have difficulties understanding and communicating with each other. At the individual level, experts with different specialties have difficulties interacting and understanding each other. The ease to communicate across such barriers in a national system with a vertical division of labour between separate organizations is especially interesting because it is here that product innovations are developed in an interaction between users and producers (Lundvall 2006).

It is a major challenge to understand the coevolution of the division of labour and the interaction that takes place within and between organizations. In some countries it is much easier to establish cooperation within and/or between organizations than it is in other countries. This will be reflected in the actual division of labour, and it affects the kind of learning and innovation that takes place in the system.

Box 9.7 National Patterns in Work Organization[17]

Table 9.2 originates from a paper by Lorenz and Valeyre (2006). The four organizational models were constructed on the basis of factor analysis of responses to surveys addressed to employees in 15 European countries.

Table 9.2 National differences in organizational models (per cent of employees by organizational class)

	Discretionary learning	Lean production learning	Taylorist organization	Simple organization
North				
Netherlands	64.0	17.2	5.3	13.5
Denmark	60.0	21.9	6.8	11.3
Sweden	52.6	18.5	7.1	21.7
Finland	47.8	27.6	12.5	12.1
Austria	47.5	21.5	13.1	18.0
Centre				
Germany	44.3	19.6	14.3	21.9
Luxemb.	42.8	25.4	11.9	20.0
Belgium	38.9	25.1	13.9	22.1
France	38.0	33.3	11.1	17.7
West				
UK	34.8	40.6	10.9	13.7
Ireland	24.0	37.8	20.7	17.6
South				
Italy	30.0	23.6	20.9	25.4
Portugal	26.1	28.1	23.0	22.8
Spain	20.1	38.8	18.5	22.5
Greece	18.7	25.6	28.0	27.7
EU-15	39.1	28.2	13.6	19.1

Source: Lorenz and Valeyre (2006).

Table 9.1 shows that people working in different national systems of innovation and competence building *have very different access* to learning by doing. It also shows that at lower income levels, there is bigger proportion of the workforce that works in either simple or Taylorist organizations. The richer the country, the more workers are employed in discretionary learning contexts. But it is also important to note that countries at similar income levels – Germany and the United Kingdom – have quite different distributions of workers between the four forms. While the proportion of workers operating in the lean production is more than 40 per cent in the United Kingdom, it is less than 20 per cent in Germany. The micro-foundation of national systems of innovation differs not only because of levels of income but also because of other systemic features.

9.4.4 Firms as sites for employee learning

Innovation indicators reflect outputs such as number of patents or inputs that are easy to measure such as R&D expenditure. When it comes to indicators of knowledge there is a strong bias in favour of knowledge that is explicit. Investment in scientific knowledge is measured by surveys on R&D and innovation. The know-how built up through learning by doing, using and interacting is much more difficult to measure. Human capital measurements may register formal investment in education but what people learn at the workplace or as consumers is not easy to capture through standard measurements.

The absence of indicators makes the area less visible for policymakers, and this contributes to a bias in innovation policy towards promoting STI rather than DUI activities (see Table 9.2).

In recent empirical work by Lorenz and Valeyre, it has been shown that there are dramatic differences between Europe's national systems in terms of how and how much an average employee learns at their workplace (Lorenz and Valeyre 2006). While in Denmark a majority of workers are engaged in 'discretionary learning', where they combine learning through problem solving with a certain autonomy in their work situation, the majority of workers in countries such as Greece and Spain are engaged in Taylorist type of work with much more limited opportunities for learning and with very little autonomy (see Box 9.7).

In a follow-up to the analysis of these national patterns of workplace learning, they have been combined with innovation indicators. The analysis shows, first, that on average countries that make intensive use of discretionary learning are most prone to engaging in 'endogenous innovation' (defined as innovations that emanate from in-house R&D efforts and result in products new to the market). But, second, it shows that strong economic performance may emanate from quite different combinations of innovation and learning modes. For instance, Denmark is not very strong in endogenous innovation but very strong in discretionary learning, while the opposite is true for another Nordic country, Finland (Arundel et al. 2006).

The national differences in what people do and learn at their workplace is a major factor structuring the national innovation system and affecting its performance; it is certainly more fundamental and difficult to change than, for instance, R&D intensity. In countries such as Finland and Korea, R&D measures of 'performance' reflect the propensity to do research within one big corporation such as Nokia and Samsung. This contrasts with indicators of competence building in working life since these refer to how competence building takes place in all parts of the economy.

9.4.5 The weak correlation between strength of the science-based and economic performance

Over the last century there has been a certain focus on the European paradox referring to the assumed fact that Europe is strong in science but weak in innovation and economic growth.[18] Similar paradoxes have been argued to exist in countries such as the Netherlands, Finland and Sweden. In an OECD report a *general result* is that for the countries included in the study it can be shown that those that 'perform well' in terms of STI indicators do not perform well in terms of innovation (OECD 2005, 29).[19] This indicates that what is registered is not so much a paradox as it is a systematic weakness in the theoretical analysis and the indicators on which it is built.

We would argue that these apparent paradoxes emanate from a narrow understanding of the innovation process. They demonstrate that heavy investment in science in the systems where organizational learning within and between firms is weakly developed and where there is a weak focus on user needs has only limited positive impact on innovation and economic growth.

This can be illustrated by data on innovation performance at the firm level – see Table 9.3. In a series of recent papers based on a unique combination of survey and register data for Danish firms, we have demonstrated that firms that engage in R&D without establishing organizational forms that promote learning and neglect customer interaction are much less innovative than firms that are strong both in terms of STI and DUI learning (Jensen et al. 2007).[20]

Table 9.3 refers to the outcome of an analysis of survey and register data for almost 700 Danish firms, and it presents different variables related to the propensity to introduce new products or services. We use sector, size and form of ownership as control variables but the focus is on a variable indicating *the mode of innovation* in the firm. We distinguish between firms that are strong in

Table 9.3 The probability that firms develop a new product or a new service

Variables	Odds ratio estimate	Coefficient estimate	Odds ratio estimate	Coefficient estimate
STI Cluster	3.529	1.2611**	2.355	0.8564**
DUI Cluster	2.487	0.9109**	2.218	0.7967**
DUI/STI Cluster	7.843	2.0596**	5.064	1.6222**
Business services			1.433	0.3599
Construction			0.491	−0.7120*
Manuf. (hi–tech) (high tech)			1.805	0.5905*
Manuf. (low and med. tech) tech)			1.250	0.2229
Other services			0.747	−0.2923
100 and more employees			1.757	0.5635*
50–99 employees			0.862	−0.1481
Danish group			0.859	−0.1524
Single firm			0.521	−0.6526*
Customized product			1.378	0.3203
Pseudo R^2	0.1247	0.1247	0.1775	0.1775
N	692	692	692	692

** = significant at the .01 level, * = significant at the .05 level.

science-based learning, firms strong in organizational learning, firms that are strong in both respects, and we use those firms that are weak in both respects as the benchmark category. To construct this variable we pursue a cluster analysis grouping the firms into the four categories.

As indicators of strong science-based learning, we use the R&D expenditure, presence of employees with academic degrees in natural science or technology and collaboration with scientists in universities or other science organizations. As indicators of experience-based learning, we take the use of certain organizational practices normally connected with learning organizations such as 'interdisciplinary work groups' and 'integration of functions' together with 'closer interaction with customers' – to signal learning by interacting and a focus on user needs.

We use firms that only make weak efforts to support science-based and experience-based learning as benchmark and the odds ratio estimate indicates how much higher the propensity to innovate is among firms strong in one or both of the modes of learning respectively. The results reported in Table 9.3 show that firms that combine the two modes are much more prone to innovate than the rest. It shows that the effect remains strong also after introducing control variables related to size and sector.

Box 9.8 How to Study National Systems?

Our interest in utilizing the innovation system perspective is not purely academic. We use this concept as a focusing device in order to better understand how innovation affects economic development at the national level. Within this broad view, many factors contribute to innovation, and it might be seen as a problem that almost all aspects of society need to be brought in to explain the actual pattern of innovation. To structure the analysis, it is useful to distinguish between the *core* of the innovation system and *the wider setting*. Both need to be included in the analysis since the aim is to link innovation to economic development.

Firms and the knowledge infrastructure constitute the core of the system. In principle, we include all firms in the core since every firm has a potential for developing, absorbing or using new technology.

The wider setting refers to institutions that contribute to competence building and shape human interaction in relation to innovation. These include, first, family pattern, education system, career patterns in labour markets, inequality and social welfare systems. Second, they include the historical record of macroeconomic stability and the access to finance. Third, they include the final demand from households and public sector organizations. Fourth, they include government and public policy directly aiming at stimulating innovation, including diffusion and efficient use.

This way of setting the scene indicates a marginal role for public policy. What is intended is rather to see public policy mainly as intervening in relation to the core and the wider setting of the national innovation system. Alternatively, we could see public policy as endogenous. To some degree, we take this perspective in Edquist and Lundvall (1993) where we demonstrate how innovation policy in Sweden and Denmark tends to reproduce rather than renew the strengths of the respective systems.

The analysis and results reported above (Table 9.3) point to the need to develop our understanding of how different forms of knowledge and different modes of innovation are combined in different national innovation systems. The analysis also explains why narrow definitions of national innovation systems that focus only on science-based innovation are of little relevance for the economic performance of firms and national innovation systems. This is not least important when it comes to analysing the barriers and opportunities for economic development in poor countries, another challenge for innovation system research (Arocena and Sutz 2000b; Cassiolato et al. 2003).

9.5 National Systems of Innovation and Economic Development

While the modern version of the concept of national systems of innovation was developed mainly in rich countries (Freeman 1982; Freeman and Lundvall 1988; Lundvall 1992; Nelson 1993; Edquist 1997), some of the most important elements actually came from the literature on development issues in the third world. For instance the Aalborg version (Andersen and Lundvall 1988) got some of its inspiration concerning the interdependence between different sectors from Hirschman (1958) and Stewart (1977). Other encouragements came from Myrdal (1968). Applying the systems of innovation approach to economic development brings into focus other research issues of general interest such as the need to understand how innovation relates to sustainable development, economic welfare and the role of government in commodifying knowledge.

Most chapters in Lundvall (1992) treat the innovation system as an ex-post rather than as an ex-ante concept. The concept refers to relatively strong and diversified systems with well-developed institutional and infrastructural support of innovation activities. The perspective is one where innovation processes are evolutionary and path dependent and systems of innovation evolve over time in a largely unplanned manner. The system of innovation approach has not, to the same extent, been applied to system building. When applied to the South, the focus needs to be shifted in the direction of system construction and system promotion – something that was central in List's ideas for catching up – and to the fact that public policy is a conscious activity that needs to stimulate and supplement the spontaneous development of systems of innovation (Muchie et al. 2003; Lundvall et al. 2006).

Box 9.9 A Method to Study National Innovation Systems

In what follows, I sketch a method to study national systems of innovation that moves from micro to macro and back again to micro. The 'model' starts from the following stylized facts:

1. Firms play the most important role in the innovation system. Firms innovate in an interaction with other firms and with knowledge infrastructure.
2. Firms' mode of innovation and learning reflects national education systems, labour markets, etc.

3. Firms belonging to different sectors contribute differently to innovation processes.

Therefore, the *first step* would be to analyse what takes place inside firms in terms of innovation in the light of organizational set-up and human resources while taking into account sector specialization.

A *second step* would be to analyse the interaction among firms and with knowledge infrastructure, including both domestic and international linkages.

A *third step* would be to explain national specificities in these respects with reference to national education, labour markets, financial markets, welfare regimes and intellectual property regimes.

A *fourth step* would be to use firm organization and network positioning as factors that explain the specialization and performance of the innovation system.

This method focuses the analysis on the central motor in the innovation system (i.e., the total population of firms, their linkages to each other and to the knowledge infrastructure). But it also recognizes that most parts of the socioeconomic system may influence how this motor works and not least how it affects the performance of the economy as a whole.

Another weakness of the system of innovation approach is that it is still lacking in its treatment of the power aspects of development. The focus on interactive learning – a process in which agents communicate and cooperate in the creation and utilization of new economically useful knowledge – may lead to an underestimation of the conflicts over income and power, connected to the innovation process. In a global context where the access to technical knowledge is becoming restricted not only by weak 'absorptive capacity' but also by more and more ambitious global schemes to protect intellectual property, this perspective gives a too rosy picture. Postcolonial and class privileges may block learning possibilities and existing competences may be destroyed for political reasons related to the global distribution of power.

Furthermore, the relationships between globalization and national and local systems need to be further researched. It is important to know more about how globalization processes affect the possibilities to build and support national and local systems of innovation in developing countries (Lastres and Cassiolato 2005). 'Borrowing' and adopting technologies that the technologically advanced countries control today is an important key to development. The combination of reverse engineering, licensing, sending scholars abroad, inviting foreign firms and experts and engaging in international scientific collaborations may be difficult to achieve but all these elements need to be considered in building the national innovation systems. When building such systems, it is a major challenge to develop national strategies that make it possible to select technologies and institutions from abroad that support innovation and competence building.

It is thus clear that the innovation system approach proposed here needs to be adapted to the situation in developing countries, if it is to be applied to system building. It is also clear that what is most relevant for developing economies is a broad definition of the NSI including not only low-tech industries but also primary sectors such as agriculture. Activities contributing to competence building need to be taken into account and narrow perspectives that focus only on the STI-mode needs to be avoided.[21]

Box 9.10 Innovation Systems and Development Thinking

As pointed out in the text, the literature on national innovation systems builds on conceptual pillars rooted in the development literature. The role of technology was an important part of the postwar debate on development. Schumpeter's (1934) concept of development contributed with two central ideas for this debate. One was the positive effects of generating new products and new processes. The other was the disruptive character of development. These two notions shaped the subsequent contributions, with Prebisch's (1950), Singer's (1950) and Myrdal's (1958) analyses of the long-term deterioration of terms of trade for primary products and of the distribution of gains between developed and developing countries.

In Latin America, a number of development studies followed Prebisch, arguing about the central role played by technical change in explaining the evolution of the capitalism and in determining the historical process of hierarchy formation of regions and countries. Furtado (1964), for instance, established an express relation between economic development and technological change pointing out that the growth of an economy was based on the accumulation of knowledge and understood development within a systemic, historically determined, view.

Inspired by Schumpeter, an important and influential literature about how firms in the developing world acquire and develop technological capabilities unfolded during the 1970s and 1980s. Key concepts were the notions of technological capabilities and learning. Several empirical studies have shown how less developed countries have managed to develop significant skills, which have led to 'efficient' production, at least in the short-term. These studies focused mostly on the capabilities of producers (e.g.

knowledge and skills required for production) (Katz 1984; Dahlman et al. 1987).

In the same period (1970s and 1980s) in Latin America, authors inspired by the Latin American Structuralist School (LASA) literature developed a number of firm-level studies where the second of Schumpeter's ideas – the disruptive character of development – was taken into account. This work was instrumental in showing not only successful stories of techno-logical upgrading but also important limitations of the capabilities and learning approaches to technology and development precisely because this approach left behind key elements, such as the role of institutions, of the macroeconomic regime and of power conflicts.

In East Asian economies, empirical investigation of successful evolution of innovation systems also helped to link the innovation systems perspec-tive to development analyses. For example, case studies of the textile and clothing and electronics industries in the Taiwan province of China and the Republic of Korea confirmed that interfirm linkages, including subcon-tracting arrangements, were crucial channels of technological learning, in some cases even more important than direct channels such as foreign direct investment (San Gee and Kuo 1998; Ernst et al. 1998).

9.5.1 Welfare and inequality in the context of innovation systems

A promising line of research is to link the perspective of Amartya Sen (1999) on welfare and inequality to the national system perspective. Sen presents a capability-based approach where development is seen as an expansion of the substantive freedoms that people enjoy. Substantive freedoms are defined as the capabilities people have to live the kind of lives they have reason to value. These include things like being able to avoid starvation and undernourish-ment, diseases and premature mortality. It also includes the freedoms of being literate, able to participate in public life and in political processes, having the ability and possibility to work and to influence one's work conditions, having entrepreneurial freedom and possibilities to take economic decisions of differ-ent kinds. Enhancement of freedoms like these is seen as both the ends and means of development.

This way of looking at development refers to the capabilities people have to act and to choose a life they value rather than to their level of income and possession of wealth. Poverty, for example, is in this perspective more a depri-vation of basic capabilities than just low income. Human capabilities rather than resource endowments are the fundamental factors of development.

Sen's approach fits well into a system of innovation approach. It is noteworthy however that learning and innovation capabilities generally do not seem to be explicitly included in this capability-based approach to development. Extending capabilities may be the result of changing the setting in which the agent operates, but even more important in the learning economy is whether the setting gives access to and stimulates a renewal and upgrading of the competences of agents.

The learning capability is thus one of the most important of the human capabilities, and it is conditioned by national institutions and forms of work organization (see, for instance, Box 9.7 for the case of Europe). It does not only have an instrumental role in development but also, under certain conditions, substantive value. When learning takes place in such a way that it enhances the capability of individuals and collectives to utilize and coexist with their environment, it contributes directly to human well-being. Furthermore, to be able to participate in learning and innovation at the work place may be seen as 'a good thing' contributing to a feeling of belonging and significance.

9.5.2 On the sustainability of innovation systems

National systems of innovation may be regarded as a tool for analysing economic development and economic growth. It aims at explaining how systemic features and different institutional set-ups at the national level link innovation and learning processes to economic growth.

But such a perspective may be too narrow. As pointed out by Freeman and Soete (1997), the ecological challenge ought to be integrated in any strategy for economic development and here we will argue that in the learning economy not only intellectual capital but also social capital is an important element in the development process. The extended perspective can be introduced as in diagram 3 below.

Table 9.4 illustrates that economic growth is faced with a double challenge in terms of sustainability and that there is an immanent risk of undermining not only the material basis of material production (Segura-Bonilla 1999) but also the knowledge base. The creation of tangible capital may be threatened

Table 9.4 Resources fundamental for economic growth – combining the tangible and reproducible dimensions

	Easily reproducible resources	**Less reproducible resources**
Tangible resources	1. Production capital	2. Natural capital
Intangible resources	3. Intellectual capital	4. Social capital

by a neglect of environmental sustainability. We will argue that the production and efficient use of intellectual capital is fundamentally dependent on social capital (Woolcock 1998). A development strategy that focuses only on production capital and intellectual capital is not sustainable.

This is equally true for developed as for developing economies. But in most developed economies there has been a long history of institution building that helps to cope with sustainability (Russia is a case where there is an imbalance between the level of technical development and institutions checking unsustainable development). Even if they are insufficient in many respects, these kinds of institutions are more developed than in the developing part of the world. A success in terms of economic growth in a less developed economy may therefore create extreme tension between growth and sustainability. Directing the efforts of the innovation system towards solving crises in ecological and social terms may be necessary in order to avoid real 'limits to growth'.

Innovation may have a positive role in bolstering sustainability. Technical innovation, for instance, in terms of developing substitutes to naturally scarce raw products, may help to overcome the fact that natural capital cannot always be reproduced. In a similar vein new social institutions may help to overcome a crisis where social capital gets fragmented. In both cases, it is important to note that the workings of unhampered market forces may, in the longer term, erode the basis of economic growth.

9.5.3 The role of the state and the commodification of knowledge

As explained, the modern version of the innovation system concept was developed in the mid-1980s. It is important to note that the early versions were *critical* both to mainstream economics and to the prevailing economic policy where weak competitiveness was seen as primarily reflecting high costs and especially high-wage costs.

The wide diffusion of the concept among policymakers took place in the 1990s. At the beginning of the new millennium, most OECD countries had adopted the concept to support the design of innovation policy. In order to understand the interpretation of the concept in policy circles, it is important to take into account the ideological and political climate that reigned during this diffusion process.

Basically the 1990s was a period with strong emphasis on market regulation and on private property rights as ideal institutions – the breakdown of the centrally planned economies in Europe gave new impetus to neoliberal strategies developed in the 1980s. This resulted in a certain degeneration of the concept. Analytical aspects of the concept that might lead to conclusions that went against the logic of markets and free trade were suppressed.

The original innovation system approach emphasized that knowledge and learning are crucial for economic performance in the current era (Lundvall 1992). But it does not follow that all knowledge should be 'commodified', and this is what seems to have become the major tendency. There is a growing trend in political circles to regard *all knowledge* as a potential commodity and to subordinate *all knowledge production* under the logic of international competitiveness. This is reflected in a movement in favour of expanding and strengthening intellectual property rights to the extreme and far beyond what promotes socioeconomic progress and as well in a strong drive towards colonizing academic knowledge and making it subordinate to market demand.

To make universities more open to society is a necessary process and expectations that the knowledge produced at universities should contribute to economic welfare are legitimate. But the current drive towards the market is driven by the lop-sided understanding of innovation as emanating almost solely from science and therefore it goes too far.

The long-term implications and costs of making scholars and universities profit-oriented seem to be neglected among the protagonists of university reforms in the Bayh–Dole spirit.[22] Scholars who are stimulated to act strategically on their own behalf and on the behalf of their institutions will certainly become less engaged in sharing their knowledge with others. Private companies might, in the short run, appreciate that universities become more profit-oriented, but they will soon experience that the barriers around the knowledge accumulated will become higher and that access to the most relevant knowledge will become more difficult.

It is even more intriguing to reflect on what awaits at the end of the current trajectory, at the point in time where the entrepreneurial university has become truly a business corporation operating in international markets. At that point we must expect that WTO restrains the current freedom of national governments to subsidize basic research taking place within universities by competition laws and trade regulations. How could it be argued that private firms (universities) that compete on global markets should be subsidized by the national government? To establish controls that make it certain that government support only goes to basic research – without affecting services sold internationally – would open up for complex legal processes. If governments wanted to go on subsidizing basic research, they might need to establish a new set of institutions.[23]

Finally, there is a need to think about the implications for the role of universities of the fact that knowledge becomes more and more fundamental for the economy as for society as a whole. The historical role of universities has been an institution that 'validates' knowledge. It has been an institution that, while aiming at the full truth of matters, at least systematically tries to establish what 'reasonably reliable knowledge' is. This is also one reason why it has been an institution with a relative autonomy in relation to the state as well as in relation to economic interests. This function is even more important in a knowledge-based society.[24]

As a kind of countervailing power to the colonizing tendency emanating from market-oriented innovation policy, we see a need to develop a wider field of politics – *knowledge politics* – that covers all aspects of knowledge production and takes into account that the production of knowledge has much wider scope than just contributing to economic growth. This includes, of course, knowledge necessary for social and ecological sustainability but not only that. In rich societies, it should be possible to afford culture, ethics and knowledge for its own sake, not only knowledge that promotes innovation and economic growth. This implies that there might be a need for establishing a new kind of 'academy of science and knowledge' that has as one of its dedicated tasks to set the limits for how far innovation policy may influence knowledge production and use.

9.5.4 Higher education, innovation and economic development

In the context of poor countries, the idea of a relative autonomy for universities may appear as a luxury that cannot be afforded. In a recent paper (Lundvall 2007), I have made an attempt to link higher education to innovation and economic development.

In less developed countries as in rich countries, the most important function of universities remains to train academic personnel and give them competences so that they can be absorbed in meaningful employment where they solve problems that are so complex that less-skilled workers would fail. Such problems will appear more frequently in economies where innovation is frequent (Nelson and Phelps 1965; Schultz 1975). Therefore the design of the university system needs to be seen as an integrated part of the formation of a national system of innovation.

The idea that universities should serve as direct sources for innovation through their 'third mission' and that this mission should involve the creation of markets for knowledge implicit in much of the triple helix literature is problematic in poor as well as in rich countries (Arocena and Sutz 2005). To establish a closer interaction with the rest of society is especially important in less developed countries where the distance between academia and real life is often very big. But rather than creating market-oriented universities, what is needed is educational reform including the wide introduction of problem-based learning as a teaching method and, in general, a closer interaction between theory and practise.

Box 9.11 The Globelics Experience

Globelics is a global research community combining scholars working on innovation studies with scholars working on development studies. It has been characterized as a network for 'researchers without borders' (www.globelics.org). The Globelics annual conferences take place in developing countries and the finance has been raised within the hosting country.

Besides the annual conferences, regional and national networks have been established in Asia, Latin America and China (see http://sdc-socialscience.com/2016-cicalics-academy-and-workshop/). Each year, 40 PhD students, coming equally from Asia, Africa, Latin America and Europe, are invited to Globelics Academy in Lisbon where world-leading scholars in innovation studies for a 10-day period give lectures and methodological advice for their thesis work. A similar Cicalics Academy takes place in China every year with a majority of Chinese students and with international lecturers. (More recently initiatives in Latin America, Africa and India have resulte in similar activities in these regions.)

The purpose of Globelics is to counterbalance the increasingly uneven global access to research networks. It gives scholars in less developed countries access to the most recent research and it opens up channels for publication of their work. It also makes it possible to share experiences among scholars from different parts of the developing world, bypassing the metropoles in the North. Several major research projects with global scope use Globelics as host – the Catch-Up project coordinated by Richard Nelson, The Brics project coordinated by Jose Cassiolato and the Unidev project coordinated by Claes Brundenius.

Globelics has a scientific board with distinguished scholars such as Christopher Freeman and Richard Nelson and with leading scholars from the South. But basically Globelics is a self-organizing global network. It draws its energy mainly from the fact that scholars from the North and the South find it highly rewarding to work together and learn from each other in a seriously committed but friendly atmosphere.

One major long-term positive effect is that young scholars from all parts of the world, sometimes working in isolation and under difficult conditions, get inspiration and support in their efforts to do good research on innovation. There is already a lively 'Globelics community' of young scholars who correspond regularly on both a scientific and a social basis.

Investment in higher education may not give substantial rates of return in a technologically stagnant economy. Since the alternative to invest in higher education is to remain in stagnation forever, our analysis needs to focus on two questions. First, how to design higher education in such a way that it helps to break the vicious circle of stagnation and stagnating demand for graduates? Second, how to design a general strategy for vitalizing national innovation systems that includes investment in higher education as important element?

9.6 Conclusions

In this chapter we went back to the origins of the concept of the national innovation system. We have argued that the original versions as developed by Christopher Freeman and the Aalborg group are more adequate tools when it comes to linking innovation to aggregate national economic performance than narrow versions that focus mainly on the science base. In the current era, there is a need both for strengthening the science base and for promoting experience-based learning. This is absolutely fundamental when it comes to linking the analysis of national innovation systems to economic development.

This implies new directions for research on innovation systems. First, it is necessary to develop a better understanding and more efficient analytical techniques to study institutional 'complementarity' and 'mismatch' in innovation systems. Second, there is a need to deepen the understanding of the production, diffusion and use of knowledge. In this connection the focus should be on interactive learning processes and on how 'social capital' evolves as a basis for interaction within and across organizational boundaries. Third, there is a need to understand and develop indicators of how and to what degree workplaces function as learning sites in different national systems. Fourth, a promising research strategy is to link organizational learning, mobility of people and network formation. Networks will always involve interaction between people, and the specific careers will have an impact on with whom and how agents interact.

Universities play an important role in the innovation system, but the triple-helix perspective, with its neglect of DUI-mode of learning, may have led to exaggerated expectations of what can and should be expected from them. Universities need to be guaranteed a minimum autonomy in order to give long-term contributions to knowledge creation and the idea that they should be completely subsumed to market forces and political control is incompatible with their role as guardians of what is 'reasonably reliable knowledge'. Their most important role in the national innovation system is not to be incubators for start-up firms or for patents; it remains the training of graduates for the labour market.

Today, as compared to the original 1992 approach, we would emphasize even more the importance of human resources. While one aspect of globalization is that codified knowledge moves quickly across borders, the most localized resource remains people, their tacit knowledge, their network relationships and their accumulated organizational experiences. Therefore all parts of the innovation system that contribute to competence building are becoming increasingly important for national performance.

Over the last decade, there has developed a big lively and productive research community primarily studying industrial dynamics in the business sector and often the contributing scholar are employed at business schools or technical universities (compare for the annual Druid (www.druid.dk) and the biannual Schumpeter conferences). There might be falling marginal returns to this kind of research and seen from the point of view of the innovation system approach, there are important issues not given sufficient attention. Five themes that have been touched on in this postscript need to be further developed in future research:

- Implications of the NSI approach for economic theory,
- NSI and economic development,
- NSI welfare states and inequality,
- Environmental sustainability of national innovation systems, and
- Innovation in the public sector.

Most of these themes will require transdisciplinary efforts combining economics with management, sociology, political science and engineering.

Notes

1 B.-Å. Lundvall (ed.). (2010), 'Post Script: Innovation System Research – Where It Came From and Where It Might Go', in *National Systems of Innovation: Towards a Theory of Innovation and Interactive Learning*, 317–49. London: Anthem.

2 In economic geography, the diffusion of the innovation system perspective has, together with the industrial district and industrial clusters approaches, contributed to the construction of a 'new economic geography' that has changed the way geographical location and agglomeration is explained (Maskell and Malmberg 1997; Cooke 2001; Clark, Feldman and Gertler 2000).

3 Several authors have presented overviews of the innovation system literature and made attempts to classify different approaches. An early contribution is McKelvey (1991). More recent ones are Balzat and Hanusch (2004) and Sharif (2006). The latter's contribution builds upon a combination of literature survey and interviews with key persons who were involved in coining the concept. An interesting critical contribution is *National Innovation System, Scientific Concept or Political Rhetoric* (Miettinen 2002), which points to the problematic and vague character of the concept as it is transferred back and forth between the academic and the public policy spheres.

4 Reinert (2003) argues that many of the ideas go further back to a succession of scholars belonging to 'the other Cannon' starting with Antonio Serra. De Liso (2006) argues that Charles Babbage may be seen as another ancestor for the innovation system concept.

5 The paper was published for the first time more than 20 years later in the journal *Industrial and Corporate Change* (Freeman 2004).

6 The IKE group had the privilege to interact with Christopher Freeman in several projects in this period, and many of our ideas were shaped in a dialogue with him (see, for instance, Freeman 1981).

7 For an overview of the current status of innovation research, see the new *Oxford Handbook on Innovation* (Fagerberg et al. 2005).

8 Adam Smith's major contribution was to link the evolving and increasingly more developed division of labour to the creation of wealth. In Lundvall (2006) I have tried to reformulate his theory, emphasizing interactive learning in the context of vertical division of labour so that it becomes more relevant for explaining innovation-based economic growth.

9 For a historical analysis of how match and mismatch is reflected in economic performance of national systems, see Freeman (1995b). In *Innovation, Growth and Social Cohesion: The Danish Model* (Lundvall 2002), I discuss the role of mismatches in the disappointing performance following 'the new economy' euphoria.

10 In 'The Invisible College of Economics of Innovation and Technological Change' (Verspagen and Werker 2003), one can see which innovation scholars define themselves as 'neo-Schumpeterians'.

11 Another point where Schumpeter's approach differs from the NSI approach is his neglect of the importance of knowledge and learning for understanding the innovation process. Schumpeter's entrepreneurs are activists who bring new combinations to the market. How the new combinations come about is left in the dark (Witt 1993, xiv).

12 In the United States, Richard R. Nelson and Nathan Rosenberg played the most important role in developing the theoretical, historical and empirical understanding of innovation.

13 The IKE group had the privilege to have him visiting as guest professor at Aalborg University for periods, and there we all became his apprentices. He was not only an outstanding scholar but also a uniquely generous person.

14 Another characteristic of the successful innovations was that the project team leader in charge of developing the innovation had certain seniority and was able to mobilize resources in critical phases of the innovation process.

15 Today we would add to this micro-foundation the nation-specific characteristics of work organization and learning at the workplace. This will be addressed in section 9.4.

16 Within this narrow logic, the neglect of learning effects from engaging in innovation will underestimate both the private and public rates of return.

17 The data originate from a survey of workers in 15 European countries on working conditions gathered by the Dublin Institute for Working and Living conditions. Discretionary learning refers to work situations where workers say that they learn a lot and that they have some freedom to organize their own work. Lean production learning refers to work situations where workers learn but where there is little discretion left for the workers to organize their own activities. Taylorist organization offers little learning and very little freedom for the worker while simple organization gives more autonomy in solving simple tasks that offer little learning opportunities.

18 This debate has triggered strong efforts to link universities to firms in Europe some-
    times going as far as seeing the ideal university as 'innovation factory'. Dosi, Llerena
    and Sylos Labini (2006) raise doubts about the basic assumption behind the paradox
    that Europe is strong in Science.

19 After comparing the performance of six countries, it is stated that 'A striking feature is
    the apparent missing link between indicators A-E and the overall performance indica-
    tors in F. '*This suggests that priorities and biases in the STI-policy system are weakly linked to general
    economic performance and policies*' (OECD 2005, 29).

20 The data in Table 9.2 are from Jensen, Johnson, Lorenz and Lundvall (2007).

21 Several authors analysing the situation of less developed countries have been critical
    to the use of the concept 'national innovation system' and have preferred to work with
    concepts such as national technological systems (Lall and Pietrobelli 2003) or national
    learning systems (Mathews 2001;Viotti 2002). To some degree I see their alternative
    conceptual proposals as reactions to the use of narrowly defined innovation systems
    with focus on STI learning. I strongly support the idea that understanding processes of
    experience-based learning is a key to the understanding of the specificities of national
    innovation systems (see Lorenz and Lundvall 2006).

22 The Bayh–Dole Act, implemented in the United States in the 1980s, gives stronger
    opportunities and incentives to universities to engage in patenting and protecting their
    knowledge. As documented by Mowery and Sampat (2004), the interpretation of the
    'success' of this reform in Europe has been exaggerated.

23 This scenario gains in realism by the fact that some major US universities would domi-
    nate 'the level playing field' and by the fact that the US government would still be able
    to pursue basic research under headings such as health, military defence and space
    technology since these can be defined as being of strategic importance for its security.

24 In order to explain this to economists it is useful to point to the generally accepted idea
    that there is a need for relative autonomy of central banks. To make sure that we can
    trust the value of money, it has been accepted that its main guardian is given a certain
    degree of autonomy. We need a similar guardian for knowledge, and it is difficult to
    find another institution/organization that is better suited to be the central bank of
    knowledge than the university.

References

Amable, B., R. Barré, and R. Boyer et al. 1997. *Les systémes d'innovation a l'ére de la globalization*.
    Paris: Economica.

Amin, A. and P. Cohendet. 2004. *Architectures of Knowledge: Firms, Capabilities and Communities*.
    Oxford: Oxford University Press.

Andersen, E. S. and B.-Å. Lundvall. 1988. 'Small National Innovation Systems Facing
    Technological Revolutions: An Analytical Framework'. In *Small Countries Facing the
    Technological Revolution*, edited by C. Freeman and B.-Å. Lundvall. London: Pinter
    Publishers, 9–36.

Archibugi, D. and B.-Å. Lundvall (eds.). 2001. *The Globalising Learning Economy: Major
    Socioeconomic Trends and European Innovation Policy*. Oxford: Oxford University Press.

Arocena, R. and Sutz, J. 2000a. 'Looking at National Systems of Innovation from the
    South'. *Industry and Innovation* 7, no. 1: 55–75.

———. 2000b. 'Interactive Learning Spaces and Development Policies in Latin America'.
    DRUID Working Papers, No. 00–13.

————. 2005. 'Latin American Universities: From an Original Revolution to an Uncertain Transition'. *Higher Education* 50: 573–92.

Arundel, A., E. Lorenz, B.-Å. Lundvall and A. Valeyre. 2006. 'The Organisation of Work and Innovative Performance: A Comparison of the EU-15', *DRUID Working Paper* No. 06–14. Aalborg: Aalborg University.

Balzat, M. and H. Hanusch. 2004. 'Recent Trends in the Research on National Systems of Innovation. *Journal of Evolutionary Economics* 14: 197–210.

Breschi, S. and F. Malerba. 1997. 'Sectoral Innovation Systems'. In *Systems of Innovation: Technologies, Institutions and Organizations*, edited by C. Edquist. London: Pinter Publishers.

Carlsson, B. and R. Stankiewitz. 1991. 'On the Nature, Function and Composition of Technological Systems'. *Journal of Evolutionary Economics* 1: 93–118.

Cassiolato, J. E., H. M. M. Lastres and M. L. Maciel. 2003. *Systems of Innovation and Development*. Cheltenham, UK: Edward Elgar.

Christensen, J. L. and B.-Å. Lundvall (eds.). 2004. *Product Innovation, Interactive Learning and Economic Performance*. Amsterdam: Elsevier.

Clark, G. L., M. P. Feldman and M. S. Gertler. 2000. *The Oxford Handbook of Economic Geography*. Oxford: Oxford University Press.

Cooke, P. 1996. *Regional Innovation Systems: An Evolutionary Approach*. London: London University Press.

————. 2001. 'Regional Innovation Systems, Clusters and the Knowledge Economy'. *Industrial and Corporate Change* 4, no. 10: 945–74.

Dahlman, C. J., B. Ross-Larson, and L. E. Westphal. 1987. 'Managing Technological Development: Lessons from the Newly Industrialized Countries'. *World Development* 15, no. 6.

De Liso, N. 2006. 'Charles Babbage, Technological change and the National System of Innovation'. *Journal of Institutional and Theoretical Economics* 162, no. 3: 470–85.

Dosi, G. 1984. *Technical Change and Economic Performance*. London: Macmillan.

————. 1999. 'Some Notes on National Systems of Innovation and Production and Their Implication for Economic Analysis'. In *Innovation Policy in a Global Economy*, edited by D. Archibugi, J. Howells and J. Michie. Cambridge: Cambridge University Press.

Dosi, G., C. Freeman, R. R. Nelson, G. Silverberg and L. Soete (eds.). 1988. *Technology and Economic Theory*. London: Pinter Publishers.

Dosi, G., P. Llerena, and M. Sylos Labini. 2006. 'Science-Technology-Industry Link and the European Paradox: Some Notes on the Dynamics of Scientific and Technological Research in Europe'. In *How Europe's Economies Learn*, edited by E. Lorenz and B.-Å. Lundvall (eds.). 203–34. Oxford: Oxford University Press.

Dosi, G., K. Pavitt and L. Soete. 1990. *The Economics of Technical Change and International Trade*. Herfordshire: Harvester Wheatsheaf.

Edquist, C. 2005. 'Systems of Innovation: Perspectives and Challenges'. In J. Fagerberg, D. Mowery and R. R. Nelson. *The Oxford Handbook of Innovation*. Norfolk: Oxford University Press.

Edquist, C. (ed.). 1997. *Systems of Innovation: Technologies, Institutions and Organizations*. London: Pinter Publishers.

Edquist, C. and B.-Å. Lundvall. 1993. 'Comparing the Danish and Swedish Systems of Innovation'. *National Innovation Systems: A Comparative Analysis*, edited by R. R. Nelson. Oxford: Oxford University Press.

Eparvier, P. 2005. 'Methods of Evolutionism and Rivalry with Neoclassical Analysis. The Example of the National System of Innovation Concept'. *Journal of Economic Methodology* 12, no. 4: 563–79.

Ernst, D., L. Mytelka, and T. Ganiatsos. 1998. 'Technological Capabilities in the Context of Export-Led Growth: A Conceptual Framework'. In D. Ernst, T. Ganiatsos, and L. Mytelka, eds., *Technological Capabilities and Export Success in Asia*. London: Routledge.

Etzkowitz, H. and L. Leydesdorff. 1995. 'The Triple Helix – University-Industry-Government Relations: A Laboratory for Knowledge-Based Economic Development'. *EASST Review* 14, no. 1: 14–19.

———. 2000. 'The Dynamics of Innovation: From National Systems and 'Mode 2' to Triple Helix of University-Industry-Government Relations'. *Research Policy* 29, no. 2: 109–123.

Fagerberg, J., D. Mowery and R. R. Nelson (eds.). 2005. *The Oxford Handbook of Innovation*. Norfolk, Oxford: Oxford University Press.

Foray, D. 2004. *The Economics of Knowledge*. Cambridge, MA: The MIT Press.

Freeman, C. (ed.). 1981. *Technological Innovation and National Economic Performance*. Aalborg: Aalborg University Press.

———. 1982. 'Technological Infrastructure and International Competitiveness'. Draft paper submitted to the OECD Ad hoc group on Science, technology and competitiveness, August 1982, mimeo.

———. 1987. *Technology Policy and Economic Performance: Lessons from Japan*. London: Pinter Publishers.

———. 1988. 'Japan: A New National Innovation Systems?'. In G. Dosi, C. Freeman, R. R. Nelson, G. Silverberg and L. Soete (eds.). *Technology and Economic Theory*. London: Pinter Publishers.

———. 1995a. 'The National Innovation Systems in Historical Perspective'. *Cambridge Journal of Economics* 19, no. 1.

———. 1995b. 'History, Co-evolution and Economic Growth'. *IIASA Working Paper* 95–76, Laxenburg: IIASA.

———. 2002. 'Innovation Systems: City-State, National, Continental and Sub-national. Mimeo, Paper presented at the Montevideo conference'. *Research Policy* 31, no. 2: 191–211.

———. 2004. 'Technological Infrastructure and International Competitiveness'. *Industrial and Corporate Change* 13, no 3: 540–52.

Freeman, C. and B.-Å. Lundvall (eds.). 1988. *Small Countries Facing the Technological Revolution*. London: Pinter Publishers.

Freeman, C. and L. Soete (eds.). 1987. *Technical Change and Full Employment*. Oxford: Basil Blackwell.

———. 1997. *The Economics of Industrial Innovation*. London: Pinter.

Furtado, C. 1964. *Development and Underdevelopment: A Structural View of the Problems of Developed and Underdeveloped Countries*. Berkeley: University of California Press.

Gee, S. and W.-J. Kuo. 1998. 'Export Success and Technological Capability: Textiles and Electronics in Taiwan, Province of China'. In *Technological Capabilities and Export Success in Asia*. D. Ernst, T. Ganiatos and L. Mytelka. London: Routledge.

Georgescu-Roegen, N. 1971. *The Entropy Law and the Economic Process*. Cambridge, MA: Harvard University Press.

Gibbons, M., C. Limoges, H. Nowotny, S. Schwartzman, P. Peter Scott and M. Trow. 1994. *The New Production of Knowledge: The Dynamics of Science and Research in Contemporary Societies*. London: Sage.

Granstrand, O. 2000. *Corporate Innovation Systems A Comparative Study of Multi-Technology Corporations in Japan, Sweden and the USA*. Chalmers University of Technology.

Hirschman, A.O. 1958. *The Strategy of Economic Development*. New Haven, CT: Yale University Press.

Jensen, M. B., B. Johnson, E. Lorenz and B.-Å. Lundvall. 2007. 'Forms of Knowledge and Modes of Innovation'. *Research Policy* 36: 680–93.

Johnson, B. 1992. 'Institutional Learning', in Lundvall, B.-Å. (ed.), *National Innovation Systems: Towards a Theory of Innovation and Interactive Learning.* London, Pinter Publishers.

Johnson, B. and B.-Å. Lundvall. 2003. 'National Systems of Innovation and Economic Development'. In *Putting Africa First, The Making of African Innovation Systems*, edited by M. Muchie, P. Gammeltoft and B.-Å. Lundvall (eds.). Aalborg: Aalborg University Press.

Johnson, B., E. Lorenz and B.-Å. Lundvall. 2002. 'Why all this fuss about codified and tacit knowledge?', *Industrial and Corporate Change* 11: 245–62.

Katz, R. 1984. 'Organizational Issues in the Introduction of new Technologies'. Working paper, Alfred P. Sloan School of Management, Massachusetts Institute of Technology.

Kline, S. J. and N. Rosenberg. 1986. 'An Overview of Innovation'. In *The Positive Sum Game*, edited by R. Landau and N. Rosenberg. Washington DC: National Academy Press.

Lall, S. and C. Pietrobelli. 2003. 'Manufacturing in Sub-Saharan Africa and the Need of a National Technology System'. In *Putting Africa First, The Making of African Innovation Systems*, edited by M. Muchie, P. Gammeltoft and B.-Å. Lundvall. Aalborg: Aalborg University Press.

Lastres, H. M. M. and J. E. Cassiolato. 2005. 'Innovation Systems and Local Productive Arrangements: New Strategies to Promote the Generation, Acquisition and Diffusion of Knowledge'. *Innovation: Management, Policy & Practice* 7, no 2.

List, F. 1841. *Das Nationale System der Politischen Ökonomie, Basel: Kyklos (translated and published under the title: The National System of Political Economy' by Longmans, Green and Co.* London.

Liu, X. and S. White. 2001. 'Comparing Innovation Systems: A Framework and Application to China's Transitional Context'. *Research Policy* 30, no 7: 1091–114.

Lorenz, E. and B.-Å. Lundvall (eds.). 2006. *How Europe's Economies Learn.* Oxford: Oxford University Press.

Lorenz, E. and A. Valeyre. 2006. 'Organizational Forms and Innovation Performance: A Comparison of the EU15'. In *How Europe's Economies Learn*, edited by E. Lorenz, and B.-Å. Lundvall. 140–60. Oxford: Oxford University Press.

Lundvall, B.-Å. 1985. *Product Innovation and User-Producer Interaction.* Aalborg: Aalborg University Press.

———. 1988. 'Innovation as an Interactive Process: From User-Producer Interaction to the National Innovation Systems'. In *Technology and Economic Theory*, edited by G. Dosi, C. Freeman, R. R. Nelson, G. Silverberg and L. Soete: London: Pinter Publishers.

———. (ed.). 1992. *National Innovation Systems: Towards a Theory of Innovation and Interactive Learning.* London: Pinter Publishers.

———. 2002. *Innovation, Growth and Social Cohesion: The Danish Model.* Cheltenham: Edward Elgar.

———. 2006. 'Interactive Learning, Social Capital and Economic Performance'. In *Advancing Knowledge and the Knowledge Economy*, edited by D. Foray and B. Kahin. Cambridge: Harvard University Press.

———. 2007. 'Higher Education, Innovation and Economic Development'. Paper presented at the World Bank's Regional Bank Conference on Development Economics, Beijing, January 16–17, 2007.

Lundvall, B. Å. and S. Borras. 1998. 'The Globalising Learning Economy – Implications for Innovation Policy'. *The European Commission*, DG XII-TSER, Brussels.

Lundvall, B.-Å. and B. Johnson. 1994. 'The Learning Economy'. *Journal of Industry Studies* 1, no. 2: 23–42.

Lundvall, B.-Å., P. Interakummerd and J. V. Lauridsen. 2006. *Asia's Innovation Systems in Transition*. London: Elgar.

Lundvall, B.-Å., B. Johnson, E. Andersen, and B. Dalum. 2002. 'National Systems of Production, Innovation and Competence-building'. *Research Policy* 31, no. 2: 213–31.

Lund-Vinding, A. 2002. *Absorptive Capacity and Innovative Performance: A Human Capital Approach, PhD Dissertation, Department of Business Studies*. Aalborg: Aalborg University.

Marshall, A. 1919. *Industry and Trade: A Study of Industrial Technique and Business Organisation*. London: Macmillan.

———. 1920. *Principles of Economics*. London, Macmillan.

Maskell, P. and A. Malmberg. 1997. 'Towards an Explanation of Regional Specialization and Industry Agglomeration'. *European Planning Studies* 5, no. 1: 25–41

Mathews, J. A. 2001. 'National Systems of Economic Learning: The Case of Technology Diffusion Management in East Asia'. *International Journal of Technology Management* 22, no. 5/6: 455–79.

McKelvey, M. 1991. 'How Do National Innovation Systems Differ?: A Critical Analysis of Porter, Freeman, Lundvall and Nelson'. In *Rethinking Economics: Markets, Technology and Economic Evolution*, edited by G. M. Hodgson and E. Screpanti. Aldershot: Elgar Publishing House.

Metcalfe, J. S. 2006. 'Marshallian Economics'. Paper presented at the International Schumpeter Society, 11th Conference, Sophia Antipolis 2006, June 21–24.

Miettinen, R. 2002. *National Innovation System, Scientific Concept or Political Rhetoric*. Helsinki: Edita.

Mjøset, L. 2001. 'Theory and Understanding in the Social Sciences'. In *International Encyclopedia of the Social and Behavioral Sciences*, edited by N. J. Smalser and P. B. Bates. Amsterdam: Pergamon/Elsevier.

———. 2002. 'An Essay on the Foundations of Comparative Historical Social Science'. *Working Paper* No. 22, ARENA, Oslo.

Mowery, D. and N. Rosenberg. 1979. 'The Influence of Market Demand upon Innovation: A Critical Review of Some recent Empirical Studies'. *Research Policy* 8, no. 2.

Mowery, D. and B. N. Sampat. 2004. 'The Bayh–Dole Act of 1980 and University–Industry Technology Transfer: A Model for Other OECD Governments?'. *The Journal of Technology Transfer* 30, no. 1–2.

Muchie, M., P. Gammeltoft and B.-Å. Lundvall (eds.). 2003. *Putting Africa First: The Making of African Innovation Systems*. Aalborg: Aalborg University Press.

Myrdal, G. 1958. *Economic Theory and Underdeveloped Regions*. London: Duckworth & Co.

———. 1968. *Asian Drama, An Inquiry into the Poverty of Nations*. New York: Penguin Books.

Nelson, R. 1984. *High-technology Policies – A Five-Nation Comparison*. Washington: American Enterprise Institute.

———. 1988. 'Institutions Supporting Technical Change in the United States'. In *Technology and Economic Theory*, edited by G. Dosi, C. Freeman, R. R., Nelson, G. Silverberg and L. Soete. London: Pinter Publishers.

———. (ed.). 1993. *National Innovation Systems: A Comparative Analysis*. Oxford: Oxford University Press.

———. 2006. *What Makes an Economy Productive and Progressive? What Are the Needed Institutions?* New York: Columbia University Press.

Nelson, R. R. and E. S. Phelps. 1965. 'Investments in Humans, Technology Diffusion and Economic Growth'. *The American Economic Review* 56, no. 1/2.

Nelson, R. R. and S. G. Winter. 1982. *An Evolutionary Theory of Economic Change*. Cambridge, MA: Belknap Press of Harvard University Press.

Nielsen, P. and B.-Å. Lundvall. 1999. 'Competition and Transformation in the Learning Economy: The Danish Case'. *Revue d'Economie Industrielle* 88: 67–90.

OECD. 1992. 'Technology and the Economy – The Key Relationships'. Paris: OECD.

––––––. 2000. 'Knowledge Management in the Learning Society'. Paris: OECD.

––––––. 2005. 'Governance of Innovation Systems', Volume 1: Synthesis Report. Paris: OECD.

Pavitt, K. 1984. 'Sectoral Patterns of Technical Change: Towards a Taxonomy'. *Research Policy* 13: 343–73.

Porter, M. 1990. *The Competitive Advantage of Nations*. London: Macmillan.

Prebisch, R. 1950. 'The Economic Development of Latin America and Its Principal Problems, United Nations'. Department of Economic Affairs, Economic Commission for Latin America.

Reinert, E. 1999. 'The Role of the State in Economic Growth'. *Journal of Economic Studies* 26, no. 4/5: 268–326.

––––––. 2003. 'The Other Canon: The History of Renaissance Economics'. In *Evolutionary Economics and Income Inequality*, edited by E. Reinert. Northampton: Edward Elgar Publishing. *Research Policy* 35, no. 5: 745–66.

Rickne, A. 2000. *New Technology-Based Firms and Industrial Dynamics: Evidence from the Technological System of Biomaterials in Sweden, Ohio and Massachusetts*. Göteborg: Chalmers University of Technology.

Rosenberg, N. 1976. *Perspectives on Technology*. Cambridge: Cambridge University Press.

Rothwell, R. 1972. *Factors for Success in Industrial Innovations: Project SAPPHO – A Comparative Study of Success and Failure in Industrial Innovation, Science Policy Research Unit*. Brighton: University of Sussex.

––––––. 1977. 'The Characteristics of Successful Innovators and Technically Progressive Firms'. *R&D Management* 7, no 3: 191–206.

Schmookler, J. 1966. *Invention and Economic Growth*. Cambridge, MA: Harvard University Press.

Schultz, T. W. 1975. 'The Value of the Ability to Deal with Disequilibria'. *Journal of Economic Literature*: 13, no. 3: 827–46.

Schumpeter, J. A. 1934. *The Theory of Economic Development: An Inquiry into Profits, Capital, Credit, Interests and the Business Cycle*. London: Oxford University Press.

––––––. 1942. *Capitalism, Socialism and Democracy*. London: Unwin.

Segura-Bonilla, O. 1999. 'Sustainable Systems of Innovation: The Forest Sector in Central America', *SUDESCA Research Paper* No 24, PhD dissertation, Department of Business Studies. Aalborg: Aalborg University.

Sen, A. 1999. *Development as Freedom*. Oxford: Oxford University Press.

Sharif, N. 2006. 'Emergence and Development of the National Innovation Systems Concept'. *Res Policy* 35, no. 5: 745–66.

Shin, J.-S. 2004. 'Studies of National Innovation Systems – Which Way to Go?', *Working Paper*, National University of Singapore.

Singer, W. H. 1950. 'U.S. Foreign Investment in Underdeveloped Areas – the Distribution of Gains between Investing and Borrowing Countries'. *American Economic Review* 40: 473–85.

Smith, A. 1776/1904. *An Inquiry into the Nature and Causes of the Wealth of Nations*, 5th edition, edited by Edwin Cannan. London: Methuen and Co., Ltd.

Stewart, F. 1977. *Technology and Underdevelopment*. London: Macmillan.

Verspagen, B. and C. Werker. 2003. 'The Invisible College of Economics of Innovation and Technological Change'. *Estudios de Economia Aplicada* 21, no. 3: 203–220.

Viotti, E. B. 2002. 'National Learning Systems: A New Approach to Technological Change in Late Industrialising Countries and Evidence from the Cases of Brazil and Korea'. *Technological Forecasting and Social Change* 69, no. 7: 653–80.

Whitley, R. 1994. 'Societies Firms and Markets: The Social Structuring of Business Systems'. In *European Business Systems, edited by* R. Whitley. London: Sage Publications.

Witt, U. 1993. *Evolutionary Economics.* Aldershot: Edward Elgar Publishers.

Woolcock, M. 1998. 'Social Capital and Economic Development: Toward A Theoretical Synthesis and Policy Framework'. *Theory and Society* 27, no. 2: 151–207.

Part IV

CONTINENTAL TRANSFORMATIONS AND GLOBAL CHALLENGES

Chapter 10

CHINA'S INNOVATION SYSTEM AND THE MOVE TOWARDS HARMONIOUS GROWTH AND ENDOGENOUS INNOVATION

Shulin Gu and Bengt-Åke Lundvall

10.1 Introduction

Observers around the world are impressed by the rapid growth of China's economy, some with hope and others with fear. Some hope that China will offer the unique experience of successful economic growth and catch-up; some see the rise of China as a threat to the current world order and to the powers that currently dominate the world in terms of economy, technology and politics.

While outside observers tend to focus on the success story of unprecedented growth, policy documents and recent domestic debates in China have pointed to the need for a shift in the growth trajectory with stronger emphasis on 'endogenous innovation' and 'harmonious development'. In this chapter, we make an attempt to capture the current characteristics of China's production and innovation system; how they were shaped by history and what major challenges they raise for the future.

In section 10.2 we present data on China's postwar growth experience. We show how the shift in policy towards decentralization, privatization and openness around 1980 established an institutional setting that, together with other factors such as the presence of a wide 'Chinese Diaspora', has resulted in extremely high rates of capital accumulation especially in manufacturing. The section ends with pointing to some inherent contradictions in the current growth pattern.

In section 10.3 we take a closer look at how the policy shift in the 1980s affected the institutional framework shaping R&D activities, in particular, and learning and innovation, in general. The attempt to break down the barrier between the science and technology infrastructure, on the one hand, and the production sphere, on the other, was highly successful as compared to the development in the former Soviet Union. But the original intentions were not fully realized. Rather than establishing markets for science and technology, the reforms led knowledge producers to engage in mergers or forward vertical integration, and they became to a large extent involved in production activities.

Referring back to the analysis of the sustainability of the growth model and the unfinished reform of the innovation system section 10.4 introduces the recent decision by China's government to promote endogenous innovation and harmonious development. Applying the innovation system perspective, we argue that these broadly defined objectives can be realized only through a strategic adjustment towards 'innovation driven growth and learning based development' and we discuss what important policy elements such a strategic adjustment needs to encompass.

In section 10.5, we conclude that imperfections in the division of labour and in the interaction between users and producers of knowledge and innovation that was behind the reforms of the 1980s remain central concerns. In order to raise the long-term efficiency of the massive accumulation of production capital, it is necessary to promote the formation of social capital and to be more considerate when exploiting natural capital.

10.2 The Transition of China's Economy

How do we explain the extraordinary growth performance of China? What are the unique features of the production system? In this section we will see how the development paths of the past define the strengths and weaknesses of the national production systems as well as the bottlenecks and challenges that confront China today. It is useful to distinguish between two periods in China in the second half of the twentieth century. The crucial shift takes place in 1978 when Deng Xiaoping took over the political leadership after Chairman Mao and initiated economic reform and the opening of the economy to international trade. The first was a period of development under a centrally planned economic regime, and the second a period with market-oriented reforms and economic transition. To characterize economic performance of the two periods, we use the data summarized by Maddison (1998) depicted in Table 10.1 and Figures 10.1 and 10.2.

At the time of the revolution, the economy was still dominated by agriculture; in 1952 about 60 per cent of GDP was generated by the agricultural

Table 10.1 Growth of China's economy 1890–1995 (at constant prices)

	1890–1952	1952–1978	1978–1995	1952–1995
Farming, Fishery & Forestry	0.3	2.2	5.1	3.4
Industry	1.7	9.6	8.5	9.2
Construction	1.6	7.2	11.1	8.7
Transport & Communications	0.9	6.0	10.0	7.6
Commerce & Restaurants	0.8	3.3	9.9	5.9
Other Services (incl. Government)	1.1	4.2	6.7	5.2
GDP	0.6	4.4	7.5	5.6
Per capita GDP	0.0	2.3	6.0	3.8
Export Volume	1.6	6.4	13.5	9.2

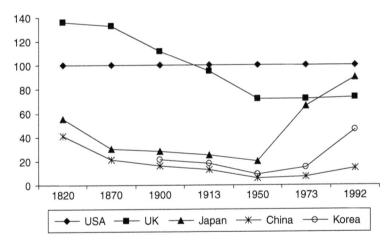

Figure 10.1 Per capita GDP in comparison (USA=100)

(primary) sector, as shown in Figure 10.2, Both the first and the second period were dominated by industrialization rather than 'postindustrialization' that took place after World War II in developed and most of the less developed countries. As a result, China ends up being highly 'industrialized' by the end of the century. In 2003, the GDP structure of China was 12.5 per cent primary, 46 per cent secondary and 41.5 per cent tertiary. The growth in manufacturing and the relative shrinkage of agriculture went on also in the 1990s,

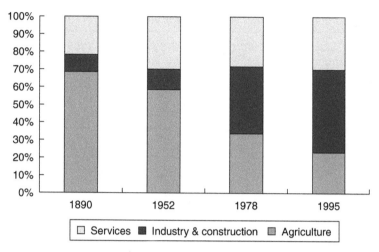

Figure 10.2 GDP structure of China's economy (at constant prices)
Source: Maddison 1998: 56, Tables 3.1 and 3.2.

and the value-added share of the service sectors remained almost unchanged until the second half of the 1990s.

But as we shall see below the economic structure looks quite different when the focus is employment rather than value added. The proportion of the labour force working in agriculture remains as high as 50 per cent in the beginning of the new millennium. The growth in manufacturing value added reflects, more than anything else, a very high rate of accumulation of fixed capital accompanied by high rates of growth in labour productivity.

Behind the high-growth rates and the restructuring of the economy in the second period lay extraordinary rates of savings and capital accumulation. In order to understand how these could be realized in a poor country like China, it is necessary to look at the institutional changes that took place with the shift in the political climate.

10.2.1 Reforms and development performance in the 1980s and 1990s

The policies transforming the economy from being centrally planned towards a market-oriented regime may be seen as following two parallel and mutually reinforcing lines of action aiming at decentralization and privatization (Wu 2003).

The first line of action, 'bureaucratic decentralization', began with increasing the autonomy of firms in decision-making on production planning, investment and acquisition of technology, marketing, pricing and personnel and with more autonomy to local governments in financial, budgetary and administrative issues. Initially, decentralization was based on ad hoc negotiations in individual cases. It was not until the mid-1990s, that nationwide reforms formalized the relationships and introduced more transparent and coherent rules. This was the period when reforms of taxation, banking system and governance structure of state-owned enterprises (i.e. 'corporatization' of previously state-ownerships) were initiated. This dynamic of policy learning where experiences from local and regional experimentation were gradually diffused at the national level has been one major characteristic of the reform period.

The second line of action loosened the restrictions first for township and village enterprises in the early 1980s and later also for private initiatives in the mid-1990s. It included the creation of 'Special Economic Zones' for –Foreign Direct Investments (FDI) with various favourable regulations. In provinces like Zhejiang, this led to private initiatives by entrepreneurs. Here limited arable land, poor mineral deposits, high population density and little accumulation in modern industry in combination with local historical experience in commercial activities led to the start-up of private firms based on small family workshops.

But most importantly, it gave the local governments bigger opportunities to engage in initiatives promoting the local accumulation of capital. They did so through establishing and expanding Township and Village Enterprises (TVEs), sometimes owned by the local governments, sometimes representing joint enterprises with private capital or through initiatives attracting private capital from local, national or international sources.

'Diaspora networks' played an important part in re-enforcing the rapid capital accumulation from foreign investment. Throughout the 1980s, the opening to FDI and international trade attracted partners mainly from the Greater China area – Hong Kong, Chinese Taipei, Singapore and overseas Chinese from other continents. It was not until the second half of the 1990s that multinational companies from North America and West Europe came into China on a large scale. In 2003 Hong Kong, together with Taiwan, remained the first and primary source of FDI, holding about half of the total FDI in China. The fact that the members of the diaspora could communicate directly with local authorities reduced investor uncertainties.

The second line of action, also called 'incremental reform', opened up new spaces for economic activities outside the entities inherited from the central planning era. As a result, the ownership structure of industrial enterprises changed rapidly. As can be seen from Figure 10.3, by 2003, each of the three types of ownership – the state-owned, FDI-dominated and other domestic – were responsible for roughly one-third of output.

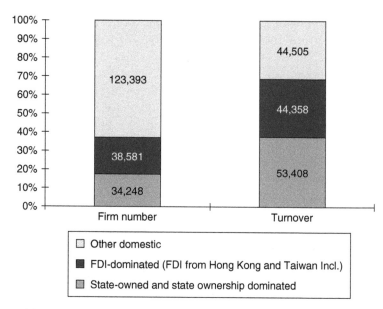

Figure 10.3 Ownership structure: Industry by 2003
Source: Based on China Statistical Yearbook 2004 http://www.stats.gov.cn/tjsj/ndsj/yb2004-c/indexch.htm

It is important to note that a big share of the firms belonging to the category of 'other domestic' enterprises primarily reflects rapid growth in the number and size of township and village firms over which local governments have some influence. The township and village enterprises that played a major role for industrialization in many regions in China outnumber both the domestic-private and the state-owned firms; they underwent a transformation from collective ownership to become privately owned since the mid-1990s.

10.2.2 Export-led growth

International trade was initially pushed by favourable policies and gradually pulled by FDI and intra-trade within global value chains. Today China's economy has reached a much higher level of openness than all other large economies in the world – developed or developing (Table 10.2 and Figure 10.4).

Export structures have been upgraded (Figure 10.5). The share of primary products, such as foodstuffs, agricultural products and mineral fuels, have been reduced from half of the total in 1980 to less than 10 per cent by 2002, while the share of manufactured goods increased to more than 90 per cent. In manufactured exports, electric and machinery products including electronic

Table 10.2 Openness of China to the global economy

	1978	1989	1997	2002	2003
GDP (¥100 million)	3,624.1	16,917.8	78,973	120,333	135,823
Sum import and export (¥100 million)	355.0	4,156.0	26,967.2	51,378.2	70,483.5

Source: Based on China Statistical Yearbook 2004; http://www.stats.gov.cn/tjsj/ndsj/
yb2004-c/indexch.htm, http://www.stats.gov.cn/tjdt/zygg/P020060109431083446682.
doc.

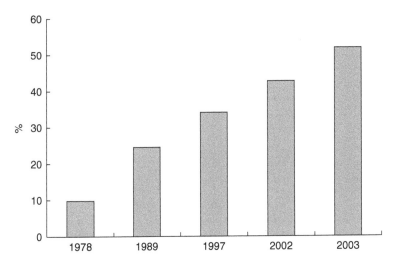

Figure 10.4 Openness to global economy
Source: Based on China Statistical Yearbook 2004; http://www.stats.gov.cn/tjsj/ndsj/
yb2004-c/indexch.htm, http://www.stats.gov.cn/tjdt/zygg/P020060109431083446682.
doc

products, demonstrated the fastest growth rate. Additionally, light and textile
products and apparel increased considerably as well.

Beyond quantitative growth, qualitative or structural change has been radical. It is useful to make a distinction between global production chains that
are driven mainly by demand factors – buyer driven chains – and those driven
mainly by supply factors – producer-driven chains (Gereffi 1999; UNIDO
2002). In the products of 'buyer-driven' chains (such as apparel, footwear and
toys) contained in category 3 and partly in category 5 in Figure 10.5, China
has become the preferred manufacturing location of a global 'Triangle' relationship. The consumption sites are largely in North America and Western
Europe, while Hong Kong and Taiwanese businesspeople play roles as relational coordinators. Many of these goods are produced in factories owned by

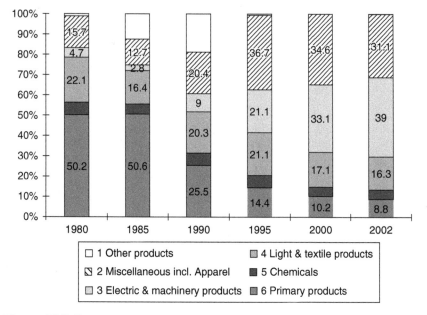

Figure 10.5 Export structure
Source: Reproduced based on Wu (2004) Table 8.7.

Taiwanese or Hong Kong investors; some are produced in Chinese-owned firms but produced in subcontracting relationships.

In the 'producer-driven' industries such as computer and IT products, which are included in category 4 in Figure 10.5, exports are mainly manufactured in factories owned by Western and Taiwanese investors. For 2003, it is reported that 61.9 per cent of high-tech export was produced by fully foreign-owned firms and 21.4 per cent by partly foreign-owned firms; altogether FDI-related manufacturing produced more than 80 per cent of high-tech export from China (China S&T Indicators 2004). This reflects overall trends of the innovation system of China characterized by easy access to foreign technology while remaining weak in local and domestic clustering. We will turn to this point in sections 10.3 and 10.4.

10.2.3 Domestic demand and investment

The domestic market has also played a role for the development in the period. Domestic demand experienced at least two rounds of surge and growth. The first round appeared through the 1980s and the first half of the 1990s, and it was led by household durables and necessities, as illustrated by color televisions in Table 10.3 and Figure 10.6. The centrally planned economy had left

Table 10.3 Growth in representative products

Year	Air conditioner 10,000 set	Color television 10,000 set	Rolled steel products 10,000 ton	Cement 10,000 ton	Passenger car 10,000 set	Microcomputer 10,000 set
1978	0.02	0.38	2,208.00	6,524.00		
1980	1.32	3.21	2,716.00	7,986.00	0.54	
1985	12.35	435.28	3,693.00	14,595.00	0.90	
1989	37.47	940.02	4,859.00	21,029.00	3.58	7.54
1990	24.07	1,033.04	5,153.00	20,971.00	3.50	8.21
1991	63.03	1,205.06	5,638.00	25,261.00	6.87	16.25
1992	158.03	1,333.08	6,697.00	30,822.00	16.17	12.62
1993	346.41	1,435.76	7,716.00	36,788.00	22.29	14.66
1994	393.42	1,689.15	8,428.00	42,118.00	26.87	24.57
1995	682.56	2,057.74	8,979.80	47,560.59	33.70	83.57
1996	786.21	2,537.60	9,338.02	49,118.90	38.29	138.83
1997	974.01	2,711.33	9,978.93	51,173.80	48.60	206.55
1998	1156.87	3,497.00	10,737.80	53,600.00	50.71	291.40
1999	1337.64	4,262.00	12,109.78	57,300.00	57.10	405.00
2000	1826.67	3,936.00	13,146.00	59,700.00	60.70	672.00
2001	2333.64	4,093.70	16,067.61	66,103.99	70.36	877.65
2002	3135.11	5,155.00	19,251.59	72,500.00	109.20	1,463.51
2003	4820.86	6,541.40	24,108.01	86,208.11	202.01	3,216.70

Source: China Statistical Yearbook 2004 Tables 14–20. http://www.stats.gov.cn/tjsj/ndsj/yb2004-c/indexch.htm.

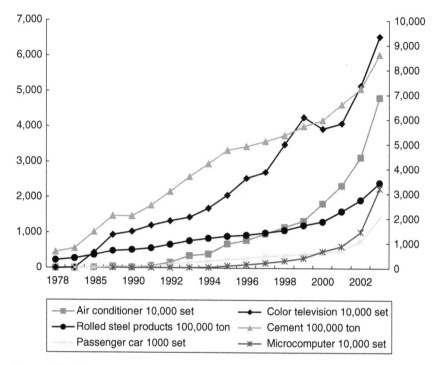

Figure 10.6 Growth in representative products
Source: China Statistical Yearbook 2004 Tables 14–20 http://www.stats.gov.cn/tjsj/ndsj/yb2004-c/indexch.htm

huge areas of shortage in consumer goods industries. The combination of bureaucratic decentralization and incremental reforms stimulated investment in the supply capacity of these industries.

The second round began around 1999 and was focused on real estate, passenger cars, personal computers and telecommunications, as illustrated by microcomputers and passenger cars in Table 10.3 and Figure 10.6. Cement and rolled steel products are intermediate products and both rounds stimulated demand for them. The second period of demand-led growth was strongly weighted towards large-scale activities such as construction and car production, which consume them in great quantities; hence one sees accelerated growth in the latter years. To expand production capacity, a very high rate of growth in investment was necessary.

The second surge of manufacturing was more directly induced by central monetary and industrial policies. In order to cope with the stagnation and deflation that appeared in 1998–99, diagnosed as caused by lack of effective demand, the government engaged in 'active fiscal policies' to increase public investment in highways, telecommunications and power generation stations. The banking system was also engaged in stimulating 'domestic demand' in consumption. It created loans for individual housing and car consumers at reduced interest rates.

10.2.4 A unique pattern of economic growth

In about a quarter of a century, China's economy has been characterized by high rates of economic growth and capital accumulation. Some of the mechanisms behind that growth pattern are unique, while some have parallels with the institutional set up that promoted capital accumulation in England in the eighteenth century (Qian 1996).

The reforms that were initiated more than 25 years ago unleashed restrained material needs. It was explicitly argued that getting some concentration of wealth among the few was a first step towards making everybody better off; this made the strife for material wealth ideologically legitimate. Slumbering entrepreneurship was awoken to engage in production and trade both within and outside the public sector. *The most important driver behind capital investment and economic growth was a specific local fusion of political and economic interests.* Local authorities and local entrepreneurs were able to promote simultaneously their political career and their own economic interests by stimulating industrial growth in their region, province, town or village. Most of the extra income created remained under local control and the incentives to reinvest the surplus were strong.

Foreign direct investment initially emanating primarily from overseas Chinese investors and subsequently from wider sources should be added to this as an important factor. Joint ventures offer good opportunities for public and private rewards for local policymakers. The same is true for attracting direct investment in purely foreign-owned enterprises to the locality. Building infrastructure and supplying cheap labour, energy and land has become a key concern for local administrators. This mixture of political and economic interests constitutes a new kind of concentration of power at the local level not always balanced by local political democracy and local rule of law, and it may explain why the local administration is less popular than the central government among Chinese citizens (Saich 2004).

The dynamics of reform has also been driven by the competition between localities to offer the most attractive framework conditions. This sometimes takes the form of offering cheap resources and lax regulations in relation to environment and workers' safety. But there are also examples of forward-looking ideas developed locally and then spread nationwide.

10.2.5 Limits to growth

The development trajectory behind the high speed of growth is now confronted with barriers for further growth. Some of these are external and refer to potential trade conflicts. Others reflect domestic problems with social and ecological sustainability. There are indications of serious weaknesses of the innovation system. The call for 'harmonious development' may be interpreted as an attempt to give new direction to the recognized unsustainable growth patterns (see below for four dimensions of unsustainability).

Remarkable global impact and trade disputes: China's economic growth has had a very visible impact on the global economy. When China's exports and imports grow with double-digit rates, it makes a major difference for the rest of the world. The impact on other countries' trade balances is such that there is an upper limit for how far the trade surplus can be increased without triggering trade quotas or other forms of retaliation. The current trend of massive penetration into global markets may not be lasting much longer.

Jobless growth: In terms of GDP structure (Figure 10.7 and Figure 10.8 compare China with four big developing or transitional economies: Brazil, South Africa, India and Russia), China appears to be overwhelmingly 'industrialized'. However, China is faced with the challenge from 'jobless growth' in the manufacturing sector. Figure 10.8 shows that in terms of employment

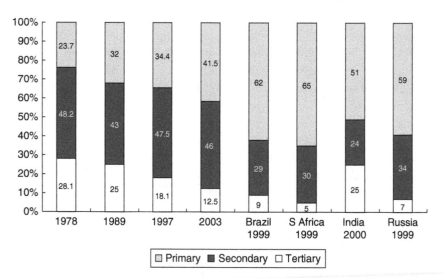

Figure 10.7 GDP structure in comparison

Source: For the data on China: Statistical Yearbook 2004 (http://www.stats.gov.cn/tjsj/ndsj/yb2004-c/indexch.htm), for the Data on Brazil, South Africa, India and Russia: World Facts and Figures at http://worldfactsandfigures.com

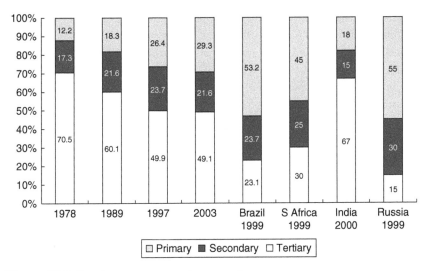

Figure 10.8 Employment structure in comparison

structure, China appears as an agricultural economy – half of the labour remains in this sector. Only India has a bigger proportion of the labour force in agriculture. Combining the two sets of data it is obvious that China is characterized by high and rapidly growing capital–labour ratio in the manufacturing sector. While there was net job creation in the first years of the reform period, the increase of employment slowed down in the 1980s and stagnated since the 1990s.

This displacement of employment exacerbates 'structural unemployment' (Lewis 1955). 'Jobless growth', in addition to inequality in wealth distribution and redistribution, entails social instability and endangers sustainable development.

Widening income gaps and negative environmental externalities: Gaps between the urban and the rural, between regions and between the rich and poor in the same region are widening. Working conditions and workers' safety have been largely neglected. Negative externalities also include environmental degradation such as air and water pollution and exploitation and wasteful use of other nonrenewable resources. The current development mode entails intense consumption of nonrenewable raw materials and energy sources. Especially when these inputs are under the control of local groups with vested interests there may be a tendency to set prices too low and to be lax in terms of safety regulations.

Slow pace in competence and competitiveness upgrading: The industrialization process has not resulted in building a widespread and robust indigenous innovation capability in Chinese firms. After 20 years of being the origin of manufactured goods 'Made in China', China's economy has not been able to embark on the track of competence upgrading. This contrasts with the catching-up history of the United States and Japan where 'Made in US' and 'Made in Japan' were preludes to the two countries, within a time span of one generation, reaching the world frontier in innovativeness and competitiveness. China remains specialized in low value-added products with profit margins trapped at a meagre 2–5 per cent, or in some areas even lower.[1]

Recent policy documents and the general debate have pointed to these problems and contradictions, and to the need for a shift in the development strategy with stronger emphasis on 'harmonious development' and 'endogenous innovation'. What adjustments of the development strategy are needed to realize the intentions signalled by these concepts?

Before we discuss this issue in section 10.4, it is necessary to analyse the reform of the innovation system that accompanied decentralization and privatization. The analysis of the reform and its outcome points to the weaknesses of the current innovation system, and it helps us to specify what reforms are required in order to make innovation endogenous and to make it contribute to harmonious development. We will argue that efforts to stimulate endogenous innovation may go hand in hand with promoting harmonious development.

10.3 The Transformation of China's Innovation System

We now turn to the transformation of the innovation system of China in the context of market-oriented economic reform. It is interesting to note that the motivation for the reform of the R&D system initiated in 1985 was 'highly systemic' in the sense that the focus was on reshaping the division of labour and the interaction between producers and users of knowledge and innovation. As we shall see, the problems that remain after the reform can also be defined as 'highly systemic'. The fundamental weakness of the system, having a negative impact both on the absorption of foreign technology and on domestic innovation, has to do with an economic structure that does not support learning by interaction in organized markets.

10.3.1 The attempt to reconfigure the user–producer relationships

China has an old civilization and historically has made important contributions to global science and technology (such as the compass, gunpowder and paper). In the older history of China, however, science and technology as it evolved in Western Europe was not regarded as important or as carrying social status. While Confucius's heritage gave high prestige to intellectuals, it was to those engaged in humanistic science and in political and administrative affairs. Scientific and technological knowledge was seen as based on practical experience rather than as a modern type of scholarship, while research and development (R&D) establishments started to be organized in the 1920s to 1930s, China only began the process of institutionalization of modern science and technology nationwide in the 1950s.

The R&D system established in the first period of development was designed in accordance with the centrally planned regime. One prominent feature was the huge size that was a reflection of the Marxist idea of science as a societal force of production and also a result of the self-reliance development strategy in the centrally planned period (see Table 10.4).

The second feature was the separation of industrial R&D centres from productive enterprises. The centrally planned regime had introduced particular mechanisms to link up R&D activity with production: all the R&D institutes, except for those belonging to the Chinese Academy of Sciences (which was assigned to be the national top organization for comprehensive natural and engineering science), were organized under the jurisdiction of sector-specific ministries or bureaus, independently outside enterprises. The ministries or bureaus took the responsibility for planning production tasks as well. They were hence in command of both R&D and production (Gu 1999, 151–76).

It is interesting to note that this model of specialization according to product category both for R&D centres and enterprises, and separation of firms from innovative activities was common for all the former centrally planned economies.[2] The organizational separation between innovation and production blocked the system from vital and intimate interactions between producers and users, which are important especially for innovation in sophisticated producer goods technology (von Hippel 1994; Kline and Rosenberg 1986; Lundvall 1988).

The institutional setting was reflected in innovation characteristics. For example, the machinery industry of China was apt at 'general purpose' machinery and weak in technologies fulfilling particular machining tasks since these could only be developed through interactive learning and close producer–user communications (Gu 1999, 127–35). The low degree of *effectiveness* of the centrally planned institutional settings was well acknowledged at the end of the 1970s. This became one important motive for the launch of reforms.

The crucial event for R&D system reform came in 1985, slightly lagging the agricultural and industrial reforms, which were started in 1978 and 1984, respectively. A 1985 decision made by the Central Committee of the Communist Party of China initiated the reforms in Science and Technology System Management.

Table 10.4 China's investment in R&D

Year	Percentage of R&D Expenditure Based on National Income	Year	Percentage of R&D Expenditure Based on GDP
1953	0.1	1978	1.5 (1.8 of national income)
1954	0.2	1979	1.5
1955	0.3	1980	1.5
1956	0.6	1981	1.3
1957	0.6	1982	1.3
1958	1.0	1983	1.4
1959	1.6	1984	1.4
1960	2.8	1985	1.2
1961	2.0	1986	1.3
1962	1.5	1987	1.0
1963	1.9	1988	0.8
1964	2.1	1989	0.8
1965	2.0	1990	0.8
1966	1.6	1991	0.8
1967	1.0	1992	0.7
1968	1.0	1993	0.7
1969	1.5	1994	0.7
1970	1.6	1995	0.6
1971	1.8	1996	0.6
1972	1.7	1997	0.6
1973	1.5	1998	0.7
1974	1.5	1999	0.8
1975	1.6	2000	1.0
1976	1.6	2001	1.1
1977	1.6	2002	1.2
1978	1.8 (1.5 of GDP)	2003	1.3

Sources: China Statistical Yearbook on Science and Technology, various issues; National Statistics Bureau 1990: 207, and http://www.sts.org.cn/KJNEW/maintitle/MainTitle.htm.

The central theme for the reform was to rearrange the relationship between knowledge producers and users and their relationships with the government. In a context where demand, supply and coordination factors were changing, reform of the science and technology system was seen as essential.

The size and complexity of the S&T system made reform crucial for the success of economic growth. By 1980, there were 4,690 research institutes affiliated with administration bodies higher than the 'county' level (i.e., to central, provincial and regional/city governments, with some additional 3,000 institutes at the county level, the lowest level of the nation's administration hierarchy with an independent budget ('White Paper' No. 1, 232–35). Some 323,000 scientists and engineers worked in these institutes. The then Prime Minister Mr. Zhao Ziyang interpreted the reform as the following:

> The current science and technology institution in our country has evolved over the years under special historical situations. The advantages embodied in this system manifested themselves in concerted efforts to tackle major scientific and technological projects, which were achieved with great success. However, there is growing evidence to show that the system can no longer accommodate the situation in the four modernizations programme, which depends heavily on scientific and technological progress. One of the glaring drawbacks of this system is the disconnection of science and technology from production, a problem, which is a source of great concern for all of us...
>
> By their very nature, there is an organic linkage between scientific research and production. For this linkage a horizontal, regular, many-leveled and many-sided channel should be provided. The management system as practiced until now has actually clogged this direct linkage, so that research institutes were only responsible to the leading departments above, in a vertical relationship, with no channels for interaction with the society as a whole or for providing consultancy services to production units. This is the root cause of the inability of our scientific research to meet our production needs over the years... This state of affairs can hardly be altered if we confine ourselves to the beaten track. The way out lies in a reform. (Zhao 1986)

10.3.2 The adaptive policy process and the recombination of competences

For reforming the S&T system, a two-pronged policy was designed. On the one hand, 'technology markets' were established to function as distributive institutions for R&D outputs (Decision: Section III). On the other hand, excellence-based allocation mechanisms were introduced for the allocation of public R&D funds (Decision: Section II). In order for R&D institutes to be able to respond to opportunities arising at the market place, some degree of autonomy in terms of hiring personnel, engaging in contracted projects and acceptance and use of contractual fees were assigned (Decision: Section VII). At the same time subsidies from the government were gradually reduced

(Decision: Sections I and II). It was expected that by push and pull, the previously publicly funded R&D institutes would move to serve their clients via regular and multiple linkages.[3]

The actual process of S&T system reform – as the reforms of the overall economic system – unfolded through trial and error and entailed continuous adjustment of policies (Shulin 1999). *The technology market solution*, central in the initial design, was soon recognized as being difficult to realize in its original form. The users were not capable of absorbing transferred technology, and the market was too small to secure R&D institutes with enough earnings. Buyers and sellers experienced serious uncertainty in assessing the use value of technology giving rise to disputes when writing and implementing contracts. As a response, in 1987 reform policy began to promote the *merger of R&D institutes* into existing enterprises or enterprise groups. The merger process was also difficult to realize, however. Huge gaps between the merging parties, from differences in work culture and administrative affiliations, were hard to overcome immediately.

In the next year (1988) the Torch Programme was launched to encourage organizations akin to *spin-off enterprises*– called *NTEs* (New Technology Enterprises) – from existing R&D institutes and universities. Local governments contributed to investment in infrastructure and supporting institutions for the New and Hi-Tech Industry Zones that became incubation bases for the NTE start-ups. Scientists and engineers, often with support from their parent institutions, went into commercial application of their inventions and expertise by means of the creation of NTEs. And by the early 1990s, reform policy included another solution to change *individual R&D institutes into production entities*. This, as well, was an adaptation to an actual evolution already realized by many industrial R&D institutes.

At the end of the 1990s, the reforms came to a form of conclusion. In 1999 an official decision pointed to the need to clarify the actual character of the previously government-run industrial technology R&D institutes. By 2001,[4] some 1,200 industrial technology R&D institutes had re-registered their business type. Of them more than 300 were *merger* cases; these institutes have cancelled their independent position and become a part of an enterprise, and 600 plus have changed to become *profitable firms* in themselves. A few have entered into a university. Table 10.5 indicates the changed structure of R&D performers. In 2000 the proportion of R&D performed by 'enterprises' increased abruptly (see line 3, Table 10.5) largely because a number of previous R&D institutes became registered enterprises or part of existing enterprises. Table 10.4 also depicts the scope of *technology market* and *spin-offs*, both grew steadily over time (lines 1 and 2), illustrating the complementary effects of various transformation means. Lines 4 and 5 and 3 show a changed

Table 10.5 Selective indicators to changes in China's NIS (all the measures at current prices)

	1985	1990	1995	2000
(1) Technology Market				
Contract fees (RMB Billion)	2.30	7.51	26.83	65.07
(2) Spin–offs				
Number of NTEs	–	1,690	12,937	20,796
Annual turnover (RMB Billion)	–	5.94	151.2	920.9
Export (USD Billion)	–	0.69	1.55	13.81
		(RMB Billion)		
(3) Domestic R&D	6.74	12.54	34.87	89.57
expenditure (RMB Billion)	(1987)			
in which Enterprises (%)		n.a.	43.7	60.0
Independent R&D institutes (%)	29.3	n.a.	42.1	28.8
Universities (%)	54.7	n.a.	12.1	8.6
	15.9			
(4) Import of capital goods	16.24	16.85	52.64	69.45
(USD Billion)				(1999)
(5) FDI (USD Billion)	1.96	3.49	37.52	40.72

Sources: China Statistical Year Book on Science and Technology, various issues.

structure in technology sources. China, not so long ago nearly closed to international exchange in technology and knowledge, has become a widely open innovation system, with enormous inflows of technology in forms of international capital goods and FDI.

Adaptive policy evolving though trial and error characterizes 'gradual reforms' in the whole process of economic transition in China. The great uncertainties associated with foreseeing the impact of major political reforms made adaptive policy learning necessary. Only policymaking that was responsive and adaptive to the feedback information on the impact could preserve the feasibility for success of any radical social innovation program (Metcalfe 1995; Gu and Lundvall 2006).

10.3.3 A review of the transformation of the innovation system

On the basis of the discussion above, Figure 10.9 illuminates the National Innovation System of China as it looked before (part A) and after (part B) the transformation. It embraces (1) *innovation actors* – R&D institutes, capital goods industries that provide embodied technology for user sectors and domestic end-product manufacturers; (2) *inflows of technology* – by means of technology licensing (TL) sample machine procurement (SMP), procurement of equipment (PE), foreign direct investment (FDI) and original equipment

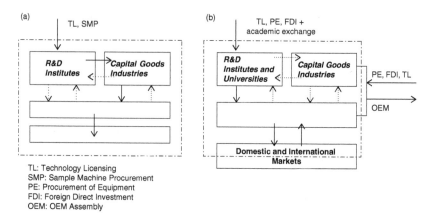

Figure 10.9 Transformation of China's NIS

manufacturing (OEM); and (3) *interactive relationships* between actors and with domestic and international markets. We use arrows with different line boldness to illustrate the intensity of the various links. It gives a first impression of what significant changes the transformation has brought into the system.

The transformation was constructive in safeguarding and recombining technological capabilities in the context of market reform and opening up to the global economy. It has supported rapid growth in the economy as a whole. For example, a number of NTEs like Huawei, Datang and Lenovo grew to become key ICT enterprises and this led to a fundamental restructuring of China's ICT industry (Shulin and Steinmueller 1996/2000). The achievements are especially impressive when comparing with Russia where scientific and technological capabilities were destroyed on a huge scale. It nonetheless leaves the system with some prominent weaknesses (see below for two major weaknesses).

Easy access to foreign technology while remaining weak in local and domestic clustering: First of all, the resulting system developed weaker domestic links and interactions than international links; although the mastery of the latter links remains rather passive, dominated by the import of foreign technology embodied in machinery and other process equipment. The *capital goods industry* has not played a role as an innovation centre for the whole economy by providing appropriately advanced production means for various users; they were instead largely integrated into the respective global value chains. Many regions of China, for which the autonomy of policy decision-making was strengthened during the market reform, are weak in *geographical proximity-based clustering or networking* even when there is some firm agglomeration. In general *potential local or domestic links along and between value chains* have been slow to develop and hard to expand. Small firms in traditional manufacturing sectors, agriculture and rural development have received inadequate support from national and regional technological infrastructure, showing a *separation between the modern and the traditional part* of the system.

Missing technological infrastructure and supportive institutional development: Second, the transformation ignored the development of technological infrastructure and supportive institutions. The remarkable aspect of the reform is that the initial intention – to establish markets for technologies for existing R&D institutes and existing enterprises – was not realized. Instead other unforeseen adaptations 'saved' the reform. A general tendency was *vertical integration of R&D and design with production activities* – either through merger into enterprises or through the establishment of downstream production. This was true not only for R&D institutes for industrial technology but also for institutes engaged in health and agricultural R&D and even for universities. As a result, the reconfiguration of the scientific and technological infrastructure was not complete during the market reforms. This has resulted in a weak capability to provide S&T inputs and supportive services to innovation in firms – a capability that is fundamentally important for knowledge based growth (Nelson 2004; David 2003).

There were several reasons for the drive towards vertical integration. One reason was the peculiar pattern of division of labour for R&D institutes inherited from the centrally planned system in which they had already been involved in many 'downstream' activities.[5] Weak absorptive capacity and less developed social capital were other reasons for the difficulties in establishing markets for technology.

The phenomenon of factories that integrated vertically within themselves all stages in the production process were common in all centrally planned economies (Granick 1967). Kornai (1980) explained this with a combination of the factories' hunger for investment and paternalistic relations with the planning authority. The *vertically integrated factories were left almost untouched* by the market reforms, and this obstructed networking in the core part of the economy. Vertically integrated enterprises survived, mainly in what had been seen as strategic sectors and especially in the machinery industry that was given high priority before the reform.

10.4 Problems, Debates and Challenges

By the second half of the 1990s, symptoms increasingly indicated that the development dynamics created by reforms were about to be exhausted and negative sides of the growth model came more into focus. The accession to WTO added to the need for China to move into a new period of economic and NIS transition. This was the background for the 1999 Decision by the Communist Party and the State Council where it declared the need for 'enhancing technological innovation, developing high technologies and promoting commercial production of S&T achievements'.[6] However there has not been much change in economic policy and in the orientation of development, except for 'active fiscal policies', which targeted material infrastructure construction and a considerable increase in public investment in R&D.

With the further accumulation of problems, the government now has decided to make 'endogenous innovation' and 'harmonious development' key components of a renewal of the development strategy. In this section we analyse the problems and introduce the policy debate around 'endogenous innovation'. Starting from the innovation system perspective and taking into account the historical transition of the system, we propose an interpretation of endogenous innovation where it is understood as a move towards innovation driven growth and learning based economic development.

10.4.1 'Endogenous innovation'[7] and policy debates

In October 2005, the Communist Party Central Committee and China's government stipulated the Guiding Vision for the 11th National Economic and Social Development Program (2006–2010). It emphasizes the importance of adjustment of development strategy, which should be economizing material inputs, upgrading economic structure and innovative capability, being friendly to environmental protection, balancing between urban and rural development and between the development in East, Middle and West regions and maintaining job creation and social equality (CCCPC 2005). The key for realizing the new strategy is endogenous innovation (zi-zhu-chuang-xin) and continuous reforms to build harmoniousdevelopment. One can see that the new strategic vision accommodates several of the problems discussed above.

Policy debates on endogenous innovation following the decision may be considered as a follow-up of earlier long-lasting debates.[8] A first focus concerns the theoretical rationale for alternative development strategies – whether the strategy should be based on comparative advantages or if it should involve strategic industrial policy aiming at catch-up and leapfrogging. Another focus of the debates relates to the buy-or-make question of technology. Here one opinion insists on the necessity to increase investment in domestic R&D so as to develop competence in core technologies and technological capabilities, national brands and to build independent capabilities in relation to defence, health care and other national specific needs. The opposite opinion argues in favour of buying/borrowing technologies from abroad; it claims that high R&D investment has, to date, brought advantages neither for the country nor for the enterprises. A third focus is on policies for FDI. Whether, and to what extent does FDI contribute to technology acquisition and upgrading? Were the policies aiming at attracting FDI by opening the huge domestic market successful? Should the favourable treatment for FDI continue or should regulatory conditions be identical for domestic and FDI-related businesses?

The debates have thus raised several different issues and have not always been clearly focused. The emphasis on promoting free market and trade liberalization in policy spheres was, to some extent, unavoidable in a period when China was engaged in economic and social transition away from a centrally planned regime. Nonetheless, the current debates may be understood as recognition that free markets alone have their limits when it comes to guide social and economic transition and development.

10.4.2 Endogenous innovation as strategic element of innovation-driven growth and learning-based economic development

In order to clarify the current debates, we believe it is necessary to elevate the central theme 'how to embark on innovation-driven growth and learning-based economic development'. Otherwise many of the debates might go nowhere.

For example, purchasing technology from overseas and the domestic development of technology are both important; they actually are complementary in most real innovation processes. To see policies that encourage domestic firms' innovation as conflicting with policies that aim to acquire foreign technologies would be misleading. Comparative advantages are necessary reference points for operational planning while strategic planning needs to consider how existing comparative advantages can be renewed and upgraded. To promote endogenous innovation, a conventional and simplistic response would be to invest more in science and technology, and re-enforce the tendency that R&D organizations move into downstream activities. It is highly questionable if such an effort would make any major difference and overcome the weaknesses in competence upgrading at the firm level and in internal clustering and dynamics.

The crucial question is how to overcome the weaknesses the Chinese economy and innovation system have encountered, and for this, it is essential to define endogenous innovation as a strategy for innovation-driven growth and learning-based development. We believe that the fundamental challenge is still to make the innovation system as a whole to work in such a way that it contributes to economic growth and harmonious development. This is actually what the Chinese government's Guiding Vision for the 11th National Economic and Social Development Program (2006–2010) declares.

10.4.3 Reconfiguring innovation systems in the context of the globalizing learning economy

The idea that economic development is a process where the degree of specialization and the division of labour grow and become more complex, and the mastery of knowledge generation and application becomes increasingly sophisticated, goes back to Adam Smith, and has been discussed widely by economic historians (e.g., Maddison 1991; Fei & Ranis 1997). Human learning, which takes place by doing and through science-based innovation, is the most important source for economic growth and involves the deepening of the division of labour and increasing scale economies as well as dynamic effects (North 1996; Lundvall and Johnson 1994). In the current context of global competition, deregulation and radical technical change the dynamic effects become increasingly important. The acceleration of the rate of change implies that the speed of learning becomes increasingly important for the competitiveness of firms and national systems. One of the authors has referred to this change in context as 'a globalizing learning economy' (Lundvall and Borras 1998; Archibugi and Lundvall 2001). China's experience shows that development in the context of globalizing learning economy has made it very essential to facilitate a rapid learning pace and intensity.

One of the major focuses of the innovation system perspective (Nelson and Winter 1982; Freeman 1987; Lundvall 1992; Nelson 1993) *is about how an innovation system generalizes and diffuses knowledge through learning.* Learning takes place in specialized R&D centres that transform local experiences and laboratory experiments into more general knowledge and diffuse it through training and publications. But learning also takes place in production and consumption. Producer learning results in productivity growth. Consumer learning results in change in the composition of final demand (Pasinetti 1981). Learning by using refers to how users of complex systems or advanced process equipment become more proficient as they experience and solve problems (Rosenberg 1982).

However, the development of new products and processes, especially capital goods and sophisticated devices, has to involve an interaction and information exchange between users and producers (Lundvall 1985). *Interactive learning* is pervasive in a modern economy, which is characteristic of sophisticated patterns in division of labour. More fundamentally, 'learning-by-interacting' generalizes and spreads the initially local learning consequences throughout the whole economy in the form of new machinery, new components or new software systems embodied knowledge and tacit and human embedded competences and business solutions (Lundvall 2006).

How a system gets interactive learning to work well is crucial for innovation and development performance of a national economy. *Interactive learning is carried out in a hybrid structure of governance* consisting of markets, organizations and networks, which we call an 'organized market' (Lundvall 1985). Perfect competition with arm's length and anonymous relationships between customers and sellers cannot support product innovation. Vertically integrated firms also exclude product innovation and an economic structure dominated by such firms would make an economy less rich in terms of learning experiences and also more rigid and therefore quite vulnerable to market turbulence (Lundvall 2006; Richardson 2002).

Learning takes place through user producer interaction where, for instance, one producer of machinery absorbs information about user experiences from many diverse users. The interaction at this level may be seen as an important dynamo for innovation-driven economic growth. Different from conventional thoughts, the perspective of interactive learning points to the *importance of the structure of production and innovation system*, the absence of a strong domestic capital goods sector would constitute a serious handicap for the innovation system. Similar considerations apply to *knowledge intensive business services*. Today such services play an increasingly important role for economic growth. While it is necessary for production enterprises to have in house R&D activities in order to be able to absorb knowledge from the outside, having access to knowledge intensive business services is a great advantage. Empirical studies from different countries show that firms that outsource the production of such services experience rapid productivity growth (Tomlinson 2001).

Network formation is crucial for the improvement of interactive learning by augmenting and mediating 'complementary' but not 'similar' innovative activities (Saxenian 1996; Baldwin and Clark 1997; Langlois 2003). *'Social capital'* supports networking and interactive learning across organizational borders (Woolcock 1998). Social capital may in this connection be defined as 'the willingness and capability of citizens and organizations to make commitments to each other, collaborate with each other and trust each other in processes of exchange and interactive learning.'

The above paragraphs illustrate the importance of applying a systemic perspective when designing an innovation policy aiming at endogenous innovation. From the NIS perspective the promotion of endogenous innovation needs to be built on an understanding of the two major themes: *interactive learning* and *system efficiency*.

The policy discussion in the following sections will draw on the ideas developed above. We see some of the major challenges for the reform of China's innovation system as having to do with a need to reconfigure user–producer relationships and to stimulate new forms for user–producer interaction in the context of innovation.

10.4.4 Innovation policies to overcome the limits to growth and foster endogenous innovation and harmonious development

At the end of section 10.2, we listed a number of problems that emanate from China's current trajectory of economic growth. At the end of section 10.3, we pointed to weaknesses of the current innovation system. In what follows we will, from the innovation system perspective, briefly present some ideas for the next transition of the innovation system that respond to these problems and weaknesses and take into account the global context.

Address domestic needs: An inexorable factor for innovation is demand characteristics; it offers both incentives and demand information. Enterprises in China should not miss the rich resources of domestic market, reflecting heterogeneous regional, habitual and cultural variation in needs and both advanced and basic needs. A general shift towards home markets would also reduce international friction in relation to trade.

One way to promote harmonious and sustained development is to direct innovation activities towards domestic social and ecological needs such as health services, education, transport, energy and environment. China has the necessary planning capacity to coordinate R&D and the development of industrial competence and qualified demand, using a pragmatic mixture of market and administrative governance.[9]

To respond to the demands emerging domestically would open ways to stimulate and nurture novel ideas for endogenous innovation. In the longer run that would eventually make it possible for China to contribute both to market demand in the international market and to human well-being. In short, addressing domestic needs is a necessary ground for 'peaceful development' and harmonious development.

Engage in product innovation and improve engineering capability: At the level of the single firm, product innovation addresses new needs in the market and therefore it may be seen as an important way to make the market grow. Process innovation, on the other hand, improves the efficiency of the production process. Both types of innovations are important for the survival of the firm. But for the innovation system as a whole product innovation may be more efficient in promoting innovation driven growth and job creation. It enriches the division of labour, and it opens up larger space for interactive learning. While product innovation creates jobs, process innovation alone tends to reduce jobs (Pianta 2005). This distinction is especially important in an economy with big labour reserves and jobless growth in its most dynamic sector.

Jobless growth results partly from lack of product innovation and partly from weak engineering capability. The weak engineering capability is reflected in the massive import of means of production such as machinery and in weak indigenous provision. Engineering capability is the ability to implement and realize innovation based on innovative ideas, which in themselves are experiencing dramatic change and improvement (Dodgson et al. 2005). Policies that stimulate domestic firms to develop new products in the form of new process equipment that can be used by domestic firms would certainly promote endogenous innovation through the stimuli for interaction at the core of the innovation system that it represents.

Product innovation takes place also in the form of new services and increasingly the knowledge intensive business services that have become strategic parts of the innovation system (Tomlinson 2001). They interact with many users that can profit from the development of more efficient services that embody the experiences of many diverse users. With a strategic perspective building a strong and dynamic sector around business services may be a necessary step towards innovation-driven growth in China. The growth of this sector has until recently been slow, and there is also a great potential for job creation in this sector.

Building user competences and institutions supporting SME competence. Since user–producer interaction is crucial for the success of innovation, it is not sufficient to merely promote the competence and knowledge creation of suppliers. One important reason why the 1985 reform did not succeed in building markets for science and technology was that the potential users did not have the competence to absorb advanced knowledge. This is why the dominant pattern was vertical integration and knowledge producers moving into production. To improve interactive learning, user competence is as important as the competence of the producer, and in China, this constitutes a major bottleneck for learning and innovation.

Competence refers to scientific capabilities as well as to the capacity to engage in learning by doing and organizational learning. To promote the building of scientific capabilities, incentives for enterprises to engage in R&D activities may be combined with incentives to hire highly educated personnel. To stimulate the diffusion of organizational learning among firms, a combination of benchmarking good practices in terms of organizational and inter-organizational learning may be combined with competence based selection and 'job rotation' among top managers.

For small and medium-sized firms in traditional sectors, including agro-food business, specific institutes and self-organized initiatives with the task of diffusing technical innovations and good organizational practice may be supported by the public sector. Such firms have the need for inexpensive access to technological services and knowledge institutions. Especially in periods of graduate engineer and scientist unemployment, giving such firms public support to hire their first engineer/graduate might be considered.

Develop a responsive science and engineering base. The 1985 reform resulted in a structure where universities and other institutions with responsibilities for basic research became strongly involved in commercial activities. With the improvement of the level of competences at the level of firms, universities and public R&D centres should redefine their roles and withdraw gradually from downstream commercial activities that are not easily combined with the search for excellence in science and technology.

Improvement of public funds management and the development of scientific community-based academic evaluation would largely increase the efficiency of knowledge production. Such a shift may actually be combined with a more intense communication with industry both in research and in higher education.[10] In the more global knowledge society, it is also important to participate in international academic communities and to expose the academic research to international competition. Such changes would certainly increase the rate of return from the increased investment in R&D that the Chinese government is beginning to implement.

Develop new forms of participatory governance of economic organizations. There are different forms of governance, and the degrees to which people tolerate social gaps also differ across the rich countries. Some advanced rich countries operate with wide social gaps while others are more egalitarian. The first group includes the United States and the United Kingdom where ordinary people are less participatory; they are expected to adapt passively to new technologies. The second group includes the small European welfare states where ordinary workers take active part in innovation as well as in sharing of the benefits that innovation creates.

In China one way to stimulate participation in the process of change is to establish cooperative ownership to firms. This might be especially relevant for densely populated agricultural regions. The International Labour Office (ILO 2003) calls for rediscovering the cooperative advantage in poverty reduction, warning at the same time that people have to learn lessons from negative experiences in the past. One of the lessons is to let the cooperatives grow through self-organization and learning; another is to support the development of the qualifications of leaders and participants.

Improving education and stimulating the mobility of skilled labour. The most fundamental and dynamic resource in the innovation system is people. Every single person is a potential user and producer of technology and knowledge. In order to enhance user competence and facilitate interaction between users and producers, improvement of education and training is one of the basic means. Universal secondary education in poor rural areas is a way to prepare residents for participation in knowledge and skill-intensive agricultural and related activities or for becoming members of new generations of urban residents.

The education system has to be modified in terms of curricula design and pedagogical methods in order to promote the problem solving capacity of students. Increasingly, interaction will depend on experts who are both creative and cooperative. Elite education needs to be complemented with universal and life-long continuous education for the strategy of endogenous innovation and harmonious development.

But not all competences emanate from formal education and training. With rapid change, the learning that takes place at work becomes more and more important. Stimulating the diffusion of 'learning organization' practices among enterprises is fundamental both for stimulating endogenous innovation and for the ongoing upgrading of skills of the workforce.

The mobility of people across organizational borders shapes social connections and interaction. Enterprise employees and managers with a university educational background will be the ones that have the least difficulties to establish collaboration with researchers at universities. Therefore, schemes that make it attractive to move back and forth between academia and the enterprise sector may be seen as especially important.

Develop networking and learning regions. Regions can be springboards for endogenous innovation, if they develop and exploit specialized strengths based on firm networks that contain tacit knowledge (Cooke and Morgan 1998). The local and regional dimension has become crucial for growth in China through reforms leading to bureaucratic decentralization. But the development towards learning regions has been less impressive. There is a need for a new incentive structure and for policy capacity building at the regional and local level. Reform should aim at rewarding innovative solutions that promote networking and save scarce resources.

There is also a need to give central government a stronger role in the redistribution of wealth between provinces and regions. Central government could also play a more important role as promoter of regional policy and managerial learning within the regions.

Table 10.6 Resources fundamental for economic growth – combining the tangible and reproducible dimensions

	Easily reproducible resources	Less reproducible resources
Tangible resources	Production capital	Natural capital
Intangible resources	Intellectual capital	Social capital

10.4.5 Social capital and endogenous innovation

In sum, endogenous innovation and harmonious development require are a new set of efforts rather different from those made in the 1980s and 1990s. It involves reforms of the institutions that support markets and make contracts trustworthy, but it also involves broader social changes that support interactions among economic agents.

Corruption and irregularities in the use of legal systems undermine trust and thereby undermine a critical prerequisite for interactive learning across organizational borders. Innovation is, because of its inherently uncertain character, especially vulnerable to lack of trust. To foster the rule of law and a competent and honest public administration is therefore an integrated element of any strategy for innovation and learning-based development. In the current context, fostering good governance, especially at the local level and at the enterprise level may be a key to enhancing innovation.

One way to illustrate the task of promoting endogenous innovation and harmonious development is to present it in terms of four types of capital (see Table 10.6).

Production capital can be relatively easily produced and reproduced. The same is true for intellectual capital. But production capital loses much of its use value when natural capital is eroded – once the land and the drinking water have been polluted, it is immensely expensive to clean it up. Intellectual capital is created through interactive learning, and it will depend strongly on social capital. In a society where people trust institutions and each other and are ready to cooperate willingly also outside the most narrow group, learning will flourish.

Endogenous innovation and harmonious development implies a growth model that gives attention not only to production capital and intellectual capital but also avoids the degradation of natural capital as a key element in a strategy favouring harmonious development. Stimulating the formation of social capital is a key to long-term success in promoting endogenous innovation. Social capital is the basis for interactive learning and therefore the lubrication that makes the innovation system work smoothly.

10.5 Conclusion

In this chapter, we have analysed the forces behind rapid growth in China. We have shown that pragmatic policies and policy learning have been central for its success. We have also pointed to challenges posed by the growth pattern and to remaining weaknesses in the innovation system.

These challenges and weaknesses are reflected in the new political signals, giving priority to the concepts of endogenous innovation and harmonious development. Building on the historical experience, we argue that the best way to interpret these concepts is to see them as signalling innovation-driven economic growth and learning-based economic development.

The global context and the historical starting point is different than it was in 1985, but the basic perspective for reform with focus on interaction between users and producers of knowledge and technology remains pertinent when designing the next major transition. Strengthening domestic demand and the competence of domestic users of technology is a key to success. Enhancing the knowledge base of strategic sectors producing process equipment and knowledge intensive business services for the market is another important element. Investing in 'social capital' – designing institutions so that citizens become more ready to collaborate and learn from each other – is a way to promote endogenous innovation.

Many aspects of both the successes and the problems that China has experienced are unforeseen in previous catch-up history and in existing theories of economic development. This is true for the limits of export-led development strategies, the inadequacy of manufactured exports in spreading learning effects, the extreme rate of substitution of capital for labour and the severe structural unemployment phenomenon. The response to these accumulated challenges sees China embark on a new development strategy characterized by endogenous innovation and harmonious development, which we have interpreted as a strategy of innovation-driven growth and learning-based development.

As China pursues harmonious development, it will become clear that it does not represent any economic threat to other countries. For those who hope China offers a uniquely successful experience, we need to point out that the actual process of adjustment unavoidably will involve uncertainties and setbacks. We wish that innovation studies can serve an instrumental and positive role and certainly believe that innovation studies can learn a lot from the transition that China will undergo in future years.

Notes

1 Low profitability of commodities made in China is common knowledge, although the 2–5 per cent is a rough estimation. For example. the TV industry, which has a

well-developed competitive advantage, has rather thin profit margins because key components for final products are imported from Japan, Korea and Taiwan. It is reported that in 2005 average net profit of the TV industry was as low as less than 3 per cent, and for some firms it was lower than 1 per cent, even though the industry had introduced flat panel TV sets one year ago and these were expected to improve the industry's profitability record. (Shangwu Shoukan (Business Watch Magazine) 28 October 2005). Ninbo City, Zhejiang province, is an important export–manufacturing base. It exported US\$ 12 billion of products such as clothing, cigarette lighters and air conditioners in 2003. Possessing weak negotiating capacity with international buyers and being engaged in the low end of value chains, the exporting firms had net profits of around 10 per cent with some lower than 5 per cent. (IT jingli shijie (CEO & CIO China) 9 November 2004).

2   See Granick (1967) for former Soviet Union and for more general discussion see Hanson and Pavitt (1987).

3   Note that the Decision recognized the diversity of R&D institutes in terms of their functions. It divided them into 'technology development type', 'basic research type', and 'public welfare and infrastructure services type'. The reduction of public funds was mainly applied to the technology development type and it was done gradually to be completed in a time span of five years. Consequently by 1991, the 2,000 plus, out of 4,000 in total, technology development institutes had had their public 'operation fees' entirely or partly cut. Roughly the sum of the reduction accounted to slightly less than RMB 1 billion (or USD\$ 200 MM) or about one-tenth of the overall government S&T budget in 1985.

4   See: http://www.sts.org.cn/report_3/documents/2002/0207.htm

5   Data show that in 1985, the centrally affiliated R&D institutes engaged mainly in 'experiment development' and 'design and production engineering'. According to international standards, half of their works were not 'R&D' but downstream innovation related activities such as 'design and production engineering' and 'diffusion and technical services'. The locally affiliated R&D institutes went even downward further. Similar phenomenon was observed in other centrally planned systems to a lesser extent.

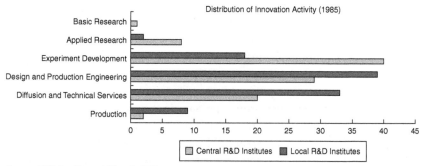

Source: 'White Paper' No. 1: 238

6   For the full document, refer to http://www.most.gov.cn/t_a3_zrfgytagg_a.jsp

7   There are different English translations of the Chinese term *zi-zhu-chuang-xin;* here we use 'endogenous innovation'. 'Independent innovation' appears quite often in English versions of Chinese media reports, to which we tend to disagree, as it is misleading. In Chinese, to put an adjective '*zi-zhu*' to 'innovation' is to emphasize that strategically

China has to be proactive to do something new and not passively stay with existing and imported technologies. Readers are better to understand the fashionable Chinese term *zi-zhu-chuang-xin* simply as 'innovation'.

8 The following is discussion based on various sources from media reports and from personal exchanges.

9 It is interesting to note that the market economy par excellence, the United States, has a much more active government policy to support science and technology than Japan and Europe. But the government programs appear as part of health- and space-related programs, not as industrial policy.

10 A stronger element of practical experience and a more problem-oriented learning method in the academic training of scientists, engineers and managers would be a most efficient way to create stronger links between universities and enterprises. The same would be true for more systematic efforts by universities to offer life-long learning to these categories. But the most important change would be coming from the increased hiring of academic personnel by the enterprises.

References

Angus, M. 1991. *Dynamic Forces in Capitalist Development, A Long-run Comparative View*. Oxford and New York: Oxford University Press.
———. 1998. *Chinese Economic Performance in the Long Run*. Paris: OECD.
Archibugi, D. and B.-Å. Lundvall (eds.). 2001. *Europe in the Globalising Learning Economy*. Oxford: Oxford University Press.
Baldwin, C. Y. and K. B. Clark. 1997. *Managing in an Age of Modularity*. Harvard Business Review, Sept/Oct.
CCCPC. 2005. The Guiding Vision for the 11th National Economic and Social Development Program (2006–2010), Beijing: Communist Party Central Committee.
China Science and Technology Indicator. 1988. (in Chinese) Centre for Science and Technology for Development of China and the Information Centre, State Science and Technology Commission, 1990.
China Statistical Yearbook. 2004. Accessible at http://www.stats.gov.cn/tjsj/ndsj/yb2004-c/indexch.htm; in 2005 the China's government has adjusted statistical date. The adjustment is accessible at http://www.stats.gov.cn/tjdt/zygg/P02006010 9431083446682.doc
China Statistical Yearbook on Science and Technology, various issues.
Christensen, J. L. and B.-Å. Lundvall (eds.). 2004. *Product Innovation, Interactive Learning and Economic Performance*. Amsterdam: Elsevier.
Cooke, P. and K. Morgan. 1998. *The Associational Economy. Firms, Regions, and Innovation*. Oxford: Oxford University Press.
David, G. 1967. *Soviet Metal-Fabricating and Economic Development, Practice versus Policy*. Milwaukee and London: University of Wisconsin Press, Madison.
David, P. A. 2003. 'The Economic Logic of "Open Science" and the Balance between Private Property Rights and the Public Domain in Scientific Data and Information: A Primer', Stanford Institute for Economic Policy Research SIEPR Discussion Paper No. 02–30.
Dodgson, M., D. M. Gann, and A. Salter. 2005. *Think, Play, Do: Technology and the New Innovation Process*. Oxford: Oxford University Press.

Dosi, G. 1982. 'Technological Paradigms and Technological Trajectories', *Research Policy* 11: 147–82.

Fei, J. C. And G. Ranis. 1997. *Growth and Development from an Evolutionary Perspective*. Malden, MA and Oxford: Blackwell Publishers.

Freeman, C. 1987. *Technology Policy and Economic Performance: lessons from Japan*. London: Pinter.

Gereffi, G. 1999. 'International Trade and Industrial Upgrading in the Apparel Commodity Chain'. *Journal of International Economics* 48: 37–70.

Granick, D. 1967. *Soviet Metal-Fabricating and Economic Development*. Madison: University of Wisconsin Press.

Gu, S. 1999. China's Industrial Technology, Market Reform and Organizational Change, Routledge in association with the UNU Press, London and New York.

ILO. 2003. 'Rediscovering the Cooperative Advantage: Poverty Reduction Through Self-Help' by Johnston Birchall, Cooperative Branch, Geneva. International Labour Office.

Janos, K. 1980. *Economics of Shortage*. Amsterdam: North Holland Publishing Company.

Jici, W. and T. Xin. 2000. 'Industrial Clusters in China: Alternative Pathways Towards Global-local Linkages'. Paper presented in International High-Level Seminar on Technological Innovation, co-sponsored by the Ministry of Science and Technology of China and United Nations University. Beijing, September 5–7.

Jinglian, W. 2003. *Dangdai zhongguo jingji gaige (China's Economic Reform, in Chinese), Shanghai yuangong chubanshe*. Shanghai: Far East Publisher.

Kline, S. J. and N. Rosenberg. 1986. 'An Overview of Innovation'. In *The Positive Sum Strategy, Harnessing Technology for Economic Growth*, edited by R. Landau and N. Rosenberg. Washington, DC: National Academy Press.

Kornai, J. *Economics of Shortage*, Vols. 1 and 2, Amsterdam: North Holland, 1980.

Langlois, R. N. 2003. 'The Vanishing Hand: the Changing Dynamics of Industrial Capitalism'. *Industrial and Corporate Change* 12, no. 2: 351–85.

———. 2003. 'The Vanishing Hand: The Changing Dynamics of Industrial Capitalism'. *Industrial and Corporate Change* 12, no. 2: 351–85.

Lewis, W. A. 1955/1970. *Theory of Economic Growth*. London: George Allen & Unwin Ltd.

Lundvall, B.-Å. 1988. 'Innovation as Interactive Process: From User-producer Interaction to the national System of Innovation'. In *Technical Change and Economic Theory*, pp. 349–69, edited by G. Dosi, C. Freeman, R. R. Nelson, G. Silverberg, and L. Soete. London and New York: Pinter Publishers..

———. 1985. *Product Innovation and User-Producer Interaction*. Aalborg: Aalborg University Press.

———. 1992. 'Explaining Inter-firm Cooperation and Innovation – Limits of the Transaction Cost Approach'. In *The Embedded Firm: On the Socioeconomics of Industrial Networks*, edited by G. Grabher. London: Routledge.

———. (ed.). 1992. *National Systems of Innovation*. London: Pinter.

———. 2006. 'Interactive Learning, Social Capital and Economic Performance'. In *Advancing Knowledge and the Knowledge Economy*, edited by D. Foray and B. Kahin. Boston: Harvard University Press.

Lundvall, B.-Å. and S. Borras. 1998. 'The Globalising Learning Economy: Implications for Innovation Policy', Brussels, DG XII-TSER, the European Commission.

Lundvall, B.-Å. and B. Johnson. 1994. 'The Learning Economy'. *Journal of Industry Studies* 1, no. 2: 23–42.

Maddison, A. 1991. *Dynamic Forces in Capitalist Development*. Oxford: Oxford University Press.

————. 1998. *Chinese Economic Performance in the Long Run*. Paris: Development Centre of the Organization for Economic Co-operation and Development.

Mark, D., D. Gann and A. Salter. 2005. *Think, Play, Do, Technology, Innovation and Organization*. Oxford: Oxford University Press.

Metcalfe, J. S. 1995. 'The Economic Foundations of Technology Policy: Equilibrium and Evolutionary Perspectives'. In *Handbook of the Economics of Innovation and Technological Change*, edited by Paul Stoneman, 409–512. Oxford UK and Cambridge, MA: Blackwell.

National Statistical Bureau, 1990. *Zhongguo kexue jishu sishi nian* (Statistics on Science and Technology of China 1949–89), Zhongguo Tongji Chubanshe (Statistics Publishing House of China).

Nelson, R. R. 2004. 'The Market Economy and the Scientific Commons'. *Research Policy* 33: 455–71.

Nelson, R. R. and G. W. Sidney. 1982. *An Evolutionary Theory of Economic Change*. Cambridge, MA and London: Belknap Press of Harvard University Press.

Nelson, R. R. (ed.). 1993. *National Innovation Systems: A Comparative Analysis*. New York and Oxford: Oxford University Press.

North, D. 1996. *Organizations, Institutions and Market Competition, Working Paper*. St Louis: Washington University.

Pasinetti, L. 1981. *Structural Change and Economic Growth*. Cambridge: Cambridge University Press.

Philip, C. and K. Morgan. 1998. *Evolutionary Processes and Regional Practices in Cooke, Philip and Kevin Morgan: The Associational Economy, Chapter 8*. Oxford: Oxford University Press.

Philip, H. and K. Pavitt. 1987. *The Comparative Economics of Research Development and Innovation in East and West: A Survey*. Chur, London, Paris, New York, Melbourne: Harwood Academic Publishers.

Pianta, M. 2005. 'Chapter 21 Innovation and Employment'. In *The Oxford Handbook of Innovation*. J. Fagerberg, D. C. Mowery and R. R. Nelson Oxford, New York: Oxford University Press.

Qian, Y. and B. R. Weingast. 1996. 'China's Transition to Markets: Market-Preserving Federalism, Chinese Style'. *Journal of Policy Reform* 1, no. 2: 149–85.

Richardson, G. B. 2002. 'The Organisation of Industry Revisited'. *Druid working paper* No. 02–15.

Rosenberg, N. 1982. *Inside the Black Box: Technology and Economics*. Cambridge: Cambridge University Press.

Saich, A. 2004. *The Governance and Politics of China*, 2nd Edition. Hampshire: Palgrave Macmillan.

Saxenian, A. 1996. 'Inside-Out: Regional Networks and Industrial Adaptation in Silicon Valley and Route 128'. *Cityscape: A Journal of Policy Development and Research* 2, no. 2: 41–60, May.

Shulin, G. 1999. *China's Industrial Technology, Market Reform and Organizational Change, Routledge in association with the UNU Press*. London and New York: 1999.

Shulin, G. and B.-Å. Lundvall. 2006. 'Policy Learning as a Key Process in the Transformation of the Chinese Innovation Systems'. In *Asian Innovation Systems in Transition*, edited by B.-Å. Lundvall, P. Intarakumnerd and J. Vang. Cheltenham: Edward Elgar Publishing Ltd.

Shulin, G. and W. E. Steinmueller. 1996/2000. 'National Innovation Systems and the Innovative Recombination of Technological Capability in Economic Transition in

China: Getting Access to the Information Revolution', *UNU/INTECH Discussion Paper* 2002–2003, Maastricht.

Tomlinson, M. 2001. 'A New Role for Business Services in Economic Growth'. In *Europe in the Globalising Learning Economy*, edited by D. Archibugi, and B.-Å. Lundvall. Oxford: Oxford University Press.

UNIDO. 2002. 'Industrial Development Report 2002–2003. Vienna: Unido.

Von Hippel, E. 1994. *The Source of Innovation*. Oxford: Oxford University Press.

Von Hippel, E. and M. Tyre. 1995. 'How Learning by Doing Is Done: Problem Identification and Novel Process Equipment'. *Research Policy* 24, no. 5: 1–12.

White Paper No. 1: State Science and Technology Commission (SSTC): *Zhongguo kexue jishu zhengce zhinan 1986, kexue jishu baipishu di'yihao* (Guide to China's Science and Technology Policy for 1986), 'White Paper on Science and Technology No. 1', 1987.

Woolcock, M. 1998. 'Social Capital and Economic Development: Toward a Theoretical Synthesis and Policy Framework'. *Theory and Society* 27, no. 2: 151–207.

Yujiro, H. 1997. 'Development Economics, from the Poverty to the Wealth of Nations'. Oxford: Oxford University Press.

Zhao, Z., 1986. Speech at the National Working Conference on Science and Technology. In: SSTC (Ed.), Guidelines for China's science and technology policy. Science and Technology, White Paper No. 1. Beijing, Science and Technology Documentary Press.Ziyang, Z. 1985. 'Speech to the National Working Conference of Science and Technology, 6 March 1985'. *White Paper* No. 1: 293–97.

Chapter 11

THE 'NEW NEW DEAL' AS A RESPONSE TO THE EURO-CRISIS

Bengt-Åke Lundvall

11.1 Introduction

While the Eurozone was originally designed to protect member countries from economic instability, it has now turned into a major source of instability for the world as a whole. Currently European leaders bring Europe ahead in the direction of a European Federation not because it is part of their vision, but because it seems to be the only way to avoid triggering a global depression.

When the Eurozone was established there were warning voices that a monetary union without a common fiscal policy would be vulnerable to external shocks. The total budget of the EU constitutes only a few percent of the total GNP for member states and therefore it cannot play the same role as the federal budget in the United States as automatic stabilizer. This is especially problematic for a currency union bringing together countries at very different levels of economic development. There were elements in the Lisbon Strategy that could have reduced the gaps between Northern and Southern Europe. But the turn towards more neoliberal solutions that took place around 2005 undermined its capacity to function as a scaffold for the Eurozone (Lundvall and Lorenz 2011).

In this chapter I show that the countries in the Eurozone now most exposed to financial speculation are the ones that have the weakest industrial structure with the biggest proportion of workplaces directly exposed to competition with emerging economies. On this background I will argue that, standing alone, neither Austrian austerity nor Keynesian policies can help establish a sustainable Eurozone. There is a need to design Keynesian policies coordinated at the European level in such a way that they promote deep institutional change in education, labour market and industrial policy in Southern Europe.

Public expenditure needs to be allocated to stimulate the learning capacity where it is weakest – this is why the solution may be referred to as a 'new new deal'. It is about redistributing learning capacities.

11.2 Innovation and the Division of Labour

The following analysis builds upon a simple theoretical model linking to each other 'innovation as an interactive process' and the dynamics of the division of labour (Lundvall 2006). According to Adam Smith the extension and deepening of the division of labour is the major mechanism behind economic growth. On the other hand, innovation is the most important mechanism behind the evolving division of labour. New products and processes give rise to new and more developed forms of specialization. The more developed division of labour opens up new interfaces for interactive learning that may stimulate further innovation. It also enhances diversity that opens up for 'new combinations' of 'distant elements'. Such new combinations are at the very core of the innovation process.

But specialization may also raise barriers between professions and disciplines, between theorists and practical people, and, not least, it may reproduce social distance between workers and bosses. One way to interpret the results to be presented below is that a mix of theory and practice at school and democracy/participation at work reduce both barriers and social distance and thereby enhance the opportunities for interactive learning and for absorbing quickly and efficiently new ideas in the production system.

In order to intervene wisely in this process, it is important to understand the role of different kinds of 'differences' for the performance of innovation systems. While high degrees of diversity in people's experiences and in sources of knowledge give a rich foundation for innovations, high degrees of inequality hamper the interaction and communication that is crucial for successful innovation. A crucial policy challenge is to combine the potential of egalitarian learning systems with open intercultural dialogue and high degrees of diversity.

11.3 The Learning Economy

The learning economy refers to acceleration in the rate of economic and technical change imposing a strong transformation pressure on open economies (Lundvall and Johnson 1994). Behind the acceleration of change lie shorter product life cycles and intensified global competition as well as politically driven deregulation. At the level of the firm, the acceleration of change is registered as an intensification of competition. At the level of the individual it is experienced as a permanent need to renew skills and competences in order to remain 'employable'. Change and learning are two sides of the same coin. The high speed of change confronts people and organizations with new problems, and to tackle the new problems requires new skills (OECD 1996). The selection by employers of more learning-oriented employees and the market selection in favour of change-oriented firms accelerates further innovation and change.

In an open economy the key to economic success is to constantly transform the economy so that the exposed activities are either upgraded or substituted for by new activities that make more intensive use of competences. It is a major task for policy to design institutions that regulate education and labour markets so that they promote processes of learning and the formation and diffusion of learning organizations in the private and public sectors. As will be demonstrated in the next section, it is not sufficient to promote R&D efforts and the training of scientists and engineers.

11.4 Modes of Innovation and Innovation Performance

In the article 'Why All This Fuss about Codified and Tacit Knowledge?' (Johnson et al. 2002), we linked the distinction between codified and tacit knowledge to innovation and learning. In 'Forms of Knowledge and Modes of Innovation' (Jensen et al. 2007), we introduced two modes of learning related to this distinction. Using a survey and register data from around 700 Danish firms, we demonstrated that firms that combine R&D efforts (STI learning) with organizational learning and interaction with customers (DUI learning) are the most innovative (see chapter 7).

In order to find out how the different aspects of establishing a learning organization tend to be combined with the capacity to handle scientific and codified knowledge, we pursued a clustering across firms using latent class analysis. The first cluster is a static or low-learning cluster and encompasses about 40 per cent of the firms. Firms belonging to the second cluster, which we refer to as the STI-cluster, encompasses about 10 per cent of the firms. They have activities that indicate a strong capacity to absorb and use codified knowledge. The third cluster, which we refer to as the DUI-cluster, is characterized by an over-average development of organizational characteristics typical for the learning organization but without activities that indicate a strong capacity to absorb and use codified knowledge. The fourth cluster includes firms using mixed strategies that combine the DUI- and STI-modes. It includes 20 per cent of the firms.

In order to examine the effect of the learning modes on the firms' innovative performance, we use logistic regression analysis as reported in Table 11.1.

Table 11.1 Logistic regression of learning clusters on product/service innovation

Variable	Model 1 (without controls)		Model 2 (with controls)	
	Odds ratio estimate	Coefficient estimate	Odds ratio estimate	Coefficient estimate
STI cluster	3.529	1.2611**	2.355	0.8564**
DUI cluster	2.487	0.9109**	2.218	0.7967**
DUI/STI cluster	7.843	2.0596**	5.064	1.6222**
Business services			1.433	0.3599
Construction			0.491	−0.7120*
Manufacturing (high tech)			1.805	0.5905*
Manufacturing (low tech)			1.250	0.2229
Other services			0.747	−0.2923
100 and more employees			1.757	0.5635*
50–99 employees			0.862	−0.1481
Danish group			0.859	−0.1524
Single firm			0.521	−0.6526*
Customized product			1.378	0.3203
Pseudo R^2	0.1247	0.1247	0.1775	0.1775
N	692	692	692	692

Notes: ** 5 significant at the 0.01 level; * 5 significant at the 0.05 level.

The dependent variable for this exercise is whether or not the firm has introduced to the market a new product or service (P/S innovation) over the last three years. The independent variables in the Model 1 specification are binary variables indicating whether or not the firm belongs to a particular cluster. In the Model 2 specification, we include control variables to account for the effects of industry, firm size, ownership structure and whether the firm produces customized or standard products.

Overall, the results of the logistic analysis show that adopting DUI-mode-enhancing practices and policies tends to increase firm innovative performance. Further, they support the view that firms adopting mixed strategies combining the two modes tend to perform better than those relying predominantly on one mode or the other.

Our results strongly suggest a need for realignment of policy objectives and priorities, given the tendency to develop innovation policy with a one-sided focus on promoting the science base of high-technology firms. Actually both, a strategy that promotes organizational learning in STI firms and one that promotes STI learning in DUI firms may have more effect on innovation than the standard solution of promoting R&D in high-tech firms that are already experienced in pursuing it.

Thinking in terms of the two modes and their evolution in the learning economy may also have implications for policy coordination and institution-building. If the main responsibility is given to a ministry of science, then the STI bias in innovation policy is reinforced. The best solution might be to establish a council with a secretariat at the level of the prime minister's office with the mandate to coordinate 'innovation and competence-building' nationwide.

11.5 How Europe's Economies Learn

Lorenz and Valeyre (2005) develop an original and informative EU-wide mapping of how employees work and learn in the private sector. In 'How Europe's Economies Learn: A Comparison of Work Organization and Innovation Mode for the EU-15' (Arundel et al. 2007), international comparisons show that there is a positive correlation between the national share of employees engaged in advanced forms of learning at the workplace and the percentage of private sector enterprises successful in the forms of innovation requiring high levels of in-house creative activity.

Cluster analysis is used to identify four different systems of work organization:

- Discretionary learning (DL)
- Lean
- Taylorist
- Traditional forms

Two of these, the discretionary-learning and lean forms, are characterized by high levels of learning and problem solving in work. The principal difference between the discretionary-learning and the lean clusters is the relatively high level of discretion or autonomy in work exercised by employees grouped in the former. Task complexity is also higher in the discretionary-learning cluster than in the lean cluster.

Discretionary learning thus refers to work settings where a lot of responsibility is allocated to the employees who are expected to solve problems on their own. Employees operating in these modes are constantly confronted with 'disequilibria' and as they cope with these, they learn and become more competent. But in this process, they also experience that some of their earlier insights and skills become obsolete.

Lean production also involves problem solving and learning, but here the problems are more narrowly defined and the set of possible solutions less wide and diverse. The work is highly constrained, and this points to a more structured or bureaucratic style of organizational learning that corresponds rather closely to the characteristics of the Japanese-inspired 'lean production' model.

The other two clusters are characterized by relatively low levels of learning and problem solving. The Taylorist form leaves very little autonomy to the employee in making decisions. In the traditional cluster, there is more autonomy but learning and task complexity is the lowest among the four types of work organization. This cluster includes employees working in small-scale establishments in personal services and transport where methods are for the most part informal and non-codified.

Table 11.2 shows that people working in different national systems of innovation and competence work and learn differently. Discretionary learning is most widely diffused in the Netherlands, the Nordic countries and to a lesser extent in Austria and Germany. The lean model is most in evidence in the United Kingdom, Ireland and Spain. The Taylorist forms are more present in Portugal, Spain, Greece and Italy, while the traditional forms are similarly more in evidence in these four Southern European countries.[1]

The share of discretionary learning is higher in Germany than in the United Kingdom or in France.

Table 11.2 indicates unequal access to learning at work across different parts of Europe. The three Nordic countries, together with the Netherlands, have few Taylorist jobs left in the economy while a majority of employees operate in jobs that are demanding both in terms of skills and in terms of autonomy.

When comparing and ranking national innovation systems the focus is normally on STI indicators. For instance, the European innovation scoreboard does not include any indicator reflecting organizational learning. The analysis pursued here shows that differences in how people work and learn across Europe are even more dramatic than differences in R&D efforts or in the intensity of training of scientific personnel.

Figure 11.1 is from a study conducted by Arundel et al. (2007). Drawing on the results from the Third Community Innovation Survey, it shows the positive correlation between the national share of employees engaged in advanced forms of learning at the workplace and the percentage of private-sector enterprises doing more radical forms of innovation. *Lead innovators* are those enterprises that have demonstrated a capacity for developing new-to-the-market innovations, and the category includes both firms that perform R&D on a continuous basis and those that do not perform R&D at all or that only do so

Table 11.2 National differences in organizational models (percentage of employees by organizational class)

	Discretionary learning	Lean production learning	Taylorist organization	Simple organization
North				
Netherlands	64.0	17.2	5.3	13.5
Denmark	60.0	21.9	6.8	11.3
Sweden	52.6	18.5	7.1	21.7
Finland	47.8	27.6	12.5	12.1
Centre				
Austria	*47.5*	21.5	13.1	18.0
Germany	*44.3*	19.6	14.3	21.9
Luxembourg	*42.8*	25.4	11.9	20.0
Belgium	*38.9*	25.1	13.9	22.1
France	*38.0*	33.3	11.1	17.7
West				
United Kingdom	34.8	40.6	10.9	13.7
Ireland	24.0	37.8	20.7	17.6
South				
Italy	30.0	23.6	20.9	25.4
Portugal	26.1	28.1	23.0	22.8
Spain	20.1	38.8	18.5	22.5
Greece	18.7	25.6	28.0	27.7
EU-15	*39.1*	*28.2*	*13.6*	*19.1*

Source: Adapted version based on Lorenz and Valeyre (2006).

occasionally. In the Arundel et al. study (2007), this group of highly creative innovators is separated out from noninnovators as well as from less ambitious firms that innovate mainly by modifying technology developed by other firms or organizations (*modifiers*) or that introduce innovations developed entirely by external sources (*followers*).

Figure 11.1 shows that countries with wide participation in discretionary learning have a bigger share of firms that develop their own innovations and innovations that are new to the market. Here it is notable that the United Kingdom stands out from the northern and most of the continental nations both for its low level of discretionary learning and its low percentage of lead

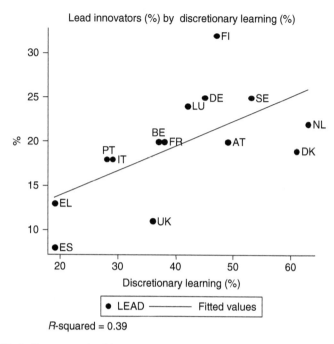

Figure 11.1 Percentage lead innovators by percentage discretionary learning

innovators. These results are compatible with other studies showing that firms with learning-organization characteristics tend to be more innovative (Lundvall and Nielsen 2007).

11.6 Education and Training for Learning Organizations

Since discretionary learning depends upon the capacity of employees to undertake complex problem-solving tasks, it can be expected that nations with a high frequency of these forms will have made substantial investments in education and training. In what follows we compare tertiary education in universities and other institutions of higher education with the continuing vocational training offered by enterprises.

Tertiary education develops both problem-solving skills and formal and transferable technical and scientific skills. While most of the qualifications acquired through third-level education will be relatively general and hence transferable in the labour market, the qualifications an employee acquires through continuing vocational training will be more firm specific. Some of this training will be designed to renew employees' technical skills and knowledge in order to respond to the firm's requirements in terms of ongoing product and process innovation.

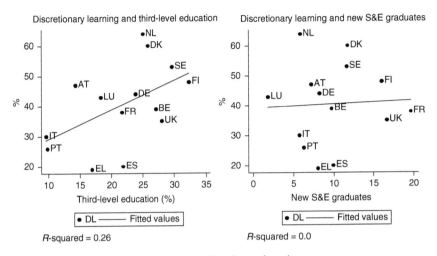

Figure 11.2 Discretionary learning and tertiary education

Figure 11.2 shows the correlations between the frequency of discretionary-learning forms and two of the four measures of human resources for innovation used in Trendchart's innovation benchmarking exercise: the proportion of the population with third-level education and the number of science and engineering graduates since 1993 as a percentage of the population aged 20–29 years in 2000.

The results show a modest positive correlation (R-squared = 0.26) between the discretionary-learning forms and the percentage of the population with third-level education and no discernible correlation between the discretionary-learning forms and the measure of the importance of new science and engineering graduates.

Figure 11.3 shows that there are fairly strong positive correlations (R-squared = 0.75 and 0.52 respectively) between the frequency of discretionary learning and the two measures of firms' investments in continuing vocational training: the percentage of private sector firms offering such training and the participants in continuous vocational education as a percentage of employees in all enterprises.[2] The results suggest that these forms of firm-specific training are key complementary resources in the development of the firm's capacity for knowledge exploration and innovation. The diagram also points to a North/South divide within Europe. The Nordic countries are characterized by relatively high levels of vocational training and by relatively high-level use of the discretionary-learning forms. This may be a factor that contributes to their relative success in the learning economy.

These results indicate that national educational systems where the emphasis is on the formal training of scientists and engineers while neglecting the

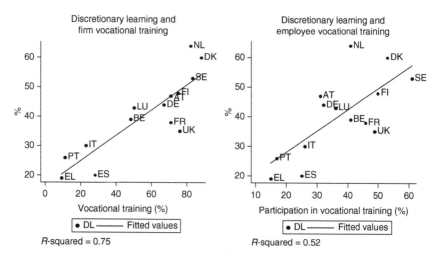

Figure 11.3 Discretionary learning and employee vocational training

broader forms of vocational training may be vulnerable in the context of the learning economy. It is notable that Portugal, Spain, Italy and Greece, which have all made considerable strides in increasing the number of science and engineering graduates but stand out for their low levels of investment in continuing vocational training, rank the lowest on the discretionary-learning scale. The more drastic the status difference and distinction between theory and practice in education programmes, the more difficult it will be to install participatory learning in the private sector. The strong element of vocational training in the Nordic countries contributes to engaging workers more actively in processes of change.

11.7 Skill Requirements in Firms Engaged in Organizational Change

Since one major role of schools is to educate and provide qualified labour, it is important to capture new tendencies in skill and competence requirements. In a socioeconomic context characterized by rapid change, it is especially interesting to analyse in what directions organizations engaged in change specify change in skill requirements. In this section, we take a closer look into how management in a selection of Danish firms refers to changes in their demand for skills. The focus is upon changes in the competences demanded within firms that have engaged in organizational change (Lundvall 2002).

A series of surveys of the Danish national innovation system (the DISKO surveys) showed among other results that organizational change involves a shift in the relative importance of tasks. Table 11.3 reveals substantial differences

Table 11.3 Changes in task content for employees during the period 1993–95 for firms that have made organizational changes (outside the parentheses) compared with firms that have not made organizational changes (in parentheses)

	More	Less	Unchanged	No answer
(a) Independence in work	72.6 (37.1)	4.2 (2.7)	21.2 (56.3)	2.0 (3.8)
(b) Professional qualifications	56.4 (36.3)	7.5 (5.3)	33.3 (53.8)	2.8 (4.4)
(c) Degree of specialization	33.9 (26.2)	20.8 (7.8)	39.3 (58.4)	6.0 (7.5)
(d) Routine character of tasks	5.6 (8.2)	41.8 (15.5)	45.0 (67.1)	7.7 (9.1)
(e) Customer contact	51.6 (29.3)	5.1 (3.1)	37.2 (59.9)	6.1 (7.6)
(f) Contact with suppliers	34.9 (18.0)	7.1 (4.3)	46.4 (62.0)	11.6 (15.6)
(g) Contact with other firms	24.7 (14.0)	5.5 (4.3)	56.8 (68.9)	13.0 (13.7)
(h) Cooperation with Colleagues	59.1 (27.1)	5.8 (4.5)	31.8 (63.3)	3.2 (5.0)
(i) Cooperation with Management	64.9 (28.6)	5.9 (4.2)	26.1 (62.2)	3.1 (4.9)

Note: Management representatives in 4,000 Danish private firms, excluding agriculture, were asked 'Did the firm introduce a non-trivial change in the organization in the period 1993–95?' The response rate was close to 50 per cent. For more detailed information, see Lundvall (2002).
Source: Lundvall (2002).

in the pattern of answers (percentage share of firms giving respectively more or less emphasis to each specific category of tasks) between the firms that have introduced new forms of organization and those that have not (numbers in parenthesis). The demand for general skills (independence in the work situation, cooperation with external partners especially customers and for cooperation with management and colleagues) has grown in both categories of firms. However, it has grown much more strongly in those firms that have pursued organizational change. There are correspondingly large differences between the two types of organizations in the rate of occurrence of a *reduction* in routine work. This response pattern gives an indication of the future direction of skill requirements.

Therefore education systems should be designed in such a way that they promote general skills in terms of communication, cooperation and creativity (to solve nonroutine problems). This model points to teaching methods that are democratic and interactive rather than authoritarian and unidirectional. Collective creativity may be stimulated by engaging students in teamwork and in solving unstructured problems with the teacher as coach.

As illustrated by Table 11.3 (see line d), the general tendency among the firms is that the amount of routine work is shrinking, while the demand for independent, creative and cooperative workers is increasing. While this trend points to a need for education to contribute to creativity, many tasks still require a capacity to pursue routine work based upon discipline-organized knowledge and with a high degree of precision in solving tasks. This is true even for the core of 'creative professions' such as architects and artists. Therefore education systems should not abandon traditional teaching methods and individual training to solve well-structured problems. On balance, however, national education systems need to give more room for stimulating both collective and individual creativity in order to cope with change and build a learning society

11.8 The Role of Universities in the Learning Economy

When it comes to linking universities to economic development, the main emphasis is currently on how universities may serve industry through direct flows of information from ongoing research. To illustrate, in a recent book with the title *How Universities Promote Economic Growth* edited by World Bank economists (Yusuf and Nabeshima 2007), the only dimension covered is the formation of university–industry links related to research. We believe that this narrow agenda, where the role of higher education is neglected, reflects a biased interpretation of the sources of innovation (as STI driven) as well as an underestimation of the importance of transmitting tacit knowledge embodied in people (Lundvall 2008).

On the basis of the data presented in the last two sections above, there may be a need to consider how well teaching programmes prepare students for the transfer and practical use of scientific knowledge. Innovation is a process requiring close interaction between individuals and organizations. Therefore, while skills in mathematics and language are fundamental, they need to be combined with social skills that make it possible to cooperate vertically in hierarchies as well as horizontally with experts with a different educational background.

This implies that teaching at universities needs to be adjusted in order to prepare the students for communication and cooperation with other categories of workers and experts. Traditional learning forms such as mass lectures neither prepare students to use the theory and methods in a real-life context nor does it replicate the kind of learning that is required in a future professional life. In professional life, most learning takes place through problem solving, often in a context of collaboration with others with a different background. *Problem-based learning and combining theoretical work with periods of practical work are obvious responses to these problems.*

The transition to a learning economy has important *implications for higher education*. One major implication is that educational institutions need to be ready to support *continuous and life-long learning*. Especially in fast-moving fields of knowledge, there is a need to give regular and frequent opportunities for experts to renew their professional knowledge. The proliferation of executive education programmes in business schools may be seen as indicating the growing insight among individuals and in management that continuously renewing competences is of great importance. But so far the opportunities for upgrading professionals skills have been offered mainly in relation to management functions. Similar programmes are needed in other areas where effective demand is less strong.

Finally, rapid change in science and technology and the need to move quickly from invention to innovation present a strong argument for keeping a reasonably *close connection between education and research* in higher education. Teachers who have little or obsolete knowledge about what is going on in current research are not helpful when it comes to giving the students useful insights into dynamic knowledge fields.

11.9 Linking Modes of Learning to Measures of Employment and Unemployment Security

EU member nations display significant differences in systems of employment and unemployment protection. Systems combining high levels of unemployment protection with relatively low levels of employment protection may have an advantage in terms of the adoption of the forms of work organization that promote learning and 'new-to-the-market' innovations. Organizations that compete on the basis of strategies of continuous knowledge exploration tend to have relatively porous organizational boundaries so as to permit the insertion of new knowledge and ideas from the outside. Job tenures tend to be short because careers are often structured around a series of discrete projects rather than advancing within an intrafirm hierarchy (Lam and Lundvall 2006).

While the absence of legal restrictions on hiring and firing will not necessarily result in the forms of labour market mobility that contribute to a continuous evolution of the firm's knowledge base, strong systems of employment protection may prove to be an obstacle. Well-developed systems of unemployment protection, however, may contribute to the development of fluid labour markets. The security such systems provide encourages individuals to commit

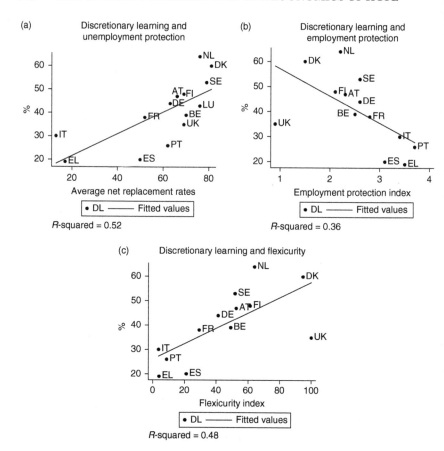

Figure 11.4 Correlations between discretionary learning and systems of social protection

Note: The unemployment protection measure shown is the average net replacement rate of in-work income over 60 months averaged across four family types and two income levels including social assistance in 1999. See OECD (2002, 40). The employment protection measure is the OECD's overall employment protection index for the late 1990s. See OECD (2000, ch. 2).

Source: Lundvall and Lorenz (2011).

themselves to what would otherwise be perceived as unacceptably risky forms of employment and career paths, and such forms of protection contribute to accumulation of knowledge for particular sectors or regions since in their absence, the unemployed workers would be under greater pressure to relocate.

Evidence in support of the view that systems of flexicurity promote the discretionary learning (DL) forms of work organization is provided in Figure 11.4. Graph (a) shows that there is a fairly strong positive correlation (*R*-squared = 0.52) between the level of unemployment protection in a nation and the frequency of discretionary learning. Graph (b) shows a negative correlation (R-squared = 0.36) between the level of employment protection and the frequency of the DL forms.

Graph (c) in Figure 11.4 shows an index of flexicurity constructed from the measures of employment and unemployment protection. The index is constructed so that a nation combining intermediate levels of both unemployment and employment security will score higher than a nation combining a high level of unemployment security with a high level of employment security, or a nation combining a low level of employment security with a low level of unemployment security.[3] The assumption is that the positive effects of a high level of unemployment protection (low level of employment protection) cannot compensate for the negative effects of a high level of employment protection (low level of unemployment protection). As the literature on flexicurity suggests, what is rather required is the right mix of flexibility and security. The index is positively correlated (R-squared = 0.48) with the frequency of the DL forms of work organization.

In the article 'Organisational Learning and Systems of Labour Market Regulation in Europe' (Holm et al. 2010), we have taken one further step towards addressing this research agenda by using multilevel logistic regression to explore the relation between individual level outcomes and national systems of labour market flexibility and regulation. The results confirm that the way work is organized is nation-specific and that it varies with the degree of labour market mobility and with the way labour markets are regulated. Again, flexicurity goes hand in hand with discretionary learning at the workplace.

11.10 Degree of Inequality in Access to Organizational Learning in Europe

An egalitarian income distribution might not be the most important dimension of social equality. If it is combined with growing gaps in competence between skilled and low-skilled workers, it might result in underemployment of the low skilled. The data referred to above on organizational models of learning in different European countries makes it possible to find indicators of such more adequate measures of inequality. In Table 11.4 we present an indicator for the social distribution of workplace learning opportunities. We distinguish between 'workers' and 'managers', and we compare their access to discretionary learning in different national systems.[4]

Table 11.4 shows that employees at the high end of the professional hierarchy have more easy access to jobs involving discretionary learning. This is true for all the countries listed. But it is also noteworthy that the data indicate that the inequality in access to learning is quite different in different

Table 11.4 National differences in organizational models (percentages of employees by organizational class)

	Discretionary learning	Share of managers in discretionary learning	Share of workers in discretionary learning	Learning inequality index*
North				
Netherlands	64.0	81.6	51.1	37.3
Denmark	60.0	85.0	56.2	35.9
Sweden	52.6	76.4	38.2	50.3
Finland	47.8	62.0	38.5	37.9
Austria	47.5	74.1	44.6	39.9
Centre				
Germany	44.3	65.4	36.8	43.8
Luxembourg	42.8	70.3	33.1	52.9
Belgium	38.9	65.7	30.8	53.1
France	38.0	66.5	25.4	61.9
West				
UK	34.8	58.9	20.1	65.9
Ireland	24.0	46.7	16.4	64.9
South				
Italy	30.0	63.7	20.8	67.3
Portugal	26.1	59.0	18.2	69.2
Spain	20.1	52.4	19.1	63.5
Greece	18.7	40.4	17.0	57.9

Note: *The index is constructed by dividing the share of 'workers' engaged in discretionary learning by the share of 'managers' engaged in discretionary learning and subtracting the resulting percentage from 100. If the share of workers and managers was the same, the index would equal 0, and if the share of workers was 0, the index would equal 100.
Source: Lundvall et al. (2008).

countries. In the Nordic countries and the Netherlands, the inequality in the distribution of learning opportunities is moderate while it is very substantial in the less-developed South. For instance, the proportion of the management category engaged in discretionary learning in Portugal is almost as high as in Finland (62% in Finland and 59% in Portugal), but the proportion of workers engaged in discretionary learning is much lower in Portugal (18.2% versus 38.2%).

The Nordic countries are egalitarian not only in terms of income distribution but also when it comes to access to workplace learning, the distribution is more equal than in Southern Europe. The combination of welfare states offering basic security, equal income distribution and low social distance is reflected in high degrees of trust and in broad participation in change. While there are tendencies towards polarization in the current context also in the Nordic countries, they still benefit from 'social capital', reducing social distance and other barriers to communication and interaction in processes of change and innovation. On the other hand we can see that the major reason for the low share of discretionary-learning jobs in the South reflects that workers – as opposed to management – do not have access to such jobs.

So, while it might be true that higher education fosters people who contribute directly to innovation, it seems to be when those people interact with broader segments of the workforce in promoting or coping with change that the innovation system as a whole turns out to be most efficient. The broader participation in change reflects a combination of increased income security offered by welfare state initiatives and equality in income distribution.

11.11 The Euro-Crisis and Europe's Uneven Development

The Euro-crisis was triggered by the financial crisis of 2007. But it is rooted in the uneven development of the countries belonging to the Eurozone. We have seen how uneven development is reflected in differences in how people work and learn at work. The differences between the South and the North are dramatic. We have also shown that the institutional characteristics of especially labour markets and education systems are highly interdependent with the frequency of the workers' access to workplace learning.

The crisis and the fear of getting the national economy into the searchlight of financial speculators force individual national governments to pursue budget cuts and make attempts to weaken trade unions and lower taxes for business. This is also the kind of 'competitive response' that German Chancellor Merkel has insisted upon as solution for Europe as a whole. But while this kind of policy might be legitimate for a small open economy such as Ireland with potential problems with the external balance, for Europe as a whole this 'small-country strategy' is self-defeating.

Not only will it cement long-term unemployment and lead to a prolonged recession, budget cuts related to education, training and active labour market policies will also contribute to making the uneven development of Europe even more serious. Deepening inequality at the national and international level will undermine social capital and interactive learning. The current version of the competitiveness/stabilization pact will aggravate rather than solve the structural crisis for the Eurozone. There is a need for a completely different approach that attacks directly the uneven development in Europe. The strategic aim of this alternative strategy should be to enhance the learning capacity in Europe with emphasis upon Southern Europe.

11.12 Policy Recommendations

On the basis of the analysis in this chapter, we recommend policy initiatives aiming at promoting innovation through reforming education systems, labour markets and working life in Southern Europe:

1. Education systems should be made robust to cope with radical unforeseen change and prepare students for participatory life-long learning.
2. Higher education should stimulate problem-based learning and combine traditional learning of disciplines with their application to real problems.
3. Universities should become more open to interaction with society and students should spend more 'learning time' outside their classroom.
4. Education systems should establish porous borders between theoretical-academic programmes and more practical-professional programmes.
5. Labour market policy should establish strong incentives for both employers and employees to upgrade skills.
6. New training programmes for those with the weakest positions in the learning society (low-skilled workers and certain ethnic minorities) should be developed.
7. A new social contract should be developed where employees respond to enhanced economic security and skill upgrading by more active participation in change.
8. Managers and employees, as well as their organizations, should be engaged in the diffusion of good practice for organizational learning.
9. At the national level, the prime minister should act as de facto chair for a new National Council for Competence Building and Innovation.

Such changes would require the engagement and positive participation of all segments of society. Government should play the role of the main driver and coach of the reform process.

11.13 The Roads Ahead for Europe

The Lisbon Strategy may be seen as an attempt to establish regional and political convergence in Europe with the ultimate aim of building a strong and cohesive union built upon the principle of solidarity. But the implementation – with emphasis on 'best-practice' and benchmarking in specific policy areas – was both too technocratic and too weak in terms of the instruments used to implement it. Neither was the strategy successful in stimulating popular participation in the project. To mobilize citizens for the European project there is a need for a vision that goes beyond the common market and 'structural reform'.

In a seminal paper written at the occasion of the conference on 'The European Identity in a Global Economy' in preparation for the Lisbon Summit under the Portuguese presidency, Manuel Castells argued that there is a need of 'a common European identity on whose behalf citizens around Europe could be ready to share problems and build common solutions' (2002, 234). After rejecting common religion and culture, he pointed to 'shared feelings concerning the need for universal social protection of living conditions, social solidarity, stable employment, workers' rights, universal human rights, concern about poor people around the world, extension of democracy to regional and local levels'. He proposed that if European institutions promoted these values, probably the 'project identity' would grow (Castells 2002).

To mobilize popular support, to reconstruct the Euro-zone and to attack uneven development in Europe, there is a need to recognize the 'social dimension' and to transform it into an Economic and Social Union (ESU). There is also a need for a shift where the fear of state intervention and the blind belief in markets is changed into a pragmatic perspective where governments are allowed to take on the tasks necessary to promote stable economic growth. Among the most important tasks, we would emphasize a redesign of all institutions and sector policies so that they respond to the fact that we are in a new phase where knowledge is the most important resource and learning the most important process.

Notes

1　Lorenz and Valeyre (2006) use logit regression analysis in order to control for differences in sector, occupation and establishment size when estimating the impact of nation on the likelihood of employees being grouped in the various forms of work organization. The results show statistically significant 'national effect' also when controlling for the structural variables, thus pointing to considerable latitude in how work is organized for the same occupation or within the same industrial sector.

2　It is also worth observing that there are fairly strong positive correlations between the frequency of leading innovators and the two measures of vocational training, R-squared = 0.47 and 0.45 respectively.

3　The index is constructed by reversing the scoring on the employment protection index such that high values correspond to low levels of protection and multiplying this reversed score by the unemployment index. The resulting flexicurity index has then been rescaled so that the maximum score is 100.

4   The class of managers includes not only top and middle management but also professionals and technicians (ISCO major groups 1, 2 and 3). The worker category includes
clerks, service and sales workers as well as craft, plant and machine operators and
unskilled occupations (ISCO major groups 4 through 9).

References

Arundel A., E. Lorenz, B.-Å. Lundvall and A. Valeyre. 2007. 'How Europe's Economies
Learn: A Comparison of Work Organization and Innovation Mode for the EU-15',
Industrial and Corporate Change 16, no. 6: 1175–210.
Castells, M. 2002. 'The Construction of European Identity'. In *The Knowledge Economy
in Europe*, edited by Maria Joan Rodrigues. Cheltenham, UK and Northampton,
MA: Edward Elgar.
Holm, J. R., E. Lorenz, B.-Å. Lundvall and A. Valeyre. 2010. 'Organisational Learning
and Systems of Labour Market Regulation in Europe'. *Industrial and Corporate Change*
19, no. 4: 1141–73.
Jensen, M. B., B. Johnson, E. Lorenz and B-Å. Lundvall. 2007. 'Forms of Knowledge and
Modes of Innovation'. *Research Policy* 36, no. 5: 680–93.
Johnson, B., E. Lorenz and B.-Å. Lundvall. 2002. 'Why All This Fuss about Codified and
Tacit Knowledge?' *Industrial and Corporate Change* 11, no. 2: 245–62.
Lam, A. and B.-Å. Lundvall. 2006. 'The Learning Organisation and National Systems of
Competence Building and Innovation'. In *How Europe's Economies Learn: Coordinating
Competing Models*, edited by E. Lorenz and B.-Å. Lundvall. Oxford: Oxford University
Press.
Lorenz, E. and A. Valeyre. 2005. 'Organisational Innovation, HRM and Labour Market
Structure: A Comparison of the EU-15'. *Journal of Industrial Relations* 47, no. 4: 424–42.
———. 2006. 'Organisational Forms and Innovative Performance: A Comparison of
the EU-15'. In *How Europe's Economies Learn: Coordinating Competing Models*, edited by
E. Lorenz and B.-Å. Lundvall, Oxford: Oxford University Press.
Lundvall, B.-Å. 2002. *Innovation and Social Cohesion: The Danish Model.* Cheltenham, UK and
Northampton, MA: Edward Elgar.
———. 2006. 'Interactive Learning, Social Capital and Economic Performance'. In
Advancing Knowledge and the Knowledge Economy, edited by D. Foray and B. Kahin.
Cambridge, MA: Harvard University Press.
———. 2008. 'Higher Education, Innovation and Economic Development'. In *Higher
Education and Economic Development*, edited by J. Y. Lin and B. Plescovic. Washington,
DC: World Bank.
Lundvall, B.-Å. and B. Johnson. 1994. 'The Learning Economy'. *Journal of Industry Studies*
1, no. 2: 23–42.
Lundvall, B.-Å. and E. Lorenz. 2011. 'From the Lisbon Strategy to EUROPE 2020'. In
Towards a Social Investment Welfare State? Ideas, Policies and Challenges, 333–51, edited by
N. Morel, B. Palier and J. Palme. Bristol: Policy Press.
Lundvall, B.-Å. and P. Nielsen. 2007. 'Knowledge Management and Innovation Performance'.
International Journal of Manpower 28, no. 3–4: 207–23.
Lundvall, B.-Å., P. Rasmussen and E. Lorenz. 2008. 'Education in the Learning
Economy: A European Perspective'. *Policy Futures in Education* 6, no. 2: 681–700.
Organisation for Economic Co-operation and Development (OECD). 1996. 'Transitions to
Learning Economies and Societies'. Paris.

————. 1999. 'OECD Science, Technology and Industry Scoreboard 1999: Benchmarking Knowledge-Based Economies'. Paris.

————. 2000. 'Employment Outlook 1999'. Paris.

S. Yusuf and K. Nabeshima (eds.). 2007. *How Universities Promote Economic Growth.* Washington, DC: World Bank.

Chapter 12

GROWTH AND STRUCTURAL CHANGE IN AFRICA: DEVELOPMENT STRATEGIES FOR THE LEARNING ECONOMY

Bengt-Åke Lundvall and Rasmus Lema

12.1 Introduction[1]

Recent press reports suggest that Africa may now be at a turning point in terms of economic growth and development. These reports point out that, although starting from a low base, Africa is now the world's fastest growing continent. However, naive optimism on this ground should be avoided (Karuri-Sebina et al. 2012). The recent growth has been concentrated in particular countries and sectors and the transformation of growth into sustainable social and economic progress will not happen automatically.

There is thus a discrepancy between the reporting of record growth rates for African economies in media and the reality of how people's living conditions have evolved over the last decade in the African high growth economies. The widely shared understanding among development scholars that registered economic growth and development must be seen as two distinct, even if related, processes has become more evident than ever. In this chapter, we will argue that in order to transform the economic upswing as measured by gross domestic product, fast-growing African countries need structural and institutional change across the economic, social and political spheres that bring them closer to what we will refer to as 'learning economies'.

The widening of the gap between reality on the ground and perceptions based on growth rates reflects partly that the increasing global demand for natural resources – especially for commodities such as oil and minerals – has led to advantageous change in terms of trade, to increased export volumes and raised the rates of GNP growth while the impact on domestic employment has often been limited and sometimes negative. The expansion of the commodity sector does not automatically create large-scale employment directly and so far it has rarely resulted in a substantial increase in job creation in upstream and downstream manufacturing and in knowledge-based services.

It has even been argued that the structural change that occurred in low-income economies with high rates of growth had a negative impact on the potential for future aggregate economic growth (McMillan and Rodrik 2011). They have pointed to the fact that the share of low productive workplaces, many of them in informal sector activities or in subsistence agriculture, has grown in the midst of the period of rapid growth. This has gone hand in hand with deindustrialization – the share of the labour force in manufacturing has fallen from an already low level.

We will take this as a starting point for an analysis of opportunities and policy options for African countries. What kind of policies and institutions are necessary in order to transform the current increase in rents from commodities exports into industrial investment and upgrading of agriculture and agro-industrial development?

This question is raised in the context of competing theories about economic development. We contrast the recommendations of neoclassical economists with those that can be derived from the classical development economics that includes scholars as Dobb, Hirschman and Sen. The theoretical perspective that we propose on this basis takes into account that we have entered a phase – the learning economy – where it is useful to take as a starting point that 'learning' is at the core of any process of development. Development is a process where individuals and organizations learn to do new things and learn to do them in new ways in conjunction with structural transformation. At the core of the process of development is competence building. In the chapter, we analyse development and learning at the micro-, macro- and meso-level.

On the basis of empirical patterns and theoretical considerations, we will discuss policy options in relation to the African reality. This is not easy. First, there are major differences between African countries – there is not one strategy that fits all. Second, in many African countries the most fundamental barriers for development are sociopolitical rather than techno-economic. Here political transformations must go hand in hand with socioeconomic and technological transformations. Finally, as outsiders to the African scene, we can refer to lessons from other parts of the world and sketch dilemmas and alternative options, but the relevance of these lessons needs to be assessed on a case-by-case basis, and the specific strategies need to be built on the basis of local experience.

12.2 Recent Developments in Africa's Economies

12.2.1 Growth and structural change

In a recent contribution, Valensisi and Davis (2011) analyse recent patterns of growth and structural change in the least developed economies, including most of the Sub-Saharan African (SSA) countries. They refer to the rapid growth between 2000 and 2009 – on average GNP has grown with 7 per cent per annum. They show that even average GDP per capita increased with as much as 5.5 per cent (growth was unevenly distributed so median growth for this group of countries was 2.2%). The authors make an effort to go behind this observed pattern of growth in order to understand the underlying structural change process.

They find that the impressive growth record was based on rapid growth in the exports of hard commodities and on a capital inflow through foreign direct investment (FDI), overseas development aids (ODA) and remittances from expatriates that allowed for a strong growth in consumer demand for services and for imported consumer goods. Agriculture grew only slowly, and in most of the least developed economies, there was deindustrialization (in two-thirds of the least developed economies the share of manufacturing was reduced from its already modest level).

The growth process and the increased demand for natural resource–based commodities did not lead to any increase in the investment ratio – on average the rate of investment remained close to 20 per cent. Most of the extra income was absorbed by middle-class consumption, and in many of the countries import grew more than exports (in 38 out of 49 countries). One problem with this pattern of growth is that it does not create sufficient number of decent jobs for the many young people in Africa. Another problem is that it establishes a vulnerable economic structure where the whole economy is dependent on single hard commodity export products.

12.2.2 Insufficient job creation and poverty reduction

The UN 2013 Economic report on Africa recognizes the problems with the current lopsided growth pattern – it is presented under the heading 'Making the Most of Africa's Commodities: Industrializing for Growth, Jobs and Economic Transformation'. It points out that the employment problem remains unsolved in most African countries.

> Strong growth across the continent has not been translated into the broad-based economic and social development needed to lift millions of Africans out of poverty and reduce the wide inequalities seen in most countries. This is because Africa's recent growth, driven by primary commodities, has low employment intensity – that is, the ability to generate jobs.' (UN 2010)

Thus the continent continues to suffer from high unemployment, particularly for youth and female populations, with too few opportunities to absorb new labour market entrants...More than 70 per cent of Africans earn their living from vulnerable employment as economies continue to depend heavily on production and export of primary commodities. Investments remain concentrated in capital-intensive extractive industries, with few forward and backward linkages with the rest of the economy. (UN 2010, 30)

The report also points out that the impact of growth on poverty reduction has been modest:

Recent data show some slight improvement in poverty reduction, even though the region will not be able to achieve the related MDGs. The proportion of people living in extreme poverty (below $1.25 a day) in Africa (excluding North Africa) has been projected to reach 35.8 per cent in 2015 against the previous forecasts of 38 per cent (UN, 2011). This slight, albeit slow, improvement is partly attributable to high and sustained economic growth since 2000. (UN 2010, 35)

The general picture is that the increase in global demand for natural resource–based commodities – especially hard commodities such as minerals – has driven growth in Africa. Combined with an inflow of financial resources this has stimulated private consumption of domestic services and imported manufactured goods. The employment impact and the impact in terms of poverty reduction have been very limited. A third problem is that the kind of structural change that has taken place with deindustrialization, growth in urban informal employment and stagnating productivity in agriculture may undermine the prospects of future economic development.

12.2.3 Growth-reducing structural change

McMillan and Rodrik (2011) pursue a simple exercise where they break down the observed aggregate growth in labour productivity into two components for the period 1990–2005. One component reflects productivity growth within sectors, and the second component is the effect that comes from moving labour from sectors with low productivity to sectors with high levels. According to the authors, most African countries have been characterized by a trend-wise move of labour from high to low productivity sectors (including urban informal sectors). This is what the authors refer to as growth-reducing structural change.

This observation goes against what should be expected since productivity gaps between sectors are extremely large in the least developed countries. Therefore, we should assume that economic development takes the form of workers moving from low to high productivity sectors. But actually, the opposite takes place in most of the observed countries. Exceptions are Ghana and Ethiopia where structural change gave a positive contribution to economic growth. According to McMillan and Rodrik, to change the dominant negative direction, there is a need to direct investment to manufacturing and especially to expand manufacturing activities with more value added to the products. According to the authors, flexible labour markets should help. Below we will propose more ambitious policies related to building learning economies as response.

12.2.4 National technological capabilities in Africa

Mayor et al. (2012) have made an attempt to map the distribution of technological capabilities in Africa. The analysis covers 30 African countries for the years 2010–11, the data used emanate from World Economic Forum, and they come either from statistical sources or from an executive survey. Technological capabilities are presented in three dimensions: (a) The available base (internet use, educated labour and research and development (R&D)), (b) government and business technological effort (technological infrastructure, enterprise performance and policies related to innovation) and (c) results (patents and the intellectual property rights regime).

The analysis leads the authors to define four clusters of countries where South Africa stands alone as a lead country followed by Morocco, Tunisia and Egypt. The countries with the weakest technological capacities are Algeria, Libya, Mauretania and Zimbabwe. It should be taken into account that most of the data originates from surveys with business leaders and so there might be a bias in favour of regimes that do not intervene with regulating business activities.

Nonetheless, the analysis illustrates that Africa is heterogeneous and that different countries face different challenges when it comes to developing and making use of technological capabilities. It is also worth noting that almost all of the lead countries have experienced political turmoil recently. We are going to turn back to this later since it indicates that investments in upgrading the skills of the young generation that are not followed by economic opportunities may lead to discontent and unrest.

12.3 What Is Development?

12.3.1 A neoclassical theory of development

If we start from neoclassical economics and deduce how less developed countries may catch-up, the focus of policy intervention would be on institutional design aiming at well-defined private property rights, including intellectual property rights. It would certainly recommend ubiquitous introduction of the market mechanism, propagate private ownership and recommend keeping the public sector as small as possible. It would advise against protectionism and hampering with international trade and capital flows. The role of government should be limited to securing a stable macroeconomic context and to guarantee private property, including intellectual property.

In cases of *obvious* market failure, government may be allowed to intervene. For instance, scientific information may be seen as a public good and therefore require state production or subsidy. But generally governments should stay out of the economic process and leave it to the market to give signals to actors. Specifically, there would be a strong emphasis on the advantages of free trade. Through the free working of comparative advantages resources would be used in the most efficient way. Since all countries have equal access to information, including technology, we would expect a general tendency towards convergence in productivity and living standards. This 'neoclassical theory of development' lies behind what has been called Washington consensus.

The recent history demonstrates that most of the countries that have built their strategy on the assumptions of neoclassical theory have failed to develop and that most of those that have prospered, especially those in Asia, have deviated from these ideas. Going further back in history, it is obvious that the rich countries did not become rich by following the neoclassical prescriptions. They protected their industries, and they showed little respect for intellectual property rights. Actually it was almost a rule that countries emulated technologies developed in other countries, often with such success that they became technology leaders. But the theory and the prescriptions remain very much alive since they are strongly supported by powerful global interest groups and institutions rooted in the developed countries.[2]

The report by Stiglitz et al. (2013) on industrial policy in Africa offers a modified version of the neoclassical development theory that use the frequency of market failure and not least the importance of knowledge and learning as arguments for a more selective and interventionist industrial policy. Actually it argues that neoclassical economics has accepted that industrial policy is now not only acceptable but also commendable. It may be noted that the authors say nothing about infant industries and trade and that there is a tendency to recommend moderate interventions with full respect for 'comparative advantage'.

12.3.2 Development economics

In the late 1940s there was a growing interest to try to explain and remedy economic underdevelopment. One of the first important contributions that triggered the debate was by Rosenstein Rodan (1943). The basic question was: How could the poor countries catch-up with rich countries? The debate was quite polarized. Some of the literature came from Marxists who saw global inequality as rooted in an imperialist system and assumed that the only way for poor countries to grow rich was a transformation towards a socialist and centrally planned economy. Others belonging to the liberal camp took the opposite view and saw underdevelopment as reflecting that markets were not free and that capitalist institutions were not sufficiently well established.

A group of scholars with mixed ideological background – Arthur Lewis, Paul Rosenstein Rodan, Hans Singer, Maurice Dobb, Amartya Sen, Albert Hirschman and others – came with more complex prescriptions for how poor countries could grow rich. They proposed that five elements were absolutely essential for development:

1. A high rate of savings and investments.
2. A first stage of import substitution increasingly to be combined with expansion of export.
3. Absorbing technological knowledge from abroad.
4. Focus on expanding the manufacturing sector.
5. An active role of the state in guiding the direction of development.

It is interesting to note that in the countries that were the most successful and competitive entrants in the world economy (Japan, Korea and China), all the five elements were present. But it is also true that in other parts of the world the attempts to combine import substitution with learning from abroad were much less successful in developing self-propelling industrial growth – at least in the long term. The less successful examples were often countries in Latin America and Africa with higher degrees of inequality and with political systems that invested less in building the domestic knowledge base necessary to learn from abroad.

So one cannot say the theory was ever proven to be wrong. Rather the experience indicated that while the five conditions listed might be necessary, they were not sufficient. In the meantime international organizations, such as the World Bank, IMF and OECD dominated by the United States, set conditions for loans and assistance that made realizing the conditions very difficult to those developing countries that became (made themselves) dependent on loans and grants.

12.3.3 Aggregate growth and structural change

Macroeconomists sometimes assume that economic growth takes place as in a corn economy with only one sector. They do so in order to keep things simple and make advanced mathematical modelling possible. This perspective misses out the very fundamental fact that growth and structural change are two sides of the same coin (Pasinetti 1981). Aggregate growth will reflect the uneven growth rates in different sectors in the economy – and in national accounts the growth of the whole is actually a weighted sum of the growth of its parts.

In this context Kutsnetz (1966) makes a very elementary but often neglected point. He shows that high rates of aggregate growth typically require that the big sectors grow rapidly. Even if a new sector grows very rapidly, its contribution to aggregate growth will, to begin with, be modest. Therefore accelerating growth in the currently dominating sectors – such as agriculture or the urban informal service sector in Africa – is an obvious way to raise income per capita in the short to medium term. A typical pattern of growth for the rich countries has been to raise productivity in agriculture, while workers have moved from agriculture to manufacturing. In Africa raising the productivity in the informal sector and to create demand for labour outside the informal sector is a major challenge.

This is important since the informal sector remains a significant and even expanding economic force in sub-Saharan Africa. The sector is estimated to account for more than 65 per cent of nonfarm employment in sub-Saharan Africa (Adams et al. 2013). In Tanzania the informal sector is estimated to account for more than 55 per cent of employment in urban areas and over the 2001–2006 period the number of workers in the informal sector increased at an annual rate of 9 per cent as compared to 4 per cent for the economy as a whole (Kahyarara and Rutasitara 2009). It is obvious that a successful industrialization strategy would reduce the relative weight of the informal sector in the long term. Given its current weight in the sub-Saharan economies measures to upgrade workers' skills and the technologies used in the informal sector would give substantial contributions to growth and welfare. The same is of course true for agriculture, which is the other major sector in terms of employment in most of the least developed economies.

Nevertheless, it is equally true that in the long term, the emergence and growth of new sectors is crucial for the wealth of the nation. The ideal new sectors would be characterized by rapid technological learning, increasing returns to scale and increasing world demand. Moreover, it must, to some degree, build on already existing domestic competences in the labour force and in enterprises. It may be a problem to foster such new sectors when the traditional big sectors have strong representation in the political system (e.g., soy producers in Argentina and the oil industry in the Northern Africa). Finding ways to align interests of dominating sectors with the formation of new sectors may be necessary to overcome such barriers.[3]

One of the most fundamental questions now debated among innovation scholars is what role the natural resource–based sectors and especially those producing hard commodities, such as minerals, oil and gas, can play in a process of industrial transformation. Is it correct that such sectors offer less potential for technological learning and for building upstream and downstream couplings as well as lateral transfer of knowledge to other sectors, or does this version of the 'resource curse' view just represent leftovers from the classical development economists? Do new perspectives on how local firms can link up to global value chains make these views obsolete? Another relevant question is if it is possible to create sufficient volume of new jobs for the young generation without industrialization. We will return to these questions in the last sections of the chapter.

12.3.4 Learning, innovation and development

Stiglitz (2011) proposes that there is a need to engage in 'rethinking development economics'. It is remarkable that he builds his argument around the concept of 'the learning society' – a concept that has been central among innovation scholars for many years. Dalum et al. (1992) presented ideas for innovation policy in the learning society in the context of the analysis of national systems of innovation (Lundvall 1992). Two years later, Lundvall and Johnson (1994) further developed this concept under the heading 'the learning economy'. As pointed out in Lundvall et al. (2009), several scholars (such as Viotti 2002) have proposed to refer to national learning systems in developing countries rather than to present them as national innovation systems. In this section, we will present a perspective on development that is rooted in our interpretation of the concept of 'the learning economy'.

An ambitious definition of development must refer not only to registered economic growth and structural change but should also take into account the welfare of individuals and to how resources and capacities are distributed among individuals, regions and classes. It also needs to take into account long-term generational perspectives. Such a definition would take into account both material conditions and mental and spiritual conditions – including positive and negative experiences – from being members of traditional and new communities. It would need to reflect experiences from different roles in life such as the roles of consumer, family member, citizen and worker. Short-term gains should be weighed against long-term costs and foregone opportunities – such as environmental degradation and depletion of nonreproducible natural resources.

Here we are going to be more modest and bring in two dimensions that tend to be neglected in the traditional view on development and economic growth. The first refers to *the quality of working life*, while the second refers to the crucial role of the uneven capacity to learn and the *uneven access to learning*. The most primitive versions of welfare economics assume that increasing the bundle of consumption goods is basically what constitutes increased welfare. This is why national income per capita is the most frequently used indicator. The perspective is implicit in the argument in favour of free trade combined with 'flexible' work arrangements.

For instance, while the positive impact of globalization on consumption opportunities is taken into account, possible negative consequences on job security and working conditions are neglected. This traditional perspective is especially problematic when it comes to assessing the economic development in Africa where increasing consumption opportunities for the middle class seem to go hand in hand with more vulnerable employment and less quality in working life for the majority of workers.

In order to understand the importance of learning, it is useful to start from Amartya Sen's definition of welfare as 'freedoms' and capabilities to realize what you regard as valuable. This is, in general, a valuable approach because it takes into account that the aspirations of people may be different in different countries and regions. We would nonetheless, in this context, like to emphasize 'access to learning' as perhaps the most fundamental freedom – especially in a society characterized by rapid change in people's private and professional lives. The two concepts – learning and development – are crucially interconnected both at the individual level and at other levels of the economy (learning organizations, learning regions and the learning economy at the aggregate level).

There are two reasons for why we should focus on learning. First, a crucial prerequisite for any kind of economic transformation is a speed-up of learning as competence building both among individuals and within organizations. Structural change is a process where people are confronted with new tasks. Second, we would argue that learning is not only of instrumental value, enhancing the productivity of the individual worker, it is also of substantive value for individuals. This is obvious for the child's development into adulthood. To block the child's process of learning to communicate and act in the society would be cruel. For most adults, a life without any learning would constitute monotony.

This perspective neither rules out that the speed of learning imposed by circumstances may become disturbingly high and create stress and sufferings, especially when the individuals have no capabilities to understand and manage the processes involved, nor does it mean that all forms of learning represent progress. And learning new things implies that old knowledge becomes obsolete. Learning as well as development will *always* involve creative *destruction*.

As new patterns take form; old ones tend to be destroyed. Often the old patterns are seen as positive by some of those living in the society. In worst cases, destruction takes place without much creation. While some form of creative destruction is necessary to lift African people out of poverty, the involvement of ordinary citizens in the management of change would make the processes of change and learning less painful.

Stiglitz (2011) argues that there is another kind of link from a learning economy perspective to inclusive development. His argument is the correct observation that the learning society will be most successful when learning is broad based and knowledge is widely spread in the economy. In a series of papers on the learning economy, we have presented a somewhat different perspective where we have shown that if left to itself, the learning economy tends to become increasingly polarized (Lundvall 1996, 2002). Only with strong and systematic government intervention aiming at strengthening the capacity of weak learners and offering them better access to learning is it possible to build strong learning societies.

12.4 Transformation Pressure, Learning Capacity and Redistribution

In a context of global competition, national economies as well as firms are exposed to a more or less intense 'transformation pressure'. For instance, the strong competition from China has put a very intense transformation pressure on manufacturing firms in Africa. The transformation pressure at the level of the manufacturing firm can be reduced in different ways. Workers may be forced to accept lower wages, the currency may be devalued or the government may introduce trade barriers to protect the domestic firms in order to promote import substitution. Another alternative is that the firms are left to themselves to cope with the intensification of the transformation pressure. They might do so by downscaling or bankruptcy. Alternatively, they may respond by engaging in organizational and technological learning resulting in a stronger competitiveness based on higher productivity and incremental product and process innovations.

When the transformation pressure is growing, it speeds up structural change in the national innovation system. Low-productivity activities will be closed down. With a sufficient population of firms with a capacity to innovate and adapt, the resources that are freed up from the firms failing will be absorbed by these new or growing high-productivity activities. However, with a weak learning capacity at the level of firms the result will be a further increase in underemployment in informal activities and unemployment. How the cost and benefits of the transformation are distributed affect how willing people will be to contribute actively to the process of transformation within the firms. The response at the national level will reflect the strength of the national innovation and competence building system.

12.4.1 Why we need to broaden the innovation system concept

One major difference between neoclassical economics and evolutionary economics is that in the evolutionary perspective history and institutions matter. The national system of innovation (NSI) concept signals that the economic structure and the current institutional set-up, both with historical roots, need to be analysed and understood in order to set policy priorities. However, it is obvious that different authors mean different things when referring to a national system of innovation. Some major differences have to do with the focus of the analysis and with how broad the definition is in relation to institutions and markets.

Authors from the United States with a background in studying science and technology policy tend to focus the analysis on 'the innovation system in the narrow sense'. They tend to regard the NSI concept as a follow-up and broadening of earlier analyses of national science systems and national technology policies (see, for instance, the definition given in Mowery and Oxley 1995, 80). The focus is on the systemic relationships between the R&D efforts in firms, science and technology (S&T) organizations, including universities, and public policy.

Freeman (1987) developed a broader concept that took into account national specificities in how firms organize innovative activities; he emphasized, for example, how Japanese firms increasingly used 'the factory as laboratory'. Researchers in Aalborg (Lundvall 1985; Andersen and Lundvall 1988) also developed a concept of innovation systems where there are other major sources of innovation than science. Innovation is seen as reflecting interactive learning taking place in connection with ongoing activities in production and sales. Therefore the analysis takes its starting point in the process of production and the process of product development assuming, for instance, that the interaction with users is fundamental for product innovation.[4]

None of these approaches, however, gave sufficient attention to the broader set of institutions shaping competence building in the economy, such as labour markets, the education and training system and their relation to systems of corporate governance, nor did they consider the broader connections between these institutional subsystems and national political cultures and welfare regimes. In order to capture this wider set of interactions in a dynamic perspective, we introduce an evolutionary framework for analysing how economies learn under the pressure of globalization.

12.4.2 Mediating transformation pressure

The starting premise is that a range of factors have resulted in an acceleration of economic change. These factors include economic globalization, policies and demands of international institutions such as deregulation of finance, population growth and technological change, etc. In many African countries, the boom in commodities exports adds to these factors. When the *transformation pressure* becomes more intense it means that firms will have to engage in change in terms of organization, technology and capabilities if they want to survive and grow. At the level of the labour market, this process will be reflected in dynamics where workers will gain, lose or change jobs while learning new (and forgetting old) skills and competences.

A crucial characteristic of a national system is how it responds to an increase in transformative pressure. The *capability to innovate and to adapt* will reflect systemic features having to do with how easy it is to establish interactive learning within and across the organizational borders (social capital) and with the preparedness to take risks (entrepreneurship). Organizational capabilities and the competence structure of the workforce play an important role. Social cohesion may be an important factor behind social capital while it might get in the way of entrepreneurship.

The mechanism for *redistribution of costs and benefits emanating from change* differs between national systems.[5] Figure 12.1 is adapted from the framework developed in Archibugi and Lundvall (2001) to link transformation pressure to the capacity to innovate and to the distribution of costs and benefits of change.

The figure reflects the view that capabilities to innovate and to adapt reflect systematic differences in national institutional arrangements at the levels of the science and technology system, labour markets, education and training and finance. These institutional subsystems will impact on how knowledge is developed and used within organizations, and these organizational differences in turn will have a bearing on innovation pace (fast or slow) and innovation style (incremental or radical).

But national differences in innovation systems need to be seen in an even broader perspective and take into account feedbacks from the distribution of costs and benefits to the capacity to innovate and to adapt. An uneven distribution may create a negative attitude to change among those who mainly register the costs and if there are high degrees of insecurity among individuals they will tend to oppose change.

A second kind of feedback mechanism goes from the ability to innovate to transformation pressure. Increasing the ability to innovate involves stimulation of entrepreneurship and the building of more flexible organizations. This

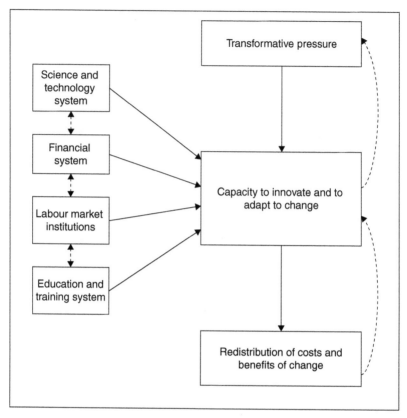

Figure 12.1 A model linking transformation pressure to the capacity to change and to the distribution of the costs and benefits of change

implies a selection of people and institutions that are more change oriented and this further increases transformation pressure.

12.4.3 Development strategies responding to transformation pressures

The simple model presented above can be used to distinguish between different developmental strategies. Washington consensus based on neoclassical assumptions recommends that governments leave it to the market to determine the transformation pressure and to install a capacity to adapt through flexible labour markets. Redistribution of costs and benefits of change should be kept at a minimum in order not to get prices and incentives wrong.

The development economists (Singer, Dobb and Sen) saw a need for less developed economies to regulate the transformation pressure shielding new industries from the full impact of international competition. It is interesting to note that they as well as the fathers of the concept of 'infant industry argument' (Hamilton and List) saw strengthening of the knowledge base of the economy as another necessary prerequisite for economic development.

Friedrich List thus insisted that 'mental capital' was more important for development than physical or financial capital. The emphasis on intangible capital, knowledge and technology has become even more clear in recent theories of economic development pointing to 'capabilities' and innovation systems as crucial for economic development. In the next section we will go deeper into how knowledge and learning links to economic development.

As we remarked above, the Asian countries were more successful using the protective strategy than countries in Latin America and Africa where the result was stagnation rather than economic growth. One explanation is that there was too little emphasis on building innovation capacity that the protection from competition from abroad was not compensated by other mechanisms, such as stimulation of domestic competition and promotion of export orientation, stimulating competitiveness and that income and access to land were more unequally distributed in Africa and Latin America.

12.4.4 Macro conditions for development

The general macroeconomic situation will affect the capacity of firms to engage in investment and innovation. This is one of the points where there is agreement among those belonging to the Washington consensus camp and those in favour of selective industrial policies promoting innovation. But there are differences in terms of focus. Washington consensus recommendations only propose financial discipline and stable prices. This perspective neglects that innovation is, to some degree, demand driven and that engaging in entrepreneurial activities is much less risky in a situation when aggregate demand is growing. Also the neoliberals propose to leave it to the market to regulate finance, something that results both in more instability and in very limited access to loans especially for small and medium enterprises.

12.4.5 Investment and finance

One of the most fundamental weaknesses of national innovation systems in Africa is the financial system. In most of the least developed countries access to capital for supporting ordinary trade, for investments in production capacity and especially for new innovative ventures is very limited. Banks do not have the routines and skills to deal with more risky projects and neither have government authorities. Therefore, the creation of new public–private institutions filling the function of development banks is crucial. This would require building new competences and here South-South learning could play an important role. Among the sources of finance to be channelled into the new institutions could be export levies on nonrenewable hard commodities.

12.4.6 Educated labour

It is obvious that education is an important prerequisite for economic development. This can be seen from the historical record of developed economies and from the recent growth of Asian countries. Basic education offering literacy and basic mathematical skills may be seen as fundamental human rights since such skills are necessary for full participation in society. Secondary and tertiary levels are of course important for economic and social development.

A major problem is that the demand for candidates with higher education is very limited in the least developed countries. This leads to an exodus of highly educated people to the rich countries and in this way the scarce resources invested in universities end up with being used in the developed countries. The 2012 UNCTAD report on the least developed countries has a theme 'the issues of brain drain and brain gain' and another on how remittances from emigrants may be mobilized for development. The report shows that from 1990–2000 the outflow of highly trained people from the least developed countries has increased and that it keeps growing in the new millennium. For many African countries, the brain drain rate (the brain drain rate is the emigrants' share of the corresponding age and educational group in the home country) is over 40 per cent. This is for instance true for Uganda, Rwanda, Somalia, Eritrea, Liberia, Sierra Leone and Gambia.

While the report discusses possible advantages of having a diaspora of trained people abroad, there is little doubt that the outflow of skilled people from the poorest to the richest countries (the United States remains the main destination) is unfair and undermines development efforts in the home countries.

The main reason for the exodus of skilled people is lack of job opportunities and substantial difference in earning between home country and the host country. In a paper on higher education, innovation and economic development (Lundvall 2008), we showed that the lack of demand reflects absence of innovation and therefore investments in higher education need to be coordinated with support to framework conditions and policies that stimulate innovation. The higher the rate of innovation, the higher is the rate of return on investments in higher education.

It is also a serious problem that the education system replicates elements from the former colonial powers. Universities train people with a strong emphasis on social science and humanities while there is a tendency to neglect the training of vocational skills and engineering. Emphasis is on narrowly defined scientific disciplines and higher education institutions often operate as academies with very limited elements of practical training. Introducing problem based learning and elements of practice in theoretical studies may reduce the problem of creating jobs for the candidates.

12.5 Public Policy and Institutional Design

As pointed out in the introduction, there are strict limits for what external experts can offer when it comes to designing and implementing public policy schemes and new institutions that support economic development. In what follows we refer to what seems to work in other contexts and what we see as general principles for promoting development.

12.5.1 Nondiscrimination as development strategy

Taking the learning economy perspective on economic development makes it clear that the inclusive formation of people's skills and their interaction is crucial. In many of the least developed economies, including those in Africa, there is discrimination to ethnic minorities and to women in terms of access to resources and citizen rights. A focus on reducing discrimination when it comes to learning, not only in terms of access to formal education – but also processes of learning in production and policy processes – expands the access to human resources and creativity. In many societies the inclusion of women and ethnic minorities can offer new potential and more commitment to economic processes.

A specific problem in Africa is the age structure with a very big share of young people. Developing new institutions that give young people a 'voice' in development issues may be a way to avoid that the youth get alienated and engage in destructive activities individually or collectively. This may be a difficult challenge in countries where there is a tradition to listen most to the old and experienced.

Such changes may be crucial also for attracting the diaspora intellectuals who often find patriarchy and authoritarianism repelling.

12.5.2 Industrial and trade policy

In a recent document from UNCTAD it is referred to some general principles for economic development:

> In recent years, UNCTAD has repeatedly argued that progressive transformation in economic structure is a prerequisite for LDCs to achieve accelerated and

sustained economic growth and poverty reduction. The policies and strategies needed to attain structural transformation will involve, inter alia,

(a) The development of a new industrial policy based on a strategic approach that reflects the specific needs and conditions of LDCs;

(b) A catalytic developmental State to compensate for the incipient and weak private sector in LDCs;

(c) Measures to encourage private investment in productive activities and public investment in basic infrastructure, including the development of skills and support institutions;

(d) The promotion of domestic technological learning and innovation and improvements in productivity in both agricultural and manufacturing sectors (UNCTAD 2013).

Our analysis above supports those principles but they are somewhat general to be implemented as such and they need to take into account the specificities of African countries' specific recent development. The UN economic report for Africa 2013 moves in that direction by demonstrating the limits of the current development patterns where natural resource rents are not transformed into investment in manufacturing and agriculture.

The UN report points to the formation of 'industrial clusters' around commodity production on the basis of private–public partnerships as the central strategy. The advantage with such an incremental strategy is that it builds on what is already there and aims at raising productivity in existing activities. However, there might be a need for more bold industrial policy strategies that take the wider perspective of the national innovation system and aim at fostering new manufacturing industries with high-learning potential. Here productivity of the whole economy could be increased by moving resources from low- to high-productivity sectors.

12.5.3 Industrial policies as learning processes

It is useful to see public policy as a learning process. There is no reason to assume that the policy makers get things right from the very beginning. For instance, we found that the original intentions of the Chinese reforms aiming at creating 'markets for knowledge' did not succeed (see chapter 10 in this book). The enterprises were not ready to procure knowledge from universities and other knowledge institutions. Instead, knowledge suppliers had to move ahead and establish their own enterprises in order to bring knowledge into use. This unintended process turned out to be an important step for China in its catch-up process, and it was accepted as such by policymakers.

When policymakers in African countries take new initiatives in industrial policy, they should be aware of the fact that it is a learning process. This involves systematically evaluating outcomes and not least registering unexpected outcomes – both positive and negative – and making sure that the next wave of initiatives takes these experiences into account.

Stiglitz et al. (2013) discuss the argument that industrial policy should be avoided in Africa because there is too little administrative capacity to pursue industrial policy in Africa. They turn down the argument. But there is little doubt that there is much for African policymakers to learn from successful catching-up economies. Programs with expert exchange between African countries and some Asian countries could be one way to speed up policy learning.

12.5.4 Environmental policy as industrial policy

As the global climate change regime moves ahead towards 2020, there will be increasing investments related to climate change mitigation and adaptation in poor countries. Substantial opportunities for funding of low-carbon innovations will arise particularly in Africa. Ensuring that the most adequate technologies are selected and that they are diffused and used in such a way that the outcome is better living conditions for the population is a major challenge.

At the same times environmental policy is an important form of industrial policy with potential for job creation. Making it more costly to use carbon-based technologies and giving support to low-carbon solutions will change not only the structure of power production but also the wider industry structure. Introducing low-carbon solutions in agriculture and in the informal sector, for instance, through new systems for recycling and repair activities can offer both investment and job opportunities.

12.5.5 The BRICS connection and below-the-radar innovation

The most recent developments in Africa with growing dependence on production of commodities and a tendency towards deindustrialization reflects the growing role of China and other major economies. It is a major task for governments in Africa to exploit the potential for a positive interaction with BRICS countries. This potential reflects that emerging economies are in a particularly strong position to advance relevant and affordable technologies because conditions in BRICS are more similar to those in the poor countries.

However, even the most 'adequate' technologies developed abroad will need to go through a process of transformation in order to become both efficient and inclusive in the specific context of African countries. The fact that the solutions may be adequate has little to do with the source of the technology but depends on the contextualization and adaptation of the technology into the local context (Arocena and Sutz 2000). Building absorptive capacity in the informal sector and in agriculture requires new types of policy initiatives.

12.5.6 The global regime for knowledge protection and sharing

Above we could see how very scarce resources used for higher education went into investments in people who then moved to rich countries that could benefit from the investments. The lack of protection of these resources can be argued in terms of the need for individual freedom to move from one country to another. The argument is weakened when it turns out that the rich countries' respect for this freedom is highly selective. Ordinary poor people with less education are effectively blocked at frontiers of the rich countries.

The lack of protection of human capital stands in strong contrast to the global rules regarding intellectual property rights. The WTO agreements on TRIPS set very strict limits for the use of knowledge developed abroad, and they have been even further restricted by bilateral agreements between the United States and the least developed countries (Sampath and Roffe 2012). The WTO agreements also include references to the duty of developed countries to engage in 'technology transfer' to the least developed economies, but those references are vague without monitoring and sanctions.

There is little doubt that the global regime for knowledge sharing and protection is biased in favour of the rich countries. To renegotiate this regime would require a coordinated effort of African countries, perhaps with a role of the African Union.

12.5.7 The natural resource curse and the need to promote manufacturing in Africa – some reflections on the implications for public policy

The data and conclusions presented under the heading 'the resource curse' in Sachs and Warner (1995) have triggered a substantial amount of analytical work as well as heated debate among economists and political scientists. Recently the topic has attracted the attention of scholars linking innovation and innovation policy to development (see for instance Katz 2006; Perez 2010; Iizuka and Katz 2011; Andersen 2012).

Some early contributions to the resource curse debate by economic historians such as Gavin Wright and Paul David demonstrated that knowledge creation and learning in direct connection with the exploitation of mineral resources have been crucial for US economic growth. Others such as De

Ferranti et al. (2002) have argued that the most important explanation of the different paths of development, where Nordic countries succeeded to develop strong and diversified economies starting from a situation of natural resource specialization, while Latin American countries failed to do so, had to do with a weak knowledge base and with an institutional set-up that did not support processes of learning.

On this basis innovation scholars have argued against a specific version of natural resource curse based on the assumptions that:

1. The learning potential and the knowledge content is limited in natural resource–based sectors.
2. Natural resource–based sectors tend to develop as enclaves with limited capacity to drive the creation of upstream and downstream manufacturing.

It is in line with the argument in this chapter that the key difference between successful and less successful growth policies lies in the nature of the learning process that promotes the economic potential of access to natural resources (Wright 2001). A crucial issue is how natural resource–related activities make use of and master new technologies and knowledge to improve production processes (De Ferranti et al. 2002). A key question is how Africa can exploit the 'window of opportunity' opened up by increased global demand for natural resources and transform it into a knowledge base that would allow for sustained and inclusive growth.

We share the scepticism to the generalized resource curse hypothesis and see the building of clusters around natural resources as one useful step towards economic development in Africa. Nevertheless, we see a need to develop further the policy implications of the criticism. We are not convinced that the natural resource base should be *the only* starting point for industrialization in Africa. The fact that most African countries import big proportions of their consumption goods from abroad indicates a potential for import substitution. Second, we see the broad-based growth of manufacturing as crucial for making Africa's economies less vulnerable and for creating jobs for the young generation. This is the case even if there is a great potential for learning and upgrading in natural resource–based sectors.

In relation to building clusters around natural resources – both mining and agriculture – we see a crucial need for building relevant capacity in *engineering and design*. Without local competence in these areas, there is no possibility to link up with global value chains with unique and high-value-added products. But the same is true for any attempt to build industrial capacity. One important reason why the attempts to realize import substitution in Latin America and Africa did not succeed is that technical training and engineering have been given too little attention as compared to general education in science, social sciences and humanities.

Notes

1   This paper was drafted to form the basis for a presentation at the AfricaLics Academy held in Algiers in October 2013. It also draws on a concept note prepared by the authors for the Globelics Seminar on Innovation and Economic Development, Dar-es-Salaam, March 2012.

2   An important factor is that, daily, thousands of young economics students are exposed to programs teaching this message. Many of those working in ministries of finance in African countries have been trained to believe in it.

3   The fact that the landed aristocracy in England became involved in trade and industry was a major factor that made the Industrial Revolution possible.

4   To a certain degree, these differences in focus reflect the national origin of the analysts. In small countries such as Denmark, as in the developing countries – a major concern of Freeman – it is obvious that the competence base most critical for innovation in the economy as a whole is not scientific knowledge. Incremental innovation, 'absorptive capacity' and economic performance will typically reflect the skills and motivation of employees as well as inter- and intra-organizational relationships and characteristics. Science-based sectors may be rapidly growing, but their shares of total employment and exports remain relatively small.

5   In the Anglo-Saxon countries the basic idea is that individuals should carry as much as possible of both benefits and costs. In the Nordic countries universal tax financed welfare systems redistribute in favour of individuals who lose their job or become handicapped. The more conservative systems in place in Continental European countries tend to redistribute through employment-tied public insurance systems. In Southern Europe, where systems of social protection are relatively weak, the family can still play an important role as redistributing mechanism. In Japan the big corporations redistribute resources to older workers who would otherwise be victims of change by offering them life-long employment.

References

Adams, A. V., S. Razmara, and S. Johansson de Silva. 2013. *Improving Skills Development in the Informal Sector: Strategies for Sub-Saharan Africa*. Washington, DC: World Bank.

Andersen, E. S. and B.-Å. Lundvall. 1988. Small National Innovation Systems Facing Technological Revolutions: An Analytical Framework (pp. 9–36). In C. Freeman and B.-Å. Lundvall (eds.). *Small Countries Facing the Technological Revolution*. London: Pinter.

Archibugi, D. and B.-Å. Lundvall (eds.). *The Globalizing Learning Economy*. Oxford: Oxford University Press, 2001.

Arocena, R. and J. Sutz. 2000. 'Looking at National Systems of Innovation from the South'. *Industry and Innovation* 7, no. 1: 55–75.

Bell, M. 2007. 'Technological Learning and the Development of Production and Innovative Capacities in the Industry and Infrastructure Sectors of the Least Developed Countries: What Roles for ODA?' *SPRU Working Paper*. Brighton: Science and Technology Policy Research, University of Sussex.

Dalum, B., B. Johnson and B.-Å. Lundvall. (1992), 'Public Policy in the Learning Society'. In Lundvall, B.-Å. (ed.). 1992. *National Systems of Innovation: Towards a Theory of Innovation and Interactive Learning*. London: Pinter Publishers.

Dantas, E. and M. Bell. 2011. 'The Co-Evolution of Firm-Centered Knowledge Networks and Capabilities in Late Industrializing Countries: The Case of Petrobras in the Offshore Oil Innovation System in Brazil'. *World Development* 39, no. 9: 1570–91.

De Ferranti *et al.* 2002. *From Natural Resources to the Knowledge Economy: Trade and Job Quality*. Washington DC: World Bank.

Freeman, C., 1987. *Technology Policy and Economic Performance: Lessons from Japan*. London: Pinter Publishers.

Kahyarara, G. and L. Rutasitara. 2009. *Survey of Working Conditions in Tanzania*. Final Report to ILO June 2009.

Kaplinsky, R. 2011. 'Schumacher meets Schumpeter: Appropriate technology below the radar'. *Research Policy* 40, no. 2: 193–203.

Karuri-Sebina, G., S. Alioune, R. Maharajh and A. Segobye. 2012. 'Fictions, Factors and Futures: Reflections on Africa's 'Impressive Growth'. *Development* 55, no. 4: 491–96.

Katz, J. 2006. 'Salmon Farming in Chile'. In *Technology, Adaptation, and Exports: How Some Developing Countries Got It Right*, edited by V. Chandra. Washington, DC: World Bank.

Kutsnetz, S. 1966. *Modern Economic Growth: Rate, Structure, and Spread*. New Haven, CT: Yale University Press.

Lundvall, B.-Å. 1985. 'Product innovation and User–Producer Interaction'. In *Industrial Development Research Series*, vol. 31. Aalborg: Aalborg University Press.

———. (ed.), 1992. *National Systems of Innovation: Towards a Theory of Innovation and Interactive Learning*. London/New York, Pinter Publishers.

Lundvall, B.-Å. and B. Johnson. 1994. 'The Learning Economy'. *Journal of Industry Studies* 1, no. 2: 23–42.

Lundvall, B.-Å., K. J. Joseph, C. Chaminade and J. Vang (eds.), 2009. *Handbook of Innovation Systems and Developing Countries: Building Domestic Capabilities in a Global Setting*. Cheltenham and Northampton, MA: Edward Elgar.

Mayor, M. G.-O., M. L. Blasquez de Hera and E. D. Ruiz. 2012. 'Empirical Study of Technological Innovation Capability in Africa'. *South African Journal of Economic and Management Science* 15, no. 4: 440–63.

McMillan. M.S. and D. Rodrik. 2011. *Globalization, Structural Change and Productivity Growth*. *NBER working paper series*. Cambridge, MA: National Bureau of Economic Research.

Morris, M., R. Kaplinsky and D. Kaplan. 2012. '"One Thing Leads to Another": Commodities, Linkages and Industrial Development'. *Resources Policy* 37, no. 4: 408–416.

Mowery, D. C. and J. E. Oxley, 1995. Inward Technology Transfer and Competitiveness: The Role of National Innovation Systems. *Cambridge Journal of Economics* 19: 67–93.

Pasinetti, L. 1981. *Structural Change and Economic Growth*. Cambridge: Cambridge University Press.

Pérez, C. (2010). Technological Dynamism and Social Inclusion in Latin America: A Resource-based Production Development Strategy. *CEPAL Review* 100: 121–141.

Rosenstein-Rodan, P. 1943. 'Problems of industrialization in Eastern and South-Eastern Europe'. *Economic Journal* 53, 202–211.

Sachs, J. D. and A. M. Warner. 1995. 'Natural Resource Abundance and Economic Growth'. *National Bureau of Economic Research Working Paper*, No. 5398, December.

Sampath, P. G. and P. Roffe. 2012. 'Unpacking the International Technology Transfer Debate: Fifty Years and Beyond'. *ICTSD Working Paper*, June.

Sen, A. 1983. 'Development: Which Way Now?' *Economic Journal* 93 (December): 745.

———. 1999. *Development as Freedom*. Oxford: Oxford University Press.

Stiglitz, J. E. 2011. 'Rethinking Development Economics'. *World Bank Research Observer* 26: 230–236

Stiglitz, J. E., J. Lin and E. Patel. 2013. 'Industrial Policy in the African Context'. *World Bank Working Paper*, S6633, World Bank.

———. 2012. 'Innovation, Technology and South-South Collaboration. Technology and Innovation Report'. New York: United Nations Conference on Trade and Development, United Nations.

UNCTAD. 2013. 'The Least Developed Countries Report, 2012, Harnessing Remittances and Diaspora Knowledge to Build Productive Capacities'. Geneva: UNCTAD.

United Nations. 2010. 'The UN 2010 Economic Report on Africa'. New York: United Nations.

———. 2013. 'The UN 2013 Economic Report on Africa'. New York: United Nations.

Valensisi, G. and J. Davis. 2011. 'Least Developed Countries and the Green Transition: Towards a Renewed Political Economy Agenda'. *Merit Working Paper*, November.

Viotti, E. B. 2002. 'National Learning Systems: A New Approach on Technological Change in Late Industrializing Economies and Evidences from the Cases of Brazil and South Korea'. *Technological Forecasting & Social Change* 69: 653–680.

Wright, G. 2001. Resources Based Growth: Then and Now. Paper Prepared for the World Bank. Stanford University, available at http://www-iepr.stanford.edu/conferences/HSTeachers_2001/resource-based-growth.pdf.

Chapter 13

NATIONAL INNOVATION SYSTEMS AND GLOBALIZATION

Bengt-Åke Lundvall

13.1 Introduction

Today the term national innovation system appears in several different domains within social science and engineering, and it is widely used in policy circles all over the world. The concept reflects an assumption that the pattern of innovation differs across countries and that such differences can be explained by systemic features. The components of the innovation system are different, and they are linked differently to each other and such differences in economic structure and institutional set up are reflected in the rate and direction of innovation.

We will take as starting point ideas presented in the very first contributions that made use of the innovation system concept, Freeman (1982) and Lundvall (1985). There is some overlap between them but the perspectives are quite different. Freeman's analysis refers to macro-phenomena and to international trade and development, while Lundvall (1985) refers to the micro level where innovation is seen as shaped by user–producer relationships. We will argue that they are complementary and that they can be used to span and dissect important themes in the more recent literature on innovation systems and global value chains.

The concept national innovation system may be seen as a new combination of two different perspectives, one developed within the IKE group at Aalborg University and one developed at Science Policy Research Unit (SPRU) at Sussex University. The concept came out of bringing together an understanding of innovation as rooted in the production system (Aalborg) and an understanding of innovation as rooted in the science and technology system (Sussex).

The Aalborg approach was inspired by the concept 'national production systems' as it was used by French Marxist structuralists such as Palloix (1969) and de Bernis (1968). Esben Sloth Andersen (1992) criticized and developed these ideas by introducing an evolutionary perspective with focus on innovation with the aim to overcome the limitations of what he saw as a too static framework. Another important inspiration for the Aalborg group's work on innovation systems came from Björn Johnson (1992) who linked innovation and learning to the socioeconomic characteristics of national institutions. Lundvall (1985) took inspiration from early works by Andersen and Johnson while studying user–producer interfaces as reflecting economic structure as well as institutional characteristics.

Scholars at SPRU were involved in a series of empirical projects that brought forward the interaction that took place in connection with innovation processes in industrial enterprises (Rothwell 1972, 1977). One of Freeman's favourite themes in lectures in the early 1980s was about how innovation studies could overcome the apparent contradiction between supply- and demand-driven innovation through understanding innovation as an interactive process. While the Aalborg research program on innovation, knowledge and economic dynamics (the IKE-group) started from the production system and developed its understanding of innovation and learning on this basis, the SPRU pioneered the mapping, comparing and analysis of national science and technology systems – a concept used by OECD already in the beginning of the 1980s. This is reflected in Freeman (1982) where the focus is on the role of *Technological Infrastructure*.

It is important to note that the two first contributions that made use of the concept (Freeman 1982 and Lundvall 1985) aimed at understanding national economic performance in terms of competitiveness and economic growth and that the analysis was critical both to mainstream economics and dominant economic policy prescriptions. They were critical to development strategies based on 'pure markets' and night watcher states and to the discourses that presented lower wages as the best cure for weak competitiveness. Both of these contributions were placed in the tradition of political economy and the power dimension was taken explicitly into account. Freeman (1982) referred to the differences between the rich and the poor countries in terms of their capacity to set the global rules of the game and pointed to the important role of state intervention to close technological gaps, while Lundvall (1985) analysed how gaps in competence and economic resources between users and producers led to 'unsatisfactory innovations' when either the user or the producer took a dominant position.

In the ensuing diffusion and use of the innovation system concept these critical dimensions were almost lost, and they were definitely marginalized.

Scholars at business schools and technological universities as well as economists in international organizations such as OECD and the World Bank used the concept in a technocratic way and neglected the power dimension.

13.2 Technological Infrastructure and International Competitiveness

Around 1980 the OECD Directorate for Science, Technology and Industry (DSTI) established a group of experts to analyse 'Science, technology and competiveness' with Sir Ingram as chairperson and Francois Chesnais as secretary. After a series of meetings, the group finalized a report in 1983 that introduced the concept of 'structural competitiveness'. The report demonstrated that short-term variations in wage costs and currency rates had only limited effects on long-term differences that reflected the 'absolute advantage' of certain countries. The report concluded that the investments in knowledge infrastructure and in human capital were crucial for the long-term economic performance of the national economy. The report's conclusions were controversial for OECD, and it was never published (officially due to limited printing capacity – sic!); some of the main results were presented in an article in STI review several years later (Chesnais 1987).

The group invited a number of external experts to write papers that gave insights into the link between science, technology and competitiveness. Christopher Freeman contributed with a paper on 'Technological Infrastructure and International Competitiveness' (Freeman 1982/2004). In this paper, he made what might be the very first reference to 'the national innovation system' (Freeman 1982, 550), and he outlined arguments for why national systems of innovation and especially technological infrastructure matter for the competitiveness of nations.

The paper is introduced by an important distinction between two different perspectives on international trade: one, prominent in standard economics where the focus is on comparative advantage and trade specialization, and a second where the focus is on absolute advantage and competitiveness. The aim of the paper is to address issues related to the second perspective. The paper refers to the Leontief paradox (1951) and to the attempts to dissolve the paradox by analysing the role that technology plays for the patterns of trade specialization (Posner 1961; Hufbauer 1966; Gruber et al. 1967). Freeman then moves on to a discussion of the literature on the role of 'non-price factors' in trade citing works by respectively Kravis and Lipsey (1971) and Posner and Steer (1979), indicating that factors related to quality and reliability are more important than price for users' selection of means of production. He also refers to 'the Kaldor paradox' (1978), showing a 'perverse' relationship between national cost levels and export shares for the 1960s and 1970s.

As Freeman points out (with the exception of Kaldor's paper) the empirical results that he quotes operate at the sector level showing that in most sectors, technology (as reflected in R&D intensity and patenting) is an important factor when it comes to explaining international specialization. They only indirectly address the question why countries remain in a dominating position for a longer period when it comes to trade and economic growth through innovation.

In order to respond to this question, he uses economic history as a method and shows how technological and economic world leadership has shifted from the Great Britain to Germany, and he gives a detailed analysis of how Japan on the basis of investment in knowledge and innovation is successfully engaged in catching-up with the United States and with the lead European countries.

One original and interesting element in Freeman's paper is his reading of Friedrich List (Freeman 1982, 552–57). He recognizes the well-known fact that List challenges the free-trade ideology of Adam Smith and that List argues in favour of protecting infant industries. But he also shows that List's most severe criticism of Adam Smith is that Smith neglects the importance of 'mental capital' and the quality of the labour force: 'His free trade theory takes into account present values, but nowhere the powers that produce them' (List 1845, 208).

According to List, it is only when you take into account the learning processes in the production sphere that you can understand why, under specific circumstances, the principle of freedom of trade may need to be subordinated to the need to foster competences in the production sphere. A related argument for protecting domestic markets is that it will attract foreign tangible and intangible capital contributing to the formation of mental capital. In both cases List's focus is on the dynamics of innovation and competence building:

> The present state of nations is the result of the accumulation of all discoveries, inventions, improvements, perfections and extertions of all generations which have lived before us; they form the mental capital of the present human race, and every separate nation is productive only in the proportion in which it has known how to appropriate these attainments of former generations, and to increase them by its own acquirements. (List 1841, 183)

Freeman concludes the paper by arguing that the international monetary systems need to recognize that there are no mechanisms that automatically will overcome major trade disequilibria since those will reflect structural factors difficult to change in the short run. In the absence of a new international economic order where surplus countries accept to transfer technologies and support the building of strong innovation systems in the deficit countries, the outcome at the global level will be deflationary. At the national level, he points to the need for public investments in education and research and in technological infrastructure. He ends the paper by arguing that these traditional priorities need to be combined with a new emphasis on understanding what kind of 'coupling' mechanisms – linking to each other education systems, scientific institutions, engineering, business and marketing – characterize the countries that have been successful in catching up.[1]

In this context he makes a reference to the research program of the IKE group at Aalborg University:

> The research at Aalborg on the inter-dependencies between various groups of firms in promoting technical progress in certain key sectors of the Danish economy is also highly relevant here. (Andersen et al. 1981; Freeman 1982, 550)

This reference points indirectly to the second early contribution to the development of the national innovation system (NIS) concept (Lundvall 1985).

13.3 Product Innovation and User–Producer Interaction

In the period 1980–84, the Aalborg group hosted a major project on the impact of the use of micro-electronics on international competitiveness – the MIKE project. At the time there were many parallel national projects going on using various methods to capture the impact on productivity, employment and balance of payment. Some of those used macroeconomic models and input–output tables, while others studied specific sectors and the impact at the level of the firm. The MIKE project defined the units of analysis as 'industrial complexes' and analysed four 'industrial complexes' that constituted important components of the Danish economy (Agro-, Office automation-, Environmental- and Textile-Industrial complexes).

The project gave special attention to the interface between users and producers of means of production that embodied information technology and studied how the specific characteristics of the user–producer relationships shaped the technologies that were developed and used. The project demonstrated several cases of producer dominance and pointed to the importance for national economic performance of giving users, including workers and consumers, stronger competences to cope with the new technologies.

Lundvall (1985) was inspired by the results obtained in the MIKE project. It addressed two sets of issues: one related to economic theory and the other related to the understanding of the innovation process. It presented innovation as an interactive process where the feedback from users' experience was seen as crucial for the success of innovation, and on this basis it demonstrated that an economy characterized either by 'pure markets' or 'pure hierarchies' would experience little (product) innovation. On this basis, it was argued that markets where new products are introduced are 'organized' markets or semi-hierarchies. The analysis pointed to the limits of neoclassical economics but also to the limits of transaction cost economics as presented in the book *Markets and Hierarchies: Analysis and Antitrust Implications* (Williamson 1975).

Second, with reference to the MIKE project's analysis of industrial complexes, it gave several examples of 'unsatisfactory innovation' reflecting a combination of uneven market power and uneven distribution of competences between the producer and the user. It also broadened the use of the concept of user–producer interaction to include universities as producers and industrial enterprises as users showing why this interaction would always be disharmonious since the user and the producer operated with different modes of learning. In this context appeared what might be the first printed reference to 'innovation system' (Lundvall 1985, 36).

There is some overlap between these two first contributions to the understanding of innovation systems. As mentioned above, while analysing the role of international specialization and competitiveness, Freeman points to the importance of 'coupling' from invention to innovation and from the original innovation (creation) to diffusion and use as well as to the complex process of 'matching scientific and technological opportunities with the needs of potential users of innovation'. The analysis in Lundvall (1985) is built on studying 'Danish' industrial complexes, but three of the four cases refer to the industrial complexes that are quite dependent on imports when it comes to the technologies used (this is especially the case for textile machinery). The paper also introduces ideas similar to what can be found in recent literature on global value chains:

> The world economic system might be regarded as a complex network of user-producer relationships connecting units dispersed in economic and geographical space … International specialization might be regarded as reflecting competition between verticals or production rather than competition between national industries. (Lundvall 1985, 34)

Some years later (in Lundvall 1988), the patterns of user–producer relationships were presented as a micro-foundation for the concept 'national innovation systems'. It was argued that the interaction with domestic users is facilitated by short distance in terms of Geography, Culture and Language. This general argument was supported by empirical analysis of trade specialization showing that there is a correlation between the specialization in a specific commodity group on the one hand and the specialization of machinery to be used in the same sector on the other. Home markets were important for those developing new production technologies (Fagerberg 1988).

Lundvall (1992a) may be seen as an attempt to combine and further develop the two perspectives presented in respectively Freeman (1982) and Lundvall (1985). In the first part of the book, the focus is on the role of economic institutions and structure in national innovation systems. The second part analyses different domains within the innovation system (work organization, cluster formation, finance, public sector and STI institutions). The third part is explicitly on the openness of national systems and refers to trade, integration and FDI.

Chapter 3 in the book used the user–producer perspective to explain why national systems remain quite resistant to the trend towards globalization (Lundvall 1992b). It is argued that domestic interaction benefits from a shared language and from nation specific economic institutions since it reduces transaction costs and raises the returns from interactive learning. In the introduction to the book, it is emphasized that all national systems are becoming increasingly open. However, this is not seen as a reason to cease further development and use of the NSI concept. It is argued that globalization makes it even more necessary to understand the historical role as well as the ongoing transformation of national innovation systems.

13.4 Each of the Origins Gives Rise to New Streams of Analysis

Each of the two pioneer contributions has stimulated specific research efforts related to innovation systems. The literature on catching-up may be seen as a logical follow-up to Freeman's reference to List and to his macro-perspective on economic development. While Freeman (1982) points to the difficulties of establishing quantitative empirical analysis given the lack of data for less developed countries, much of the work on catching up has been empirical and aimed at testing his hypotheses. More specifically, this literature has tested the relative importance of 'openness' vs. factors related to the strength of the national innovation system. In the next section we summarize the main results from this literature.

The literature on cluster formation and regional innovation systems developed by economic geographers may be seen as a follow-up to the analysis of user–producer interaction in *Product Innovation and User-Producer Interaction* (Lundvall 1985). To begin with, this literature gave major emphasis to the importance of local interaction. Later on it developed the analysis and pointed to complementarity between global (pipelines) and local (buzz) interaction.

This evolution of ideas about interaction in space was interconnected with an analysis of distinct kinds of knowledge and different forms of learning. Below we will focus on how this literature has developed its view of the role of distance in connection with the interaction that characterizes the innovation process.

13.5 What Are the Prerequisites for Catching-Up?

Fagerberg's contributions on competitiveness and catching up may be seen as following a trajectory that was outlined in Freeman's paper from 1982. While Freeman with reference to lack of data, especially for the least developed countries, used qualitative and historical arguments to indicate the importance of technology for national economic development, Fagerberg, starting with his PhD thesis (1988b), has engaged in a life-long effort to analyse quantitative data in order to sort out what are the main factors that contribute to economic growth and international competitiveness in countries at different levels of development (Fagerberg 1993, 1994, 2010, 2011).

His works show that technological capabilities (the national innovation system) and factors having to do with 'governance' are crucial for economic development, while factors cherished within Washington consensus such as 'openness' (to trade and FDI) and the prevalence of Western political institutions do not favour economic development – especially not in the least developed countries. In 'The Changing Global Economic Landscape: The Factors That Matter', where Fagerberg (2010) summarizes much of his work on why growth rates differ, he demonstrates that a broader definition of 'openness' is significant for economic development. Openness to ideas, to entrepreneurial effort and to people (including tolerance to minorities), is positively correlated with national economic performance.

These conclusions are in line with the main results presented in 'The Role of Foreign Technology and Indigenous Innovation in the Emerging Economies: Technological Change and Catching-Up' (Fu, Pietrobelli and Soete 2011). Their analysis aims at understanding the role of national and international sources of knowledge and innovation. It is built on an extensive literature review on the impact of FDI, and it refers to a different type of data than the empirics used by Fagerberg (their evidence is from case studies of global value chains in emerging economies), and they find that:

> The evidence suggests that, despite the potential offered by globalization and a liberal trade regime, the benefits of international technology diffusion can only be delivered by parallel indigenous innovation efforts and the presence

of modern institutional and governance structures and a conducive innovation system. (Fu et al. 2011, 1210)

They conclude that 'without indigenous innovation the income gap between rich and poor countries will never be closed'.

These results support Freeman's 1982 analysis where he, with reference to Friedrich List, argues that building national technological infrastructure and a strong national knowledge base should be a major focus for development strategies. Fagerberg's analysis adds to that perspective the importance of governance (rule of law, intellectual property rights, corruption) as well as openness to ideas. Neither Fagerberg's nor the analysis of value chains in emerging economies indicate that the least developed countries would benefit from engaging in 'free trade' and from more free access for foreign capital without simultaneously building technological capabilities and 'upgrading' national governance.

13.6 Interactive Learning in Regional Systems of Innovation

While much of Jan Fagerberg's work may be seen as following the trajectory outlined by Freeman (1982), economic geographers used some of Lundvall's (1985) core ideas in a similar way to develop further the analysis of why certain activities tend to be located together in a specific region. The analysis of processes of innovation and not least the diffusion of innovation was, of course, not new for this interdisciplinary discipline. Torsten Hägerstrand's seminal contributions on time and space models were linked to an analysis of innovation diffusion in space including reflections on the importance of face-to-face interaction. His dissertation (1953) represented a major milestone.

In the entrance to the 1990s, Krugman and colleagues (Krugman 1991; Krugman and Venables 1995) presented quantitative growth models that signalled 'the new economic geography'. Their models took aboard most of the main assumptions characterizing neoclassical economics but loosened up for some – most importantly they allowed for increasing returns to scale, oligopolistic competition and costs of transport. This invasion of a rather narrow economics perspective – where it was assumed that regional agglomerations could be explained by rational behaviour of fully informed agents – left many economic geographers uncomfortable. Neither did it match well with the classical approach of Hägerstrand who, while using quantitative modelling, always emphasized the human and cultural dimensions of geography and preferred to work within an evolutionary perspective where uncertainty is seen as fundamental for outcomes.

In this climate, many economic geographers and experts on regional development saw the new perspectives emerging within innovation studies developed by heterodox economists as a more relevant inspiration for their research. The concept of interactive learning was used in Cooke and Morgan (1990) to explain economic agglomeration in Europe. The combination of the specific focus on user–producer interaction (Lundvall 1985), the more general concepts of innovation systems (Lundvall 1988) and 'the learning economy' (Lundvall and Johnson 1993) inspired concepts such as 'the learning region' and the 'regional innovation systems'. Nordic scholars such as Maskell and Malmberg (1997) and Asheim (1996) took some of these concepts as the basis for developing theoretical and empirical works in new directions.

Further developments by Aalborg economists of the understanding of different types of knowledge and modes of innovation (Lundvall and Johnson 1994; Jensen et al. 2007) also influenced this literature. A major argument for why proximity between users and producers was critical to innovation was that important components of knowledge are tacit (for in depth analysis, see Gertler 2007; Asheim and Coenen 2005). But it was also recognized that knowledge may be more or less codified in different sectors and in different technologies and that this fact was important for understanding differences across industries in their degrees of localization and internationalization.

One of the most important contributions was the paper by Michael Storper (1995) who made use of ideas from Lundvall (1985) to introduce 'untraded interdependencies' as a key concept aimed at giving regional economics a new theoretical foundation. Here he argued that vertical linkages such as those between producers and professional users were only one example of 'untraded interdependencies'; others were related to the employment contracts and were reflected in informal labour market institutions at the regional level. Such relationships could be more or less hierarchical and be more or less built on trust. While most other scholars in economic geography draw rather practical implications from the analysis, using it primarily to argue that proximity is important and using it to explain the formation of clusters, Storper brought forward and further developed the underlying theoretical ideas. He summarizes his conclusions in three points:

1. Technological change is path dependent.
2. It is path dependent because it involves interdependencies between choices made over time – choices are sequenced in time, not simultaneous, and often irreversible.
3. These choices have a spatial dimension which is closely tied to their temporal uncertainty and interdependence. Some interorganizational dependencies within the division of labour, that is input–output or network

relations, involve some degree of territorialization. But in all cases where organizations cluster together in territorial space in order to travel along a technological trajectory, they have interdependencies that are untraded, including labour market relationships, and 'conventions', or common languages and rules for developing, communicating and interpreting knowledge (though direct input–output relations may also play a role here).

Storper (1995) was not unaware that globalization was an ongoing process but he argued that those who saw it as a hegemonic trend that met with little resistance had given too much attention to techno-economic input–output relations and too little to untraded interdependencies, including those not related to user–producer interactions. He used the concept of localized 'economic conventions' related to the knowledge system and to labour markets as signifying such interdependencies.

The work by Edward Lorenz with colleagues on national differences in the organization of work may be seen as a follow-up of these ideas. Such differences constitute an important but neglected dimension of Europe's national innovation systems and learning economies. In Lorenz and Valeyre (2006), it is demonstrated that work is organized quite differently in different national systems within Europe and that workers have very different access to jobs offering access to learning. In 'How Europe's Economies Learn: A Comparison of Work Organization and Innovation Mode for the EU-15' (Arundel et al. 2007), it is demonstrated that there is significant correlation between national performance in terms of innovation and the predominant forms of work organization. These differences typically reflect both differences in formal institutions surrounding the labour markets and 'conventions' strongly rooted in national systems.

The first wave of research on regional clustering taking Lundvall (1985, 1988) as inspiration emphasized the forces that lead to agglomeration and often it was assumed that agglomeration could be explained by the character of knowledge exchange in connection with local input–output or user–producer relationships. At the level of national innovation systems, it was also assumed that user–producer relationship could explain the relative stability in international specialization. Empirical work did not always support this perspective and increasingly it was found that:

1. The vertical couplings between firms within regional cluster were not always highly developed. Increasingly, the vertical division of labour in product chains was further developed and different steps were distributed at different locations, sometimes at locations across the globe.

2. While the interaction with domestic customers and suppliers was more frequent when developing new products, the less frequent interaction

with distant customers and suppliers outside the national system played an important role especially in connection with path-breaking and more radical innovations. Firms and clusters that combined 'local buzz' with 'global pipelines' were more viable and performed better than those depending only on local interaction.

These observations emphasized the need to combine a national perspective with a wider view, a need reinforced by the globalization of financial markets, by economic integration in Europe and by the increasing number of firms that behave as if they were footloose. In the introduction to the *Handbook in Economic Geography* (Clark et al. 2000), these are the main arguments for why a national perspective is insufficient. Nevertheless, the conclusion is still that the national systems matter. It is actually said that 'As representatives of political agency they may be more important than ever.' Where the authors see a weakening of the role of national systems is especially in the tendency towards decoupling between private economic interest and enterprise and the home nation.

13.7 The Global Value Chain Approach

It is interesting to note that in the *Handbook on Economic Geography* (Clark et al. 2000), there is only one reference to 'global commodity chains' in spite of the fact that the introduction argues that global and subnational economic processes should be given more attention. This reflects that the community of scholars who developed the global value chain approach had their belonging to development studies – a subdiscipline clearly separated from regional studies and from the community of scholars working on issues related to economic geography in the North.

The main research question in recent global value chain research is: How does the character of the global production chain contribute to or hinder the upgrading of activities in firms located in less developed economies? The complementary question is how the character of the chain affects the distribution of value produced along the chain. This leads to the third question: Does the integration of local firms into global chains contribute to economic development in developing countries?

One early major contribution to this field of research was the edited book by Gereffi and Korzeniewicz (1994). The book brought together contributions by scholars with different backgrounds. Some of the contributions were case studies while others were historical or theoretical. The main theoretical references were to respectively Immanuel Wallerstein's contribution on 'the world system and global commodity chains' (1974) and to Michael Porter's work on 'competition and innovation' (1990. The most important analytical step taken was Gereffi's distinction between producer-driven and user-driven value chains. This constituted the beginning of a discourse on 'governance' that later became dominated by references to transaction cost analysis.

Another important reference is to Humphrey and Schmitz (2002). Those two scholars have affiliation with IDS at Sussex University. During the 1990s, their focus was on how the new understanding of industrial districts and cluster formation developed in Europe could inspire strategies for industrial development in developing countries (Humphrey 1995; Schmitz 1995, 1999; Humphrey and Schmitz 1996). Schmitz introduced the concept 'collective efficiency' as characterizing successful clusters, a concept close to untraded interdependencies and shared economic conventions.

Humphrey and Schmitz (2002) is an important paper since it marks a bridging between the global value chain literature and the cluster literature as it emanated from The Institute for Development Studies at Sussex University. It is also important since it, on a few pages, introduces some fundamental concepts that have shaped the value chain discourse onwards. First it makes the distinction between four forms of industrial upgrading:

1. New process
2. New product
3. New function
4. New sector

As compared to the innovation literature, the third form of upgrading is of special interest since it goes beyond technical innovation. It may be seen as a form of innovation resulting in a 'new organization'. In the context of the global value chain literature, it has a more specific connotation, and it is assumed to be of great strategic importance. The value chain is seen as encompassing different functions spanning from exploitation of natural resources and manufacturing to R&D and marketing. It is assumed that firms that control the R&D and marketing functions can extract more value than those firms that are engaged exclusively in natural resource extraction or manufacturing. Even when firms succeed in developing new products and more efficient processes, they might gain little in terms of value if they remain a producer without access to R&D or without a strong position in the end-user markets. For the demand-driven chains, the most important factor is the control of end-user markets, including establishing a strong brand. For the producer-driven chains, the most important form for functional upgrading is related to the building of R&D capacity. Multinational firms that control these functions are assumed to be able to dominate and 'organize' the whole value chain.

The second conceptual contribution relates to different degrees of dominance, and it refers to the governance of networks. The analysis takes Oliver Williamson's transaction cost theory (1975) as its starting point. It is argued that four types of relationships can be distinguished in the value chain:

1. Arm's length market relations
2. Networks
3. Quasi-hierarchies
4. Hierarchy

The dominating form will depend on a series of factors. Quasi-hierarchies may reflect a combination of monopoly position of the buyer, need for speedy response among suppliers, limited capacity of suppliers and complexity in the product. It is argued that in a dynamic perspective, the entrance of local firms into quasi-hierarchies may support upgrading at least in terms of products and processes.

The paper points to the importance of understanding the role of global linkages for firm level upgrading. But it also specifies that in order to be successful, integration needs to be combined with investing in knowledge within the firm and that the more demanding forms of upgrading require a strong innovation system and active innovation policies.

A further step towards developing the understanding of governance of global chains was based on the work by Sturgeon on modular production networks. Sturgeon (2002) argues that the modularization of information technology production chains should be seen in the light of transaction cost theory. By standardizing and codifying interfaces between those producing components and the major computer firms, it has been possible to reap scale economies in production without imposing inhibitive transaction costs. It is argued that this is 'a new American model of industrial production' that can be applied in other sectors and set new global standards for the organization of value chains.

Gereffi et al. (2005) take these ideas into account and propose five different modes of governance:

a) Hierarchy
b) Captive
c) Relational
d) Modular
e) Market

It is assumed that the further down we get on this list, the less significant is the element of dominance. As compared to the categories used by Humphrey and Schmitz (2002), captive corresponds to semi-hierarchical, while the network category has been divided into two types of networks – relational and modular.

Three different characteristics are used to explain why a transaction interface takes on a specific form:

1. The complexity of information and knowledge transfer
2. The extent to which the information can be codified
3. The capabilities of suppliers

What is new as compared to Humphrey and Schmitz (2002) is that complexity now is explicitly related to information and knowledge and especially the emphasis is on the codifiability of the information. This is a theme that Aalborg economists have addressed in a number of papers where the emphasis has been on the limited codifiability of crucial elements of knowledge – especially codifiability is limited for what they refer to as 'know-how' and 'know-who' (Lundvall and Johnson 1994; Johnson et al. 2008).

13.8 Relating the Global Value Chain Approach to the Original NSI Contributions

The global value chain literature may be seen as combining elements from the two original NSI contributions referred to above. It makes an attempt to address the fundamental question raised by Freeman in connection with his interpretation of Friedrich List: Under what circumstances does participation in trade and openness to FDI have positive impact on the knowledge base of the economy?

There is also much overlap between the global value chain literature and Lundvall (1985). Lundvall (1985) does propose that most markets are organized and that they are infiltrated by hierarchical relationships – uneven access to resources and competences are seen as resulting in 'unsatisfactory innovation' especially when technologies are systemic. Other important overlaps are the references to Oliver Williamson's 'transaction cost analysis' and the idea that the character of knowledge as more or less codified – or technologies as more or less modularized – matters for the predominant form of governance.

Therefore, combining the innovation system perspective and the value chain perspective may be a way to reestablish the critical intentions in the original contributions by Freeman and Lundvall. As mentioned, much of the more recent literature and policy prescriptions have become technocratic and marginalized issues related to social phenomena such as power and trust.

But there are of course important differences as well. While the analysis of Freeman aimed at pursuing analysis at the aggregate level, something that was followed up in Fagerberg's work, most of the empirical work in the global value chain community is located at the level of the firm, the cluster or the value chain as a whole.

As Adrian Wood (2001) has pointed out, there is a need to establish an analytical link from upgrading at the level of the single firm to the development of a whole economy. Without such a link, there is no way that one can conclude that upgrading of a single firm or one single cluster of firms will contribute to economic development at the country level. This 'fallacy of composition' may actually be the weakest point in the global value chain analysis. What might be good for the single firm might not be good for a cluster, a region or a national economy.

When it comes to the micro-foundation for innovation systems and value chains, there are also important differences. Lundvall (1985) and especially the economic geographers who made use of and further developed his ideas have insisted on the in depth analysis of why specific activities become located together. Here the focus has been on the character of knowledge and learning processes as well as on localized 'institutions' and 'economic conventions'.

The global value chain literature tends to give less emphasis to analysing cultural, economic and political geography. This reflects that globalization is seen predominantly as bringing institutional convergence between national economies. This contrasts with the innovation system perspective where globalization is seen as a process that might make specific national patterns more disparate leading to divergence not only in terms of economic structure but also in terms of institutions.

The value chain analysts tend instead to give more weight to relative costs. Their starting point is empirical observations of increasingly global commodity chains, and to some degree, they seem to take for given that national governments have to respect the principles of comparative advantage. It is paradoxical that value chain analysis developed mainly by sociologists has ended up with a somewhat uncritical use of relative cost and transaction cost theory.

13.9 On the Importance of Building a Strong National Innovation System

Another issue where the two streams of thought diverge in terms of emphasis relates to the relative importance of domestic technological capacity and outcomes of participation in global value chains. The paper by Giuliani et al. (2005) is interesting since it makes an attempt to present a picture of local versus global interaction in Latin America on the basis of no less than 40 case studies. Their conclusions are that you find elements of 'collective efficiency' in most clusters while the form it takes depends on sector as well as regional and national context. They also confirm that in order to explain how integration in global value chains affects upgrading in the firm, you need to take into account the characteristics of regional and national systems of innovation and especially the firms' own efforts to engage in capacity building.

This corresponds to what is found in 'Learning and Catching up in Different Sectoral Systems: Evidence from Six Industries' (Malerba and Nelson 2011). Studying 'catching-up' in six sectoral innovation systems, they find that industries differ in terms of how they link up with international firms. In some successful cases of catching-up (automobiles in Korea), the access to foreign technology was crucial while in other cases (software, semiconductors and agro-food), multinationals operated as customer lead firms in global value chains. But again, in order to explain success and failure in catching-up – a phenomenon that could be referred to as 'sectoral upgrading' – they find that it is necessary to link the analysis of sector performance to the characteristics of national innovation system.

But the analysis of a wider set of cluster developments or of sectoral systems does not solve the 'fallacy of composition'-problem. Even if it can be shown that most clusters can benefit from firms' integration in global value chains and that specific sectors in a national system are characterized by catching-up, it does not follow that this will contribute to economic and social upgrading at the national level. This is not to degrade the importance of case studies and sector studies, but it is a strong argument for combining different methods including analysis at the macro level in order to make it possible to establish links from micro and meso levels to what happens at the national level.

13.10 Conclusion

The two first papers that made use of the concept 'innovation system' (Freeman 1982 and Lundvall 1985) had in common a critical perspective on economic theory and on economic policy. They introduced the concept in two different contexts. Freeman analysed the importance of building a strong technological infrastructure at the national level, while Lundvall analysed the interaction taking place at the level of the market between users and producers of new products.

Freeman (1982) has inspired Fagerberg's work on catching-up at the level of national systems. Fagerberg has developed methods to analyse in quantitative terms what Freeman derived as hypotheses on the basis of historical material. Lundvall (1985) inspired economic geographers such as Morgan,

Cooke, Gertler, Maskell and Asheim who developed further the analysis of forms of knowledge in the context of geographic space. Michael Storper enriched the analysis by linking 'nation specific conventions' to 'untraded interdependencies'.

The global value chain literature is overlapping with the two original contributions to the innovation system analysis. It shares Freeman's assumption that capacity building (upgrading) is crucial for economic development and his concern that not all participation in international trade will contribute to that. It shares with Lundvall (1985) the assumption that most markets are organized (taking the form of networks) with patterns of dominance, and it also links the degree of codification to transaction cost analysis.

There is, however, a tension between the two perspectives, and this tension can be linked to the issue of convergence versus divergence among national systems of innovation. Transnational value chains would be easier to establish if national systems become less disparate in terms of institutional set-up and mode of innovation. On the other hand, international diversity in terms of specialization in production, knowledge and in terms of income/cost levels can be seen as a underlying driver of the formation of global value chains.

In order to understand the dynamics of convergence and divergence, the most important step might be to analyse in some detail the evolution of codes of communication used in more or less local or global forms of interaction. There is little doubt that the multinational enterprises that play the most active part in shaping value chains also engage in developing codes that can overcome gaps in culture and competences. An interesting question is how this affects competence building worldwide. Codification of tacit knowledge is not costless. Literature on the codification of expert systems shows that what comes out of the codification process is less rich in terms of complexity and nuance than the original expert knowledge.

The global value chain approach and the national innovation system approach differ also when it comes to the focus and the level of analysis. While the focus of the system of innovation approach has been on the role of governments in building national infrastructure and on the role of domestic linkages, the focus of global value chain analysis has been on trade policies and transnational linkages. Freeman's insistence (see Sharif 2006) that innovation system analysis should give more weight to understanding macro-phenomena rather than just doing case and sectoral studies has not been taken up on a big scale among those working on innovation systems.[2]

Among those who have done it most systematically, we find Fagerberg, Dosi and Verspagen.

To link the transformation of economic structures to the process of economic growth and development is a major methodological challenge and it is of major importance for the design of trade, industry and technology policy. In classical development economics, the growth of manufacturing activities (assumed to be characterized by increasing returns to scale and steep learning curves) was seen as a crucial prerequisite for high rates of aggregate growth. This was presented as motivation for trade and industry policy aiming at import substitution. An interesting and promising recent approach is to link national economic performance not to specific sectors but to the characteristics of the technology predominant in the domestic high growth sectors (Lee 2013).

An open and critical discussion between the national innovation system proponents and the global value chain scholars will prove fruitful when it comes to building an agenda for development research and when it comes to developing strategies for development. This assumption takes inspiration from the fact that the few countries that have been successful in catching-up (Korea, Taiwan, Japan and China) have followed strategies where they gave attention both to building strong national innovation systems and to joining global value chains.

Current ideological campaigns in Latin America and in Africa by experts close to the Bretton Woods institutions (the World Bank and the International Monetary Fund – sometimes supported by OECD) present joining global value chain as a *sufficient* road to development and *as a substitute for* sector specific industrial and trade policy. This ideological drive undermines the credibility of the analytical literature on global value chains. There is no indication that Africa can enter a sustained development trajectory without strong government intervention just relying on the interaction with foreign multinational enterprises.

One ambitious goal for the research agenda could be to follow up on Freeman's interpretation of Friedrich List and develop a distinction between patterns of participation in the global economy that strengthen the national knowledge base (enhance mental capital) and patterns that undermine it. It could also address the more specific question: Under what circumstances will the participation in global value chains contribute to learning and upgrading at the level of the firm, at the level of a sector and to economic and social development at the national level? Such an analysis would be helpful in defining strategies for 'managing the openness of national systems of innovation'. The idea propagated by neoliberal economists that every single entrance of a domestic firm into a global value chain is promoting national economic development is of course naive.

Notes

1   The ideas of structural competitiveness and the importance of national innovation systems for international competitiveness became more widely accepted in the 1990s and in the first year of the third millennium – at least in public discourse. The Euro-construction, the Euro-crisis and the EU response to it, with a competitiveness pact that puts all the burden of adjustment on lowering wages and living standards in the south of Europe, is tragic evidence that those in charge of European economic policy have no understanding of the real dynamics of competitiveness (Lundvall and Lorenz 2012).

2   As Freeman puts it in an interview, 'most of the people working on Innovation Systems prefer to work at the micro level and they are a bit frightened still of the strength of the neoclassical paradigm at the macroeconomic level, and I think that's where they have to work. You have to have an attack on the central core of macroeconomic theory. It is happening but not happening enough, not strongly enough argued.' (Sharif 2006 745–66)

References

Andersen, E. S. 1981. 'The Importance of the Home Market for the Technological Development and the Export Specialisation of the Manufacturing Industry'. Technical Innovation and National Economic Performance: An IKE Seminar. Aalborg: Aalborg University Press.

Andersen, E. S., 1992. 'Approaching National Innovation Systems'. In *National Innovation Systems*, edited by B.-Å Lundvall. London: Pinter.

Andersen, E. S. and B.-Å. Lundvall. 1988. 'Small National Innovation Systems Facing Technological Revolutions: An Analytical Framework'. In *Small Countries Facing the Technological Revolution*, edited by C. Freeman and B.-Å. Lundvall. London: Pinter Publishers: 9–36.

Arundel, A., E. Lorenz, B.-Å. Lundvall and A. Valeyre. 2007. 'How Europe's Economies Learn: A Comparison of Work Organization and Innovation Mode for The EU-15'. *Industrial and Corporate Change* 16, no. 6: 1175–1210.

Asheim, B. T. 1996. 'Industrial Districts as 'Learning Regions': A Condition for Prosperity'. *European Planning Studies*, 4 no. 4: 379–400.

Asheim, B. T. and L. Coenen. 2005. 'Knowledge Bases and Regional Innovation Systems: Comparing Nordic Clusters'. *Research Policy* 34, no. 8: 1173–90.

Bathelt, H., A. Malmberg, and P. Maskell. 2004. 'Clusters and Knowledge: Local Buzz, Global Pipelines and the Process of Knowledge Creation'. *Progress in Human Geography* 28, no. 1: 31–56.

Chesnais, F. 1987. 'Science, Technology and Competitiveness'. *STI Review* 1: 85–129.

Clark, G. L., M. Feldman and M. Gertler. 2000. *The Oxford Handbook of Economic Geography*. Oxford: Oxford University Press.

Cooke, P. and K. Morgan. 1990. *Learning through Networking: Regional Innovation and the Lessons of Baden-Wurtemberg*. RIR Report No. 5. University of Wales, Cardif.

Cooke, P. 1992. 'Regional Innovation Systems: Competitive Regulation in the New Europe'. *Geoforum* 23: 365–82.

———. 1006. *Regional Innovation Systems: An Evolutionary Approach*. London: London University Press.

———. 2001. 'Regional Innovation Systems, Clusters and the Knowledge Economy'. *Industrial and Corporate Change* 4, no. 10: 945–74.

De Bernis, G. D, 1968. 'Les industries industrialisantes et l'intégration économique régionale', Archives de l'ISEA, 1968/1.

Dosi, G., K. Pavitt and L. Soete. 1990. *The Economics of Technical Change and International Trade*. Herefordshire: Harvester Wheatsheaf.

Fagerberg, J. 1988. *Technology, Growth and Trade. Schumpeterian Perspectives*. University of Sussex, Brighton (D.Phil. thesis).

———. 1993. 'A Technology Gap Approach to Why Rates Differ'. *Research Policy* 22, no. 2: 103.

———. 1994. 'Technology and International Differences in Growth Rates', *Journal of Economic Literature* 32: 1147–75.

———. 2010. 'The Changing Global Economic Landscape: The Factors That Matter'. In *The Shape of the Division of Labour: Nations, Industries and Households*, edited by M. Robert,R. M. Solow and J.-P. Touffut. Cheltenham: Edward Elgar Publishing: 6–31.

———. 2011. 'Domestic Demand, Learning, and the Competitive Advantage of Nations: an Empirical Analysis'. In *Competition, Competitive Advantages, and Clusters*. 131–47. Oxford: University Press.

Fagerberg, J. and Srholec, M. 2013. 'Knowledge, Capabilities and the Poverty Trap: The complex interplay between technological, social and geographical factors'. In *Knowledge and the Economy*, 113–37, edited by P. Meusburger, J. Glückler and M. el Meskioui. New York: Springer.

Freeman, C. 1982. 'Technological Infrastructure and International Competitiveness'. Draft paper submitted to the OECD Ad hoc group on Science, technology and competitiveness, August 1982, mimeo. Later published as Freeman, C. (2004), 'Technological Infrastructure and International Competitiveness'. *Industrial and Corporate Change* 13: 540–52.

———. (ed.), 1981. *Technological Innovation and National Economic Performance*. Aalborg: Aalborg University Press.

Freeman, C. and Lundvall, B.-Å. (eds.). 1988. *Small Countries Facing the Technological Revolution*. London: Pinter Publishers.

Freeman, C. and Soete, L. 1997. *The Economics of Industrial Innovation*. London: Pinter Publishers.

Fu, X., C. Pietrobelli and L. Soete, 2011. 'The Role of Foreign Technology and Indigenous Innovation in the Emerging Economies: Technological Change and Catching-Up'. *World Development* 39: 1204–1212.

Gereffi, G. and M. Korzeniewicz. 1994. *Commodity Chains and Global Capitalism*. Santa Barbara, CA: ABC-CLIO.

Gertler, M. S. 2007. 'Tacit Knowledge in Production Systems: How Important Is Geography?' In *The Economic Geography of Innovatio*, 87–111, edited by K. E. Polenske. Cambridge: Cambridge University Press.

Gereffi, G., G. J. Humphrey and T. Sturgeon. 2005. 'The Governance of Global Value Chains'. *Review of International Political Economy* 12. 78–104.

Giuliani, E., Rabellotti, R. and Pietrobelli, C. 2005. 'Upgrading in Global Value Chains: Lessons from LatinAmerican Clusters', *World Development* 33 (4): 549–73.

Gruber, W., D. Mehta and R. Vernon. (1967), 'The R & D Factor in International Trade and International Investment of United States Industries,' *Journal of Political Economy*, no. 1: 20–37.

Hägerstrand T. 1953. *Innovation Diffusion as a Spatial Process (English translation by Pred, A, 1967)*. Chicago: University of Chicago Press.

Hufbauer, G. C. 1966. *Synthetic Materials and the Theory of International Trade*. Cambridge, MA: Harvard University Press.

Humphrey, J. 1995.' Industrial Reorganization in Developing Countries: From Models to Trajectories.' *World Development* 23, no. 1, 149–162.

Humphrey, J. and H. Schmitz. 1998. Trust and Inter-firm Relations in Developing and Transition Economies. *Journal of Development Studies* 34, no. 4: 32–61.

———. 2002. 'How Does Insertion in Global Value Chains Affect Upgrading in Industrial Clusters?' *Regional Studies* 36. 1017–27.

Jensen, M. B., B. Johnson, E. Lorenz and B.-Å. Lundvall. 2007. 'Forms of Knowledge and Modes of Innovation'. *Research Policy* 36: 680–93.

Johnson, B. 1992. 'Institutional Learning'. in *National Innovation Systems: Towards a Theory of Innovation and Interactive Learning*, edited by B.-Å. Lundvall. London: Pinter Publishers.

Kaldor, N. I978. 'The Effect of Devaluations on Trade in Manufactures'. In *Further Essays on Applied Economics*, pp. 99–118. London: Duckworth.

Kravis, I. and R. E. Lipsey. 1971. *Price Competitiveness in World Trade*. New York: Columbia University Press.

Krugman, P. 1991. 'Increasing Returns and Economic Geography'. *Journal of Political Economy* 99: 483–99.

Krugman, P. and A. J. Venables. 1995. 'Globalization and the Inequality of Nations'. *Quarterly Journal of Economics* 110: 857–880.

Lee, K. 2013. *Schumpeterian Analysis of Economic Catch-Up: Knowledge, Path-Creation and the Middle Income Trap*. Cambridge: Cambridge University Press.

Leontief, W. 1953. 'Domestic Production and Foreign Trade, The American Capital Position ReExamined'. *Proceedings of the American Philosophical Society* 97: 332–49.

List, F. 1845. *The National System of Political Economy*. London: Longmans, Green and Co.

Lorenz, E. and B.-Å. Lundvall (eds.). 2006. *How Europe's Economies Learn*. Oxford: Oxford University Press.

Lorenz, E. and Valeyre, A. 2006. 'Organizational Forms and Innovation Performance: A Comparison of the EU15'. In *How Europe's Economies Learn*, 140–60, edited by E. Lorenz, and B.-Å. Lundvall. Oxford: Oxford University Press.

Lundvall, B.-Å. 1985. *Product Innovation and User-Producer Interaction*. Aalborg: Aalborg University Press.

———. 1988. 'Innovation as an Interactive Process: From User-Producer Interaction to the National Innovation Systems'. in *Technology and Economic Theory*, edited by G. Dosi, C. Freeman, R. R. Nelson, G. Silverberg and L. Soete. London: Pinter Publishers.

———. (ed.). 1992a. *National Innovation Systems: Towards a Theory of Innovation and Interactive Learning*. London: Pinter Publishers.

Lundvall, B.-Å. 1992b. 'User-producer relationships, national systems of innovation and internationalisation'. In National Systems of Innovation: Towards a Theory of Innovation and Interactive Learning, ed. B.-Å. Lundvall, pp. 45–67. London: Pinter.

Lundvall, B.-Å. and Lorenz, E. 2012. 'Social Investment in the Globalising Learning Economy: A European Perspective'. In *Towards a Social Investment Welfare State? Ideas, Policies, Challenges*, 235–60. N. Morel, B. Palier and J. Palme. Bristo: Policy Press.

Malerba, F. and L. Orsenigo. 1997. 'Technological Regimes and Sectoral Patterns of Innovative Activities'. *Industrial and Corporate Change* 6: 83–117.

Malerba, F. and R. R. Nelson. 2011. 'Learning and Catching Up in Different Sectoral Systems: Evidence from Six Industries'. *Industrial and Corporate Change* 20: 1645–1675.

Maskell, P. and A. Malmberg. 1997. 'Towards an Explanation of Regional Specialization and Industry Agglomeration'. *European Planning Studies* 5: 25–44.

Palloix, C. 1969. *Problèmes de croissance en économie ouverte*. Paris: Maspero.

Pietrobelli, C. and R. Rabellotti. 2011. 'Global Value Chains Meet Innovation Systems: Are There Learning Opportunities for Developing Countries?' *World Development* 39: 1261–69.

Porter, M. 1990. *The Competitive Advantage of Nations*. London: Macmillan.

Posner, M. V. 1961. 'International Trade and Technical Change'. *Oxford Economic Papers*. October.

Posner, M. and A. Steer. 1979. 'Price Competitiveness and the Performance of Manufacturing Industry'. In *De-industrialisation, Heinemann,* edited by F. Blackaby. Aldershot: Gower Publishing.

Rothwell, R. 1972. 'Factors for Success in Industrial Innovations: Project SAPPHO – A Comparative Study of Success and Failure in Industrial Innovation'. *Science Policy Research Unit.* University of Sussex, Brighton.

———. 1977. 'The Characteristics of Successful Innovators and Technically Progressive Firms'. *R&D Management* 7: 191–206.

Schmitz, H. 1995. 'Small Shoemakers and Fordist Giants: Tale of a Supercluster'. *World Development* 23: 9–28.

———. 1999. 'Global Competition and Local Cooperation: Success and Failure in the Sinos Valley, Brazil'. *World Development* 27, no. 9: 1627–50.

———. (ed.). 2004. *Local Enterprises in the Global Economy: Issues of Governance and Upgrading.* Cheltenham: Edgar Elgar.

———. 2006. 'Learning and Earning in Global Garment and Footwear Chains'. *European Journal of Development Research* 18: 546–71.

Sharif, N. 2006. 'Emergence and Development of the National Innovation Systems Concept'. *Research Policy* 35: 745–66.

Storper, M. 1995. 'The Resurgence of Regional Economics, Ten Years Later: The Region as a Nexus of Untraded Interdependencies'. *European Urban and Regional Studies* 2: 191–221.

Sturgeon, T.J. 2002. 'Modular Production Networks: A New American Model of Industrial Organization'. *Industrial and Corporate Change* 11: 451–96

Wallerstein, I. 1974. *The Modern World System*. New York: Academic Press.

Williamson, O. E. 1975. *Markets and Hierarchies: Analysis and Antitrust Implications.* London: Macmillan.

Wood, A. 2001. 'Value Chains: An Economist's Perspective'. *IDS Bulletin Special Issue on The Value of Value Chains* 32, no. 3: 41–46.

Part V
ECONOMICS OF HOPE OR DESPAIR: WHAT NEXT?

Chapter 14

THE LEARNING ECONOMY AND THE ECONOMICS OF HOPE

Bengt-Åke Lundvall

This chapter addresses global issues regarded through the focusing device of 'the learning economy'. The form is brief and essayistic. The chapter begins with reflections on the basic concepts and their roots. With reference to the three chapters on Europe, China and Africa (chapter 10, 11 and 12), it is shown that while problems and opportunities are context specific, they often originate from developments in another region. On this basis, the essay points to the need for new forms of global governance that can promote learning worldwide. It ends with some ideas for a research agenda.

14.1 The Economics of Hope

The economics of hope alludes to a book with this title bringing together articles written by Christopher Freeman (1992). The essays cover topics related to science policy, innovation and competitiveness linking science and technology to broader social and environmental issues. They are critical to the dominant paradigm in economics and to public policy, but they combine criticism with constructive ideas about where to go. Freeman was critical of how modern capitalism produced inequality and exploited natural resources. He was, however, equally critical of dystopian perspectives where current negative trends were projected into the future and ending in catastrophic scenarios.

The perspective presented in this book is somewhat different. Freeman's starting point was science and science policy, and his most important reference was to the Marxist physicist J. D. Bernal who established analytical links between science and society. Both Freeman and Bernal built their conditional optimism on the assumption that science and technology has a lot to offer in terms of solutions to the world's problems, if the institutional setting allowed it to serve society. In this book the starting point is the learning economy, where human interaction and learning at different levels spanning from the organizations, the regions and the nations shape what is happening in the world. Freeman's conditional optimism was based on the potential that science-based learning could offer, while this book broadens the perspective and gives more attention to the potential of experience-based learning.

14.2 The Learning Economy

The learning economy concept has three dimensions – it is normative as well as descriptive and analytical. First, the concept describes characteristics of the current economy where the capacity and the opportunity to learn are crucial for economic performance. Second, it is analytical making use of distinctions between different forms of knowledge and different modes of learning. Third, it is based on the normative assumption that learning contributes to human well-being and emancipation.

The concept is based on an understanding of all human beings as having the capacity to learn. Learning does not only refer to expanding cognition and developing skills, but the values and ideas that people adopt will reflect their experiences. The motivations that drive people will reflect experiences as well as the expectations from others. There is no fixed human nature. This perspective comes close to George Herbert Mead's theory of social interaction and Dewey's pragmatist understanding of learning.

This perspective gives ground for conditional optimism since it opens up for major and generalized change in human behaviour. The fact that the level of trust shows great variation across societies illustrates that context matters. The effective imposition of the smoking ban in most countries in the world has led to unexpected changes in attitudes to smoking, and this illustrates that even when major economic interests with great lobbying resources are against it, state regulations that affect human behaviour can be implemented.

14.3 Experience-Based Learning Is Not Always Progressive

Learning can result in criminal skills and bad habits. Enterprises may learn to become more proficient in producing and marketing products that are dangerous and unhealthy. Learning has a positive connotation in common with concepts such as knowledge, technical change and innovation. However, while more knowledge and more innovation is a prerequisite *for* 'progress', it is not *equal to* 'progress'. It is therefore a collective task both to promote learning and to give direction to processes of learning.

Learning will from time to time result in situations of 'lock-in' where individuals, organizations and the whole economy get stuck because of what has been learnt. Organizations and whole industries may establish capabilities that become obsolete – the mechanical industry had great problems with mastering information technology. The population in a region may have learnt activities no longer in demand – one major reason for the success of the IT industry in the Silicon Valley was the absence of heavy industry experience in the region.

Experience-based learning will, if standing alone, mainly promote incremental change along the existing trajectories. Such gradual processes result in gains in wealth, and they are necessary when it comes to absorbing radical innovations and transforming them into valuable outcomes. However from time to time, the old technological trajectory may be depleted and a new one is needed; especially when facing situations of underdevelopment and major crises, there is a need for opening up new trajectories. In such situations, external interventions giving new direction both to STI- and DUI-modes of learning are necessary. The most powerful institution that can intervene in the economy is, of course, the state.

Governments have limited capacity to intervene, and it should not be used to fine-tune processes of learning. First it should be used to establish framework conditions that support the capacity to adapt and innovate in society. This involves the design and implementation of research, education, labour market, energy, environment and innovation policy. It also involves policies that aim at redistributing the costs and benefits of change (see figure 12.1 in chapter 12).

The second major task is, from time to time, to open up new techno-economic trajectories. The state has an important role as a collective entrepreneur. Historically, the state has played a key role in initiating the Industrial Revolution in England as well as in fostering the information technology revolution in the United States. Today, governments face the important task of opening up a green techno-economic trajectory.

14.4 Europe as a Learning Economy

The concept 'the learning economy' was inspired by research on innovation and industrial dynamics in Denmark. Empirical studies demonstrated that private firms that engaged in interactive learning with customers and workers performed better than those that did not. When comparing economies in Europe, a similar pattern was discerned at the national level. The countries in Europe with wide participation in 'discretionary learning' turned out to be more engaged in radical innovations than the rest (chapter 8). Together these observations give ground for optimism. If democratizing the economy – giving consumers and workers voice and reducing inequality – contributes to strong national economic performance, the future looks bright.

The Lisbon Strategy from 2000 was influenced by such an optimistic view. But the strategy had, from the very beginning, two competing sources of inspiration. One reflected the idea of an egalitarian knowledge-based development. It was reflected in the objective set for 2010 'to make Europe the most competitive knowledge-based region in the world with more and better jobs and with social cohesion'. The other source was mainstream economics, as practiced by OECD economists, and it was reflected in the call for more flexible labour markets, principally meaning that wages should adjust more quickly to changes in the demand for labour.

Already halfway through the planning period (around 2005), the strategy became mainly oriented towards increasing flexibility and the objectives set for investment in knowledge and promoting learning were never given high priority. This reflected that the ideas of the knowledge-based and learning economy were never taken seriously among those who were in charge of economic policy. In the wake of the financial crisis, the coordination of economic policy was given up, and it was agreed that each member country should increase its own competiveness by reducing costs and by austerity policies (see chapter 11 and the next section)

14.5 Europe's Austerity Response to the Financial Crisis

International competitiveness is an ideologically loaded concept. In the dominant discourse, it is assumed that firms compete on the basis of low prices and, therefore, low costs are seen as the most important source of competitiveness. Since wages constitute the major element in costs, a direct link is established between the national wage rate and competitiveness. Increasingly, the debate brought in the costs of financing the public sector as another factor that undermines 'competitiveness' through its direct or indirect impact on the national cost level. It followed that raising wages and expanding the public sector became seen as undermining competitiveness while austerity was seen as the right way to enhance it.

In chapter 13, we refer to the controversial analytical work at OECD in the early 1980s on the link between science and technology, on the one hand, and competitiveness, on the other. One major conclusion from this work was that while costs matter in the short term, other factors are decisive for long-term competitiveness, or for what the group referred to as 'structural competitiveness'. Among those factors, the strength of the knowledge base of the economy and the strength of its 'national system of innovation' were found to be of crucial importance (chapter 13).

This more nuanced understanding of what constitutes competitiveness became (with some delay) more widely accepted within OECD, and in the beginning of the 1990s, it was combined with a new understanding of the economy as being 'knowledge based'. As mentioned, this new perspective was part of the background for the Lisbon Strategy. But the 2007 financial crisis changed the discourse, and the original link between austerity and competitiveness was reestablished.

In the wake of financial speculations against the weak members of the Eurozone, a radical shift in policy perspective took place. A 'competitiveness pact' was established where each single country on its own should assure that their economic policy and economic fundamentals were acceptable to finance capital or to 'the market'. This turn of events had far-reaching consequences for Europe and for the rest of the world. One consequence was that the efforts to build a strong national knowledge base were given even lower priority. Among the victims of austerity policy were investments in research, education and training.

The character of Europe's competitiveness strategy is important for the world economy as a whole. When all the European countries focus on lowering costs and reducing the volume of public expenditure, it contributes to weak effective demand and to economic stagnation at the world level. The neglect of investment in knowledge and learning undermines innovation and growth from the supply side. The focus on austerity weakens trade unions and reduces the capacity of governments to redistribute income to the poor. The final outcome is economic stagnation combined with growing inequality.

The challenge for Europe is to reinvent the original intentions behind the European Union so that they fit into the context of the globalizing learning economy. This requires a new kind of internal solidarity with priority given to investments in knowledge in the weak countries and breaking the current tendency towards increasing inequality. It also requires a change of the competitiveness discourse and practice so that Europe carries its fair share of world investment in knowledge. This will require strong political leadership and a readiness to go against the interests of global finance.

14.6 China's Growth and Investment in Knowledge

When the Lisbon strategy was developed around 2000, the US economy was used as benchmark for Europe and there were few references to the economic development in China in the background documents. Today, it is generally recognized that China's high rate of growth, together with high growth rates in other BRICS countries, has had an enormous impact on the rest of the world. Less attention has been given to the exceptionally high rate of investment in knowledge in China. Since 2000, China is the single country in the world that has given full attention to the role of knowledge and innovation, and as a result, the global knowledge landscape has changed.

When aggregate economic growth of GNP reached more than 10 per cent per annum in China, the investment in knowledge was growing at double that rate. Research and development (R&D) expenditure, the annual number of PhD graduates and the number of scientific publications were all growing with around 20 per cent per annum. While the R&D intensity remained unchanged during the period 2000–2015 at around 1.5 per cent in a stagnating Europe, it grew from 0.8 per cent to 1.5 per cent in the rapidly growing Chinese economy.

This massive investment in knowledge has not been accompanied by a corresponding effort to build a learning economy, however. Most Chinese firms operate with hierarchical forms of organization, and there is little room for creative contributions from employees. This becomes a growing problem in a society where there is explosive growth in the number of highly educated young scholars. The problem is reflected in the reluctance of overseas Chinese to come back and work in China and in a tendency among young people to prefer to work for foreign companies offering more room for organizational learning.

It is a major challenge for China's leaders and enterprises to realize the potential of combining this major effort to promote STI-mode of learning with a stronger emphasis on the DUI-mode. When workers, consumers and citizens take on more participatory roles in the economy, it would become the first real test of the potential offered by the learning economy hypothesis (chapter 10).

14.7 Growth and Structural Change in Africa

China's high growth rates have had major impacts on all major regions in the world. China became a host for foreign direct investments from Europe and the United States, and outsourcing led to structural change with loss of jobs in manufacturing in the OECD area. The increased demand for natural resource–based commodities from China contributed to high-growth rates in Latin America and Africa.

However so far, the high-growth rates in Africa have not spread and benefited the majority of the population. The African countries have become increasingly specialized in natural resource–based hard commodities such as oil and other minerals, and as a result, their economies have become even more vulnerable to shifts in global demand. Deindustrialization and growth in the share of the informal sector characterize structural change since the beginning of the millennium. The present form of economic growth cannot overcome Africa's problems of poverty, hunger, massive youth unemployment and food import dependence (chapter 12).

Joining global value chains and learning from foreign companies is not sufficient to open up a different trajectory leading towards industrialization and job creation (chapter 13). There is a need for strong and selective intervention in terms of industry and trade policy, to give strong priority to build technological infrastructure and to establish STI learning in relation to some selected sectors including the sectors that produce food and energy. Such top-down efforts would need to be supported by local initiative and mobilization.

The challenge for Africa is that domestic governments are weak and rentier interests strong, while international partners tend to benefit from the lop-sided growth. Some believe that the African Union could play a role in shaping a common strategy. Since it is crucial to finance new activities, there would be a need for a stronger role of the African Development Bank. Others look at China's growing presence and assume that the rising costs in manufacturing in China combined with Chinese entrepreneurship could offer new opportunities for Africa.

While this chapter is being written, there has been a massive increase in the number of refugees coming to Europe from war zones in Syria, Iraq and Afghanistan – among them are also an increasing number of young African illegal emigrants hoping to get away from poverty and unemployment. The first reaction has been the attempts to build Fort Europe to stop illegal immigrants from entering. Given the global communication infrastructure and the proximity between Africa and Europe, it is doubtful if these efforts can succeed. It is possible that failure and self-interest would trigger European collaboration with African countries aiming at job creation in Africa.

14.8 Europe, China and Africa – Different but Interconnected Challenges

The development of the austerity strategy with weak investments in knowledge and learning in Europe has a negative impact on world economic growth, while China's high rates of growth and strong investment in knowledge have had the opposite effect. The increased demand for natural resources has led to strong but lop-sided economic growth in Africa. The lop-sided character of growth is one factor explaining the growing number of emigrants now coming into Europe.

It is obvious that the world economy is strongly interconnected and that political choices made in one part of the world have major impact on living conditions in other parts. This stands in contrast to the fact that the organization of political processes predominantly is organized within the single nation state. This interdependence becomes most dramatic, tangible and visible in periods of worldwide crises.

The financial crisis had as prerequisite the deregulation of financial markets led by the United States and the United Kingdom and supported by multilateral organizations such as IMF. Governments let financial speculation become a main driver of the economy and allowed financial bubbles to emerge. Enterprises changed their attention and activities as it became increasingly worthwhile to engage in financial transactions as compared to engaging in innovation and investing in production capacity. The process of innovation and growth in the real sector was undermined and the result was financial instability and major crises. The deregulation strategies of the countries that host the world leading financial centres (the United States and the United Kingdom) pursued policies that imposed enormous social and economic costs on the rest of the world.

The environmental crisis and global warming affect many parts of the world, but the most strongly affected are poor people living in tropical regions in Africa. The polluters are located in other parts of the world. The movement of heavy industry from Europe and the United States to locations in Asia is reflected in the changing patterns of CO_2 emissions. In this area, the need for international agreements has been generally recognized, but the readiness to engage in binding agreements is limited and even binding agreements go without sanctions for those signing them. One major argument slowing down progress is that commitments would undermine the competitiveness of domestic firms.

The ongoing refugee crisis may be seen as reflecting demographic crises in different parts of the world. In parts of Europe and Japan, the nativity is so low that population stagnates, and as a result there is an aging population. In Africa and parts of Asia, the population keeps growing at high rates, and as a result, the proportion of young people is high. Limited job opportunities in these parts of the world give strong incentives to the young to move from the South to the North. In the North, the major interest is to receive and integrate well-educated immigrants who give positive economic contributions to the national economy.

In what follows, these three worldwide crises will be confronted with the learning economy concept. They have in common that they are based on systemic weaknesses resulting in unsustainable paths of development. They also have in common that there is a need for new types of coordination at the global level. Finally, they have in common that a solution will require that the entrepreneurial state gives a new direction to knowledge creation and learning. Market forces will, if left alone, only aggravate the problems.

14.9 Financialization, Innovation and Learning

Through deregulations of finance, the world economy has become dominated by a process of financialization. This is reflected in an increasing role of financial motives, financial markets, financial actors and financial institutions in the operation of the domestic and international economies. This new global regime is supported by the financial–industrial complex combining the interests of financial institutions, public regulators and experts.

The concept of an industrial complex alludes to the military–industrial complex, that is, to a strong social and political constellation. Within the complex, experts move between functions in organizations serving as regulators, suppliers and customers. Participants in the complex share the understanding of what technological trajectory to follow, and they stand together in defending the autonomy of the complex.

The current position of the financial–industrial complex represents a major threat to the learning economy. Rather than fulfilling the role of channelling capital to innovation and productive investments, it serves its own interests. The swarms of 'financial innovations' that went ahead of the global financial crisis are perhaps the most striking examples of how innovations can have destructive consequences. Those financial innovations made it possible for an increasing share of transactions to take place inside the complex while taxing the rest of the economy.

In spite of the discrediting effect of the crisis, the financial–industrial complex has actually strengthened its position with regard to national governments. Financial institutions give grades to national policy strategies. Good grades are given to austerity while the kind of reforms and public investments that enhance the long-term capacity to innovate and learn are neglected or regarded and treated as negative. Grading involves sanctions where bad grades result in high capital costs or even a complete closing of the access to international loans.

In the wake of the most recent financial crisis, regulations to repair some of the most obvious flaws in the global and national financial systems were implemented at the international and national level. But the regulations have not changed the basic dynamics of the system. Expansionary monetary policy has resulted in assets price inflation making the rich richer, but zero interest rates have not led to new investments and economic growth. New asset price raises take place in a context of economic stagnation. As a result, new bubbles threaten to burst and give rise to the next financial crisis.

One way to reform the financial system and move its focus from speculation towards innovation would be to introduce national and regional development banks with public ownership and a clear mandate to build the foundation of knowledge-based growth. It would require strong political leadership ready to confront the financial–industrial complex as it operates at the national and global level. Critical research on the functioning of finance and the formation of independent expertise would be helpful in this process. Today, most 'experts on finance' are insiders and support the strong position of the financial–industrial complex.

To avoid major depressions as triggered by financialization, there is a need for global cooperation on a new foundation where the focus is on knowledge-based development rather than on monetary discipline. The current institutional setting where the IMF and the World Bank tend to support rather than control the financial–industrial complex needs to be changed.

In this context, the recent collaboration of major development banks from BRICS countries (Brasil, Russia, India, China and South Africa) resulting in an alternative World Development Bank is of major interest. Global cooperation could result in a Tobin tax on speculation with incomes allocated to strengthening the knowledge base and innovation systems in the least developed countries.

Policy learning will be required and in this case the resistance to change is strong, well-organized and supported by the current economic philosophy. Historical experience shows, nonetheless, that when the survival of the system is threatened, necessary reforms will be implemented. Perhaps the sufficient willingness to learn will require yet another major world economic crisis.

14.10 Coordinated Efforts to Establish a Green Trajectory

This section relates economic growth to sustainable development from an innovation and learning economy perspective, taking into account that so far innovations have driven economies towards more intensive and extensive use of both renewable and nonrenewable natural resources. Nonetheless, it is impossible to envisage any successful strategy for environmental survival that does not make full use of knowledge and innovation. Therefore the struggle is not for or against advancing knowledge and stimulating innovation but rather a struggle about giving new directions for innovation and learning.

In order to reduce the environmental impact in terms of natural resources, low entropy energy and ecosystems resilience, the focus evidently has to be on the creation and utilization of knowledge. Final demand should be, increasingly, addressed towards goods and services with low environmental impact and technological and organizational knowledge should systematically be developed towards this goal. Progress in any of the following dimensions would move the economy in the right direction:

a) New processes (production, transport and logistics) requiring less resource input per unit of production.

b) Substituting nonrenewable with renewable resources
c) New products which are more long lasting and more recyclable
d) A change in the sectorial composition of the economy towards less resource intensive production activities
e) A change in the location of economic activities that reduce resource use for transport
f) New forms of agglomerations and new principles for housing that reduce resource use

A significant amount of current innovation efforts undermine sustainability. One example is product innovations for consumers that are designated and designed exclusively to stimulate consumers' appetite for new models. Another example is process innovations that lead to more resource use per unit of value produced. Therefore it is necessary to redefine innovation policy from 'general innovation support' towards 'directed innovation support'.

Guidance may take the form of a combination of taxes, subsidies, public production, public procurement, standard settings and prohibitions. One important criterion for selecting and designing policy tools must be how they affect innovation and learning. There is, for instance, a scholarly literature on how the design of standards may respectively promote or slow down innovations. Measures should be designed not so that they freeze procedures. They should give freedom in choice of method as long as the outcome is that specific green objectives are reached.

One argument against guidance is that the measures taken are costly and that given the uncertainty regarding the future, we should postpone the introduction of such measures, while we in the meantime create more knowledge through R&D efforts. This is the current position of Bjørn Lomborg – the sceptical environmentalist. It reveals a fundamental lack of understanding of the innovation process. One well-established conclusion from innovation research is that effective new solutions can only be developed in a process where the outcomes of research efforts are continuously applied. The feedback from users to producers is of crucial importance for developing useful technologies.

Nation states dominate political governance. They have the most powerful tools when it comes to intervention. In some cases, nation states have realized the potential of building green competitiveness strategies. This has taken place with windmills in Denmark, electrical cars in California and wind and solar power in China. In the case of China, the scale of government intervention in promoting renewable energy has been raised as a problem in the WTO. One factor reducing national efforts in the West is resistance to selective government intervention and market dogmatism.

A green innovation strategy would require a speed up of innovation and of restructuring of the economy. This has implications for finance of innovation and investment. To channel finance into new green industries, there will be a need to establish 'green development banks' where governments play an important role of determining the direction of investment. Not when it comes to picking specific projects but when it comes to promoting specific new industries that need to be promoted in order to build a green production and innovation system.

This restructuring will of course be reflected in shifts in the demand for labour. There will be sectors where specific jobs disappear while new jobs in other sectors are created and many existing jobs will require new skills and new perspectives on how to do things. Very ambitious combinations of education, life-long learning and labour market policies will be required in order to transform green innovations into wide production and use. Not least will there be a need for new kinds of education and for retraining of engineers, designers, skilled workers and managers. Institutions that support the learning economy will be crucial for the transformation.

Initiatives at the national level cannot stand alone. Therefore, in parallel with national efforts, there is a need to design global cooperation. So far much of the attention in connection with global cooperation has been on reaching agreements on targets for reduction of the amount of CO_2 produced. Changing the perspective and giving more attention to how to promote innovation in green technologies would help getting out of the current stalemates. The establishment of international problem based 'mega-science' and mega-technology projects, where scholars and enterprises collaborate and share knowledge relevant for solving ecological problems (water, desertification, renewable technologies), would be one way to make national agreements in this area more realistic. Global engineering universities with a strong profile in terms of sustainability technologies could be another type of new institutions that could move things in the right direction.

If these different initiatives were taken, a new kind of innovation system would emerge. It would be a system where the different components converged towards new objectives and gradually accepted new norms for what is acceptable in terms of environmental conditions. The attention would be much more turned towards how innovations impact the environment. The performance indicators used to measure progress would be different and consumers would have found new ways to satisfy their need for stimulation and newness,

It is an open question if the capitalist process of production and accumulation can become environmentally sustainable. It is, of course, important not to 'confuse the limits of one particular development paradigm, with the limits to growth of the system in general' (Freeman 1992). It is clear, however, that the scale of the problem requires radical changes not only in technologies but also in values, institutions, policies and consumption patterns to develop what Christopher Freeman (1992) two decades ago termed a 'green techno-economic paradigm'.

There are no technical barriers to moving the innovation system in this direction. However, the political and institutional barriers are huge. Vested interests, nationalism, financialization, pro-market dogma and political short termism constitute barriers for change. Nevertheless, new ways of tackling the ecological crisis will have to be developed as problems become more serious.

14.11 Demographic Crises and Migration in the Context of the Globalizing Learning Economy

The rate of world population growth is unevenly distributed between countries and continents. When combined with worldwide communication and with big and growing gaps in living standards, it results in growing flows of migration between continents. In this section, the focus is on the impact of migration on innovation systems and the learning economy.

The integration of foreign workers coming from a radically different culture represents a challenge for the OECD and especially for countries with the most developed learning economies. It is not surprising that Denmark and Netherlands combine the highest degrees of workers' participation in organizational learning with weak performance in terms of integrating immigrants with a different ethnical background in the labour market. These two countries are culturally homogenous, and it has allowed organizational learning to take place on the basis of tacitness and implicit rules.

This style of learning excludes those who do not understand the informal rules, and for integration to take place, more explicit rules and more hierarchical forms of management tend to be implemented. This is reinforced by the impact of immigration on the industrial structure. More ample access to low-skilled workers with modest wage demands makes it possible to prolong the life of sectors and workplaces characterized by Taylorist or simple work organization.

In order to safeguard some of the basic qualities of the learning economy, major investments in training immigrants both outside and inside the enterprise sector are crucial. Such training must combine upgrading of skills with elements of cultural integration. This is important not only to avoid ethnic conflicts and the formation of ghettos but also in order to avoid a regression towards hierarchical forms of work organization and low-quality jobs with limited room for discretionary learning. Such investments require a partnership between the state, the workers' organizations and the private sector.

Other migration flows, driven less by poverty and war, are important in shaping the global knowledge landscape. The migration of experts and scientists is an important vehicle for transferring both explicit and tacit knowledge across continents. Scientists of Chinese and Indian origin constitute a big share of all natural scientists at US universities. Others work in high-tech companies. This reflects that the interest among US-born students has been directed more towards other fields of knowledge than science and technology. Chinese and Indian scholars have been attracted to the United States and to Europe by academic freedom and more attractive material conditions.

Recently this outflow of scholars from China and India has begun to be combined with a flow back to the countries of origin. The successful industrial transformations in the North-east Asia (Korea, Taiwan, Singapore and China) have all benefited from the absorption of returnees who have brought both specific scientific and technological capabilities and insights in how to organize finance, marketing and research back from experience-based learning abroad. Additionally, the returnees have been instrumental in building network relationships between their new home base and the enterprises and institutions abroad. The original brain drain has, to some degree, turned into brain circulation.

This beneficial effect cannot be seen in Africa. The rather small proportion of well-trained professionals, scientist and engineers in Africa are attracted to OECD countries offering better working and living conditions. In some African countries, around half of all doctors and nurses work in Europe while there is acute shortage of health personnel in the country of origin. So far, there are few signs of a flow back from the rich countries. While there are ample problems in Africa that require high-level expertise, the effective demand for this kind of knowledge is weak. Lundvall (2008) argues that the low level of effective demand for knowledge in less developed countries reflects lack of innovation, and that expanding higher education without a major drive for innovation and structural change tends to result in further brain drain.

The above brief notes on how migration between Europe, the United States, China and Africa relates to the learning economy serve to illustrate the interdependence between continents when it comes to building a strong knowledge base. There is much attention in WTO trade agreements to intellectual property rights that protect the interests of major multinational firms that have a technological lead. Much less attention is given to protect the interests of African countries that use scarce resources to educate professionals who end up working in Europe or the United States.

The combination of high rates of population growth and high rates of poverty in Africa will lead to a future mass emigration to Europe that will prove to be impossible to absorb with or without building Fort Europe. Today many European countries are reducing their development aid in order to finance the inflow of refugees and immigrants. This will aggravate future problems. What is required is a new global regime where African countries are supported in their effort to create new activities and jobs. At the core of this regime should be compensation for brain drain and new and more generous rules for international knowledge sharing.

14.12 Learning in Geographical Space – towards a New Research Agenda

This section presents the contours of a research agenda that may be seen as a follow-up to the analysis and issues raised in this book. There is one overarching question that needs to be given more satisfactory answer than those given by current research: *How do different forms of globalization and different forms of opening up of national innovation systems affect the creation, diffusion and use of knowledge at the local, national and global level?* When this question has been answered, there are several follow-up questions to be answered: *What are the implications for public policy at the national (or regional) level in different parts of the world? What are the implications for the rules of the game at the global level?*

One of the most fundamental assumptions driving economic policy is that expanding international trade contributes to economic growth and welfare. When countries specialize, they become more productive, and consumers become better off. In chapter 12 on Africa, we showed how a whole continent as a result of trade specialization had ended with a lop-sided structure with limited potential for learning and job creation. In chapter 13, we raised doubts about the beneficial effects of joining global value chains in the absence of local capacities and a strong national innovation system. A fundamental research question is: *What are the dynamic effects of reducing trade barriers on the knowledge base and learning capability?*

New trade agreements are propagated with the argument that they raise the level of income. When they get implemented, it turns out that the promises made were exaggerated. More important is that the gains take the form of one discrete raise. Research should ask the question: *What is the impact of specific trade agreements on the dynamic performance of the national innovation system?*

Referring back to the three crises discussed, here we should also ask: *How do new trade agreements and existing rules for international economic interaction contribute to respectively financial stability, environmental sustainability and poverty reduction?* The costs of 'free trade' in these three dimensions need to be taken as seriously as the benefits. The fact that it is possible for the United States to make complaints via WTO when China subsidizes green technologies illustrates that there are such costs. Another example is that the WTO regime makes it possible to sanction poor countries with much less political strength that engage in active industrial and trade policy.

The starting point for the research presented in this book was the analysis of the interaction between users and producers that takes place in processes of product innovation. This analysis inspired research on national systems of innovation. One reason for studying *national* systems is that some forms of knowledge as well as some modes of interactive learning are localized. A fundamental research question is: *What happens to knowledge exchange and interactive learning between users and producers involved in innovative activities when the distance between them goes from local and national to global?* The answer will show how degrees of codification, modularization and standardization of knowledge will change as we move from local to global interaction.

In chapter 2 it was shown that hierarchical user–producer relationships tend to lead to 'unsatisfactory innovations'. When we go to interaction at the global level, we would expect that in most instances, users or producers located in less developed countries are much weaker in terms competence or economic resources. A relevant research question is: *How does the big knowledge gap between global partners affect the direction of innovation?*

The national innovation system concept has been challenged by economic geographers and trade economists who point to the increasing importance of respectively local and global interaction. In this book, it is assumed that economic development requires a developmental state that supports innovation and learning – sometimes in the form of major interventions to establish new trajectories in terms of technology and industrial development. Nevertheless, it is also recognized that states in weak economies are themselves weak. This raises several research questions: *What is the role of the state at different levels of development when it comes to regulating and managing the openness of the economy and when it comes to building national institutions that make it possible to benefit from increased openness?*

Globalization is a process that has been stimulated by technological change and pushed by politics. Information and communication technologies and deregulation of finance are important factors. Sometimes, the fact that millions (most of them Chinese!) have been lifted out of poverty is ascribed to the globalization process and to the growth in international trade. However, the performance of the world economy in terms of productivity and growth is not impressive. This raises the final and most difficult research question: *How does the current form of globalization, where local tacit knowledge is transformed into global standardized knowledge, contribute to the world's production, diffusion and use of knowledge?*

14.13 Conclusions

There are different interpretations of world development and different interpretations of where current trends are leading. Global warming, financial instability and demographic challenges are three major global challenges which have in common, first, that market forces alone cannot be expected to lead to acceptable and sustainable outcomes and, second, that nation state governance alone is insufficient. In an era with strong neoliberal pro-market ideology in international organizations and growing nationalism, it is tempting to end up with a pessimist view of the world.

However, such pessimism is myopic and underestimates the potential of humankind to overcome what may look like a hopeless struggle to break disastrous trends. Through history, there have been major crises with great human costs. Some of those reflected natural disasters, others an incapacity to manage major epidemics, periods of climate change and major wars that were initiated by imperialistic hunger for power and resources. Nonetheless, there has been progress in important dimensions. Today more people than ever before in history can live a longer life with more peace and security, with sufficient nutrition and with capacity to read and follow what is going on in the world through different media.

There is little doubt that capitalist development has contributed to the raise in productivity and to the increased diversity of the world economy, which are prerequisites for the raise in living standards and in their turn constitute the basis for better health, nutrition and education. Competition is a major factor driving innovation. The profit motive and the search for enrichment is one reason why individuals work hard and entrepreneurs constantly look for new opportunities. Markets are useful institutions that reduce the need for administrative decisions. This is important since the capacity to make knowledgeable and wise decisions is limited – sometimes it is absent because of the self-interest among decision-makers.

Therefore neoliberal economists, who hail the market and raise doubts about the size and role of the public sector, have got some of the historical evidence on their side. But they tend to abstract from the other set of prerequisites for the raise in productivity and increased diversity. State regulation of working conditions and the formation of trade unions played an important role in making capitalist growth socially sustainable. The most successful countries had a strong state that promoted general education before the beginning of, or at very early stages of the industrialization process. Since the beginning of the millennium, China drives world economic growth and leads investments in knowledge on the basis of a mix of planning and markets.

While the West struggles against religious fundamentalism resulting in terror, it has failed to recognize that it has developed an *economic fundamentalism* that stands in the way of making full use of the potential offered by science, technology and experience-based learning. This book presents an alternative perspective that we refer to as 'the Economics of Hope'. The starting point is that knowledge is seen as the most important resource in the economy and learning as the most important process. This gives hope because knowledge has unique characteristics in terms of scarcity. Learning is a cumulative process, and the more you use knowledge, the more it grows. Knowledge can be shared with others without making it less useful, and one excellent way to learn more is through sharing knowledge with others. Young university professors experience this when they prepare and execute their first courses. When our societies draw the full implications from such a perspective, many problems can be solved and well-being can be enhanced.

References

Freeman, C. 1992. *The Economics of Hope: Essays on Technical Change, Economic Growth, and the Environment*. London: Pinter Publishers.
Lundvall, B.-Å. 2008. 'Higher Education, Innovation and Economic Development'. In *Higher Education and Economic Development*, edited by J. Y. Lin and B. Plescovic. Washington, DC: World Bank.

CONTRIBUTORS

Anthony Arundel is professor of innovation at the Australian Innovation Research Centre, University of Tasmania, and concurrently a professorial fellow at United Nations University – Maastricht Economic and Social Research Institute on Innovation and Technology, Maastricht. His research covers the innovative activities of firms, public administrative agencies and universities, and using data from innovation surveys.

Shulin Gu is research professor at the Institute of Policy and Management, Chinese Academy of Sciences, Beijing. She also serves as advisory research professor at China Institute of Science and Technology Policy and at Tsinghua University, Beijing. Her research areas include S&T policy, S&T system reform in China, innovation and development studies, innovation policy, institutional change, inclusive and 'green' innovation.

Morten Berg Jensen is associate professor of business statistics at the Department of Economics and Business, Aarhus University, Denmark. He holds a doctoral degree from the same university. He specializes in research involving quantitative analysis of problems related to innovation systems, open and user driven innovation, and health economics.

Björn Johnson is senior associate professor and reader in economics at Aalborg University, Copenhagen, Denmark. His earlier research dealt with regional aspects of consumer behavior, comparative economic systems and comparative analysis of strategies in economic policy. His current research is in the field of institutional economics with a focus on the relations between technical and institutional change and economic development.

Rasmus Lema is associate professor at the Department of Business and Management at Aalborg University, Copenhagen, Denmark. He is an interdisciplinary social scientist with a DPhil in development studies from the University of Sussex, UK. Focusing on research issues at the intersection between innovation and development studies, his current work concentrates on globalization and innovation in sustainable energy sectors in developing countries.

Edward Lorenz is professor of economics at the University of Nice-Sophia Antipolis, France, and adjoint professor at Aalborg University, Copenhagen, Denmark. He was awarded a PhD in economics by the University of Cambridge (1983). His research focuses on international comparative analysis of business organization, employment relations and innovation systems. He has published regularly in major peer-reviewed journals including *Research Policy* and *Industrial and Corporate Change*.

Bengt-Åke Lundvall is professor of economics at the Department of Management and Business, Aalborg University, Copenhagen, Denmark. He is the founder of the global research network on innovation and competence building, GLOBELICS. His research is about the management and economics of innovation and knowledge. Together with Chris Freeman he introduced the concept the National Innovation System and together with Björn Johnson he developed the concept of the Learning Economy.

Antoine Valeyre has recently retired as senior researcher with expertise in work organization, working conditions and labor markets economics. He has served as research fellow in several research centres of the National Center for Scientific Research such as Centre d'Etudes de l'Emploi and Equipe de recherche sur les inégalités sociales at Centre Halbwachs. He has published articles and books linking modes of organization to work satisfaction and working conditions.

INDEX